Lecture Notes in Artificial Int

Edited by J. G. Carbonell and J. Siekmann

Subseries of Lecture Notes in Computer Science

Matteo Baldoni   Ulle Endriss (Eds.)

Declarative
Agent Languages
and Technologies IV

4th International Workshop, DALT 2006
Hakodate, Japan, May 8, 2006
Selected, Revised and Invited Papers

 Springer

Series Editors

Jaime G. Carbonell, Carnegie Mellon University, Pittsburgh, PA, USA
Jörg Siekmann, University of Saarland, Saarbrücken, Germany

Volume Editors

Matteo Baldoni
Università degli Studi di Torino, Dipartimento di Informatica
via Pessinetto 12, 10149 Torino, Italy
E-mail: baldoni@di.unito.it

Ulle Endriss
University of Amsterdam, Institute for Logic, Language and Computation
Plantage Muidergracht 24, 1018 TV Amsterdam, The Netherlands
E-mail: ulle@illc.uva.nl

Library of Congress Control Number: 2006938418

CR Subject Classification (1998): I.2.11, C.2.4, D.2.4, D.2, D.3, F.3.1

LNCS Sublibrary: SL 7 – Artificial Intelligence

ISSN   0302-9743
ISBN-10   3-540-68959-1 Springer Berlin Heidelberg New York
ISBN-13   978-3-540-68959-1 Springer Berlin Heidelberg New York

Springer is a part of Springer Science+Business Media

springer.com

© Springer-Verlag Berlin Heidelberg 2006
Printed in Germany

Typesetting: Camera-ready by author, data conversion by Scientific Publishing Services, Chennai, India
Printed on acid-free paper   SPIN: 11961536   06/3142   5 4 3 2 1 0

Preface

The workshop on Declarative Agent Languages and Technologies (DALT), in its fourth edition this year, is a well-established forum for researchers interested in sharing their experiences in combining declarative and formal approaches with engineering and technology aspects of agents and multiagent systems. Building complex agent systems calls for models and technologies that ensure predictability, allow for the verification of properties, and guarantee flexibility. Developing technologies that can satisfy these requirements still poses an important and difficult challenge. Here, declarative approaches have the potential of offering solutions that satisfy the needs for both specifying and developing multiagent systems. Moreover, they are gaining more and more attention in important application areas such as the Semantic Web, Web services, security, and electronic contracting.

DALT 2006 was held as a satellite workshop of AAMAS 2006, the fifth International Joint Conference on Autonomous Agents and Multiagent Systems, in May 2006 in Hakodate, Japan. Following the success of DALT 2003 in Melbourne (LNAI 2990), DALT 2004 in New York (LNAI 3476), and DALT 2005 in Utrecht (LNAI 3904), the workshop again provided a discussion forum to both (a) support the transfer of declarative paradigms and techniques to the broader community of agent researchers and practitioners, and (b) to bring the issue of designing complex agent systems to the attention of researchers working on declarative languages and technologies.

This volume contains the 12 contributed articles that were selected by the Programme Committee for presentation at the workshop as well as three invited articles, originally presented as short papers at AAMAS 2006, that were extended by their authors. The volume also includes the article "Producing Compliant Interactions: Conformance, Coverage, and Interoperability" by Amit K. Chopra and Munindar P. Singh. Professor Singh, from North Carolina State University, was the invited speaker for this edition of DALT.

We would like to thank all authors for their contributions, the members of the DALT Steering Committee for their precious suggestions and support, and the members of the Programme Committee for their excellent work during the reviewing phase.

October 2006

Matteo Baldoni
Ulle Endriss

Workshop Organization

Workshop Organizers

Matteo Baldoni — University of Turin, Italy
Ulle Endriss — University of Amsterdam, Netherlands

Programme Committee

Marco Alberti — University of Ferrara, Italy
Natasha Alechina — University of Nottingham, UK
Grigoris Antoniou — University of Crete, Greece
Matteo Baldoni — University of Turin, Italy
Cristina Baroglio — University of Turin, Italy
Rafael Bordini — University of Durham, UK
Keith Clark — Imperial College London, UK
Ulle Endriss — University of Amsterdam, Netherlands
Benjamin Hirsch — Technical University Berlin, Germany
Shinichi Honiden — National Institute of Informatics, Japan
John Lloyd — Australian National University, Australia
Viviana Mascardi — University of Genoa, Italy
John-Jules Ch. Meyer — Utrecht University, Netherlands
Enrico Pontelli — New Mexico State University, USA
M. Birna van Riemsdijk — Utrecht University, Netherlands
Chiaki Sakama — Wakayama University, Japan
Wamberto Vasconcelos — University of Aberdeen, UK
Christopher Walton — University of Edinburgh, UK
Michael Winikoff — RMIT University, Melbourne, Australia

Additional Reviewers

Giovanni Casella
Valentina Cordì
John Knottenbelt

Steering Committee

João Leite — New University of Lisbon, Portugal
Andrea Omicini — University of Bologna-Cesena, Italy
Leon Sterling — University of Melbourne, Australia
Paolo Torroni — University of Bologna, Italy
Pınar Yolum — Bogazici University, Turkey

Table of Contents

Producing Compliant Interactions: Conformance, Coverage, and Interoperability

Amit K. Chopra and Munindar P. Singh

North Carolina State University

Abstract. Agents in an open system interact with each other based on (typically, published) protocols. An agent may, however, deviate from the protocol because of its internal policies. Such deviations pose certain challenges: (1) the agent might no longer be conformant with the protocol—how do we determine if the agent is conformant? (2) the agent may no longer be able to interoperate with other agents—how do we determine if two agents are interoperable? (3) the agent may not be able to produce some protocol computations; in other words, it may not cover the protocol—how we determine if an agent covers a protocol?

We formalize the notions of conformance, coverage and interoperability. A distinctive feature of our formalization is that the three are orthogonal to each other. Conformance and coverage are based on the semantics of runs (a run being a sequence of states), whereas interoperability among agents is based upon the traditional idea of *blocking*. We present a number of examples to comprehensively illustrate the orthogonality of conformance, coverage, and interoperability.

Compliance is a property of an agent's execution whereas conformance is a property of the agent's design. In order to produce only compliant executions, first and foremost the agent must be conformant; second, it must also be able to interoperate with other agents.

1 Introduction

We investigate the topic of an agent's compliance with a protocol by checking its design for conformance with the protocol and interoperability with other agents. Our agents are set in an open environment, and thus expected to be autonomous and heterogeneous. The interactions of agents are characterized in terms of protocols. The autonomy of an agent is reflected in its policies, which affect how it interacts with others, possibly resulting in deviations from the given protocol.

Deviations complicate the task of determining compliance. To take a simple example, a customer in a purchase protocol may send reminders to a merchant at its own discretion even though the protocol did not encode sending reminders. Some deviations can be flagrant violations. For example, a customer may not pay after receiving the goods it ordered. What can we say about the compliance of these agents? Sending a reminder seems like an innocuous deviation from protocol, whereas not sending the payment appears more serious. One could argue that sending reminders could have been easily incorporated into the protocol. However, when we consider that deviations in protocol are a manifestation of the individual policies of agents, the number of possible deviations from a protocol is potentially infinite. As more deviations are encoded, the resulting

M. Baldoni and U. Endriss (Eds.): DALT 2006, LNAI 4327, pp. 1–15, 2006.

protocol would become large and unwieldy. If each deviant protocol were published as a separate protocol, too many niche protocols would arise. It is better to maintain a smaller number of general protocols and to entertain deviations from such protocols. However, not all deviations are acceptable from the point of view of compliance.

1.1 Compliance: Conformance and Interoperability

For an agent to be compliant with a protocol, first and foremost it must be conformant with the protocol. While agent compliance can only be checked by monitoring the messages the agent exchanges with its peers at runtime, conformance can be verified from its design. The design of an agent involves two primary components: protocols and policies. Protocols are the public part of the design and can be considered fixed for the set of agents that adopt specific roles in the protocol. However, the policies are private to each agent, and potentially unique to each agent. Hence, the design of an agent is a function of its policies. An agent is conformant with a protocol if it respects the semantics of the protocol. A useful criterion when considering conformance is the satisfaction of commitments. Our definition of conformance supports commitments, but it is more general.

The distinction between conformance and compliance is important: an agent's design may conform, but its behavior may not comply. This may be not only because of the agent's failure or unreliable messaging (which do not concern us here), but also because an agent's design may preclude successful interoperation with its peers. In other words, even though an agent is individually conformant, it may not be able to generate compliant computations because of the other agents with whom it interacts, apparently according to the same protocol. Interoperability is distinct from conformance; interoperability is strictly with respect to other agents, whereas conformance is with respect to a protocol.

1.2 Coverage

A protocol may offer a number of alternative execution paths. Some of those paths may be impossible for an agent who deviates from the protocol. Such a reduction in possible paths may be viewed as a reduction in the capabilities of an agent. Conversely, the agent's design may make it possible to interact along paths unforeseen in the protocol. Such an addition may be viewed as an increase in the capabilities of an agent. Informally, we say an agent covers a protocol if it capable of taking any of the paths in the protocol.

This notion of coverage is an important one: if an agent covers a protocol it would appear to be at least as flexible as the protocol. That is, the agent can handle whatever the protocol can "throw" at it. Moreover, in some settings it may be institutionally required that an agent cover a protocol. For example, a tax official must report discrepancies in reviewed filings to the main office; the official cannot ignore them.

1.3 Contributions and Organization

Our contributions include (1) an account of conformance and coverage based on a semantics for protocols suitable for open systems; (2) showing how conformance, coverage, and interoperability are orthogonal concerns; and (3) establishing that in order to only produce compliant interactions, one has to consider both an agent's conformance with the protocol, and its interoperability with other agents.

Section 2 presents the representation of protocols as transition systems. Section 3 discusses the way in which an agent may deviate from protocol. Section 4 defines conformance and coverage. Section 5 discusses the interoperability of agents. Section 6 shows that conformance, coverage, and interoperability are orthogonal; it also discusses the relevant literature.

2 Protocols

We represent protocols as transition systems; the transition systems are similar to those described by $C+$ specifications [5]. The *signature* of a transition system is the set σ of constants that occur in it. Here σ^{act} and σ^{fl} represent the sets of actions and fluents, respectively. Each constant c is assigned a nonempty finite domain $Dom(c)$ of symbols. An *interpretation* of σ is an assignment $c = v$ for each $c \in \sigma$ where $v \in Dom(c)$.

Informally, a transition system is a graph with states as vertices and actions as edges. A state s is a particular interpretation of σ^{fl}, the set of fluents; a transition is a triple $\langle s, e, s' \rangle$ where s and s' are states, and e is an interpretation of σ^{act}, the set of actions. In addition, the initial and final states are marked.

Definition 1. A transition system is a $\langle \sigma^{fl}, \sigma^{act}, S, s_0, F, \delta \rangle$, where σ^{fl} is the set of fluents, σ^{act} is the set of actions, S is the set of states such that $S \subseteq 2^{\sigma^{fl}}$, $s_0 \in S$ is an initial state, $F \subseteq S$ is the set of final states, $\delta \subseteq S \times E \times S$ is the set of transitions, where $E \subseteq 2^{\sigma^{act}}$.

Figure 1 shows the transition system of a purchase protocol. The protocol has two roles: *merchant* (*mer*) and *customer* (*cus*) engaging in the steps below:

1. The customer sends a *request* for quotes to the merchant.
2. The merchant responds either by sending an *offer* for the goods for which the customer requested a quote, or by indicating the nonavailability of requested goods in which case the protocol ends. By sending an offer, the merchant creates the conditional commitment *CC(mer, cus, a_price, an_item)* meaning that if the customer pays price *a_price*, then the merchant will send the goods *an_item*.
3. The customer can respond to the offer by either sending an *accept*, or a *reject*. Accepting the quote creates a conditional commitment *CC(cus, mer, an_item, a_price)*, meaning that if the merchant sends the goods, then the customer will pay. If the customer sends a *reject*, the protocol ends.
4. If the customer sends a *payment* to the merchant, then *CC(cus, mer, an_item, a_price)* is discharged and *CC(mer, cus, a_price, an_item)* is reduced to *C(mer, cus, an_item)* meaning that the merchant is now committed to sending the goods. But if the merchant sends *an_item* to the customer, then *CC(mer, cus, a_price,an_item)* is discharged and *CC(cus, mer, an_item, a_price)* is reduced to *C(cus, mer, a_price)* meaning that the customer is now committed to paying for the goods.
5. If the customer has paid in the previous step, then the merchant sends the goods, thereby discharging its commitment. But if the merchant has sent the goods in

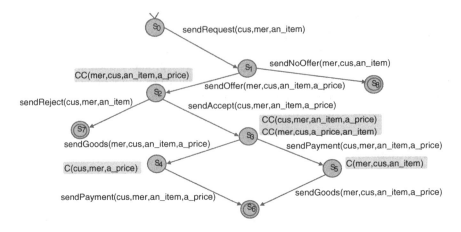

Fig. 1. A purchase protocol

the previous step, then the customer sends the payment, thereby discharging its commitment. In either case, no commitments or conditional commitments hold in the resulting state, which is a final state of the protocol.

Table 1 shows the interpretation of states in the transition system. An action starting with 'send' represents a single message exchange between roles with the *sender* role and *receiver* role as the first and second arguments, respectively. The fluents *initial* and *final* mark the start state and the final states respectively.

We now introduce some definitions related to transition systems.

Definition 2. A path in a transition system is a series of transitions $\langle s_0, e_0, s_1 \rangle$, $\langle s_1, e_1, s_2 \rangle$, ...,$\langle s_{f-1}, e_{f-1}, s_f \rangle$ such that s_0 is the initial state, and s_f is a final state.

A path may be abbreviated as $\langle s_0, e_0, s_1, e_1, \ldots, e_{f-1}, s_f \rangle$. Given a path $\rho = \langle s_0, e_0, s_1, \ldots, s_i, e_i, \ldots, e_{f-1}, s_f \rangle$, we say $e_i \in \rho$ $(0 \le i < f)$, and $s_i \in \rho$ $(0 \le i \le f)$.

We restrict our attention to two-party protocols. All the actions performed by the agents are communications. We further assume about the transition system of any protocol or agent that (1) only one action is performed along any transition; (2) in any transition $\langle s, e, s' \rangle$, $s \not\equiv s'$; (3) there exist no transitions $\langle s, e, s' \rangle$ and $\langle s, e', s' \rangle$ such that $e \equiv e'$ (in other words, no two distinct actions cause a transition into the same destination state from the same origin state); (4) the transition system is deterministic; and (5) along any path in the transition system, an action is performed at most once.

Definition 3. A *run* in a transition system is a series of states $\langle s_0, s_1, \ldots, s_f \rangle$ such that there exists a path $\langle s_0, e_0, s_1, e_1, \ldots, e_{f-1}, s_f \rangle$ in the transition system.

For example, the protocol of Figure 1 has the runs: $\langle s_0, s_1, s_8 \rangle$, $\langle s_0, s_1, s_2, s_7 \rangle$, $\langle s_0, s_1, s_2, s_3, s_4, s_6 \rangle$, and $\langle s_0, s_1, s_2, s_3, s_5, s_6 \rangle$. Note that given the above restrictions, each run maps to a unique path and vice versa.

Definition 4. The t-span $[T]$ of a transition system T is the set of paths in T.

Table 1. States in Figure 1

State	Fluents
s_0	*initial*
s_1	*request(cus, mer, an_item)*
s_2	*request(cus, mer, an_item), offer(mer, cus, an_item, a_price),* *CC(cus, mer, an_item, a_price)*
s_3	*request(cus, mer, an_item), offer(mer, cus, an_item, a_price),* *accept(cus, mer, an_item, a_price), CC(cus, mer, an_item, a_price),* *CC(mer, cus, a_price, an_item)*
s_4	*request(cus, mer, an_item), offer(mer, cus, an_item, a_price),* *accept(cus, mer, an_item, a_price), goods(mer, cus, an_item, a_price),* *C(cus, mer, a_price)*
s_5	*request(cus, mer, an_item), offer(mer, cus, an_item, a_price),* *accept(cus, mer, an_item, a_price), pay(cus, mer, an_item, a_price),* *C(mer, cus, an_item)*
s_6	*request(cus, mer, an_item), offer(mer, cus, an_item, a_price),* *accept(cus, mer, an_item, a_price), goods(mer, cus, an_item, a_price),* *pay(cus, mer, an_item, a_price), final*
s_7	*request(cus, mer, an_item), offer(mer, cus, an_item, a_price),* *reject(cus, mer, an_item, a_price), final*
s_8	*request(cus, mer, an_item), no_offer(mer, cus, an_item), final*

Notice that t-span is thus defined for protocols, role skeletons, and agents.

For example, $\{\langle s_0, s_1, s_2, s_7 \rangle, \langle s_0, s_1, s_8 \rangle, \langle s_0, s_1, s_2, s_3, s_4, s_6 \rangle, \langle s_0, s_1, s_2, s_3, s_5, s_6 \rangle\}$ is the t-span of the purchase protocol of Figure 1.

3 Deviating from Protocol

A role skeleton is a projection of a protocol onto a particular role; it is the transition system of the role. Figure 2 shows the customer skeleton. A customer's policies are combined with the customer role to create a new transition system representing the customer agent. Saying an agent is conformant with a protocol is the same as saying it is conformant with the role it adopts in the protocol; the same holds for coverage. Also note that if the transition system of an agent is identical to the skeleton of the role it adopts, we shall say that the agent *follows* the role.

The policies that go into designing an agent may be such that it follows a protocol. Or, they may be such that the agent encodes deviations from the protocol. Below, we list some common kinds of deviations.

Narrowing. The t-span of an agent is a proper subset of the t-span of the role skeleton it adopts: a typical reason for this would be to simplify its implementation.

Example 1. As shown in the agent's transition system in Figure 3, the customer requires the goods to arrive before it sends the payment. Essentially, the customer has removed a run from the role skeleton, namely, the run in which payment happens before the delivery of goods. ∎

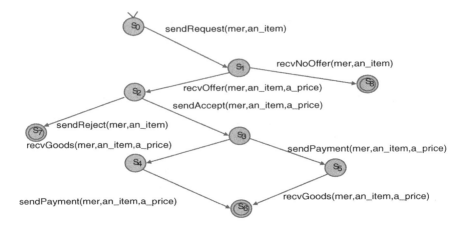

Fig. 2. Customer role skeleton

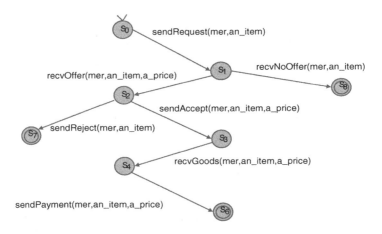

Fig. 3. Customer who sends payment only after receiving goods

Broadening. The t-span of the role skeleton is a proper subset of the t-span of the agent that adopts that role: a typical reason for this would be to handle scenarios not encoded in the protocol.

Example 2. The customer agent sends a reminder to the merchant about its commitment to send goods. Thus, in addition to the original runs, the customer agent includes the run in which it sends a reminder. For the sake of brevity, Figure 4 only shows the additional run; the remaining runs are as in Figure 2.   ∎

Lengthening. The t-span of an agent is similar to that of the role skeleton except that some runs in the t-span of the agent are longer than the corresponding runs in the role skeleton: the reason is that additional actions happen along the path corresponding to the run.

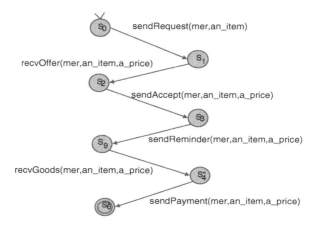

Fig. 4. The run in which customer sends a reminder

Example 3. If we replace the run $\langle s_0, s_1, s_2, s_3, s_4, s_6 \rangle$ in the customer role skeleton (shown in Figure 2) with the run in which a reminder is sent (shown in Figure 4), then it represents an example of lengthening.

Example 4 illustrates the shortening of runs.

Example 4. Consider the customer of Figure 5. After receiving goods, the customer does not send payment for them. State s_4 is a final state for this customer.

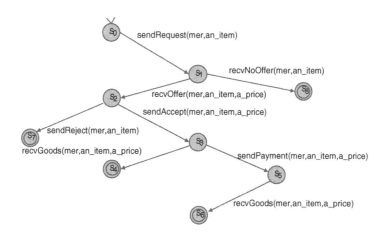

Fig. 5. Customer who does not pay for received goods

Gating. An agent may broaden or lengthen a protocol in such a way that it expects to receive additional messages from its partners in order to proceed.

Example 5. The customer agent may ask for warranty information upon receiving the goods, in which case it expects the merchant to send the information before it makes the payment. The customer is thus "gated" upon the receipt of warranty information. Figure 6 shows the additional run; the remaining runs are as in Figure 2.

Note that combinations of the above deviations are also possible. Example 5, for instance, represents a case of both gating and broadening. It is also possible that an agent represents narrowing as in Example 1, and at the same time represents broadening and gating as in Example 5.

4   Conformance and Coverage

What can we say about the conformance of the customer agent in each of the above examples? Clearly, no customer is following the purchase protocol. Then, are they are all nonconformant? If we look at the agents from the point of view of commitments, it sheds some light on their conformance. No commitments remain unsatisfied in any run in the customers in Examples 1, 2, 3, and 5. We would expect that these customers are determined conformant to their roles. The customer of Example 4, however, has a pending commitment (to pay) in its final state s_4. Consequently, this customer should be determined to be nonconformant.

Similarly, what can we say about the coverage of the customer agent in each of the above examples? Based on the discussion of coverage in Section 1, we would expect the customers in Examples 2 and 5 to be determined to be covering the protocol, whereas the customers in Examples 1 and 4 to be determined to be noncovering. The customer of Example 3 is more interesting: it could be identified as noncovering since one of the runs of the protocol is missing. However, this run has been replaced by a run that sends a reminder: the replacement run is quite similar to the missing run. Sending a reminder does not affect the commitments. Hence, we would expect the customer in Example 3 to be covering.

Our definitions of conformance and coverage rely on the notion of run subsumption [6]. In the following, we briefly discuss run subsumption, then we formally define conformance and coverage.

We introduce *state similarity* to compare states. A state-similarity function f maps a state to a set of states, i.e., $f : \mathbf{S} \rightarrow 2^{\mathbf{S}}$. From f, we induce a binary relation $\approx_f \subseteq \mathbf{S} \times \mathbf{S}$, where $\approx_f = \{(s, f(s)) : s \in \mathbf{S}\}$. We require f to be such that $\approx_f$ is an equivalence relation. For example, commitments could be used to compare states. Two states are *commitment similar* if the same set of commitments hold in them.

Let $\prec_\tau$ be a temporal ordering relation on states in a run τ. That is, $s \prec_\tau s'$ means that s occurs before s' in τ.

Definition 5. A run τ_j subsumes τ_i under a state-similarity function f, denoted by $\tau_j \gg_f \tau_i$ if for every state s_i that occurs in τ_i, there exists a state s_j that occurs in τ_j such that $s_j \approx_f s_i$, and for all s'_i that occur in τ_i, if $s_i \prec_{\tau_i} s'_i$ then there exists s'_j that occurs in τ_j such that $s_j \prec_{\tau_j} s'_j$ and $s'_j \approx_f s'_i$.

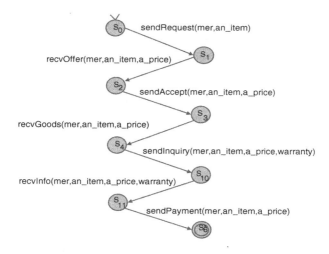

Fig. 6. The run in which the customer asks for warranty information

Run subsumption is reflexive, transitive, and antisymmetric up to state similarity [6]. Longer runs subsume shorter runs, provided they have similar states in the same temporal order.

The closure of a protocol is a span that is closed under run subsumption. That is, if a run is in the closure, then all the runs that subsume it (under some state-similarity function) are also in the closure. Closures are unique (under a particular state-similarity function), and provide a firm basis for comparing protocols; a different closure may be obtained by changing the state-similarity function. For the purposes of this paper, we will use the commitment-similarity function.

Definition 6. The closure of a protocol P under a state-similarity function f is given by $[\![P]\!]_f = \{\tau \mid \forall \tau' \in [P] : \tau \gg_f \tau'\}$.

Definition 7. An agent α is conformant with a protocol P under a state-similarity function f if $[\alpha] \subseteq [\![P]\!]_f$.

As expected, Definition 7 renders the customers in Examples 1, 2, 3 and 5 conformant with the protocol, and the customer in Example 4 nonconformant with the protocol.

Definition 8. An agent α covers a protocol P under a state-similarity function f, if for each $\tau \in [P]$, there exists a $\tau' \in [\alpha]$ such that $\tau' \gg_f \tau$.

As expected, Definition 8 renders the customers in Examples 2, 3 and 5 as covering the protocol, and the customers in Examples 1 and 4 as noncovering.

5   Interoperability

Section 4 defines the conformance of an agent with respect to its role skeleton. A conformant agent respects the semantics of the protocol: it encodes only runs in the closure of the protocol. However, just because an agent is conformant does not mean it can always successfully interoperate with other conformant agents. Let us consider the examples below involving conformant customer and merchant agents; the merchant, in particular, follows its role in the protocol.

It is worth considering the idea of how protocols can be operationally interpreted. An agent may ignore messages that are not in its vocabulary (i.e., do not occur in its t-span). Or an agent may ignore all messages that are unexpected, specifically including those that are in the vocabulary but arrive out of order.

Example 6. The customer sends reminders as shown in Figure 4. The reminders are not in the t-span of the protocol, but are in its closure. Thus they are allowed but may not be implemented by agents playing other roles. Such reminders do not cause a problem in interoperation: the merchant cannot handle reminders, but can ignore them.

Example 6 is benign in that even though the customer does something the merchant does not expect, both can execute the protocol to completion. Therefore, we expect these agents to be rendered interoperable.

Example 7. The customer sends payment only upon receipt of goods (as in Figure 3) from a merchant. Even though, the customer and merchant are individually conformant with their respective roles, they exists the possibility of a deadlock: the customer waits for the merchant to send goods first, and the merchant waits for the customer to send payment first.

Because of the possibility of a deadlock, we expect the agents in Example 7 to be rendered noninteroperable.

Example 8. The customer agent asks for warranty according to the run shown in Figure 6. The merchant cannot fulfill the customer's warranty information request: the merchant simply ignores the request. And the customer would not send payment until it receives the warranty information.

We expect the agents in Example 8 to be rendered noninteroperable. In this example, noninteroperability causes a violation of a customer's commitment to pay.

5.1   Verifying Interoperability

The interoperability of two agents depends upon the computations that they can jointly generate. The agents may act one by one or in true concurrency. Definition 9 captures the above intuitions for a product transition system of a pair of agents.

Definition 9. Given two agents $\alpha_1 := \langle \sigma_1^{fl}, \sigma_1^{act}, S_1, s_{0_1}, F_1, \delta_1 \rangle$ and $\alpha_2 := \langle \sigma_2^{fl}, \sigma_2^{act}, S_2, s_{0_2}, F_2, \delta_2 \rangle$, the product transition system $\alpha_\times = \alpha_1 \times \alpha_2$ is given by $\alpha_\times := \langle \sigma_\times^{fl}, \sigma_\times^{act}, S_\times, s_{0_\times}, F_\times, \delta_\times \rangle$ where,

- $\sigma_\times^{fl} = \sigma_1^{fl} \cup \sigma_2^{fl}$
- $\sigma_\times^{act} = \sigma_1^{act} \cup \sigma_2^{act}$
- $S_\times = S_1 \times S_2$

- $s_{0_\times} = (s_{0_1}, s_{0_2})$
- $F_\times = F_1 \times F_2$
- $\delta_\times \subseteq S_\times \times E_\times \times S_\times$ where $E \subseteq 2^{\sigma_\times^{act}}$ such that $\langle s, e, s' \rangle \in \delta_\times$, where $s = s_1 \times s_2$ and $s' = s'_1 \times s'_2$, $(s_1, s'_1 \in S_1)$, $(s_2, s'_2 \in S_2)$, if and only if
  - $\langle s_1, e, s'_1 \rangle \in \delta_1$, or
  - $\langle s_2, e, s'_2 \rangle \in \delta_2$, or
  - $e = (e_1, e_2)$ and $\langle s_1, e_1, s'_1 \rangle \in \delta_1$ and $\langle s_2, e_2, s'_2 \rangle \in \delta_2$.

The technical motivation behind Definition 9 is that it accommodates the transitions that would globally result as the agents enact the given protocol. When the agents act one by one, the transitions are labeled with an action from their respective σ^{act}. When the agents act concurrently, the transitions are labeled by a pair of actions, one from each agent.

Interoperability can become challenging in light of the fact that communication between agents is asynchronous. The essence of these challenges is that an agent might block indefinitely upon doing a receive. We verify the interoperability of agents by analyzing their product transition system for the absence of such problems.

The sending of a message m by an agent α is represented by $send(\alpha, m)$. Similarly, receiving a message is represented by $recv(\alpha, m)$. When the identity of the agent does not matter, we write only $send(m)$ and $recv(m)$ instead. Below $x, y, \ldots$ range over messages $m_1, m_2, \ldots$, and $\alpha, \beta, \ldots$ are agents.

Definition 10. An action a strictly precedes an action b on a path ρ in the product transition system, denoted by $a \prec_\rho b$, if and only if $a \in e_i$ and $b \in e_j$ such that $e_i, e_j \in \rho$ and $i < k$. If we change the index condition to $i \leq k$, we say $a \preceq_\rho b$.

Next, we identify all the pathological paths in the product, i.e., those that can be never be realized during execution. A kind of pathological path is one whose execution is impossible under considerations of asynchrony, for instance, a path where the receipt of a message happens precedes its sending. Another kind of pathological path can be identified when we associate angelic determinism with attempted receipts of messages. The idea is that if an action $send(\alpha, x)$ happens, and it it is possible to execute one of either $recv(\beta, x)$ or $recv(\beta, y)$ ($x \neq y$), then $recv(\beta, x)$ is executed. Definition 11 allows for angelic nondeterminism on receives; specifically, it identifies paths that appear "bad" as they appear to block on a receive, but are "saved" by angelic nondeterminism.

Definition 11. A path $\rho = \langle \ldots, s_i, e_i, s_j, \ldots \rangle$ is said to be locally matched by a path $\rho' = \langle \ldots, s_i, e'_i, s_k, \ldots \rangle$ in the product transition system if and only if

- $recv(\alpha, x) \in e_i$ and $send(\beta, x)$ never occurs on ρ, and
- $recv(\alpha, y) \in e'_i$ and $send(\beta, y)$ occurs on ρ'.

Definition 12 defines a product transition system that contains only paths that can be realized (paths which block are considered realizable).

Definition 12. A causal product transition system based on two agents is a transition system whose set of paths is a subset of the paths of the product transition system of the two agents such that it contains no path $\rho = \langle \ldots, s_i, e_i, s_{i+1}, \ldots \rangle$ that satisfies one of the conditions below:

- for some i, $e_i = recv(x)$ or $e_i = (recv(x), send(y))$, such that $recv(x) \prec_\rho send(x)$, or
- it is locally matched.

Definition 13. A path $\rho = \langle \ldots, s_i, e_i, s_{i+1}, \ldots \rangle$ in the product transition system is a deadlock path if and only if $e_i = (recv(x), recv(y))$ and $recv(x) \prec_\rho send(x)$ and $recv(y) \prec_\rho send(y)$.

Note that Definition 12 does not consider $e_i = (recv(x), recv(y))$ as they might be the indication of deadlocks. However, it might remove other paths that are an indication of deadlocks, for example, ρ where $recv(\alpha, x) \prec_\rho recv(\beta, y)$ and $recv(\alpha, x) \prec_\rho send(\beta, x)$ and $recv(\beta, y) \prec_\rho send(\alpha, y)$. However, from the construction of the product, if there is such a path ρ in the product, there must be a corresponding deadlock path ρ'. Hence, ρ may be removed without compromising our ability to detect deadlocks.

Definition 14. A path $\rho = \langle \ldots, s_i, e_i, s_{i+1}, \ldots \rangle$ is a blocking path if and only if for some $recv(x) \in e_i$, there occurs no $send(x)$ on the path.

Definition 15. A path $\rho = \langle \ldots, s_i, e_i, s_{i+1}, \ldots \rangle$ is an out-of-order path if and only if $recv(\alpha, x) \preceq_\rho recv(\alpha, y)$ and $send(\beta, y) \preceq_\rho send(\beta, x)$.

Definition 16. Two agents are interoperable if and only if in the causal product of their transition systems

- there exists no deadlock path, and
- there exists no blocking path, and
- there exists no out-of-order path.

As expected, Definition 16 renders the agents in Example 6 interoperable. Also as expected, it renders the agents in Examples 7 and 8 as noninteroperable; it also renders the customer in Example 4 noninteroperable with a merchant that follows protocol. In fact, if the customer and merchant each follows their roles, they will be rendered noninteroperable (and rightly so) because of the nonlocal choice between sending goods and sending payment. It may be argued that a protocol with nonlocal choice is inherently incomplete and, therefore, may be considered as an abstract protocol. For such protocols further negotiation is necessary between the agents or their designers to ensure interoperability.

6 Discussion

We have defined conformance and coverage in a way that respects the semantics of the protocol. Although we have used a commitment-based semantics, the semantics primarily depend on the state-similarity function. Our definitions of conformance and coverage allow agents flexibility in their interactions, which is crucial in open settings. By contrast, interoperability is strictly about an agent receiving a message it expects to receive. In that manner, interoperability is less semantic, and imposes strict restrictions on agents to interoperate.

6.1 Proving Orthogonality

We prove the orthogonality of conformance, coverage, and interoperability with the help of examples. We have already seen that agents that follow the customer and merchant roles respectively in the purchase protocol of Figure 1 are not interoperable. Now we consider a variant of the purchase protocol which does not have the pay-before-goods path. Specifically, let's consider the protocol of Figure 1, but without the run $\langle s_0, s_1, s_2, s_3, s_5, s_6 \rangle$. Let this variant be P'. Figure 3 would then depict the customer role skeleton; the merchant's role skeleton would be symmetric except that the sends and receives would be swapped. Table 2 considers the conformance and coverage of different merchant agents with respect to P', and the agents' interoperability with a customer that follows the customer role. (Figure 7 shows the paths that the table refers to.) It is clear from the table that the conformance, coverage, and interoperability are orthogonal concerns, because examples of all possible combinations of their truth and falsity exist.

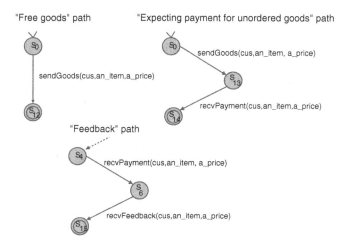

Fig. 7. Some runs used in Table 2

6.2 Literature

Baldoni *et al.* [2] and Endriss *et al.* [4] present alternative formalizations of conformance and interoperability. Both formalizations, however, violate the orthogonality of conformance and interoperability with the result that many agents that should be considered conformant in a practical setting—and are determined to be conformant according to our formalization—are rendered nonconformant in theirs. For example, they would both determine the customer who sends reminders to be nonconformant. Agents that are conformant by our definition, but gate on some message not in the role they are playing, seem to present a problem. Such agents would not be interoperable with agents that are conformant but do not send the message being gated upon. Importantly,

Table 2. Orthogonality of conformance (**C**), coverage (**V**), and interoperability (**X**)

Merchant agents	C	V	X
Only has path expecting payment for unordered goods	×	×	×
Has additional free goods path and no reject path	×	×	✓
Has additional path expecting payment for unordered goods	×	✓	×
Has additional free goods path	×	✓	✓
Has the goods-pay path gated on feedback and no reject path	✓	×	×
Has no reject path	✓	×	✓
Has the goods-pay path gated on feedback	✓	✓	×
Follows role	✓	✓	✓

such agents could potentially violate their commitments because of the gating; in other words, they could potentially produce noncompliant executions. For example, the customer in Example 5 would violate its commitment to pay if it fails to receive the warranty information.

Deeming such an agent nonconformant would, however, be unduly restrictive. The noninteroperability of such an agent with other agents could be detected, and special measures taken to ensure that an agent does not blindly enter such interactions. Specifically, such measures include developing agents who can negotiate with others about the possibilities of deviating from their chosen roles. Even if the agents involved cannot negotiate—then the agents are effectively noninteroperable—this situation is more acceptable than potentially violating a commitment. Our formalization of conformance and interoperability supports such scenarios.

Approaches based on verifying compliance at runtime [1,7] are important in the context of open systems since agents may behave in unpredictable ways; also it is necessary to have independent arbiters in case of disputes involving agents. Such approaches are complementary to this work.

6.3   Directions

A possible direction is to extend this work to more general protocols and agents: specifically, multiparty protocols and agents with infinite runs. Also, this work may be tied together with work on protocol transformations [3]: it would be interesting to be able to determine which transformers, when applied to a protocol, would preserve conformance, coverage, and interoperability.

References

1. M. Alberti, D. Daolio, P. Torroni, M. Gavanelli, E. Lamma, and P. Mello. Specification and verification of agent interaction protocols in a logic-based system. In *Proceedings of the 19th ACM Symposium on Applied Computing (SAC 2004)*, pages 72–78, 2004.
2. M. Baldoni, C. Baroglio, A. Martelli, and V. Patti. Verification of protocol conformance and agent interoperability. In *6th International Workshop on Computational Logic in Multi-Agent Systems (CLIMA VI)*, pages 265–283, 2005.

3. A. K. Chopra and M. P. Singh. Contextualization of commitment protocols. In *Proceedings of the Fifth International Joint Conference on Autonomous Agents and Multiagent Systems*, 2006.
4. U. Endriss, N. Maudet, F. Sadri, and F. Toni. Protocol conformance for logic-based agents. In *Proceedings of the 18th International Joint Conference on Artificial Intelligence*, pages 679–684, 2003.
5. E. Giunchiglia, J. Lee, V. Lifschitz, N. McCain, and H. Turner. Nonmonotonic causal theories. *Artificial Intelligence*, 153(1-2):49–104, 2004.
6. A. U. Mallya and M. P. Singh. An algebra for commitment protocols. *Journal of Autonomous Agents and Multiagent Systems special issue on Agent Communication (JAAMAS)*, Apr 2006.
7. M. Venkatraman and M. P. Singh. Verifying compliance with commitment protocols: Enabling open Web-based multiagent systems. *Journal of Autonomous Agents and Multi-Agent Systems*, 2(3):217–236, Sept. 1999.

Towards Theory Translation[*]

Dejing Dou[1] and Drew McDermott[2]

[1] Computer and Information Science
University of Oregon
Eugene, OR 97403, USA
`dou@cs.uoregon.edu`
[2] Computer Science Department
Yale University
New Haven, Connecticut 06520, USA
`drew.mcdermott@yale.edu`

Abstract. Ontologies play a key role in agent communication and the emerging Semantic Web to define a vocabulary of concepts and their relationships. Different agents and web services may use vocabularies from different ontologies to describe their data. The current research on ontology mapping and ontology translation mainly focuses on how to map and translate vocabularies and associated data instances from one ontology to another. However, more complicated true statements, such as axioms (rules), are used or being developed to describe the relationships among the concepts. When extending one ontology using complicated true statements (theory) from another, we must confront the problem of *theory translation*, which is difficult because of the *asymmetry of translation*. In this paper, using an inferential approach we call *axiom derivation*, we show how to translate complex axioms between different time ontologies. We also prove the validity of our algorithm.

1 Introduction

Ontologies, which can be defined as the formal specification of a vocabulary of concepts and the relationships among them, play a key role in agent communication and the emerging Semantic Web [3]. Multiple agents and Semantic Web services often need to share data, in spite of the fact that they describe similar domains using different vocabularies, or use the same symbols to mean different things. This *semantic heterogeneity* problem has received significant attention. (See [21] for a survey.) We can distinguish several different problems:

1. *Ontology matching and mapping:* Finding correspondences (matchings) and mappings between the concepts of two ontologies. The mappings are often equivalences, subclass-superclass (or subproperty-superproperty) relationships and other more complicated relationships.

---

[*] This work was partly supported by the DARPA DAML project, under contract F30602-00-2-0600. This is an invited paper that is extended from our short paper "Deriving Axioms across Ontologies" in AAMAS2006 [12].

M. Baldoni and U. Endriss (Eds.): DALT 2006, LNAI 4327, pp. 16–28, 2006.

2. *Ontology translation:* Translating a dataset (assertions) or a query expressed using one ontology (or set of ontologies) into a form that uses a different ontology (or set).
3. *Theory translation:* Translating more complicated true statements (theory), such as axioms, of one ontology into the vocabulary of another while preserving their validity.

Significant works [10,17,20,5] cover the first category while others [15,7,9,14,8] concern the second. In this paper we focus on the third.

Ontologies constrain the meanings of vocabularies by expressing relationships among their symbols, such as subset-superset links, role declarations, and the like. Complex relationships can be expressed only with logical theory, such as axioms (rules). For example, to overcome the expressivity limitation of OWL (Web Ontology Language [2]), the research on OWL Rule languages [16] has proposed a Horn clause rules extension to represent the relationships among properties. On the other hand, the semantic mappings between the concepts of different ontologies also can be represented as logical axioms. For example, the research on MAFRA [17] and C-OWL [4] can represent the mappings between the contents of different ontologies by extending DAML+OIL [1] and OWL syntax and semantics. Our previous work on OntoMerge [13,14] has used first order bridging axioms to represent semantic mappings. It is well known that complex mapping rules can not be generated fully automatically; human experts may need to help the process based on the mapping suggestions from automatic or semi-automatic ontology mapping tools such as those described in [10,17,20,5].

Normally, the data instances and queries can be automatically translated from the source ontology to the target ontology once the semantic mappings have been discovered and presented to translators [7,9,14,8]. However, little research has been done on translating the axioms or other complicated true statements (theory) automatically, which raises the possibility that important semantic constraints will be lost in translation. It is important to represent theories in different vocabularies and preserve their validity.

In this paper, we will first use one inferential framework to unify the ontology translation and theory translation for facts, queries, axioms and other complicated true statements. One assumption of our framework is that the mappings between the concepts from different ontologies are represented as Horn-like mapping rules, which we call *bridging axioms*. We point out that it is the *asymmetry of translation* that makes the translation of axioms and other complicated theories difficult. We then describe an algorithm called *axiom derivation* for translating theories, such as those axioms in time ontologies, from one ontology to another by both forward and backward chaining. We also prove the validity of our algorithm.

2   Framework and Previous Work

2.1   Merged Ontologies and Bridging Axioms

In this section we briefly review our previous work on ontology translation. We assume that in order to translate facts from one ontology to another there must be a *merged ontology* in which all the relevant symbols are allowed to interact. For example, consider a pair of genealogy ontologies $Gonto_1$ and $Gonto_2$. The former uses the symbols husband and married while the latter uses male_partner, spouse, and in_marriage. The matchings (correspondences) between them can be represented as:

husband $\longrightarrow$ male_partner, spouse
married $\longrightarrow$ in_marriage

but these correspondences only hint at the actual semantic relationships, which can be expressed exactly using these axioms (rules):

$$(\forall x, y)\text{husband}(x, y) \rightarrow \text{male\_partner}(x, y) \tag{1}$$

$$(\forall x, y)\text{husband}(x, y) \leftrightarrow \text{spouse}(x, y) \tag{2}$$

$$(\forall x, y)\text{married}(x, y) \leftrightarrow \text{in\_marriage}(x, y) \tag{3}$$

where x and y are universal variables to represent male and female respectively. We call these axiomatic mapping rules *bridging axioms*. We have developed *Web-PDDL* as a strongly typed first-order logic language with Lisp-like syntax, to express Horn-like bridging axioms. These axioms are embedded in a *merged ontology* complete with namespace declarations and type-equivalence rules. For example, to represent axiom 2, we use the following Web-PDDL expression:

```
(forall (x - @Go1:Male y - @Go1:Female)
    (iff  (@Go1:husband x y)
          (@Go2:spouse x y)))
```

where Go1 and Go2 are prefixes of $Gonto_1$ and $Gonto_2$. These correspond to XML namespaces, and when Web-PDDL is translated to RDF [19], that is exactly what they become. The hyphen notation is used to declare a constant or variable to be of a type T, by writing "x - T".

However, unlike typical Horn clauses, bridging axioms can have conjunction of predicates on the conclusion side (see more examples later in Section 5). The predicates in bridging axioms can have built-in (but non-recursive) functions as arguments. Based on our previous experience with mapping different pairs of ontologies, this form is expressive enough for most mappings found by mapping tools or human experts.

2.2   Inferential Ontology Translation

We will use the symbol $\rightsquigarrow$ to indicate translation: $\alpha \rightsquigarrow \beta$ means that β is the translation of α. We call the ontology O_s that α uses the *source* ontology and O_t, the one β uses, the *target*. In the case of sets of assertions ("datasets"), we stipulate that the translation of α_d is simply the strongest set of assertions, β_d, in O_t entailed by α_d. A consequence of this stipulation is that

$$(KB; \alpha_d) \rightsquigarrow \beta_d \ only \ if \ (KB; \alpha_d) \models \beta_d$$

where we add to the left-hand sides the symbol KB to refer to the merged ontology which includes bridging axioms (mapping rules). It means we use entailment ($\models$) to define dataset translation: if all the bridging axioms in KB and all the assertions in α_d are true, then all the assertions in β_d should be true. Alternatively, we say that β_d is a logical (or semantic) consequence of KB and α_d. The only way to guarantee this entailment is to use sound inference ($\vdash$) in first order theory. In other words, "$\rightsquigarrow$" entails soundness, so we actually can use $\vdash$ to implement dataset translation:

$$(KB; \alpha_d) \rightsquigarrow \beta_d \ \Leftrightarrow \ (KB; \alpha_d) \vdash \beta_d \ \Rightarrow \ (KB; \alpha_d) \models \beta_d$$

This definition means that β_d is the largest set of assertions that can be derived from KB and α_d by inference.

Similarly, if α_q is a query in O_s, its translation is a query β_q in O_t such that any answer (set of bindings) to β_q is also an answer to α_q. In other words:

$$(KB; \alpha_q) \rightsquigarrow \beta_q \ only \ if \ (KB; \theta(\beta_q)) \models \theta(\alpha_q)$$

for any substitution θ, which is from the facts in the target database. It means we still use entailment ($\models$) to define the query translation. It is easy to get, for any substitution θ,

$$(KB; \alpha_q) \rightsquigarrow \beta_q \ \Leftrightarrow \ (KB; \theta(\beta_q)) \vdash \theta(\alpha_q)$$
$$\Rightarrow \ (KB; \theta(\beta_q)) \models \theta(\alpha_q)$$

where a sound inference ($\vdash$) can actually implement and guarantee the entailment. The point is that β_q need not be (and seldom is) *equivalent* to α_q, in the sense that any answer to one is an answer to the other. All we need is that any answer to β_q be an answer to α_q. If we take O_s to be $Gonto_2$ and O_t to be $Gonto_1$, the query male_partner($?x, ?y$) in $Gonto_2$ will be translated into the query husband($?x, ?y$) in $Gonto_1$. But the set of all husbands is not equivalent to the set of all male partners, since husbands are only one kind of male partners.

In order to use bridging axioms for inferential ontology translation, we built a special purpose first-order theorem prover called OntoEngine. OntoEngine has both forward chaining and backward chaining reasoners using generalized modus ponens [22]. The dataset translation can be implemented by a forward chaining reasoner and the query translation can be implemented by a backward chaining reasoner. Our framework has been evaluated by using OntoEngine on several real ontology translation tasks. Some of them need OntoEngine to process large sets of data. The results of experiments show that the translation for both data and queries works efficiently [14,11].

3   Asymmetry and Composition of Theory Translation

3.1   Asymmetry of Translation

In the previous section, we have shown that a genealogy ontology $Gonto_1$ has two concepts (properties): husband and married. There may be a first-order logic axiom to describe their relationship:

$$(\forall x, y)\text{husband}(x, y) \rightarrow \text{married}(x, y) \qquad (4)$$

We also know that another genealogy ontology $Gonto_2$ has male_partner, spouse and in_marriage as mapped properties. Some facts (assertions) expressed in the language of $Gonto_1$, can be translated into the language of $Gonto_2$ by simply replacing corresponding properties:

$$\text{husband}(\text{John}, \text{Mary}) \rightsquigarrow \text{male\_partner}(\text{John}, \text{Mary})$$

$$\text{husband}(\text{John}, \text{Mary}) \rightsquigarrow \text{spouse}(\text{John}, \text{Mary})$$

$$\text{married}(\text{John}, \text{Mary}) \rightsquigarrow \text{in\_marriage}(\text{John}, \text{Mary})$$

The translations are correct in terms of the semantics of $Gonto_1$ and $Gonto_2$, where husband can be thought of as spouse and a special kind of male_partner. However, if we use the same technique to translate the axiom (4) of $Gonto_1$ to $Gonto_2$, we get:

$$(\forall x, y)\text{male\_partner}(x, y) \rightarrow \text{in\_marriage}(x, y) \qquad (5)$$

$$(\forall x, y)\text{spouse}(x, y) \rightarrow \text{in\_marriage}(x, y) \qquad (6)$$

It is obvious that (5) is not always true since a man is a partner of a woman doesn't mean that he must be in a marriage with her; (5) is not a valid axiom in $Gonto_2$. But (6) is true as an axiom in $Gonto_2$. Why is it that the translation from (4) to (6) is correct, but the translation from (4) to (5) is not correct?

Given our inferential ontology translation framework, translation exhibits certain asymmetries that one must be wary of. Query translation is different from assertion translation. We will subscript the symbol $\rightsquigarrow$ with a "Q" to indicate the query case ($\rightsquigarrow_Q$), and with a "D" (for "data") to indicate the assertion or dataset case($\rightsquigarrow_D$). (We leave the subscript off in those cases where the context allows either reading.) In addition, if β_t is the translation of α_s:

$$(KB; \alpha_s) \rightsquigarrow \beta_t$$

that doesn't mean α_s is the translation of β_t:

$$(KB; \beta_t) \rightsquigarrow \alpha_s$$

Slightly less obviously, if $(KB; P) \rightsquigarrow Q$ we can't conclude $(KB; \neg P) \rightsquigarrow \neg Q$.

3.2 Composition of Theory Translation

Instead (not surprisingly), negation ends up involving the same duality as query translation. Assume that R is an expression which can be derived from KB and $\neg P_s$ by inference. Using the deduction theorem in first-order logic and considering that $\neg P_s \rightarrow R$ is equivalent to $\neg R \rightarrow P_s$, we know that

$$
\begin{aligned}
(KB; \neg P_s) \vdash R &\Leftrightarrow KB \vdash (\neg P_s \rightarrow R) \\
&\Leftrightarrow KB \vdash (\neg R \rightarrow P_s) \\
&\Leftrightarrow (KB; \neg R) \vdash P_s
\end{aligned}
$$

This gives us a way to translate negations. We can think of P_s as a "ground query" ($\theta(P_s) = P_s$): Given P_s, try to find a Q'_t, which satisfies $(KB; Q'_t) \vdash P_s$. But this is just the problem of translating the query P_s: $(KB; P_s) \rightsquigarrow_Q Q'_t$.

Therefore, if the query translation of P_s is Q'_t, $\neg Q'_t$ can be derived from KB and $\neg P_s$ by the data translation and vice versa:

$$
\begin{aligned}
(KB; P_s) \rightsquigarrow_Q Q'_t &\Rightarrow (KB; \neg P_s) \rightsquigarrow_D \neg Q'_t \\
(KB; P_s) \rightsquigarrow_D Q'_t &\Rightarrow (KB; \neg P_s) \rightsquigarrow_Q \neg Q'_t
\end{aligned}
$$

Theory, such as axioms, are usually more complex than a typical dataset element, and it would be useful if we could attack this complexity by translating the pieces of a complex formula and composing the results. The presence of asymmetry means that care is required in doing the composition. For conjunctions and disjunctions, composition of translation is straightforward. It is easy to show that if we know that

$$
(KB; P_{s1}) \rightsquigarrow Q_{t1} \; ; \; (KB; P_{s2}) \rightsquigarrow Q_{t2}
$$

then

$$
\begin{aligned}
(KB; P_{s1} \wedge P_{s2}) &\rightsquigarrow Q_{t1} \wedge Q_{t2} \\
(KB; P_{s1} \vee P_{s2}) &\rightsquigarrow Q_{t1} \vee Q_{t2}
\end{aligned}
$$

But when we encounter a negation we must flip from "D" mode to "Q" mode or vice versa.

Since every complicated true statement (theory) in first-order can be put into CNF [1], we just need to consider the translation of negations and disjunctions. The composition of the translation of disjunctions is straightforward. In the following section, we will describe an algorithm for translating implications (e.g., axiom (4)), which includes translating negations. It actually shows that we can translate any true statement (theory) from one ontology to another ontology, after we transform the theory to CNF form.

---

[1] Conjunctive normal form (CNF): a conjunction of clauses, where each clause is a disjunction of literals. Literals can have negations and variables. For example, the implication $P_{s1} \rightarrow P_{s2}$ can be transformed to its equivalent $\neg P_{s1} \vee P_{s2}$.

4   Axiom Derivation

4.1   Conditional Facts and ICF Axioms

To explain our approach to theory (axiom) translation, we first show how to translate *conditional facts* using OntoEngine. A conditional fact is a formula of the form:

$$P_1 \wedge \cdots \wedge P_i \cdots \wedge P_n \rightarrow Q_1 \wedge \cdots \wedge Q_j \wedge \cdots \wedge Q_m$$

where all $P_i (1 \leq i \leq n)$ and $Q_j (1 \leq j \leq m)$ are ground atomic formulas (facts). The axioms, such as axioms 4 and horn-like bridging axioms, can be put in this form which we call *ICF (Implicative Conjunction Form)*, but of course axioms have quantified variables:

$$\forall v_1 \ldots \exists v_k \ldots v_l, \; P_1 \wedge \cdots \wedge P_i \cdots \wedge P_n \rightarrow Q_1 \wedge \cdots \wedge Q_j \wedge \cdots \wedge Q_m$$

where the v are quantified and typed variables, some universal (e.g., v_1) and some existential.

It is unusual but not unheard of for people to need to express that some facts are true only if some other facts are also true:

$$precedes(deathof(Roosevelt), \; endof(WW2)) \rightarrow$$
$$president(Truman, \; endof(WW2))$$

"If Roosevelt died before the end of World War 2, then Truman was president at the end of World War 2."

4.2   Conditional Fact Translation

Conditional fact translation is the translation of a conditional fact from the source ontology to the target ontology. This is a typical example for which we need to consider asymmetry of translation since the translation of implications actually includes the translation of negations and disjunctions. For example, suppose we have a simple conditional fact in $Gonto_1$:

$$@\mathsf{Go1} : \mathsf{husband}(A, B) \rightarrow @\mathsf{Go1} : \mathsf{married}(A, B)$$

where Go1 is the prefix of $Gonto_1$ (adopting some syntax from Web-PDDL) and A and B are a male and a female. We want to translate this conditional fact to $Gonto_2$ which has prefix Go2.

Considering the asymmetry of translation, the antecedent @Go1:husband(A,B) can be translated to @Go2:spouse(A,B) by the query translation with backward chaining, and the conclusion @Go1:married(A,B) can be translated to @Go2: in_marriage(A,B) by data translation with forward chaining. We know the result

$$@\mathsf{Go2} : \mathsf{spouse}(A, B) \rightarrow @\mathsf{Go2} : \mathsf{in\_marriage}(A, B)$$

is a true statement in $Gonto_2$.

In summary, the algorithm to do conditional fact translation is:

Procedure CFT(C_s, M)

input: conditional fact C_s in the source ontology O_s, bridging axioms M between O_s and the target ontology, O_t

output: translated conditional fact C_t in O_t

steps:

1. Let Ant_s be the antecedent of C_s and Con_s be the conclusion of C_s (C_s: $Ant_s \rightarrow Con_s$.)
2. Get the antecedent of C_t, Ant_t, by backward chaining of Ant_s with M from O_s to O_t.
3. Get the conclusion of C_t, Con_t, by forward chaining of Con_s with M from O_s to O_t.
4. Return C_t as $Ant_t \rightarrow Con_t$.

It should be obvious that this process yields a valid result, in the sense that the translated fact follows from the original fact and the axioms. If backward chaining from the antecedent fails to find any goals in the target ontology, then the antecedent of the translated conditional fact will be empty, or false, making the translation itself equivalent to true — and hence useless.

4.3   Extending Conditional Facts Translation to Axiom Derivation

The translation of ICF axioms can still be thought of as an inference process called *axiom derivation*, if we can transform the axioms to conditional facts and transform the conditional facts back to axioms. The idea is to substitute Skolem constants for the variables temporarily. (A similar technique was used in [18].) In general, axiom derivation can be broken into three steps:

From ICF axioms to conditional facts: we can use Universal Elimination and Existential Elimination [22] to transform ICF axioms to conditional facts. Suppose that we have an axiom in the source ontology O_s:

$$(\forall x, y)@\text{O\_s} : \text{P}(x, y) \rightarrow$$
$$(\exists z)@\text{O\_s} : \text{Q}(x, z) \wedge @\text{O\_s} : \text{R}(z, y)$$

We can substitute the universal quantified variables with constants (e.g., Atx and Bty) and substitute the existential quantified variables with uniquified Skolem terms (e.g., Skz01):

$$@\text{O\_s} : \text{P}(\text{Atx}, \text{Bty}) \rightarrow$$
$$@\text{O\_s} : \text{Q}(\text{Atx}, \text{Skz01}) \wedge @\text{O\_s} : \text{R}(\text{Skz01}, \text{Bty})$$

Conditional facts translation: suppose that the target ontology is O_t and we already have the merged ontology of O_s and O_t. The conditional fact in O_s can be translated to O_t. By backward chaining from the antecedent and forward chaining from the conclusion, we finally get a conditional fact in O_t:

$$@\text{O\_t} : \text{S}'(\text{Atx}, \text{Ctc}) \wedge @\text{O\_t} : \text{T}'(\text{Ctc}, \text{Bty}) \rightarrow$$
$$@\text{O\_t} : \text{U}(\text{Atx}, \text{Skz01}) \wedge @\text{O\_t} : \text{V}(\text{Skz01}, \text{Skd02})$$
$$\wedge @\text{O\_t} : \text{W}(\text{Bty}, \text{Skz01})$$

where Ctc is a constant and Skd02 is a new generated Skolem term by forward chaining.

From conditional facts to ICF axioms: we can use Universal Generalization [18] and Existential Introduction [22] to transform conditional facts back to ICF axioms.

We can use Universal Generalization to replace all constants which have substituted universal variables with universal variables. For example, Atx, Bty and Ctc can be replaced by x, y and c. We also can use Existential Introduction to replace all Skolem terms with existential variables. Skz01 and Skd02 can be replaced by z and d. Therefore, the generated ICF axiom looks thus:

$$(\forall x, y, c)@\text{O\_t} : S'(x, c) \wedge @\text{O\_t} : T'(c, y) \rightarrow$$
$$(\exists z, d)@\text{O\_t} : U(x, z) \wedge @\text{O\_t} : V(z, d) \wedge @\text{O\_t} : W(y, z)$$

4.4 Proof of Axiom Derivation

It's not so obvious that this procedure works, but we can prove that it does.

Theorem: Any axiom developed by the above procedure is a logical consequence of the axioms of the merged ontologies.

Proof: It suffices to show that the negation of the axiom is inconsistent with the merged ontology. As usual, we assume the axiom is in ICF form:

$$Y_1 v_1 \ldots Y_k v_k (R_1 \wedge \cdots \wedge R_i \wedge \cdots \wedge R_n \rightarrow T_1 \wedge \cdots \wedge T_m)$$

where the v_j are quantified variables and Y_j are the quantifiers, some universal and some existential. The axiom this is derived from is

$$X_1 u_1 \ldots X_k u_k (P_1 \wedge P_2 \wedge \ldots \wedge P_n \rightarrow Q_1 \wedge \ldots \wedge Q_m)$$

where the u_i are quantified variables and the X_i are also the quantifiers, some universal and some existential.

What we will actually show is that a weakened version of the negation of the axiom is inconsistent; from which it follows that a strong version is inconsistent as well. Negating the axiom flips the quantifiers, so the existentials become universals and vice versa. We weaken the negation of the axiom by moving all the existentials inward. If $(\exists x \forall y)(\ldots)$ is true, then so is $(\forall y \exists x)(\ldots)$. We can then use the resolution procedure to derive a contradiction. Skolemizing the weakened version turns the (originally) universally quantified variables into Skolem constants and the (originally) existentially quantified variables into free variables. In addition, the conclusion becomes disjunctive, so that we have a list of clauses:

$$R'_1 \quad R'_2 \quad \ldots \quad R'_n$$
$$\neg T'_1 \vee \neg T'_2 \vee \ldots \vee \neg T'_m$$

Now we mimic the deductions performed during our axiom derivation procedure, running them in reverse. That is, if we inferred $\theta(R_1 \wedge \ldots \wedge R_k)$ from R_i using a backward-chaining rule $R_1 \wedge \ldots \wedge R_k \rightarrow P_i$, where P_i and R_i unify with substitution θ, we now infer $\theta'(R_i')$ from $\theta'(R_1' \wedge \ldots)$. The unification then is possible now, because R_i' is derived from R_i by replacing some Skolem constants with different Skolem constants (possibly losing some of their arguments). The resulting θ' is less restrictive than the original θ, so the process can be repeated until variants of the original P_i are derived. Similarly, we can run the forward chaining from T_1 backward to Q_1, resulting in a smaller clause (with some free variables substituted) $\neg T_2'' \vee \ldots \neg T_m''$. We now repeat the procedure for T_2'', and so forth, until the empty clause is derived. *Q.E.D.*

5   Axiom Derivation for Different Time Ontologies

We want to evaluate our axiom derivation algorithm in some real application scenarios. We are especially interested in the translation between complex ontologies which have large sets of axioms. For example, several time ontologies, such as Cyc time [2], SUMO [3] time, and OWL-Time (formerly DAML-Time) [4], describe temporal concepts and their relationships which are represented using large sets of logic axioms (e.g., the OWL-Time ontology has around 180 first order axioms.)

Researchers have manually built some mappings among the concepts of some time ontologies, but have not talked about how to represent the axioms in different time ontologies. In this paper, we use an example to illustrate the automatic translation of axioms from the Cyc time ontology to the OWL-Time ontology.

For example, one of the axioms in the Cyc time ontology can be represented in Web-PDDL as following:

```
(forall (te1 - TemporalThing da2 - Date)
  (if (dateOfEvent te1 da2)
      (and (startingDate te1 da2)
           (endingDate te1 da2))))
```

It is an axiom to describe the relationship between three properties: dateOfEvent, startingDate and endingDate. This axiom means if some event happens on a specific date, it must begin and end on the same date. The task for OntoEngine is to represent this axiom in the OWL-Time ontology.

We have manually generated the bridging axioms between the Cyc time and OWL-Time ontologies. Here are some examples (cyc and ot are the prefixes for the Cyc time and OWL-Time ontologies.):

```
(forall (e1 - @cyc:Eventuality d2 - @cyc:Date)
        (iff (@cyc:dateofEvent e1 d2)
             (exists (ti - @ot:Interval)
                     (and (@ot:during e1 ti)
                          (@ot:int-during ti d2)))))
```

---

[2] http://www.cyc.com/cycdoc/vocab/time-vocab.html
[3] http://ontology.teknowledge.com/
[4] http://www.isi.edu/~pan/OWL-Time.html

```
(forall (t1 - @cyc:TimeInterval d2 - @cyc:Date)
        (iff (@cyc:startingDate t1 d2)
             (exists (ti - @ot:Instant)
                     (and (@ot:begins ti t1) (@ot:inside ti d2)))))

(forall (t1 - @cyc:TimeInterval d2 - @cyc:Date)
        (iff (@cyc:endingDate t1 d2)
             (exists (ti - @ot:Instant)
                     (and (@ot:ends ti t1) (@ot:inside ti d2)))))
  . . .
```

Where the Cyc time ontology's Date type is treated as a specialization (sub-type) of TimeInterval. With those bridging axioms, OntoEngine can do axiom derivation from the Cyc time ontology to the OWL-Time ontology.

First, that axiom in the Cyc time ontology will be transformed to a conditional fact:

```
(:objects T1 - @cyc:TemporalThing D2 - @cyc:Date)

(if (@cyc:dateOfEvent T1 D2)
    (and (@cyc:startingDate T1 D2)
         (@cyc:endingDate T1 D2)))
```

Then OntoEngine can do backward chaining from the antecedent, (@cyc:dateOfEvent T1 D2), and forward chaining from both (@cyc:startingDate T1 D2) and (@cyc:ending Date T1 D2). Finally the translated conditional fact in OWL-Time ontology can be transformed back to an axiom in the OWL-Time ontology:

```
(forall (e - Eventuality d - Interval)
  (if (exists (t - Interval)
              (and (during e t) (int-during t d)))
      (exists (ti1 ti2 - Instant)
              (and (begins ti1 t) (inside ti1 d)
                   (ends ti2 t) (inside ti2 d)))))
```

It is interesting that this generated axiom does not belong to those 180 existing axioms in the OWL-Time ontology. It is a new axiom. However, it does make sense to describe the relationships between an event and a time interval: during the interval the event happens but it may not be through the whole interval. The total 44 axioms in the Cyc time ontology can be automatically translated to 18 axioms in the OWL-Time ontology in 2 seconds using OntoEngine. Not all axioms in the Cyc time ontology can be translated to the OWL-Time ontology because those two ontologies do not have exactly the same concepts.

This real example shows that some time ontologies may have different axioms from other time ontologies, although they have very similar concepts (i.e., types and properties). If we fail to port the axioms from one to another, we lose important aspects of the semantics of the terms involved.

6 Related Work

A lot of other ontology translation work [7,9] focuses on term rewriting between different ontologies or different ontology languages, but does not use inference. To the best of our knowledge, the only other work on axiom (theory) translation is [6]. This work presents a formalism for knowledge translation based on the theory of contexts [18]. The authors define knowledge translation in terms of truth, and like us they propose using a theorem prover to perform translations. However, the paper doesn't say exactly *how* the theorem-proving process would work. We have shown that a special-purpose inference engine using backward and forward chaining can be used in an efficient mechanism for translating axioms.

7 Conclusion

Complex ontologies require complicated true statements (theory), such as logic axioms (rules). Many relationships among their symbols simply can't be expressed any other way. Based on our formal framework and inference engine for inferential ontology translation, this paper has described and proved the correctness of an *axiom derivation* algorithm for theory translation from one ontology to another.

We have shown that theory translation is necessary in some real application scenarios in which ontologies have large sets of axioms, such as different time ontologies. Although our algorithm is provably correct, practical application requires further work on problems of incompleteness and redundancy. Our algorithm does not by itself guarantee that the axioms we produce are complete, nor does it avoid producing axioms that are already present in the target ontology. Those are problems for future research for theory translation.

Acknowledgements

We would like to thank Haizheng Zhang and Prof. Victor Lesser from the University of Massachusetts, Amherst, for their help with presenting the poster of our short paper [12] in AAMAS2006. We also would like to thank Paea LePendu for his help with the design of the poster.

References

1. DAML+OIL web ontology language.
   http://www.w3.org/TR/daml+oil-reference.
2. OWL Web Ontology Language.
   http://www.w3.org/TR/owl-ref/.
3. T. Berners-Lee, J. Hendler, and O. Lassila. The Semantic Web. *Scientific American*, 284(5), May 2001.
4. P. Bouquet, F. Giunchiglia, F. van Harmelen, L. Serafini, and H. Stuckenschmidt. C-OWL: Contextualizing Ontologies. In *International Semantic Web Conference*, pages 164–179, 2003.

5. P. Bouquet, B. Magnini, L. Serafini, and S. Zanobini. A SAT-based algorithm for context matching. In *CONTEXT*, pages 66–79, 2003.
6. S. Buvac and R. Fikes. A Declarative Formalization of Knowledge Translation. In *Proceedings of the ACM CIKM conference*, 1995.
7. H. Chalupsky. Ontomorph: A Translation System for Symbolic Logic. In *Proceedings of the KR conference 2000*, pages 471–482, 2000.
8. Ó. Corcho and A. Gómez-Pérez. A Layered Model for Building Ontology Translation Systems. *Int. J. Semantic Web Inf. Syst.*, 1(2):22–48, 2005.
9. M. Dell'Erba, O. Fodor, F. Ricci, and H. Werthner. Harmonise: A solution for data interoperability. In *I3E 2002*, 2002.
10. A. Doan, J. Madhavan, P. Domingos, and A. Y. Halevy. Learning to Map Between Ontologies on the Semantic Web. In *International World Wide Web Conferences (WWW)*, pages 662–673, 2002.
11. D. Dou and P. LePendu. Ontology-based Integration for Relational Databases. In *SAC '06: Proceedings of the 2006 ACM symposium on Applied computing*, pages 461–466, 2006.
12. D. Dou and D. McDermott. Deriving Axioms across Ontologies. In *Proceedings of International Joint Conference on Autonomous Agents and Multi-Agent Systems (AAMAS'06)*, pages 952–954, 2006.
13. D. Dou, D. V. McDermott, and P. Qi. Ontology Translation on the Semantic Web. In *Proceedings of the International Conference on Ontologies, Databases and Application of Semantics (ODBASE)*, pages 952–969, 2003.
14. D. Dou, D. V. McDermott, and P. Qi. Ontology Translation on the Semantic Web. *Journal of Data Semantics*, 2:35–57, 2005.
15. T. Gruber. Ontolingua: A Translation Approach to Providing Portable Ontology Specifications. *Knowledge Acquisition*, 5(2):199–220, 1993.
16. I. Horrocks and P. F. Patel-Schneider. A proposal for an OWL rules language. In *WWW*, pages 723–731, 2004.
17. A. Maedche, B. Motik, N. Silva, and R. Volz. MAFRA - A MApping FRAmework for Distributed Ontologies. pages 235–250, 2002.
18. J. McCarthy and S. Buvac. Formalizing context (expanded notes). In A. Aliseda, R. van Glabbeek, and D. Westerstahl, editors, *Computing Natural Language*. University of Chicago Press, 1997.
19. D. V. McDermott and D. Dou. Representing Disjunction and Quantifiers in RDF. In *International Semantic Web Conference*, pages 250–263, 2002.
20. P. Mitra, G. Wiederhold, and M. Kersten. A graph-oriented model for articulation of ontology interdependencies. In *Proceedings of Conference on Extending Database Technology (EDBT 2000)*, 2000.
21. N. F. Noy. Semantic Integration: A Survey Of Ontology-Based Approaches. *SIGMOD Record*, 33(4):65–70, 2004.
22. S. Russell and P. Norvig. *Artificial Intelligence: A Modern Approach*. Prentice-Hall, Inc, 1995.

The Complexity of Model Checking Concurrent Programs Against CTLK Specifications*

Alessio Lomuscio and Franco Raimondi

Department of Computer Science
University College London – London, UK
{a.lomuscio,f.raimondi}@cs.ucl.ac.uk

Abstract. This paper presents complexity results for model checking formulae of **CTLK** (a logic to reason about time and knowledge in multi-agent systems) in concurrent programs. We apply these results to evaluate the complexity of verifying programs of two model checkers for multi-agent systems: MCMAS and Verics.

1 Introduction

Multi-agent systems (MAS) are a successful paradigm employed in the formalisation of many scenarios [33,34], including communication protocols, security protocols, autonomous planning, etc. In many instances, MAS are modelled by means of multi-modal logics with modal operators to reason about temporal, epistemic, doxastic, and other properties of agents.

As MAS being modelled grow larger, however, automatic techniques are crucially required for the formal verification of MAS specifications. Accordingly, various authors have investigated the problem of verification for MAS [35,3,1,13,28,18,30]. In particular, [35,3,1] reduce the problem of model checking MAS to the verification of temporal-only models, while [28,18,30,13] extend traditional model checking techniques to the verification of MAS. Model checking [9] was traditionally developed for the verification of hardware circuits using temporal logics. Various tools are available for the verification of temporal logics [28,23,7,16], and complexity results for model checking temporal logics are well known [8,31,32,19]. In contrast, model checking for MAS is still in its infancy. In particular, to the best of our knowledge, the complexity of model checking for MAS has been little explored [15].

In this paper we review various complexity results for temporal and multi-modal logics and we investigate the complexity of model checking the logic **CTLK** in concurrent programs. The main result of this paper is presented in Section 3, where we show that the problem of model checking formulae of **CTLK** in concurrent programs is PSPACE-complete. This result allows to establish complexity results for the problem of verifying MCMAS [22] and Verics [28] programs.

This paper is organised as follows. Temporal logics, model checking, and complexity classes are briefly reviewed in Sections 2.1 – 2.3; Section 2.4 introduces the logic

---

* The present paper is an extended version of [21]. The authors acknowledge support from the EPSRC (grants GR/S49353 and CASE CNA/04/04).

M. Baldoni and U. Endriss (Eds.): DALT 2006, LNAI 4327, pp. 29–42, 2006.

CTLK and presents some results for model checking extensions of temporal logics. Section 3 contains the main result of this paper: the proof of PSPACE-completeness for model checking **CTLK** in concurrent programs. Section 4 presents an application of this result to the evaluation of the complexity of verifying programs for two tools, MCMAS[22] and Verics [28]. We conclude in Section 5.

2   Notation and Preliminaries

2.1   Temporal Logics and Model Checking

CTL   The language $\mathbf{L}_{CTL}$ of Computational Tree Logic (CTL, [24,9]) is defined over a set of atomic formulae $AP = \{p, q, \dots\}$ as follows:

$$\varphi ::= p|\neg\varphi|\varphi \vee \varphi|EX\varphi|E[\varphi U\psi]|EG\varphi.$$

The remaining temporal operators to express eventuality and universality can be derived in standard way, for instance: $EF\varphi = E(\top U\varphi)$, and $AG\varphi = \neg EF\neg\varphi$ [17].

CTL formulae are interpreted in *Kripke models*. A Kripke model M for CTL is a tuple $M = (S, R, V, I)$ where S is a set of states, $R \subseteq S \times S$ is a serial transition relation (the *temporal* relation), $V : S \rightarrow 2^{AP}$ is an evaluation function, and $I \subseteq S$ is a set of initial states. A *path* $\pi =< \pi_0, \pi_1, \pi_2, \cdots >$ of M is an infinite sequence of states in S such that $(\pi_i, \pi_{i+1}) \in R$ for all $i \geq 0$.

Satisfiability of a CTL formula φ at a state $s \in S$ of a given model M is defined inductively as follows:

$s \models p$ iff $p \in V(s)$,
$s \models \neg\varphi$ iff $s \not\models \varphi$,
$s \models \varphi_1 \vee \varphi_2$ iff $s \models \varphi_1$ or $s \models \varphi_2$,
$s \models EX(\varphi)$ iff there exists a path π such that $\pi_0 = s$ and $\pi_1 \models \varphi$,
$s \models E[\varphi U\psi]$ iff there exists a path π such that $\pi_0 = s$ and a $k \geq 0$
                  such that $\pi_k \models \psi$ and $\pi_i \models \varphi$ for all $0 \leq i < k$,
$s \models EG(\varphi)$ iff there exists a path π such that $\pi_0 = s$ and $\pi_i \models \varphi$ for all $i \geq 0$.

We write $M \models \varphi$ if φ is satisfied at all states of the Kripke model M (notice that some authors write $M \models \varphi$ when φ is satisfied in the set of initial states I of M; the two approaches are equivalent from a complexity point of view).

Model Checking.   Model checking is the problem of establishing (possibly in automatic way) whether or not a formula φ is satisfied on a given model M. While this check may be defined for a model M of any logic, traditionally the problem of model checking has been investigated mainly for temporal logics. Various tools have been developed for temporal logics [23,16,7,28]. Typically, a tool for temporal logic model checking provides a programming language to describe a Kripke model S and implements efficient techniques for the automatic verification of formulae (see Section 2.3).

2.2   Turing Machines and Complexity Classes

In this section we follow the presentation given in [29]. A k-string Turing machine ($k \geq 1$) is a tuple $TM = (K, \Sigma, \delta, s)$ where K is a set of states, Σ is a set of symbols (the alphabet of TM), δ is a transition function, and $s \in K$ is an initial state. Additionally, a Turing machine TM is equipped with k "heads" (one for each string) to read symbols from a certain position on the string, signposted by a "cursor". The transition function $\delta : K \times \Sigma^k \to (K \cup \{h," yes"," no"\}) \times (\Sigma \times \{\Rightarrow, \Leftarrow, -\})^k$ is the *program* of the machine and describes the evolution of the machine. The special symbols $\{\Rightarrow, \Leftarrow, -\}$ denote the direction of the cursor of TM, and $\{h," yes"," no"\}$ are special halting states for TM. At the beginning of a run, TM is provided with an input string $x \in \Sigma^*$ and the heads are at the beginning of each string. We refer to [29] for more details.

The output of a Turing machine TM on input x is denoted by $TM(x)$, and it is defined to be *yes* (resp. *no*) if TM halts on state *yes* (resp. *no*) on input x. If the machine halts in state h, then $TM(x)$ is defined to be the string on the last tape. A language $L \subseteq \Sigma^*$ is *decided* by a Turing machine TM if, for all strings $x \in L$, $TM(x) = yes$.

A k-string *non-deterministic* Turing machine is a tuple $NTM = (K, \Sigma, \Delta, s)$, where Δ is a transition *relation* $\Delta \subseteq K \times \Sigma^k \times (K \cup \{h," yes"," no"\}) \times (\Sigma \times \{\Rightarrow, \Leftarrow, -\})^k$.

A language $L \subseteq \Sigma^*$ belongs to the *complexity class* TIME($f(n)$) if there exists a deterministic Turing machine deciding L in time $f(n)$. A language $L \subseteq \Sigma^*$ belongs to the *complexity class* SPACE($f(n)$) if there exists a deterministic Turing machine deciding L in space $f(n)$ [29]. NTIME and NSPACE are non-deterministic complexity classes defined analogously for non-deterministic Turing machines.

Important complexity classes are L (logarithmic space), NL (non-deterministic logarithmic space), P (polynomial time), NP (non-deterministic polynomial time), PSPACE (polynomial space). The following inclusions hold: $L \subseteq NL \subseteq P \subseteq NP \subseteq PSPACE$ [29].

2.3   Model Checking Concurrent Programs

In many practical instances, when using model checkers, states and relations of temporal models are not listed *explicitly*. Instead, a *compact description* is usually given for a model M. Various techniques are available to provide succinct descriptions (variables, program constructors, etc). In this paper we focus on *concurrent programs* [19]. Concurrent programs offer a suitable framework to investigate the complexity of model checking when compact representations are used because, as exemplified in Section 4, various techniques can reduced concurrent programs[1].

Formally, a program is a tuple $D =< AP, AC, S, \Delta, s^0, L >$, where AP is a set of atomic propositions, AC is a set of actions, S is a set of states, $\Delta : S \times AC \to S$ is a transition function, s^0 is the initial state, and $L : S \to 2^{AP}$ is a valuation function.

---

[1] Notice that some authors [31] define the problem of establishing whether or not a formula φ holds on a model whose description is given in a compact way with the term *symbolic model checking*. On the other hand, other authors [25] define *symbolic model checking* to be a technique that "avoids building a state graph by using Boolean formulas to represent sets and relations." To avoid confusion, we will refer to symbolic model checking in the latter, stricter sense.

Given n programs $D_i =< AP_i, AC_i, S_i, \Delta_i, s_i^0, L_i > (i \in \{1, \ldots, n\})$, a concurrent program $D_C =< AP_C, AC_C, S_C, \Delta_C, s_C^0, L_C >$ is defined as the parallel composition of the n programs D_i, as follows:

- $AP_C = \cup_{1 \le i \le n} AP_i$;
- $AC_C = \cup_{1 \le i \le n} AC_i$;
- $S_C = \prod_{1 \le i \le n} S_i$;
- $(s, a, s') \in \Delta_C$ iff
    - $\forall 1 \le i \le n$, if $a \in AC_i$, then $(s[i], a, s'[i]) \in \Delta_i$, where $s[i]$ is the i-th component of a state $s \in S$.
    - if $a \notin AC_i$, then $s[i] = s'[i]$;
- $L_C(s) = \cup_i L_i(s[i])$.

(in the remainder, we will drop the subscript C when this is clear from the context)

CTL formulae can be interpreted in a (concurrent) program D by using the standard Kripke semantics for CTL formulae in a model $M = (S, R, V)$. Indeed, the set of states S of M can be taken to be set of states S of D, the temporal relation R can be defined by Δ, and the evaluation function V can be defined by L (we refer to [19] for more details). By slight abuse of notation, we will sometimes refer to the programs D_i and to D with the term "Kripke models".

Summary of Known Results for Temporal Logics Model Checking. Traditionally, the complexity of temporal logics model checking has been investigated assuming that models are given explicitly. In this approach, complexity is given as a function of the size of the model and of the size of the formula. Known results are reported in Table 1.

Table 1. The complexity of model checking for some temporal logics

Logic	Complexity
CTL [8,31]	P-complete
LTL [32]	PSPACE-complete
CTL* [8,32]	PSPACE-complete
μ-calculus [19]	MC$\in$ NP $\cap$ co-NP

The complexity of model checking concurrent programs against CTL specifications is investigated in [19]; the authors analyse first the *program complexity* of model checking, i.e., the complexity of model checking as a function of the size of the model only (with a fixed formula). Results are presented in Table 2.

Based on these results, the authors of [19] employ automata-based techniques to evaluate the complexity of model checking as a function of the size of the formula and the sum of the sizes of the concurrent programs constituting D. Their results are presented in Table 3.

Table 2. Program complexity of model checking for some temporal logics in concurrent programs

Logic	Program complexity
CTL	NLOGSPACE-complete
CTL*	NLOGSPACE-complete
μ-calculus	P-complete

Table 3. Program complexity and complexity of model checking for some temporal logics

Logic	Program complexity	Complexity
CTL	PSPACE-complete	PSPACE-complete
CTL*	PSPACE-complete	PSPACE-complete
μ-calculus	EXPTIME-complete	EXPTIME

2.4 CTLK

CTLK is an extension of CTL with epistemic operators [10]. Well-formed **CTLK** formulae are defined by the following grammar:

$$\varphi ::= p \mid \neg\varphi \mid \varphi \vee \varphi \mid EX\varphi \mid EG\varphi \mid E[\varphi U \psi] \mid K_i\varphi.$$

The formula $K_i\varphi$ expresses the fact that agent i *knows* φ.

CTLK formulae can be interpreted in a Kripke model $M = (W, R_t, \sim_1, \ldots, \sim_n, V)$ where W is a set of states, $R_t \subseteq S \times S$ is a serial transition relation (the *temporal* relation), $\sim_i \subseteq S \times S$ are equivalence relations (the *epistemic* relations), and $V : S \to 2^{AP}$ is an evaluation function for a given set AP of atomic propositions. Formulae are interpreted in a standard way, by extending the interpretation of CTL formulae of Section 2.1 with the following:

$$M, w \models K_i\varphi \text{ iff for all } w' \in W, \sim_i (w, w') \text{ implies } M, w' \models \varphi,$$

Notice that **CTLK** is a multi-dimensional logic obtained by the fusion (or independent join) [12,2] of CTL with $\mathbf{S5}^n$, where n is the number of distinct epistemic modalities.

CTLK formulae can be interpreted in concurrent programs: the temporal operators of **CTLK** are interpreted as in [19], while epistemic operators are evaluated by defining epistemic accessibility relations based on the equivalence of the components of the states of a conxcurrent program (a similar approach can be found in [10]). Specifically, let $D = < AP, AC, S, \Delta, s^0, L >$ be a concurrent program obtained by the parallel composition of n programs $D_i = < AP_i, AC_i, S_i, \Delta_i, s_i^0, L_i > (i \in \{1, \ldots, n\})$. Notice that a state $s \in S$ is a tuple $(s_1, \ldots, s_n)$ such that, for all $i \in \{1, \ldots, n\}$, $s_i \in S_i$. We define two states $s = (s_1, \ldots, s_n)$ and $s' = (s'_1, \ldots, s'_n)$ to be related via the epistemic accessibility relation $\sim_i$ iff $s_i = s'_i$, i.e., two states of S are related via the epistemic relation $\sim_i$ iff the i-th components of the two states are identical.

Known Results About Model Checking Temporal-Epistemic Logics. An upper bound for "explicit" model checking formulae on Kripke models is given by the following theorem.

Theorem 1. ([10], p.63) *Consider a Kripke model $M = (W, R_1, \ldots, R_n, V)$ for a normal modal logic (e.g. $\mathbf{S5}^n$, $\mathbf{K}$, etc.) and a formula φ. There is an algorithm that, given a model M and a formula φ, determines in time $O(|M| \times |\varphi|)$ whether or not $M \models \varphi$.*

The time complexity for model checking fusion (independent join) of logics can be derived using the following theorem [11]:

Theorem 2. *Let $M = (W, R_1, R_2, V)$ be a model for the fusion of two logics $\mathbf{L}_1$ and $\mathbf{L}_2$, and φ a formula of $\mathbf{L}_1 \oplus \mathbf{L}_2$ (where $\oplus$ denotes the fusion of two logics). The complexity of model checking for $\mathbf{L}_1 \oplus \mathbf{L}_2$ on input φ is:*

$$O(m_1 + m_2 + n \cdot n) + \sum_{i=1}^{2}((O(k) + O(n)) \cdot C_{\mathbf{L}_i}(m_i, n, k))$$

where $m_i = |R_i|$, $n = |W|$, $k = |\varphi|$, and $C_{\mathbf{L}_i}$ is the complexity of model checking for logic $\mathbf{L}_i$, as a function of m_i, n and k.

The following lower bound can be shown:

Lemma 1. *Model checking is P-hard for the logic $\mathbf{K}$, for $\mathbf{D}$, and for any normal logic obtained by fusion (aka independent join), in which one of the components is either $\mathbf{K}$, or $\mathbf{D}$, or CTL.*

Proof. Following the approach of [31] for CTL, by reduction of a P-complete problem to model checking. Consider SAM2CVP (synchronous alternating monotone fanout 2 circuit value problem [14]). Any circuit can be reduced to a Kripke model for $\mathbf{K}$ or for $\mathbf{D}$ (but not to models for other logics, such as $\mathbf{T}$, where accessibility relations are constrained). Consider then the formula $\varphi = \Diamond\Box\Diamond \ldots \Box\Diamond 1$. The circuit evaluate to 1 iff $M, w_0 \models \varphi$.

The lemma above gives an immediate P-completeness result for the logic **CTLK** *with common knowledge*. Indeed, a P-time algorithm is provided in [26] for model checking epistemic operators and common knowledge in $\mathbf{S5}^n$, and CTL is known to be P-complete (see Table 1).

3   The Complexity of Model Checking CTLK in Concurrent Programs

Similarly to temporal logics, model checkers for multi-modal logics accept a "compact" description of Kripke models. In this section we present a proof for the PSPACE-completeness of the problem of model checking **CTLK** in concurrent programs; this result will be employed in Section 4 to investigate the complexity of existing tools.

Following the approach of Section 2.3, we will analyse the complexity of model checking a concurrent program $D = < AP, AC, S, \Delta, s^0, L >$ obtained by the parallel composition of n programs $D_i = < AP_i, AC_i, S_i, \Delta_i, s_i^0, L_i >$.

We first introduce some lemmas that will be used in the proof of the main theorem. Lemma 3 states that, if the formula $EG\varphi$ is true at a state s of a model M, then φ is true on a path of length $|M|$ starting from s *and vice-versa*. Corollary 4 states that, if $E[\varphi U \psi]$ is true at a state s of a model M, then there is a state s' on a path starting from s at a distance not greater than $|M|$ from s, in which $s' \models \psi$, and such that φ holds in all states from s to s'. Moreover, we report three well known theorems, as variations of these will be used in the proof of Theorem 7.

Theorem 3. *Given a Kripke model $M = (S, R, V, I)$ for CTL, a state $s \in S$, and a formula φ, $M, s \models EG\varphi$ iff there exists a path π starting from s of length $|\pi| \geq |M|$ s.t. $M, \pi_i \models \varphi$ for all $0 \leq i \leq |M|$.*

Proof. If $M, s \models EG\varphi$, then there exists a path π from s such that, for all $i \geq 0$, $M, \pi_i \models \varphi$; as the relation R is serial, this path is infinite (so, obviously, $|\pi| \geq |M|$).

Conversely, if there is a path π from s of length $|\pi| \geq |M|$, then such a path must necessarily include a backward loop. As $M, \pi_i \models \varphi$ for all i in this loop, it suffices to consider the (infinite) trace generated by this loop to obtain a (semantical) witness for $M, s \models EG$.

Theorem 4. *Given a Kripke model $M = (S, R, V, I)$ for CTL, a state $s \in S$, and two formulae φ and ψ, $M, s \models E[\varphi U \psi]$ iff there exists a path π starting from s s.t. $M, \pi_i \models \psi$ for some $i \leq |M|$, and $M, \pi_j \models \varphi$ for all $0 \leq j \leq i$.*

Proof. If $M, s \models E[\varphi U \psi]$, by the definition of the until operator, there must exist a state s' in which ψ holds, and φ holds in every state from s to s'. Moreover, the state s' cannot be at a "distance" greater than $|M|$ from s.

The other direction is obvious.

The proof of Theorem 7 requires a procedure for establishing whether or not two states $s, s' \in S$ of a Kripke model M are connected via a temporal path. Moreover, the same proof requires a procedure to convert a non-deterministic Turing machine into a deterministic one. Both problems are in fact instances of the same problem: reachability of two nodes in a graph. Formally, given a graph G and two nodes $(x, y) \in G$, REACHABILITY is the problem of establishing whether there is a path from x to y or not. The following known theorems are related to REACHABILITY.

Theorem 5. (Savitch's Theorem) REACHABILITY $\in$ SPACE($\log^2(n)$).

Corollary 1. ([29], p.150) NSPACE($f(n)$) $\subseteq$ SPACE($f^2(n)$).

Notice that, by Corollary 1, NPSPACE = PSPACE.

Theorem 6. ([29], p.153) NSPACE($f(n)$) = co $-$ NSPACE($f(n)$).

We are now ready to provide a proof for the main claim of this section:

Theorem 7. *Symbolic model checking for **CTLK** is PSPACE-complete.*

Proof. Proof idea: Given a formula of φ of **CTLK** and a concurrent program D, we define a non-deterministic polynomially-space bounded Turing machine T that halts in an accepting state iff $\neg\varphi$ is satisfiable in D (i.e. iff there exists a state $s \in S$ s.t. $D, s \models \neg\varphi$). Based on this, we conclude that the problem of model checking is in co-NPSPACE. From this, considering Corollary 1 and Theorem 6, we conclude that symbolic model checking for **CTLK** is PSPACE-complete (the lower bound being given by the complexity of symbolic model checking CTL).

Proof details: T is a multi-string Turing machine whose inputs are D and φ. T operates "inductively" on the structure of the formula φ (see also [6] for similar approaches), by calling other machines ("sub-machines") dealing with a particular logical operator. The input of T includes the states of the program S_i ($1 \leq i \leq n$), the transition relations, the evaluation functions and all the other input parameters of each Δ_i. This information can be stored on a single input tape, separated by appropriate delimiters. The formula φ is negated, and then it stored on the same tape. The following is a description of the "program" of T.

The machine T starts by guessing a state s and by verifying that s is reachable from the initial state; if it is not, the machine halts in a "no" state. The algorithm of Theorem 5 can be used here, but notice that a polynomial amount of space is needed to store a state of D (as it is the product of states of D_i); this algorithm uses the transition relations Δ_i encoded in the input tapes to verify reachability. In the remainder of this proof, we assume that whenever a new state is "guessed", it is also checked for reachability from the initial state.

The computation proceeds recursively on the structure of $\neg\varphi = \psi$ by calling one of the machines described below. Each machine accepts a state s and a formula, and returns either 0 (the formula is false in s) or 1 (the formula is true in s). Notice that each machine can call any other machine. The following is a description of the formula-specific machines:

- The machine T_p for atomic formulae simply checks whether or not the state is in $L(s)$; if it is, then the machine returns 1. Otherwise, it returns 0.
- The machine $T_\neg$ for formulae of the form $\psi = \neg\psi'$ calls the appropriate machine for ψ' and returns the opposite.
- The machine $T_\vee$ for disjunction of the form $\psi = \psi' \vee \psi''$ first calls the machine for ψ', and then for ψ'', and returns the appropriate result.
- The machine T_{EX} for formulae of the form $\psi = EX(\varphi')$ is as follows: Consider the machine that guesses a state $s' \in S$, checks whether it is reachable with a temporal transition from s, and then calls the sub-machine for φ' (if s' is not reachable, the machine halts in a "no" state). Notice that this sub-machine will return 1 iff it can "guess" an appropriate successor where φ' holds, and it uses at most a polynomial amount of space. By Corollary 1, it is possible to build a *deterministic* machine based on this non-deterministic machine returning either 0 or 1 in polynomial space; T_{EX} is taken to be this "deterministic" machine.
- The machine T_{EG} for formulae of the form $\psi = EG(\varphi')$ is as follows: consider a machine executing the following loop:

```
s-now = s;
counter = 0;
do
   guess a state s';
   check that s' is reachable from s-now;
        if s' is not reachable, return 0;
   if (f does not hold in s') then
      return 0;
   else
      s-now = s';
   end if
   if (counter > |M|)
     return 1;
   else
     counter = counter + 1;
   end if
end do
```

Based on Lemma 3, this machine guesses a path of length greater than $|M|$ (this value can be computed by considering the size of the input) in which φ' holds. When (and if) such a path is found, the machine returns 1 (notice that this machine uses a polynomial amount of space and always halts). By Corollary 1, it is possible to build a deterministic machine T_{EG} in PSPACE that returns 1 iff there exists a path of length greater than $|M|$ in which φ' holds.

 - The machine T_{EU} for formulae of the form $\psi = E[\varphi'U\psi'']$ is as follows. Consider the machine executing this code:

```
s-now = s;
counter = 0;
do
   if ( psi'' holds in s-now) then
     return 1;
   else
     if ( psi' does not hold in s-now) then
       return 0;
     else
       guess a state s';
       check that s' is reachable from s-now;
           if s' is not reachable return 0;
       s-now = s';
       counter = counter + 1;
     end if
   end if
   if ( counter > |M| )
     return 0;
   end if
end do
```

This machine implements the idea of Corollary 4: it tries to find a state s' in which ψ'' holds and which is at a distance not greater than $|M|$ from s. As in the previous cases, the machine is non-deterministic, it uses a polynomial amount of space, and it always halts; thus, by Corollary 1, a deterministic machine T_{EU} can be built that uses only a polynomial amount of space.

- The machine T_K for formulae of the form $\psi = K_i\varphi'$ is as follows. Consider a sub-machine that guesses a state $s' \in S$, checks whether it is reachable with an *epistemic* transition from s (i.e. it checks whether the i-th component of the two states are equal), and then calls the sub-machine for $\neg\varphi'$. Notice that this sub-machine will return 1 iff it can "guess" a appropriate successor where $\neg\varphi'$ holds, and it uses at most a polynomial amount of space. By Corollary 1, it is possible to build a *deterministic* machine T_K based on this non-deterministic machine returning either 0 (if a state in which $\neg\varphi$ holds is reachable form s), or 1 (if no such state exists) in polynomial space.

Each of the machines above uses at most a polynomial amount of space, and there are at most $|\varphi|$ calls to this machines in each run of T. Thus, T uses a polynomial amount of space. □

Notice that this proof differs from the proof of PSPACE-completeness for symbolic model checking CTL presented in [19]. The authors of [19] investigate the complexity of various automata and apply these results to the verification of branching time logics. Unfortunately, it does not seem that their technique can easily extended to epistemic modalities. Thus, the proof above provides an alternative proof of the upper bounds for symbolic model checking CTL, which can be easily extended to CTLK.

4   Applications

MCMAS [22] and Verics [28] are two tools for the automatic verification of multi-agent systems via model checking. Both tools allow for the verification of **CTLK** formulae in Kripke models. MCMAS uses *interpreted systems* [10] to describe Kripke models in a succinct way. Verics employs *networks of automata*. Both approaches can be reduced to *concurrent programs*, and *vice-versa*; thus, Theorem 7 allows to establish PSPACE-completeness results for the problem of verifying MCMAS and Verics programs.

4.1   The Complexity of Model Checking MCMAS Programs

MCMAS [22] is a symbolic model checker for interpreted systems. Interpreted systems [10] provide a fine grain semantics for temporal and epistemic operators, based on a system of *agents*. Each agent is characterised by a set of local states, by a set of actions, by a protocol specifying the actions allowed in each local state, and by an evolution function for the local states. MCMAS accepts as input a description of an interpreted system and builds a *symbolic* representation of the model by using Ordered Binary Decision Diagrams (OBDDs, [4]). We refer to [10,22,30] for more details. An excerpt of a sample input file for MCMAS is reported in Figure 1.

```
Agent SampleAgent
 Lstate = {s0,s1,s2,s3};
 Lgreen = {s0,s1,s2};
 Action = {a1,a2,a3};
 Protocol:
   s0: {a1};
   s1: {a2};
   s2: {a1,a3};
   s3: {a2,a3};
 end Protocol
 Ev:
   s2 if ((AnotherAgent.Action=a7);
   s3 if Lstate=s2;
 end Ev
end Agent
```

Fig. 1. MCMAS input file (excerpt)

An interpreted systems described in MCMAS can be reduced to a concurrent program: each agent is associated with a program $D_i =< AP_i, AC_i, S_i, \Delta_i, s_i^0, L_i >$, where AC_i is the set of actions for agent i, S_i is the set of local states for agent i, and the evolution function Δ_i is the one provided for the agent.

In the formalism of interpreted systems an agent's evolution function may depend on the other agents' actions. Thus, we modify the definition of a concurrent program $D =< AP, AC, S, \Delta, s^0, L >$ obtained by the composition of n programs D_i (one for each agent), as follows:

- $AP = \cup_{1 \leq i \leq n} AP_i$,
- $AC = \prod_{1 \leq i \leq n} AC_i$,
- $S = \prod_{1 \leq i \leq n} S_i$,
- $(s, a, s') \in \Delta$ iff $\forall 1 \leq i \leq n, (s[i], a, s'[i]) \in \Delta_i$,
- $L(s) = \cup_i L_i(s[i])$.

Notice that, instead of taking the union, AC is now the *Cartesian* product of the agents' actions AC_i, and the transition function is modified accordingly. Thus, given an interpreted system and a **CTLK** formula φ described in the formalism of MCMAS, it is possible to obtain a concurrent program D of size equal to the original MCMAS description (modulo some constant), so that the Turing machine T defined in Section 3 can be employed to perform model checking of φ. Hence, we conclude that model checking MCMAS programs is in PSPACE.

Conversely, the problem of model checking a formula φ in the parallel composition of n programs $D_i =< AP_i, AC_i, S_i, \Delta_i, s_i^0, L_i >$ can be reduced to an MCMAS program. Indeed, it suffices to introduce an agent for each program, whose local states are S_i and whose actions are AC_i. The transition conditions for the agent can be taken to be Δ_i, augmented with the condition that a transition between two local states is enabled if all the agents including the same action in AC_i perform the transition labelled with the particular action.

It is worth noticing that the actual implementation of MCMAS requires, in the worst case, an exponential time to perform verification. Indeed, MCMAS uses OBDDs, and it is known [5] that OBDDs may have a size which is exponential in the number of variables used.

4.2 The Complexity of Model Checking Verics Programs

Verics [28] is a tool for the verification of various types of timed automata and for the verification of **CTLK** properties in multi-agent systems. In this section we consider only the complexity of verification of **CTLK** properties in Verics.

A multi-agent system is described in Verics by means of a network of (un-timed) automata [20]: each agent is represented as an automaton, whose states correspond to local states of the agent. In this formalism a single set of action is present, and automata synchronise over common actions.

The reduction from Verics code to concurrent programs is straightforward: each automaton is a program D_i and no changes are required for the parallel composition presented in Section 2.3, and similarly a concurrent program can be seen as a network of automata. Thus, we conclude that the problem of model checking Verics programs is PSPACE-complete.

Notice that the actual implementation of Verics performs verification by reducing the problem to a satisfiability problem for propositional formulae. Similarly to MCMAS, this reduction may lead to exponential time requirements in the worst case.

5   Conclusion

In this paper we have reviewed various results about the complexity of model checking for temporal logics, both for "explicit" and for symbolic model checking. We have extended some of these results to richer logics for reasoning about knowledge and time. In particular, we have presented Theorem 7 which provides a result for the complexity of symbolic model checking **CTLK**. To the best of our knowledge, no other complexity results for symbolic model checking temporal-epistemic logics are available, with the exception of [26,27]. The authors of [26,27] investigate the complexity of model checking for LTL extended with epistemic operators and common knowledge in synchronous/asynchronous systems with perfect recall. Let $\mathcal{L}_{X,U,K_1,...,K_n,C}$ be the full language of this logic. Complexity results are presented in Table 4. Intuitively, model checking for these semantics is more complex than for the "standard" Kripke semantics (also called "observational" semantics by the authors), because perfect recall causes local states to be unbounded strings, thus "generating" an infinite set of worlds, upon which model checking should be performed.

Our work differs from [26,27] in analysing the problem of *symbolic* model checking for the generic framework of concurrent programs, in which models are not described explicitly: in turn, the generic result in Theorem 7 provides a concrete methodology to investigate the complexity of verifying MCMAS and Verics programs.

Finally, the work presented here is similar in spirit to [15] where complexity results for the verification of ATL against simple reactive modules are presented.

Table 4. Complexity of MC for some perfect recall semantic

Language	Complexity
$\mathcal{L}_{K_1,\ldots,K_n,C}$, synchronous	PSPACE-hard
$\mathcal{L}_{K_1,\ldots,K_n,C}$, asynchronous	undecidable
$\mathcal{L}_{X,K_1,\ldots,K_n,C}$, synchronous	PSPACE-complete
$\mathcal{L}_{X,U,K_1,\ldots,K_n}$, synchronous	non-elementary
$\mathcal{L}_{X,U,K_1,\ldots,K_n,C}$, synchronous	undecidable

References

1. M. Benerecetti, F. Giunchiglia, and L. Serafini. Model checking multiagent systems. *Journal of Logic and Computation*, 8(3):401–423, 1998.
2. P. Blackburn, M. de Rijke, and Y. Venema. *Modal Logic*, volume 53 of *Cambridge Tracts in Theoretical Computer Science*. Cambridge University Press, 2001.
3. R. H. Bordini, M. Fisher, C. Pardavila, and M. Wooldridge. Model checking AgentSpeak. In J. S. Rosenschein, T. Sandholm, W. Michael, and M. Yokoo, editors, *Proceedings of the Second International Joint Conference on Autonomous Agents and Multi-agent systems (AAMAS-03)*, pages 409–416. ACM Press, 2003.
4. R. E. Bryant. Graph-based algorithms for boolean function manipulation. *IEEE Transactions on Computers*, 35(8):677–691, 1986.
5. R. E. Bryant. On the complexity of VLSI implementations and graph representations of boolean functions with application to integer multiplication. *IEEE Trans. Comput.*, 40(2):205–213, 1991.
6. A. Cheng. Complexity results for model checking. Technical Report RS-95-18, BRICS - Basic Research in Computer Science, Department of Computer Science, University of Aarhus, Feb. 1995.
7. A. Cimatti, E. M. Clarke, E. Giunchiglia, F. Giunchiglia, M. Pistore, M. Roveri, R. Sebastiani, and A. Tacchella. NUSMV2: An open-source tool for symbolic model checking. In *Proceedings of the 14th International Conference on Computer Aided Verification (CAV'02)*, volume 2404 of *LNCS*, pages 359–364. Springer-Verlag, 2002.
8. E. M. Clarke, E. A. Emerson, and A. P. Sistla. Automatic verification of finite-state concurrent systems using temporal logic specifications: A practical approach. *ACM Transactions on Programming Languages and Systems*, 8(2):244–263, 1986.
9. E. M. Clarke, O. Grumberg, and D. A. Peled. *Model Checking*. The MIT Press, Cambridge, Massachusetts, 1999.
10. R. Fagin, J. Y. Halpern, Y. Moses, and M. Y. Vardi. *Reasoning about Knowledge*. MIT Press, Cambridge, 1995.
11. M. Franceschet, A. Montanari, and M. de Rijke. Model checking for combined logics with an application to mobile systems. *Automated Software Engineering*, 11:289–321, 2004.
12. D. Gabbay and V. Shehtman. Products of modal logics, part 1. *Logic Journal of the IGPL*, 6(1):73–146, 1998.
13. P. Gammie and R. van der Meyden. MCK: Model checking the logic of knowledge. In *Proceedings of 16th International Conference on Computer Aided Verification (CAV'04)*, volume 3114 of *LNCS*, pages 479–483. Springer-Verlag, 2004.
14. R. Greenlaw, H. J. Hoover, and W. L. Ruzzo. *Limits to Parallel Computation: P-Completeness Theory*. Oxford University Press, 1995.

15. W. v. Hoek, A. Lomuscio, and M. Wooldridge. On the complexity of practical atl model checking knowledge, strategies, and games in multi-agent systems. In *Proceedings of the fifth international joint conference on Autonomous agents and multiagent systems (AAMAS'06)*, Hakodake, Japan. ACM Press. To appear.
16. G. J. Holzmann. The model checker SPIN. *IEEE transaction on software engineering*, 23(5):279–295, 1997.
17. M. R. A. Huth and M. D. Ryan. *Logic in Computer Science: Modelling and Reasoning about Systems*. Cambridge University Press, Cambridge, England, 2000.
18. M. Kacprzak, A. Lomuscio, and W. Penczek. From bounded to unbounded model checking for temporal epistemic logic. *Fundamenta Informaticae*, 63(2,3):221–240, 2004.
19. O. Kupferman, M. Y. Vardi, and P. Wolper. An automata-theoretic approach to branching-time model checking. *Journal of the ACM*, 47(2):312–360, 2000.
20. A. Lomuscio, T. Łasica, and W. Penczek. Bounded model checking for interpreted systems: preliminary experimental results. In M. Hinchey, editor, *Proceedings of FAABS II*, volume 2699 of *LNCS*. Springer Verlag, 2003.
21. A. Lomuscio and F. Raimondi. The complexity of model checking concurrent programs against CTLK specifications. In *Proceedings of the fifth international joint conference on Autonomous agents and multiagent systems (AAMAS'06)*, pages 548–550, Hakodake, Japan, 2006. ACM Press.
22. A. Lomuscio and F. Raimondi. MCMAS: A model checker for multi-agent systems. In H. Hermanns and J. Palsberg, editors, *Proceedings of TACAS 2006, Vienna*, volume 3920, pages 450–454. Springer Verlag, March 2006.
23. K. McMillan. The SMV system. Technical Report CMU-CS-92-131, Carnegie-Mellon University, Feb. 1992.
24. K. McMillan. *Symbolic model checking: An approach to the state explosion problem*. Kluwer Academic Publishers, 1993.
25. K. L. McMillan. *Symbolic Model Checking*. Kluwer Academic Publishers, 1993.
26. R. Meyden. Common knowledge and update in finite environments. *Information and Computation*, 140(2):115–157, 1998.
27. R. v. Meyden and H. Shilov. Model checking knowledge and time in systems with perfect recall. In *Proceedings of Proc. of FST&TCS*, volume 1738 of *Lecture Notes in Computer Science*, pages 432–445, Hyderabad, India, 1999.
28. W. Nabialek, A. Niewiadomski, W. Penczek, A. Pólrola, and M. Szreter. VerICS 2004: A model checker for real time and multi-agent systems. In *Proceedings of the International Workshop on Concurrency, Specification and Programming (CS&P'04)*, volume 170 of *Informatik-Berichte*, pages 88–99. Humboldt University, 2004.
29. C. H. Papadimitriou. *Computational Complexity*. Addison-Wesley, 1994.
30. F. Raimondi and A. Lomuscio. Automatic verification of multi-agent systems by model checking via OBDDs. *Journal of Applied Logic*, 2005. To appear in Special issue on Logic-based agent verification.
31. P. Schnoebelen. The complexity of temporal logic model checking. In *Proceedings of the 4th Conference Advances in Modal Logic (AiML'2002)*, volume 4 of *Advances in Modal Logic*, pages 437–459. King's College Publications, 2003.
32. A. P. Sistla and E. M. Clarke. The complexity of propositional linear temporal logic. *Journal of the ACM*, 32(3):733–749, 1985.
33. M. Wooldridge. *Reasoning about Rational Agents*. MIT Press, 2000.
34. M. Wooldridge. *An introduction to multi-agent systems*. John Wiley, England, 2002.
35. M. Wooldridge, M. Fisher, M. Huget, and S. Parsons. Model checking multiagent systems with MABLE. In *Proceedings of the First International Conference on Autonomous Agents and Multiagent Systems (AAMAS-02)*, pages 952–959, Bologna, Italy, July 2002.

Dynamic Model Checking
for Multi-agent Systems

Nardine Osman, David Robertson, and Christopher Walton

School of Informatics, The University of Edinburgh, Edinburgh EH8 9LE, UK
N.Osman@sms.ed.ac.uk, {dr,cdw}@inf.ed.ac.uk

Abstract. This paper is concerned with the problem of obtaining predictable interactions between groups of agents in open environments when individual agents do not expose their BDI logic. The most popular approaches to this in practise have been to model interaction protocols and to model the deontic constraints imposed by individual agents. Both of these approaches are appropriate and necessary but their combination creates the practical problem of ensuring that interaction protocols are meshed with agents that possess compatible deontic constraints. This is essentially an issue of property checking dynamically at run-time. We show how model checking can be applied to this problem.

1   Introduction

One of the most fundamental challenges of multi-agent system engineering is to enable predictable, reliable interaction amongst groups of agents without requiring a deep standardisation of the way in which they are engineered and while preserving as much as possible their autonomy in individual reasoning. It is not plausible that agents built independently and with no agreement on forms of interaction could be predictably reliable, so researchers have searched for ways of standardising some aspects of coordination in the hope that this small amount of standardisation would provide predictability sufficient for important tasks. Two contrasting approaches to this problem have emerged:

- The use of explicit *models of interactions* (in a generic process or state-machine language) along with mechanisms by which agents can locate, reason about and participate in models of interaction that they judge appropriate. These are built to describe forms of interaction (thus are detached from individual agents) and are typically accessed when an agent anticipates it wants to initiate or join that type of interaction.
- The specification of constraints imposed by individual agents on the interactions they will allow: *deontic constraints*. These are built locally for an individual agent and typically accessed when a specific interaction is anticipated with an individual agent.

These two approaches are compatible, in the sense that they attack different aspects of a similar problem. They have not, however, been combined. Hitherto,

M. Baldoni and U. Endriss (Eds.): DALT 2006, LNAI 4327, pp. 43–60, 2006.

this has not been a major problem, because neither approach had significant user communities. Those now are developing so that it is of practical importance to have a way of answering the question "Given an interaction model and an agent with given deontic constraints wishing to participate in that model, could that combination work?" This is a difficult question because both interaction models and deontic constraints are sophisticated logical objects, so the inference involved is not (say) simple term matching or subsumption. It is also difficult because in practise the question must be answered automatically and in real time, so inference mechanisms must be self contained and efficient. This involves an engineering balance which we explore in the rest of this paper.

In Section 2, we explain in detail the distinction we make between interaction and deontic definitions, relating those in Section 3 to model checking. Interaction models are shared between agents and are therefore portable. In Section 4, we explain how this is achieved in the LCC language and demonstrate how this links cleanly to the types of process calculi used in model checking. Section 5 then defines the language used to describe properties checked by our system, while the model checking algorithm (which is surprisingly compact) is summarised in Section 6.

2   Motivation and Design Goals

Let us consider the following example. For finding and reserving a suitable vacation package consisting of booking a flight ticket and a hotel reservation, a customer agent contacts a broker to find a suitable travel agent. The broker searches for appropriate agents for the given scenario. The scenario is similar to the travel agent use case of [1]. Figure 1 presents an overview of the interaction while Figure 2 defines the section of the interaction model corresponding to the communication between the customer and travel agents (I_{CT} of Figure 1). The interaction starts when a customer agent (C) provides the travel agent (T) with its vacation's start date, end date, and its destination (SD, ED, D). The travel agent forwards this information to the airline web services (As) for retrieving quotations (FL) which are forwarded to the customer agent. After the customer selects a flight (Fx), the travel agent searches the hotel directory (HD) and sends a detailed list of hotel options (HL) back to the customer. The customer selects a hotel (Hx), the travel agent computes the total amount (TA) to be paid, and the customer sends its payment details (PD). The travel agent verifies the payment details with the credit card web service (CD), which either provides a signed payment authorisation ($PId, Sign$) or the reason (R) for payment failure. If the payment is authorised, a copy is sent to the airline and hotel agents (A and H) for confirming the booking. Otherwise, the customer is informed of the failure and it might either choose to retry sending payment details or quit the interaction.

In addition to the interaction rules (Figure 2), the objects involved may also lay down their own set of restrictions: their deontic rules. Table 1 provides a sample of such rules. For example, the customer agent's request for booking both

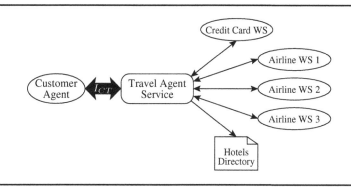

Fig. 1. Overview of the travel agent scenario

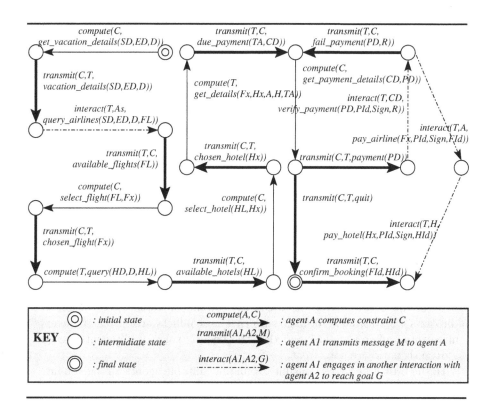

Fig. 2. The rules of interaction between the customer and travel agent (I_{CT} of Figure 1)

a plane ticket and a hotel requires the travel agent to be capable of querying the hotel directory. The broker then needs to verify Rule 1 which states that an agent A may query a directory D only if it has access to it ('+' implies an action is

Table 1. A sample of deontic rules

#	Rule	Enforced by	Description
1-	$(A, D, +query(D, \_, \_)) \leftarrow$ $(A, D, +access).$	Broker	Broker verifies that an agent is capable of performing a query on a directory by verifying that it has access to the directory
2-	$(A, self, +access) \leftarrow$ $member(A, syta).$	Hotel directory	Hotel directory allows A to access it only if it was a member of $syta$
3-	$(A, \_, +get\_payment\_details(\_, CD)) \leftarrow$ $customer(A, CD).$	Broker	Broker verifies that customer agent A is capable of paying its bills by verifying that it is a customer of the selected credit card web service CD
4-	$(CD, \_, +authenticate(X.509)).$	Travel agent	Travel agent needs to ensure that the credit card web service CD is capable of authenticating itself with $X.509$ certificate
5-	$(self, \_, -encrypt(X)) \leftarrow$ $\neg(X = OpenPGP).$	Customer agent	Customer agent is prohibited to use any encryption other than $OpenPGP$

permitted while a '$-$' implies it is prohibited). The success of this rule, however, is dependent on other agents' deontic rules. For example, the hotel directory may enforce its own rule (Rule 2) which states that an agent A may access it only if it is a member of the Student and Youth Travel Association ($stya$). Rules may be used to address issues such as access control (Rule 1), authorisation (Rule 2), authentication and trust (Rule 4), security (Rule 5), and others (Rule 3). While some of these rules (e.g. Rules 1 and 3) are a requirement for the broker to fulfil, others (e.g. Rules 2, 4 and 5) are a requirement for other agents and services engaged in this scenario (see 'Enforced by' column of Table 1). However, it is the broker's responsibility to make sure that no conflicts arise from the agents' requirements and constraints, and that the deontic rules of all agents engaged in a given scenario are consistent.

With the broker being responsible for finding suitable agents for a given interaction protocol, it should also be capable of verifying, at interaction time, that the protocol it has instantiated with agents is likely to work. This, however, relies on the correctness of the interaction protocol as well as the compatibility of the chosen agents. For example, trying to ally the customer agent with a travel agent that does not have access to a hotel directory will result in a scenario failure, regardless of whether the interaction protocol itself is error free or not. This requires a verifier that can handle both interaction and deontic constraints, and is capable of operating automatically at run-time. The broker could then use such a verifier to verify an instance of the interaction protocol — the interaction protocol for a given set of agents.

3   Implementation Plan

Our goal is to achieve a verifier which could be used by agents at interaction time for verifying MAS through the verification of the interaction and deontic rules. Figure 3 illustrates the move from the design to the implementation plan.

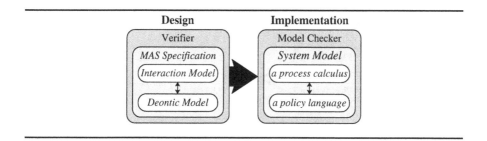

Fig. 3. Implementation plan

As illustrated by the travel agency example, the broker agent will need to verify the interaction protocol for various deontic rules until a team of collaborating agents is reached. In open systems consisting of autonomous agents, it is necessary for agents to be capable of automatically verifying, at run-time, dynamic protocols affected by dynamic deontic rules. For this reason, we choose model checking from amongst other verification techniques because it provides a fully automatic verification process which could be carried out by the agents during interaction time.

For specifying interaction protocols, which deal with coordinating messages between agents, we choose process calculus. Process calculus is a calculus for representing concurrent and distributed processes, and accounts for the non-deterministic and non-terminating nature of these processes. Its success in efficiently describing the rules for coordinating messages makes them especially appealing for specifying interaction protocols of MAS.

Policy languages, on the other hand, have been widely used in hardware systems and networks for expressing deontic rules — the rules of obligations, permissions and prohibitions. Policy languages address issues such as security, trust negotiation, access control mechanism, authorisations, etc. This makes them good candidates for specifying agents' deontic rules.

Implementing the Model Checker. The model checking problem can be defined as follows: *Given a finite transition system S and a temporal formula ϕ, does S satisfy ϕ?* The model checking process is divided into three stages: modelling, specification, and verification. The system to be verified must first be modelled in the language of the model checker S. The properties to which the system model is verified upon should be specified using the model checker's temporal logic ϕ. Both the system model and the properties specification are fed to the model checker for the verification stage. The model checker is, essentially, an algorithm that decides whether a model S satisfies a formula ϕ. Some model checkers may also provide a counter example when the property is not satisfied. This is traditionally used to aid the human debugging process. Since humans are not involved in our automatic checking, we do not need our model checker to generate counter examples. Figure 4 provides a representation of the model checking process.

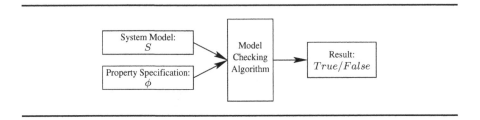

Fig. 4. The model checking process

Our system model S is a bundle of interaction and deontic rules (Figure 3). For specifying the interaction rules of the system model, we choose the Lightweight Coordination Calculus (LCC) (Section 4) mainly for two reasons (refer to Section 8 for details): (1) it supports the attachment of a deontic layer to the interaction layer, and (2) it supports the use of a dynamic local model checker. For defining the property specifications ϕ, we choose a modified version of the modal μ-calculus (Section 5) basically for its contribution to the compact size of our dynamic model checker. Finally, a logic-based local model checking algorithm (Section 6) is chosen for implementing our verifier.

The result is a significantly small sized model checker (based solely on the rules of Figures 8 and 11) implemented in tabled Prolog. The use of computational logic allows us to efficiently compute constraints, which is essential for verifying deontic constraints. Furthermore, the local model checking technique implies that the state-space is not constructed beforehand, but generated and traversed one step at a time until a solution is reached. The use of tabled Prolog for performing local model checking throws the burden of searching the state-space on the tabled Prolog system, keeping the model checker small and simple. This relatively efficient and extremely compact model checker can be used automatically by agents at run-time.

4   Lightweight Coordination Calculus (LCC)

LCC is the calculus used for specifying interaction protocols of MAS. It is based on the concept of agents playing roles and sharing a dialogue framework for achieving distributed coordination. An interesting and important aspect of LCC is its capability to define the interaction protocol without having to specify details of agents involved in this interaction. This supports our requirement for separating the interaction layer from the agent layer. Furthermore, the constraints in the LCC language provide the link needed for connecting the deontic layer to the interaction layer (Section 4.1). The use of LCC, however, has several other advantages. Its syntax presents it as a process calculus which makes it suitable to be used as our model checker's description language (Section 4.3). The syntax also presents it as a logic programming language [2] which affects the efficiency of our constraints' computation (Section 8). Finally, LCC is a lightweight calculus whose only requirement on agents that want to engage in an interaction is to be able to apply the transition rules of Figure 8 (the clause expansion mechanism). This lightweight nature along with its clause expansion mechanism provides the support needed for a dynamic local model checker (Section 6.1).

4.1 LCC Syntax

The LCC interaction framework is the set of clauses specifying the expected message passing behaviour. Its syntax is given in Figure 5.

$$
\begin{aligned}
Framework &:= \{Clause, \ldots\} \\
Clause &:= Agent :: ADef \\
Agent &:= a(Role, Id) \\
ADef &:= null \leftarrow C \mid Agent \leftarrow C \mid Message \leftarrow C \mid \\
&\quad ADef \; then \; ADef \mid ADef \; or \; ADef \mid \\
&\quad ADef \; par \; ADef \\
Message &:= M \Rightarrow Agent \mid M \Leftarrow Agent \\
C &:= Term \mid C \wedge C \mid C \vee C \\
Role &:= Term \\
M &:= Term
\end{aligned}
$$

null denotes an event which does not involve message passing.
Term is a structured term in Prolog syntax.
Id is either a variable or a unique agent identifier.

Fig. 5. Syntax of the LCC dialogue framework

Agents, in LCC, are defined by their roles and identifiers. A framework is composed of a set of clauses. A clause gives each agent role a definition that specifies its acceptable behaviour. An agent can either do nothing (usually used for internal computations), take a different role, or send/receive messages ($M \Rightarrow A$, $M \Leftarrow A$). Agent definitions can get more complex by using the sequential (*then*), choice (*or*), parallel composition (*par*), and conditional ($\leftarrow$) operators. The conditional operator is used for linking constraints to message passing actions. These constraints can be used to link the interaction model to the deontic model.

Example: The Travel Agency Scenario. To illustrate the specification of systems with LCC, let us consider a section of the travel agency scenario. Figure 6 models the interaction between the customer and the travel agent described earlier in Figure 2. The first two clauses specify the interaction rules of the two roles played by the customer agent. The interaction starts when the agent retrieves it vacation details: start date SD, end date ED, and destination D. It then sends these details to the travel agent, receives a list of available flights FL, selects an appropriate flight Fx, sends its choice to the travel agent, receives a list of available hotel options HL, selects a hotel Hx, sends its choice to the travel agent, receives the bill of amount TA to be paid via credit card CD, and finally takes a different role *paying_customer* for paying its bill. The role *paying_customer* is responsible for retrieving the payment details (e.g. credit card number, expiry date, etc.). Then it either receives a message confirming its bookings (*confirm_booking*), or a message informing it of the reason R for the payment's failure. In the latter case, the agent might either decide to retry its payment ($a(paying\_customer(T, CD), C)$) or send a *quit* message to the travel agent to conclude the interaction.

Similarly, the last two clauses specify the travel agent's rules governing its interaction with the customer. To keep the example simple and short, Figure 6 omits role definitions dealing with the travel agent's interaction with other agents, e.g. *query_airlines*, *get_airline_replies*, and *pay_services*.

4.2   LCC Clause Expansion

This section explains the clause expansion mechanism of LCC which supports decentralised coordination. The mechanism also directly affects our choice of model checking technique: local model checking (see Section 6.1).

Decentralised coordination is achieved by sending the protocol along with the messages. When an agent needs to send a message to another agent, the tuple $(I, M, A, R, \mathcal{P})$ is transmitted, where I identifies the interaction, M the message, A the receiving agent, R the receiving agent's role in the interaction, and $\mathcal{P}$ the protocol. The protocol itself consists of three elements: a set of LCC clauses P_F that defines the protocol framework, a set of clauses P_S that defines the current protocol state, and a set of clauses K defining the common knowledge. The protocol framework is the original protocol which remains unchanged throughout an interaction. The protocol state consists of those clauses which are constantly modified to keep track of the current protocol state. Common knowledge in LCC is the knowledge needed to carry out a given interaction protocol. It is specific to the given interaction. Please refer to [3] for further details.

Figure 7 describes the algorithm of LCC's coordination mechanism. The algorithm is triggered when an agent receives a tuple of the form $(I, M, A, R, \mathcal{P})$.

Upon receiving a tuple $(I, M, A, R, (P_F, P_S, K))$, the agent checks whether a copy of its own protocol state exists in P_S by checking for a clause matching its role R and Id A. If such a clause does exist, then it is retrieved. Otherwise, the agent's original clause is retrieved from P_F. The incoming message M is added to the list of incoming messages M_i and the transition rules of Figure 8

$a(customer(T), C)$ ::
 $vacation\_details(SD, ED, D) \Rightarrow a(travel\_agent(\_, \_, \_), T)$
  $\leftarrow get\_vacation\_details(SD, ED, D)$ then
 $available\_flights(FL) \Leftarrow a(travel\_agent(\_, \_, \_), T)$ then
 $chosen\_flight(Fx) \Rightarrow a(travel\_agent(\_, \_, \_), T)$
  $\leftarrow select\_flight(FL, Fx)$ then
 $available\_hotels(HL) \Leftarrow a(travel\_agent(\_, \_, \_), T)$ then
 $chosen\_hotel(Hx) \Rightarrow a(travel\_agent(\_, \_, \_), T)$
  $\leftarrow select\_hotel(HL, Hx)$ then
 $due\_payment(TA, CD) \Leftarrow a(travel\_agent(\_, \_, \_), T)$ then
 $a(paying\_customer(T, CD), C).$

$a(paying\_customer(T, CD), C)$ ::
 $payment(PD) \Rightarrow a(verify\_payment(\_, \_, \_), T)$
  $\leftarrow get\_payment\_details(CD, PD)$ then
 $(confirm\_booking(FId, HId) \Leftarrow a(verify\_payment(\_, \_, \_), T)$
 or
  $(fail\_payment(PD, R) \Leftarrow a(verify\_payment(\_, \_, \_), T)$ then
   $(a(paying\_customer(T, CD), C)$
    $\leftarrow retry\_payment(CD)$
  or
   $quit \Rightarrow a(verify\_payment(\_, \_, \_), T)$
    $\leftarrow \neg retry\_payment(CD)))).$

$a(travel\_agent([As], HD, CD), T)$ ::
 $vacation\_details(SD, ED, D) \Leftarrow a(customer(\_), C)$ then
 $a(query\_airlines([As], SD, ED, D), T)$ then
 $a(get\_airline\_replies([As], [], FL), T)$ then
 $available\_flights(FL) \Rightarrow a(customer(\_), C)$ then
 $chosen\_flight(Fx) \Leftarrow a(customer(\_), C)$ then
 $null \leftarrow query(HD, D, HL)$ then
 $available\_hotels(HL) \Rightarrow a(customer(\_), C)$ then
 $chosen\_hotel(Hx) \Leftarrow a(customer(\_), C)$ then
 $due\_payment(TA, CD) \Rightarrow a(customer(\_), C)$ then
 $a(verify\_payment(CD, H, A), T)$
  $\leftarrow get\_airline\_agent(Fx, A) \wedge get\_hotel\_agent(Hx, H)$

$a(verify\_payment(CD, H, A), T)$ ::
 $payment(PD) \Leftarrow a(paying\_customer(\_, \_), C)$ then
 $a(verify\_payment(PD, CD, PId, Sign, R), T)$ then
 $(a(pay\_services(H, A, PId, Sign, FId, HId), T)$
  $\leftarrow R = null$ then
 $confirm\_booking(FId, HId) \Rightarrow a(paying\_customer(\_, \_), C))$
 or
 $(fail\_payment(PD, R) \Rightarrow a(paying\_customer(\_, \_), C)$
  $\leftarrow \neg R = null$ then
  $(a(verify\_payment(CD, H, A), T)$
  $or \; quit \Leftarrow a(paying\_customer(\_, \_), C))).$

Fig. 6. LCC interaction model of Figure 2

are applied. The agent's new protocol state replaces the old one (if it existed) in P_S resulting in a new protocol state P_{Sn}. Finally, messages that need to be sent to other agents will be transmitted via the tuple $(I, M_x, A_x, R_x, (P_F, P_{Sn}, K))$.

For the agent to perform a transition step, the transition rules of Figure 8 are applied exhaustively. The rules state that $M \Leftarrow A$ can perform a transition $in(M)$ to the empty process nil by retrieving the incoming message M. $M \Rightarrow A$ can perform a transition $\overline{out}(M)$ to nil by sending the message M. $null$ can perform the transition $\#$ to nil ($\#$ represents internal computations). $A \leftarrow C$

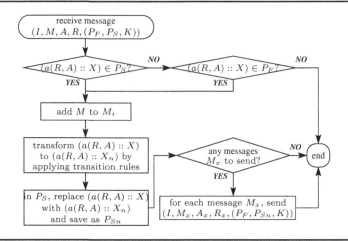

Fig. 7. LCC's coordination mechanism

can perform a transition to E if C is satisfied and A can perform a transition to E. A, with definition $A :: B$, can perform a transition to E if B can perform a transition to E. $A \, or \, B$ can perform a transition to E if either A or B can perform a transition to E. $A \, par \, B$ can perform a transition either to $E \, par \, B$ if A can perform a transition to E, or to $A \, par \, E$ if B can perform a transition to E. $A \, par \, B$ can also perform the transition τ to $E \, par \, F$ if both A and B can perform transitions to E and F, respectively. Finally, $A \, then \, B$ can perform a transition to B if A can perform a transition to the empty process nil; otherwise, it can perform a transition to $E \, then \, B$ if A can perform a transition to E.

4.3   LCC: Process Calculus for Modelling MAS

LCC ,the calculus used for both specifying the interaction model and building the executable model, is also a process calculus. We propose a model checker that accepts LCC as its description language. The LCC protocol, capturing the actual system to be checked, is directly fed to the model checker. This avoids the complexity of modelling the system in another language, and the possibility of introducing errors in doing so. Eliminating this step also contributes to the remarkably small size of the model checker.

Comparing LCC to traditional process calculi: an agent in the LCC language is equivalent to a process. The syntax of an LCC process, as defined earlier, is:

$$ADef := null \leftarrow C \mid Agent \leftarrow C \mid Message \leftarrow C \mid$$
$$ADef \; then \; ADef \mid ADef \; or \; ADef \mid$$
$$ADef \; par \; ADef$$

Similar to traditional process calculi, an agent can be defined in terms of other agents, i.e. an agent can take a different role ($Agent = a(Role, Id)$). The

$$\frac{}{M \Leftarrow A \xrightarrow{in(M)} nil}$$

$$\frac{}{(A \leftarrow C) \xrightarrow{\#(X)} A} \; sat(C) \wedge X \; in \; C$$

$$\frac{}{M \Rightarrow A \xrightarrow{\overline{out(M)}} nil}$$

$$\frac{A \xrightarrow{a} E}{(A \leftarrow C) \xrightarrow{a} E} \; sat(C) \wedge (a \neq \#/\_)$$

$$\frac{}{null \xrightarrow{\#} nil}$$

$$\frac{A \xrightarrow{a} E}{A \; par \; B \xrightarrow{a} E \; par \; B}$$

$$\frac{B \xrightarrow{a} E}{A \xrightarrow{a} E} \; A ::= B$$

$$\frac{B \xrightarrow{a} E}{A \; par \; B \xrightarrow{a} A \; par \; E}$$

$$\frac{A \xrightarrow{a} E}{A \; or \; B \xrightarrow{a} E}$$

$$\frac{A \xrightarrow{a} E \quad B \xrightarrow{\overline{a}} F}{A \; par \; B \xrightarrow{\tau} E \; par \; F}$$

$$\frac{B \xrightarrow{a} E}{A \; or \; B \xrightarrow{a} E}$$

$$\frac{A \xrightarrow{a} nil}{A \; then \; B \xrightarrow{a} B}$$

$$\frac{A \xrightarrow{a} E}{A \; then \; B \xrightarrow{a} E \; then \; B} \; E \neq nil$$

$sat(C)$ is *true* if the constraint C can be satisfied.
nil is the empty process which can not perform any actions.
$in(M)$ is the action of receiving a message M.
$\overline{out}(M)$ is the action of sending a message M.
$\#/\_$ is the action of internal computations.
a is any action (message passing or internal computations).
$\overline{a}$ is the co-action of a. A message input action is the co-action of its output action, and vice versa. Note that internal computational actions do not have co-actions.
τ is a complete internal action. It is the result of carrying out an action and its co-action in parallel.
$X \; in \; C$ implies that X is a term in the conjunction of terms C.

Fig. 8. LCC's transition rules

actions an agent can take are restricted to message passing actions. $M \Rightarrow A$ and $M \Leftarrow A$ are used for sending and receiving messages, respectively. This is similar to Milner's CCS value passing actions $a(x)$ and $\overline{a}(x)$ where x represents the message sent and a represents the channel between the two communicating agents. However, LCC names the processes involved rather than the channels. The sequential operator *then* is similar to Hoare's CSP's sequential operator [;] rather than CCS's prefix operator [.]. The choice operator *or* is equivalent to [+] in CCS. Similarly, the parallel composition operator *par* (in the current version of LCC) is equivalent to [||] in CCS. LCC also defines a conditional operator $\leftarrow$ equivalent to *if C then E* in CCS. LCC's empty process *null* is similar to CCS's *nil* process. The *null* process is usually used in LCC when an agent needs to carry out internal computational actions (see Figure 8).

5 μ-Calculus: A Modified Version

The previous section introduces LCC which we use in parallel with deontic constraints for modelling MAS scenarios. This constitutes the system model M. We now introduce a modified version of the μ-calculus which is used for specifying properties ϕ. The system model M is then fed to the model checker along with property specifications ϕ to verify whether or not M satisfies ϕ.

5.1 μ-Calculus Syntax and Semantics

The syntax and semantics of the μ-calculus are provided by Figure 9 [4].

The semantics imply that a state E always satisfies tt, and never ff. The propositional variable Z is satisfied if E belongs to the valuation of Z. E satisfies $\phi_1 \wedge \phi_2$ if it satisfies both ϕ_1 and ϕ_2, and it satisfies $\phi_1 \vee \phi_2$ if it satisfies either ϕ_1 or ϕ_2. $\langle A \rangle \phi$ is satisfied if E can take an action a, element of A, to state F, such that F satisfies ϕ. Similarly, $[A]\phi$ is satisfied if for all actions a_i that E can take to F_i, where a_i is an element of A, then F_i satisfies ϕ. $\nu Z.\phi$ is satisfied if E belongs to the union of all post-fixed points, while $\mu Z.\phi$ is satisfied if E belongs to the intersection of all pre-fixed points.

The modifications we made to the language is that A, the set of actions, may now contain message passing actions as well as non-communicative actions $\#(C)$, where C is a constraint to be satisfied by some agent or any other constraint we would like to verify.

Compared to other temporal logics, the μ-Calculus has a simpler syntax yet more complex formulae. This simplified syntax is another reason behind the compact model checker (see Figure 11).

5.2 μ-Calculus for Specifying MAS Properties

Choosing the right temporal logic is crucial since it controls which behavioural aspects of the system model may be verified. In what follows, we give an idea of the type of properties that may be verified using our modified μ-calculus version.

Let us consider the travel agency scenario of Figure 6. The broker needs to verify that certain properties are satisfied. For example, the customer is interested in an interaction that guarantees providing flight and hotel quotations. Property 1 verifies the message passing actions of an interaction protocol. It states that if the customer agent requests a vacation package (by sending the *vacation_details* message), then the travel agent will always eventually send back a list of flights and hotels (by sending the *available_flights* and *available_hotels* messages).

Syntax:

$$\phi ::= \text{tt} \mid \text{ff} \mid Z \mid \phi_1 \wedge \phi_2 \mid \phi_1 \vee \phi_2 \mid \langle A \rangle \phi \mid [A]\phi \mid \nu Z.\phi \mid \mu Z.\phi$$

Semantics:

$$
\begin{aligned}
&E \models \text{tt} \\
&E \not\models \text{ff} \\
&E \models Z && \text{iff } E \in V(Z) \\
&E \models \phi_1 \wedge \phi_2 && \text{iff } E \models \phi_1 \text{ and } E \models \phi_2 \\
&E \models \phi_1 \vee \phi_2 && \text{iff } E \models \phi_1 \text{ or } E \models \phi_2 \\
&E \models \langle A \rangle \phi && \text{iff } \exists F \in \{E' : E \xrightarrow{a} E' \text{ and } a \in A\}.F \models \phi \\
&E \models [A]\phi && \text{iff } \forall F \in \{E' : E \xrightarrow{a} E' \text{ and } a \in A\}.F \models \phi \\
&E \models \nu Z.\phi && \text{iff } E \in \bigcup\{S : S \subseteq \|\phi\|\} \\
&E \models \mu Z.\phi && \text{iff } E \in \bigcap\{S : \|\phi\| \subseteq S\}
\end{aligned}
$$

tt and ff are the logical *true* and *false*, respectively.
Z is a propositional variable.
A is a set of actions
E and F are states of the transition system.
S is a set of states.
$V(Z)$ is the set of states satisfying Z.

Fig. 9. μ-Calculus syntax and semantics

$$
\begin{aligned}
\nu Z.\, & [-]Z \wedge \\
& [out(vacation\_details(\_,\_,\_), a(travel\_agent(\_,\_,\_),\_))] \\
& \quad (\; \mu Y.\langle - \rangle \text{tt} \wedge \\
& \quad\quad [in(available\_flights(\_), a(travel\_agent(\_,\_,\_),\_))] \\
& \quad\quad\quad (\; \mu X.\langle - \rangle \text{tt} \wedge \\
& \quad\quad\quad\quad [in(available\_hotels(\_), a(travel\_agent(\_,\_,\_),\_))]X))
\end{aligned}
\tag{1}
$$

Property 1 is read as follows: It is always the case $(\nu Z.[-]Z)$ that if a request for a vacation package is made $(out(\,vacation\_details(\,\_,\_,\_),$ $a(travel\_agent(\_,\_,\_),\_)))$ then eventually $(\mu Y.\langle - \rangle \text{tt})$ a list of available flights and hotels will be received $(in(available\_flights(\_), a(travel\_agent(\_,\_,\_),\_))$ and $in(available\_hotels(\_), a(travel\_agent(\_,\_,\_),\_)))$.

While property 1 above verifies the correctness of the message passing actions, our modified version of the μ-calculus allows us to test for non-communicative actions as well. This gives way to verifying deontic rules in parallel with inter-action rules. For example, the broker will need to verify that the travel agent is capable of accessing the hotel directory. Property 2 models this: In every run of the interaction, it is always the case that the hotel directory is eventually queried. The property is said to be satisfied if the LCC constraint $query(HD, D, HL)$ on the *travel_agent* role of Figure 6 can be satisfied. However, this property holds only if the deontic rules of the travel agent and the hotel directory provide the travel agent with the access needed to perform its query (see Rules 1 and 2 of Table 1).

$$\mu Z. \langle \#(query(HD, \_, \_))\rangle \mathbf{tt} \vee (\langle - \rangle \mathbf{tt} \wedge [-]Z) \tag{2}$$

6   The Model Checker

Following the introduction of the LCC and the μ-calculus languages used for specifying system models and temporal properties, respectively, this section introduces the model checker's technique and algorithm. Model checking LCC protocols suggests — given its logic programming nature along with its clause expansion mechanism — the use of a logic based local model checker.

6.1   Local Model Checking

In LCC, agents' actions are a result of the transition rules applied to the protocols (Figure 8). With each transition, the agent is traversing the state-space graph (or the transition graph [4]). For example, the transition graph of the process $a(paying\_customer(CD, T), C)$ of Figure 6 is provided by Figure 10. The state s_0, the initial state of this process, can only take a transition $out(payment(PD))$ to state s_1, where $payment(PD)$ is the message sent and in is the name of the channel between the two communicating agents, the customer and the travel agent. The interaction proceeds, traversing the transition graph one step at a time. Note that when model checking a system, the transition graph of the whole system is used.

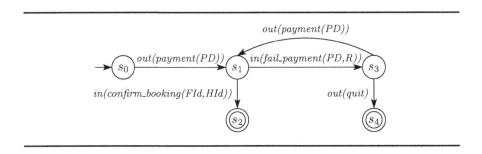

Fig. 10. Transition Graph of process $a(paying\_customer(CD, T), C)$ of Figure 6

The nature of the LCC language and its transition rules proposes the use of a local model checker. While global model checking is based on generating the whole state-space, local model checking partially constructs the state-space one step at a time until a solution is reached. Model checking approaches based on tableaux systems (e.g. [5]) provide such a solution. Termination, in such scenarios, is then to be addressed. We refer to the XMC model checker for inspiration.

The XMC system [6] is a model checker built on top of XSB [7], a tabled Prolog system. The concept of caching in tabled Prolog ensures termination, avoids redundant subcomputations, and computes the well-founded model of normal logic programs. We rationally reconstruct the XMC model to accept LCC models and our verified version of μ-calculus. The result is a simplified and remarkably compact model checker that is based solely on the μ-calculus' proof rules as well as LCC's transition rules (Figures 11 and 8, respectively). This significantly simplified version does not affect the model checker's efficiency discussed in Section 8, the base of which is the XSB system.

6.2 Model Checking Algorithm

We now define our model checking algorithm as follows. A system S is said to satisfy a formula ϕ if its initial state E satisfies ϕ. Hence, the initial state E and the formula ϕ are passed to the model checker. Model checking is then performed in a top-down manner based on the μ-calculus semantics presented in Figure 9. Rules concerning the verification of $E \models \text{tt}$, $E \not\models \text{ff}$, $E \models Z$, $E \models \phi_1 \wedge \phi_2$, $E \models \phi_1 \vee \phi_2$, $E \models \langle A \rangle \phi$ and $E \models [A]\phi$ can easily be encoded in Prolog. The challenge is dealing with the greatest and least fixed point formulae. Prolog, by nature, computes the least fixed point solution. The greatest fixed point, however, is the dual of the least fixed point, i.e. the greatest fixed point formula is satisfied if the least fixed point of the negated formula fails to be satisfied. In XSB, this can be achieved by making use of the negation predicate $sk\_not/1$ in addition to the tabled environment which ensures that a least fixed point solution is found if it does exist in the table.

The result is a simple, straightforward, and compact XSB coded model checker: the code is directly translated into XSB from Figure 11, where $E \xrightarrow{A} F$ follows LCC's transition rules of Figure 8. However, this simple and straightforward algorithm limits the μ-calculus to the alternation-free fragment where nesting of least and greatest fixed-point operators is prohibited. That is because formulae with alternation result in loops through negation which are not easily handled by XSB.

7 Related Work

In this field, different verification techniques have been applied to various aspects of multi-agent systems. In [8] and [9], message passing actions affect the mental states of agents (or the beliefs, desires, and intentions). The verification process is carried by testing the mental states of the agents involved in an interaction. Consequently, the verified system's results hold for a particular set of agents. The approach presented in this paper separates the interaction layer from the agents BDI layer. The verification process does not require access to the agents' BDI models (only deontic constraints specific to the interaction are required). Moreover, the model checker is dynamic. This allows it to be invoked at runtime to verify properties affected by interaction and/or dynamic deontic rules.

[10] offers a technique which separates the mental state of agents from the social state of an interaction. Both the system specification and the properties to

$$models(E, \mathtt{tt}) \qquad \leftarrow \mathtt{true}$$
$$models(E, \phi_1 \vee \phi_2) \leftarrow models(E, \phi_1) \vee models(E, \phi_2)$$
$$models(E, \phi_1 \wedge \phi_2) \leftarrow models(E, \phi_1) \wedge models(E, \phi_2)$$
$$models(E, \langle A \rangle \phi) \quad \leftarrow \exists F. \, ((E \xrightarrow{A} F) \wedge models(F, \phi))$$
$$models(E, [A]\phi) \quad \leftarrow \forall F. \, ((E \xrightarrow{A} F) \rightarrow models(F, \phi))$$
$$models(E, \mu Z.\phi) \quad \leftarrow models(E, \phi)$$
$$models(E, \nu Z.\phi) \quad \leftarrow dual(\phi, \phi') \wedge \neg models(E, \phi')$$

Fig. 11. The modal μ-calculus proof rules

be verified are written in DLTL. Verification is carried based on the use of Buchi automata. Model checking is then applied to the proof of the formulas to be verified. This makes the verification process a complex process based on a combination of model checking and other techniques. This paper proposes a simple and automatic technique which allows the agents themselves to perform the verification process at run-time, which is one of the main contributions of this paper.

[11] and [12] also separate the mental state from the social state. These approaches strictly limit the verification process to verifying message passing actions only. The approach presented in this paper allows the model checker to verify message passing actions of the interaction model as well as deontic constraints affecting the interaction. This is made possible by introducing the modified version of the μ-calculus of Section 5 which permits the verification of constraints in LCC which are essentially a link to the deontic constraints.

[13] differs from all other techniques since it focuses on the evolution of knowledge in MAS. The system is a Real Time Interpreted System. The temporal logic used is TECTLK — a logic for knowledge and real time. All system states should be represented by bit vectors and are, hence, encoded before the verification process is initiated. These then undergo a translation process and the resulting propositional formula is fed to a SAT solver for verification. This technique differs from the one presented in this paper since it verifies the change of knowledge in MAS. Furthermore, all system states need to be encoded before the verification process can take place. This paper proposes a technique which requires only the initial state of the system. Local model checking is then used to incrementally generate the state-space until a solution is reached. This is applied via the proof rules of Figure 11 and the transition rules of Figure 8. The whole process is an automatic process that could be carried out by agents at run-time.

8   Conclusion

This paper presents a model checker which may be invoked at run-time by agents for verifying instances of the interaction protocol. Each of the languages chosen

— LCC, policy languages, or μ-calculus — contribute to the following features of the model checker:

1. **LCC for supporting the attachment of a deontic model to the interaction model**
   Policy languages are essentially a tuple of the form $(s,o,<sign>a)$ which permits or prohibits — depending on the *sign* of a — a subject s from executing action a on object o. Additionally, conditions may be attached to rules (see Table 1). In short, policy languages are a set of constraints. Constraints in LCC could then act as a window to the dynamic, agent specific set of deontic rules. For example, constraint $query(HD, D, HL)$ of the travel agency interaction protocol triggers deontic Rules 1 and 2 of Table 1.

2. **Logic-based programming for efficient constraint computing**
   The use of computational logic results in a model checker that deals efficiently with constraints and complex data structures. This is crucial for us since our system model makes heavy use of constraints and structured terms.

3. **A compact size model checker for agents to use at run-time**
   The use of the modal μ-calculus along with local model checking techniques, which is suggested by the transition rules of LCC, results in an very simple and compact model checker. The model checker is constructed from the rules of Figures 8 and 11 and encoded in XSB. This throws the burden of searching the state-space on the underlying XSB system. As a result, the small size of the model checker makes it a good candidate to be used by agents at run-time.

   As for efficiency, the model checker has worked well when tested on some scenarios. For example, the verification of property 2 of Section 5.2 with five agents involved — a customer agent, a travel agent, an airline agent, a hotel agent, and a credit card agent — consumes 0.039 sec of CPU time and 2.18MB of memory when run on a P4 2GHz machine. A more complex example, an auction system with a set of three bidders, consumes 0.868 sec and 51MB. These are preliminary results only, and further tests and evaluation still needs to be taken.

4. **LCC for supporting dynamic model checking of dynamic system models**
   The decentralised coordination mechanism driven by the clause expansion mechanism of LCC allows agents to verify dynamic deontic rules as well as dynamic interaction protocols at run-time. This is made possible by retrieving the current protocol state at run-time along with the current deontic rules, and feeding this information to the model checker.

References

1. He, H., Haas, H., Orchard, D.: Web services architecture usage scenarios. W3C Working Group Note (2003) http://www.w3.org/TR/2004/NOTE-ws-arch-scenarios-20040211/.
2. Robertson, D.: Multi-agent coordination as distributed logic programming. In: International Conference on Logic Programming. Volume 3132 of Lecture Notes in Computer Science., Sant-Malo, France, Springer (2004) 416–430

3. Robertson, D.: A lightweight coordination calculus for agent social norms. In: Proceedings of Declarative Agent Languages and Technologies workshop at AAMAS, New York, USA (2004)
4. Stirling, C.: Modal and Temporal Properties of Processes. Texts in Computer Science. Springer-Verlag (2001)
5. Stirling, C., Walker, D.: Local model checking in the modal mu-calculus. Theoretical Computer Science **89**(1) (1991) 161–177
6. Ramakrishnan, C.R., Ramakrishnan, I.V., Smolka, S.A., Dong, Y., Du, X., Roychoudhury, A., Venkatakrishnan, V.N.: XMC: a logic-programming-based verification toolset. In: Computer Aided Verification. Lecture Notes in Computer Science, Springer (2000) 576–580
7. Sagonas, K., Swift, T., Warren, D.S.: XSB as an efficient deductive database engine. In: Proceedings of the 1994 ACM SIGMOD international conference on Management of data (SIGMOD '94), ACM Press (1994) 442–453
8. Wooldridge, M., Fisher, M., Huget, M.P., Parsons, S.: Model checking multi-agent systems with mable. In: Proceedings of the first international joint conference on Autonomous agents and multiagent systems (AAMAS '02), New York, USA, ACM Press (2002) 952–959
9. Benerecetti, M., Giunchiglia, F., Serafini, L.: Model checking multiagent systems. Journal of Logic and Computation **8**(3) (1998) 401–423
10. Giordano, L., Martelli, A., Schwind, C.: Verifying communicating agents by model checking in a temporal action logic. In: Proceedings of Logics in Artificial Intelligence, 9th European Conference, JELIA 2004. Volume 3229 of Lecture Notes in Computer Science., Lisbon, Portugal, Springer (2004) 57–69
11. Walton, C.: Model checking agent dialogues. In: Proceedings of the Workshop on Declarative Agent Languages and Technologies (DALT '04). Lecture Notes in Computer Science, Springer-Verlag (2005)
12. Wen, W., Mizoguchi, F.: Analysis and verification of multi-agent interaction protocols. In: Proceedings of the Sixth Asia-Pacific Software Engineering Conference (APSEC '99), Takamatsu, Japan, IEEE Computer Society (1999) 252–259
13. Woźna, B., Lomuscio, A., W.Penczek: Bounded model checking for knowledge and real time. In: In Proceedings of the 4th International Joint Conference on Autonomous Agents and Multi-agent systems (AAMAS'05), ACM Press (2005) 165–172

Automating Belief Revision for AgentSpeak

Natasha Alechina[1], Rafael H. Bordini[2], Jomi F. Hübner[3],
Mark Jago[1], and Brian Logan[1]

[1] School of Computer Science
University of Nottingham
Nottingham, UK
{nza,bsl}@cs.nott.ac.uk,
mark.jago@nottingham.ac.uk
[2] University of Durham
Dept. of Computer Science
Durham, UK
r.bordini@durham.ac.uk
[3] Univ. Regional de Blumenau
Dept. Sistemas e Computação
Blumenau, SC, Brazil
jomi@inf.furb.br

Abstract. The AgentSpeak agent-oriented programming language has recently been extended with various new features, such as speech-act based communication, internal belief additions, and support for reasoning with ontological knowledge, which imply the need for belief revision within an AgentSpeak agent. In this paper, we show how a polynomial-time belief-revision algorithm can be incorporated into the *Jason* AgentSpeak interpreter by making use of *Jason*'s language constructs and customisation features. This is one of the first attempts to include automatic belief revision within an interpreter for a practical agent programming language.

1 Introduction

After almost a decade of work on abstract programming languages for multi-agent systems, practical multi-agent platforms based on these languages are now beginning to emerge. On such language is AgentSpeak, and in particular its implementation in *Jason* [7]. AgentSpeak continues to evolve, and a number of AgentSpeak extensions have been reported in the literature and incorporated into *Jason*. Some of these new features, such as internal belief additions, speech-act based communication, and support for reasoning with ontological knowledge, have led to a greater need for *belief revision* as part of an AgentSpeak agent's reasoning cycle. However, in common with other mature agent-oriented programming languages [5], AgentSpeak does not currently provide automatic support for belief revision. While the current *Jason* implementation provides a simple form of belief *update*, which can be customised for particular applications, the problem of belief-base consistency has, so far, remained the responsibility of the programmer.

M. Baldoni and U. Endriss (Eds.): DALT 2006, LNAI 4327, pp. 61–77, 2006.

The lack of support for belief revision in practical agent programming languages is understandable, given that known belief revision algorithms have high computational complexity. However recent work by Alechina, Jago and Logan has changed this picture. In [2] they presented a polynomial time belief revision algorithm for resource bounded agents. The algorithm is theoretically well-motivated, in the sense of producing revisions that conform to a generally accepted set of postulates characterising *rational* belief revision. In this paper, we show how this work can be incorporated into the *Jason* AgentSpeak interpreter by making use of *Jason*'s language constructs and customisation features. In doing so, we also clarify the desired outcome of belief contraction in AgentSpeak from the logical point of view.

The problem of how to incorporate belief revision into a practical agent programming language has been largely ignored in the literature. There has been some initial work on belief revision in an *abstract* programming language, for example, in [24]. In [10], Clark and McCabe show how the Go! agent programming language can be extended to incorporate dependency (or reason) maintenance. In their approach, the removal of a belief B automatically results in B being removed from justifications of other beliefs, and if B was the only justification, then those beliefs are automatically removed. However, the removal of sufficient beliefs to prevent B being re-derived is left to the programmer. We believe our approach is one of the first attempts to include automatic *belief revision* within an interpreter for a practical agent programming language.

The remainder of the paper is organised as follows. In Sections 2 and 3 we give a brief overview of AgentSpeak programming and its implementation in *Jason*. In Section 4, we state our desiderata for belief revision in AgentSpeak, and in Section 5 we summarise the main points of the algorithm first presented in [2]. We then discuss the integration of the belief revision algorithm into *Jason* in Section 7, and in Section 8 we give a simple example which illustrates the importance of belief revision in practical programming of multi-agent systems. Finally, we conclude and outline directions for future work.

2   AgentSpeak

The AgentSpeak(L) programming language was introduced in [22]. It is based on logic programming and provides an elegant abstract framework for programming BDI agents. The BDI architecture is, in turn, the predominant approach to the implementation of *intelligent* or *rational* agents [27], and a number of commercial applications have been developed using this approach.

An AgentSpeak agent is defined by a set of ground (first-order) atomic formulæwhich comprise its *belief base*, and a set of plans which form its *plan library*. An AgentSpeak plan has a *head* which consists of a triggering event (specifying the events for which that plan is *relevant*), and a conjunction of belief literals representing a *context*. The conjunction of literals in the context must be a logical consequence of that agent's current beliefs if the plan is to be considered *applicable* when the triggering event happens (only applicable plans can be chosen for execution). A plan also has a *body*, which is a sequence of basic actions or (sub)goals that the agent has to achieve (or test) when the plan is triggered. *Basic actions* represent the atomic operations the agent can perform to change the environment. Such actions are also written as atomic formulæ, but using a set of *action symbols* rather than predicate symbols. AgentSpeak distinguishes two types of *goals*: achievement goals and test goals. Achievement goals are formed by prefixing atomic formulæ with the '**!**' operator, while test goals are prefixed with the '**?**' operator. An *achievement goal* states that the agent wants to achieve a state of the world where the associated atomic formula is true. A *test goal* states that the agent wants to test whether the associated atomic formula is a logical consequence of its beliefs.

An AgentSpeak agent is a *reactive planning system*. Plan exeecution is triggered by the *addition* ('**+**') or *deletion* ('**-**') of beliefs due to perception of the environment, or to the addition or deletion of goals as a result of the execution of plans triggered by previous events.

A simple example of an AgentSpeak program for a Mars robot is given in Figure 1. The robot is instructed to be especially attentive to "green patches" on rocks it observes while roving on Mars. The AgentSpeak program consists of three plans. The first plan says that whenever the robot perceives a green patch on a certain rock (a belief addition), it should try and examine that particular rock. However this plan can only be used (i.e., it is only applicable) if the robot's batteries are not too low. To examine the rock, the robot must retrieve, from its belief base, the coordinates it has associated with that rock (this is the reason for the test goal in the beginning of the plan's body), then achieve the goal of traversing to those coordinates and, once there, examine the rock. Recall that each of the achievement goals will trigger the execution of some other plan.

```
+green_patch(Rock)
    :   not battery_charge(low)
    <-  ?location(Rock,Coordinates);
        !traverse(Coordinates);
        !examine(Rock).

+!traverse(Coords)
    :   safe_path(Coords)
    <-  move_towards(Coords).

+!traverse(Coords)
    :   not safe_path(Coords)
    <-  ...
```

Fig. 1. Examples of AgentSpeak Plans for a Mars Rover

The two other plans (note the last one is only an fragment) provide alternative courses of action that the rover should take to achieve the goal of traversing towards some given coordinates. Which course of action is selected depends on its beliefs about the environment at the time the goal-addition event is handled. If the rover believes that there is a safe path in the direction to be traversed, then all it has to do is to take the action of moving towards those coordinates (this is a basic action which allows the rover to effect changes in its environment, in this case physically moving itself). The alternative plan (not shown here in full) provides an alternative means for the agent to reach the rock when the direct path is unsafe.

3 Jason

The *Jason* interpreter implements the operational semantics of AgentSpeak as given, e.g., in [8]. *Jason* [1] is written in Java, and its IDE supports the development and execution of distributed multi-agent systems [6]. Some of the features[2] of *Jason* are:

- speech-act based inter-agent communication (and annotation of beliefs with information sources);
- annotations on plan labels, which can be used by elaborate (e.g., decision-theoretic) selection functions;
- the possibility to run a multi-agent system distributed over a network (using SACI or some other middleware);
- fully customisable (in Java) selection functions, trust functions, and overall agent architecture (perception, belief-revision, inter-agent communication, and acting);
- straightforward extensibility (and use of legacy code) by means of user-defined "internal actions";
- clear notion of *multi-agent environments*, implemented in Java (this can be a simulation of a real environment, e.g., for testing purposes before the system is actually deployed).

3.1 Extensions to AgentSpeak

Recent work appearing in the literature has made important additions to AgentSpeak, which have also been (or are in the process of being) implemented in *Jason*. Below we briefly discuss some of these features, focusing on those that have particular implications for belief revision.

Belief additions. This is one of the earliest extensions of the AgentSpeak language, and one of the most important from the point of view of belief revision. Experience with AgentSpeak has shown that the execution of some plans could be greatly facilitated by allowing a plan instance being executed to add derived beliefs to the agent's belief base. A formula such as $+bl$ in the body of a plan, has the effect of adding the belief literal bl to the belief base. Together with the ability to exchange beliefs and plans with other agents (see below), such derived beliefs can result in the agent's belief base becoming inconsistent (i.e., both b and $\sim b$ are in the belief base, for some belief b)[3]. Unless the programmer intends to make use of paraconsistency, this is clearly undesirable, yet it is *not* checked or handled automatically in the current version of *Jason*.

Speech-act based communication and plan exchange. Another important addition, first proposed in [17], is the extension of the AgentSpeak operational semantics to allow speech-act based communication among AgentSpeak agents. That work gave semantics to the change in the mental attitudes of AgentSpeak agents when receiving messages from other agents (using a speech-act based language). This involves not only changes

---

[1] *Jason* is *Open Source* (GNU LGPL) and may be obtained from http://jason.sf.net.
[2] As of this writing, the current version of *Jason* is v0.8.
[3] The '$\sim$' operator denotes strong negation in *Jason*.

in beliefs and goals, but also the plans used by the agent. The latter allows agents to exchange know-how with other agents in the form of plans for dealing with specific events [3]. The intuitive idea is that if one does not know how to do something, one should ask someone who does. To implement this idea of *cooperation* through plan exchange between agents, it was necessary to enable agents to retrieve plans for a given triggering event for which the agent has no applicable plan, and also to annotate plans with *access specifiers* (e.g., to prevent private plans being accessed by other agents) or with indications of what the agent should do with the retrieved plan once it has been used for a particular event (e.g., discard it, or keep it in the plan library for future reference). However the ability to exchange beliefs and plans with other agents increases the chances of the agent's belief base becoming inconsistent.

Prolog-like Rules. An extension currently being implemented in **Jason** is that the belief base will no longer be just a set of ground literals, but will also have Prolog-like rules. This is similar to the 3APL implementation [11], where the belief base is effectively a Prolog program. The lack of such rules forced AgentSpeak programmers to use plans for deriving useful information, and the consequence of this was that programs were less clear because theoretical and practical reasoning were mixed together. With this addition, we now have a clear separation between rules that allow agents to derive conclusions that follow from their current belief state and plans which allow agents to decide how to act. However, for uniformity, we do not use the Prolog syntax for the body of rules; instead, we use the same syntax as used in the context of AgentSpeak plans (with the same expressive power).

Ontological reasoning. Ontologies are presently being used in various agent-based applications (see, e.g., [9]). In [18], the AgentSpeak-DL extension of AgentSpeak was proposed which aimed at incorporating ontological reasoning within an AgentSpeak interpreter. The language was extended so that the belief base can include Description Logic [4] operators. In addition to the usual ABox (factual knowledge in the form of ground atomic formulæ), the belief base can also have a TBox (containing definitions of complex concepts and relationships between them). This results in a number of changes in the interpretation of AgentSpeak programs: (i) queries to the belief base are more expressive as their results do not depend only on explicit knowledge but can also be inferred from the ontology; (ii) the notion of belief update must be refined so that following the addition of a property of an individual, the resulting belief base is consistent with the agent's concept descriptions; (iii) the search for a plan (in the agent's plan library) that is relevant for dealing with a particular event is more flexible as this is not based solely on unification, but also on the subsumption relation between concepts; and (iv) agents may share knowledge by using web ontology languages such as OWL.

The issue of belief revision is clearly important in the context of ontological reasoning, and this is another motivation for the work presented here. In particular, consider item (ii) above. For example, if the belief base contains both $unstable(p)$ and $\neg dangerous(p)$, and the TBox contains $unstable \sqsubseteq dangerous$ then the agent's belief state is inconsistent. However, simply ignoring the belief addition $unstable(p)$ since it would cause an inconsistency in the belief base, or always forcing such additions and removing the contradicting belief instead, are both clearly unacceptable.

Belief annotations. Another important change in the version of AgentSpeak interpreted by ***Jason*** is that atomic formulæ now can have "annotations". An annotation is a list of terms enclosed in square brackets immediately following a predicate. For example, the annotated belief "green_patch(r1)[doc(0.9)]" could be used by a programmer to represent the fact that rock r1 is believed to have a green patch in it, and this is believed with a degree of certainty (doc) of 0.9. Within the belief base, an important use of annotations is to record the sources of information for a particular belief. A (pre-defined) term source(s) is provided for that purpose, where s can be an agent's name (to denote the agent that has communicated that information), or two special atoms, percept and self, which denote, respectively, that a belief arose from perception of the environment, or from the agent explicitly adding a belief to its own belief base as a result of executing a plan. The initial beliefs that are part of the source code of an AgentSpeak agent are assumed to be internal beliefs (i.e., as if they had a [source(self)] annotation), unless the belief has any source explicit annotation given by the user. For more on the annotation of sources of information for beliefs, see [17].

As will be seen below, annotations can be used to support context sensitive belief revision, where beliefs of a particular type or from a particular source are preferred to others when an inconsistency arises.

3.2   Belief Update in *Jason*

Users can customise certain aspects of the (practical) reasoning of a ***Jason*** agent by overriding methods of the **Agent** class. This includes, for example, the three user-defined selection functions that are required by an AgentSpeak interpreter. One of the methods of the **Agent** class that can be overridden, which is of interest here, is the brf method. This represents the *belief revision function* commonly found in agent architectures (although the Agents literature often assumes that this function is used mainly for belief update, rather than belief revision).

In the current version of ***Jason***, the brf method takes a list of additions to the belief base, and is used for both belief *update* and belief revision. Belief update following perception of the environment results in a call to brf with literals in the list of additions representing the percepts[4]). It is assumed that all perceptible properties are included in the list of additions: all current beliefs no longer within the list of percepts are deleted from the belief base, and all percepts not currently in the belief base are added to it. For other changes in the belief base, the default brf method in ***Jason*** simply adds to the belief base any belief addition executed within a plan, as well as any information from permitted sources; the source is annotated on the belief added to belief base, so that consideration of the degree of trust in any particular belief can be taken by the programmer. At present, belief additions (from whatever source) are *not* checked for consistency, with the result that the belief base can become inconsistent, unless sufficient care is taken by the programmer.

---

[4] The fact that a literal is a percept rather than other forms of information is explicitly stated in the annotations: all percepts have a source(percept) annotation.

4   Requirements for Belief Revision in AgentSpeak

We have two main objectives in adding belief revision to AgentSpeak. First the belief revision algorithm should be theoretically well-motivated, in the sense of producing revisions which conform to a generally accepted set of postulates characterising *rational* belief revision. Second, we want the resulting language to be practical, which means that the belief revision algorithm must be efficient. Our approach draws on recent work [2] on efficient (polynomial-time) belief revision algorithms which satisfy the well-known AGM postulates [1] characterising rational belief revision and contraction.

The theory of belief revision as developed by Alchourron, Gärdenfors, and Makinson in [13,1,14] models belief change of an idealised rational reasoner. The reasoner's beliefs are represented by a potentially infinite set of beliefs closed under logical consequence. When new information becomes available, the reasoner must modify its belief set to incorporate it. The AGM theory defines three operators on belief sets: expansion, contraction, and revision. *Expansion*, denoted $K + A$, simply adds a new belief A to K and the resulting set is closed under logical consequence. *Contraction*, denoted by $K \dot{-} A$, removes a belief A from the belief set and modifies K so that it no longer entails A. *Revision*, denoted $K \dot{+} A$, is the same as expansion if A is consistent with the current belief set, otherwise it minimally modifies K to make it consistent with A, before adding A.

Contraction and revision cannot be defined uniquely, since in general there is no unique maximal set $K' \subset K$ which does not imply A. Instead, the set of "rational" contraction and revision operators is characterised by the AGM postulates [1]. The basic AGM postulates for contraction are:

(K$\dot{-}$1) $K \dot{-} A = Cn(K \dot{-} A)$ (closure)
(K$\dot{-}$2) $K \dot{-} A \subseteq K$ (inclusion)
(K$\dot{-}$3) If $A \notin K$, then $K \dot{-} A = K$ (vacuity)
(K$\dot{-}$4) If not $\vdash A$, then $A \notin K \dot{-} A$ (success)
(K$\dot{-}$5) If $A \in K$, then $K \subseteq (K \dot{-} A) + A$ (recovery)
(K$\dot{-}$6) If $Cn(A) = Cn(B)$, then $K \dot{-} A = K \dot{-} B$ (equivalence)

where $Cn(K)$ denotes closure of K under logical consequence.

AGM style belief revision is sometimes referred to as *coherence* approach to belief revision, because it is based on the ideas of coherence and informational economy. It requires that the changes to the agent's belief state caused by a revision be as small as possible. In particular, if the agent has to give up a belief in A, it does not have to give up believing in things for which A was the sole justification, so long as they are consistent with the remaining beliefs.

While AGM belief revision provides an appealing definition of rational belief revision, it is generally considered to apply only to idealised agents, because of the assumption that the set of beliefs is closed under logical consequence. To model AI agents, an approach called belief base revision has been proposed (see for example [16,19,25,23]). A belief base is a finite representation of a belief set. Revision and contraction operations can be defined on belief bases instead of on logically closed belief sets. However the complexity of these operations ranges from NP-complete (full meet revision) to low in the polynomial hierarchy (computable using a polynomial number of calls to an NP oracle which checks satisfiability of a set of formulæ) [21]. The reason for the high complexity is the need to check for classical consistency while performing the operations. One way around this is to weaken the language and the logic of the agent so that the consistency check is no longer an expensive operation (as suggested in [20]). This is also the approach taken in [2] and adopted here.

Another strand of theoretical work in belief revision is the *foundational*, or *reason-maintenance* approach to belief revision. Reason-maintenance style belief revision is concerned with tracking dependencies between beliefs. Each belief has a set of justifications, and the reasons for holding a belief can be traced back through these justifications to a set of foundational beliefs. When a belief must be given up, sufficient foundational beliefs have to be withdrawn to render the belief underivable. Moreover, if all the justifications for a belief are withdrawn, then that belief itself should no longer be held. Most implementations of reason-maintenance style belief revision are incomplete in the logical sense, but tractable.

In the next section we present an approach to belief revision and contraction for resource-bounded agents which allows for both AGM and reason-maintenance style belief revision. AGM-style contraction by A removes beliefs which imply A, but does not remove beliefs for which A is the sole justification. In contrast, reason-maintenance style contraction in addition removes beliefs for which A is the sole justification. Both AGM and reason-maintenance contraction have the same polynomial-time complexity and satisfy the AGM postulates with the exception of the recovery postulate $(K\dot{-}5)$.

5   The Belief Revision Algorithm

In this section we briefly describe the contraction algorithm introduced in [2]. We define AGM-style contraction by a literal A as the removal of A and sufficient literals from the agent's belief base so that A is no longer a consequence of the beliefs in the belief base. We explain in more detail in Section 6 what we mean by "consequence"; for the moment, we assume that a belief is derivable if it has been asserted using the agent's plans or has been inferred using ontological definitions and the literals in the agent's belief base.

The inferential relationships between the beliefs in the agent's belief base can be represented as a directed graph, where the nodes are beliefs and *justifications*. A justification consists of a belief literal and a *support list* containing the beliefs which were used to derive that literal, for example: $(A, [B, C])$, where A was derived from B and C. If A has been derived in several different ways, for example, from B, C and from D (where B, C and D are in the belief base), the graph contains several justifications for A, for example $(A, [B, C])$ and $(A, [D])$. We say a belief is *independent* if it has at least one non-inferential justification, e.g., beliefs acquired by perception, communicated beliefs, and the literals in the belief base when the agent starts. Non-inferential justifications are of the form $(D, [])$, i.e., the support list is empty. In the graph, each justification has one outgoing edge to the belief it is a justification for, and an incoming edge from each belief in its support list. We assume that each support list s has a designated *least preferred* member $w(s)$. Intuitively, this is a belief which is not preferred to any other belief in the support list, and which we would be prepared to discard first, if we have to give up one of the beliefs in the list. We discuss possible preference orderings and their computation in the next section. We assume that we have constant time access to $w(s)$.

The algorithm to contract by a belief A is as follows:

```
For each of A's outgoing edges
    to a justification (C, s),
    remove (C,s) from the graph.

For each of A's incoming edges
    from a justification (A, s),
        if s is empty:
            remove (A, s);
        else:
            contract by w(s);
Remove A.
```

To implement reason-maintenance style contraction, we also recursively remove beliefs which have no incoming edges.

The algorithm runs in time $O(kr + n)$, where k the maximal number of beliefs in any support list, r is the number of plans, and n the number of literals in the belief base [2]. Indeed, the upper bound on the number of steps required to remove justifications corresponding to plan instances is $r(k + 1)$ (one constant time operation for each belief in the context of the plan and one for the belief asserted by the plan). Removing all justifications corresponding to foundational beliefs costs n steps. The last step in the contraction algorithm (removing a belief) is executed at most n times. Reason-maintenance style contraction adds one extra traversal of the justification graph, but has the same complexity.

In [2], it was shown that the contraction operator defined by the algorithm above satisfies (K$\dot{-}$1)–(K$\dot{-}$4) and (K$\dot{-}$6); (K$\dot{-}$5) is not satisfied. To give an example, suppose B can be derived using A (but not vice versa). If we contract by B, then A is also removed from the belief base. When we expand by B, A is not restored to the belief base.

5.1 Preferred Contractions

In general, an agent will prefer some contractions to others. In this section we focus on contractions based on preference orders over individual beliefs, e.g., degree of belief or commitment to beliefs. We assume that an agent associates an *a priori* quality with each non-inferential justification for its independent beliefs. For example, communicated information may be assigned a degree of reliability by its recipient which depends on the degree of reliability of the speaker (i.e., the speaker's reputation), percepts may be assumed to be more reliable than communicated information, and so on.

For simplicity, we assume that quality of a justification is represented by non-negative integers in the range $0, \ldots, m$, where m is the maximum size of the belief base. A value of 0 means the lowest quality and m means highest quality. We take the preference of a literal A, $p(A)$, to be that of its highest quality justification:

$$p(A) = max\{qual(j_0), \ldots, qual(j_n)\},$$

where $j_0, \ldots, j_n$ are all the justifications for A, and we define the quality of an inferential justification to be that of the least preferred belief in its support:[5]

$$qual(j) = min\{p(A) : A \in \text{ support of } j\}.$$

This is similar to ideas in argumentation theory: an argument is only as good as its weakest link, yet a conclusion is at least as good as the best argument for it. This approach is also related to Williams "partial entrenchment ranking" [26] which assumes that the entrenchment of any sentence is the maximal quality of a set of sentences implying it, where the quality of a set is equal to the minimal entrenchment of its members. While this approach is intuitively appealing, nothing hangs on it, in the sense that any preference order can be used to define a contraction operation, and the resulting operation will satisfy the postulates.

To perform a preferred contraction, we preface the contraction algorithm given above with a step which computes the preference of each literal in the belief base, and for each justification, finds the position of a least preferred member of the support list. The preference computation algorithm can be found in [2]. We then simply run the contraction algorithm to recursively delete the weakest member of each support in the dependency graph of A.

We define the *worth* of a set of literals Γ as $worth(\Gamma) = max\{p(A) : A \in \Gamma\}$. In [2], it was shown that the contraction algorithm removes the set of literals with the least worth. More precisely:

Proposition 1. *If contraction of the set of literals in the belief base K by A resulted in removal of the set of literals Γ, then for any other set of literals Γ' such that $K - \Gamma'$ does not imply A, $worth(\Gamma) \leq worth(\Gamma')$.*

The proof is given in [2]. Computing preferred contractions involves only modest computational overhead. The total cost of computing the preference of all literals in the belief base is $O(n \log n + kr)$, where n the number of literals in the belief base, k is the maximal number of beliefs in any support list, and r the number of plans. As the contraction algorithm is unchanged, this is also the additional cost of computing a preferred contraction. Computing the most preferred contraction can therefore be performed in time linear in $kr + n$.

6   Belief Revision in AgentSpeak

The belief revision algorithm presented above was developed for rule based agents, where rules could easily be interpreted as corresponding to logical implications. However the execution of AgentSpeak plans cannot always be interpreted as corresponding to logical derivations. In this section we show how the algorithm can be applied in the context of AgentSpeak and briefly discuss the notion of consistency which our contraction algorithm maintains between the beliefs of an AgentSpeak agent.

---

[5] Literals with no supports (as opposed to an empty support) are viewed as having an empty support of the lowest quality.

The original version of the algorithm presented in [2] assumed a forward-chaining rule-based agent, with rules of the form $A_1, \ldots, A_n \rightarrow B$, which fires its rules to quiescence (i.e., until no more rules are applicable). To define for those agents what it means for the belief base to be consistent and what it means for a belief to be derivable, we interpret rules as Horn clauses and literals as atomic formulæof predicate logic, and postulate that the agent "reasons" using a single inference rule of *generalised modus ponens*:

$$\frac{\delta(A_1), \ldots, \delta(A_n), \qquad \forall \bar{x}(A_1 \wedge \ldots \wedge A_n \rightarrow B)}{\delta(B)}$$

where δ is a substitution function which replaces all free variables of a formula with constants. In [2], the resulting logic is called W. Clearly, the language of W is weaker than the language of full classical logic (e.g., it does not have disjunctions). The deductive power of the logic is also weaker; for example, from $A \rightarrow B$ and $\neg A \rightarrow B$ the agent cannot derive B, as it would have been possible in classical logic. It was shown in [2] that the beliefs of a quiescent forward-chaining agent are closed with respect to consequence in W, and that the contraction algorithm restores consistency in the sense of W; that is, after contraction by A the agent can no longer derive A in W from its beliefs.

Since not all rule-based agents fire their rules to quiescence, [2] also analysed belief contraction in the non-quiescent case. In that case, the agent's beliefs at each point in time are closed with respect to the set of rule instances *which have been applied by the agent up to that point in time*. Even this is not exactly true if the agent uses refractory rule firing, that is, each rule instance is only fired once. This means that if $A(x)$ implies $B(x)$, $A(a)$ is in the belief base, $B(a)$ is derived and then removed, $B(a)$ can not be re-derived again using the same rule. However in this paper we ignore refractory rule firing and take "derivable" to mean "derivable using previously fired rule instances". In effect, we over-approximate the set of literals the agent can derive with respect to refractory rule firing.

As noted above, the execution of AgentSpeak plans cannot always be interpreted as corresponding to logical derivations. We therefore assume that, in future versions of **Jason**, plans that can be used to derive a new belief on the basis of currently held beliefs will be annotated by the programmer to indicate that they are relevant for belief revision. We call such plans *declarative-rule plans*. A declarative-rule plan of the form "$te : l_1 \& \ldots \& l_n \mathrel{<-} bd$", where te is a triggering event and bd a plan body starting with belief addition $+bl$, is interpreted as an implication $l_1, \ldots, l_n \rightarrow bl$; if the triggering event, te, is itself a belief addition, it is included in the antecedent as well: $te, l_1, \ldots, l_n \rightarrow bl$. When declarative rules or ontological reasoning are used to check if a plan is applicable, e.g., if a plan with literals $l_1, \ldots l_n$ in its context is applicable not because $l_1, \ldots, l_n$ are in the belief base, but because other literals $m_1, \ldots, m_n$ are, and the agent's declarative rules or ontological reasoning entails $m_i \sqsubseteq l_i$ for each i, we interpret this as a plan instance with $m_1, \ldots, m_n$ in its context. A belief is then derivable if it is derivable from the belief base using the plan instances used so far, with the results of the declarative rules or ontological reasoning substituted in the actual plan instances; so instead of, e.g., $l_1, \ldots, l_n \rightarrow bl$ in the implications, we have $m_1, \ldots, m_n \rightarrow bl$

where $m_1, \ldots, m_n$ are the belief literals in the belief base which were actually used for the plan to be considered applicable, given the agent's declarative or ontological rules.

We say that a belief base of an AgentSpeak agent is consistent if a contradiction is not derivable by generalised modus ponens from the contents of the belief base and the agent's plans (represented as implications) which were used in the agent's execution so far. In particular, after contracting by bl, bl is not re-derivable from the corresponding set of implications and atomic beliefs in the logic W.

7 Implementation of Belief Revision in *Jason*

Future versions of *Jason* will incorporate an implementation of the belief revision algorithm described above. The belief revision functionality will be split between the existing brf and a new buf responsible for belief update. Perception of the environment will be followed by a call to buf with the literals in the list of additions representing the list of percepts. As in the current version of *Jason*, it is assumed that all perceptible properties are included in the list of additions: all current beliefs no longer within the list of percepts are deleted from the belief base, and all percepts not currently in the belief base are added to it. All other additions to the belief base are handled by brf. Belief additions in plans annotated for belief revision result in a call to brf with the new belief as argument. If the new belief is inconsistent with the current belief base, brf may discard it or may delete some other belief(s) to allow the new belief to be consistently added to the belief base. Which beliefs are actually deleted is determined by a user-specified preference order (see below).

The directed graph used by the belief revision algorithm is implemented in terms of two lists for each belief: a "dependencies list" (the literals that allowed the derivation of the belief literal in question), and a "justifies list" (which other beliefs the literal in question justifies, i.e., it appears in their dependencies list). The new brf method maintains two special annotations for each belief in the belief base "dep([...]), just([...])" which record the dependencies and justifies lists for the belief respectively. The literals to populate these two lists are retrieved from the intention that generated the belief change. For example, if the top of the intention structure that generated a belief change $+bl$ has a plan instance of the form "te : l_1 & $\ldots$ & l_n <- bd", where te is a triggering event and bd a plan body in which $+bl$ is the first action, the support list of the justification is simply the (ground) literals from the plan context, "$[l_1,\ldots,l_n]$". If the triggering event, te, is itself a belief (addition), the literal in te is included together with the context literals in the support list as noted above. If a belief was added as a result of a plan being applicable using declarative rules or ontological reasoning, e.g., if the literal l_1 is not in the belief base, but some other literal l is, and $l \sqsubseteq l_1$ is an instance of an declarative or ontology rule, then l will be in the support list for bl instead of l_1. For each literal in the support list $l_1, \ldots, l_n$ we add the justification to the literal's "justifies" list. We also record the time at which the justification was added to the relevant list.

In addition to the "dependencies" and "justifies" lists, the belief revision algorithm also requires the definition of a partial order relation specifying contraction preference. To allow for user customisation, this is defined as a separate method that can also be overridden. The default definition of this method gives preference to perceived information over communicated information (as also happens in [24]), and in case of information from sources of similar reliability, it gives preference to newer information over older information (this is why the time when a justification was inserted is also added as an annotation).

During belief update and revision, the "dependencies" and "justifies" lists are updated to reflect the beliefs (and their justifications) which have been removed from the agent's belief base. Deletion of beliefs as a result of belief update results in the appropriate changes to the justification structure and belief base: with AGM-style revision, the deleted belief is removed from the "dependencies" lists of all other beliefs in the belief base; with reason-maintenance style revision, any beliefs in whose "justifies" list a deleted belief appears are also deleted. The buf method also removes any justification which has a deleted perceptual belief in its support list, and marks the justified belief as a self-supporting (independent) belief. This additional bookkeeping reflects the special status of perceptual beliefs: perceptual beliefs can trigger or justify the addition of other beliefs, but their deletion is not in itself a reason for removing a derived belief. When an inconsistency is detected during belief revision, brf determines which of the two beliefs is less preferred, and then (recursively) deletes the least preferred belief in the "dependencies" list of the contracted belief. With reason-maintenance style revision, any beliefs in whose "justifies" list a deleted belief appears are also deleted.

The implementation described above is conservative in revising only the agent's belief state. The agent's plans are considered part of the agent's program and are not revised (though revising plans, in particular those received from other agents, would be an interesting extension). Similarly, when revising beliefs derived using ontological rules, we assume the ontology used by the agent to be immutable and consistent, and that it is consistent with every other ontology it references. Moreover, *intention* revision remains the responsibility of the programmer. Changes in the agent's intentions following the removal of beliefs to restore consistency, or changes in beliefs as a consequence of intention reconsideration, must be programmed using the appropriate *Jason* mechanisms. All belief changes, regardless of whether they are internal, communicated, or perceived can lead to the execution of a plan which could be used, for example, to drop an intention. If the belief revision algorithm has to remove any beliefs to ensure consistency, this will also generate the appropriate (belief-deletion) internal events, which in turn can trigger the execution of a such plans to revise the agent's intentions.

8   An Example

To illustrate the importance of belief revision in the context of AgentSpeak (or, more generally, an agent programming language), we present a simple scenario of an agent that buys stocks from the stock market. The agent receives financial information (or guesses) from other agents, some of which can be trusted (or are currently considered trustworthy), and it also has access to Web Services which filter relevant newspaper stories and provide symbolic versions of such news for stock market agents. As these web services are authenticated, this corresponds to actual perception of the "environment".

Suppose our agent receives a message $\langle \text{ag1}, tell, \text{salesUp(c1)} \rangle$ and its plan library has the following plan:

```
+salesUp(C)[source(A)]
  : wellManaged(C) & trust(A)
    <- +goodToBuy(C).
```

When the plan is executed, the brf() method will then add goodToBuy(c1)[source(ag1)] to the belief base with [salesUp(c1), wellManaged(c1), trust(ag1)] in its "dependencies" list, and goodToBuy(c1) is added to the "justifies" lists of the beliefs salesUp(c1), wellManaged(c1), and trust(ag1). In the context of the overall agent program, the idea is that if the agent ever comes to have the goal of buying stocks, it can make use of beliefs such as goodToBuy, together with various other conditions, to decide which specific stocks to buy.

Now assume that, from the financial news web service, the agent acquires the belief stocks(c2,10)[source(percept)], which means that company c2's stocks are up by 10 points, and the agent also believes that rival(c2,c1) (i.e., that companies c2 and c1 are competitors), so that increase in the stocks of one of them tends to lead to a decrease in the other's stocks. Assume further that the agent happens to have the following plan:

```
+stocks(C,P)
  : P > 5 & rival(C,R)
    <- +~goodToBuy(R).
```

When the plan is executed, the attempt to simply add ~goodToBuy(c1) to the belief base would not be carried out because it would result in an inconsistent belief state. With the default contraction preference relation, it is not difficult to see that, in this instance, the algorithm would contract by goodToBuy(c1) because its support is based on communicated information which is less reliable than the observed information from which ~goodToBuy(c1) was derived.

As can be seen, the belief revision algorithm takes care of ensuring that inconsistencies, such as goodToBuy(c1) and ~goodToBuy(c1)) being believed simultaneously, never occur in the belief base. Moreover, the data structures used by the algorithm (the dependencies and justifications lists) allow it to automatically revise the belief base in ways that previously would have required significant programming effort. For example, suppose the agent receives news that a crooked CEO has just been fired from c1. The agent is likely to have a plan to update its beliefs about c1 being well managed as a consequence of such new information about the CEO. If the user has chosen the *reason-maintenance style* of the algorithm, and there is no other justification for goodToBuy, then the algorithm would remove not only the wellManaged(c1) belief, but also the goodToBuy(c1) belief because the latter depends on the former. Similarly if for some reason the agent later finds out that ag1 is not trustworthy after all.

However, if the user opts for AGM-style revision, removing wellManaged would *not* remove goodToBuy. Although in this example the reason-maintenance style is arguably more appropriate, in other applications the coherence style might be more useful. In either case, it is clear that without the use of automatic belief revision, it would be very difficult for a programmer to ensure that revision occurs appropriately in all situations. The programmer would either have to develop an application-specific brf method, or else write specific plans to handle *all possible belief change events* that might affect any derivations the agent can make.

9   Conclusions and Future Work

As multi-agent programming languages become richer, it becomes harder for programmers to ensure that the belief states of agents developed using these languages are kept consistent. In this paper we briefly summarised the rationale for including automatic belief revision in an agent programming language. Using the AgentSpeak programming language as an example, we showed how a number of features recently added to the language have dramatically increased the need for automatic belief revision. We motivated the choice of the polynomial-time belief revision algorithm presented in [2], and described its integration into the ***Jason*** AgentSpeak interpreter. We also gave a simple example which illustrates the usefulness of such an automatic belief revision mechanism in a practical multi-agent system scenario, and sketched how it can significantly reduce the programming efforts required. We believe that other agent-oriented programming languages and their platforms [5], which currently push responsibility for maintaining a consistent belief state onto programmers, can also benefit from our approach.

A limitation of the work presented here is that we only consider plans which correspond to classical implication; in particular, we don't consider negation as failure in plan contexts. Belief revision in the presence of negation as failure would be an interesting problem to consider, since it corresponds to belief revision in default logic. Another interesting question to be considered in further work is the need for belief revision as a consequence of intention reconsideration. On the more practical side, we plan to develop large-scale agent applications to assess the performance of ***Jason*** with belief revision.

Acknowledgements

Rafael Bordini gratefully acknowledges the support of The Nuffield Foundation (grant number NAL/01065/G).

References

1. C. E. Alchourrón, P. Gärdenfors, and D. Makinson. On the logic of theory change: Partial meet functions for contraction and revision. *Journal of Symbolic Logic*, 50:510–530, 1985.
2. N. Alechina, M. Jago, and B. Logan. Resource-bounded belief revision and contraction. In *Proceedings of the 3rd International Workshop on Declarative Agent Languages and Technologies (DALT 2005)*, number 3904 in LNCS, pages 141–154, Utrecht, the Netherlands, July 2005. Springer-Verlag.
3. D. Ancona, V. Mascardi, J. F. Hübner, and R. H. Bordini. Coo-AgentSpeak: Cooperation in AgentSpeak through plan exchange. In N. R. Jennings, C. Sierra, L. Sonenberg, and M. Tambe, editors, *Proceedings of the Third International Joint Conference on Autonomous Agents and Multi-Agent Systems (AAMAS-2004), New York, NY, 19–23 July*, pages 698–705, New York, NY, 2004. ACM Press.

4. F. Baader, D. Calvanese, D. McGuinness, D. Nardi, and P. Patel-Schneider, editors. *Handbook of Description Logics*. Cambridge University Press, Cambridge, 2003.

5. R. H. Bordini, M. Dastani, J. Dix, and A. El Fallah Seghrouchni, editors. *Multi-Agent Programming: Languages, Platforms and Applications*. Number 15 in Multiagent Systems, Artificial Societies, and Simulated Organizations. Springer, 2005.

6. R. H. Bordini, J. F. Hübner, et al. *Jason: A Java-based Agentspeak interpreter used with SACI for multi-agent distribution over the net*, manual, release version 0.7 edition, August 2005. http://jason.sourceforge.net/.

7. R. H. Bordini, J. F. Hübner, and R. Vieira. *Jason* and the Golden Fleece of agent-oriented programming. In Bordini et al. [5], chapter 1.

8. R. H. Bordini and Á. F. Moreira. Proving BDI properties of agent-oriented programming languages: The asymmetry thesis principles in AgentSpeak(L). *Annals of Mathematics and Artificial Intelligence*, 42(1–3):197–226, Sept. 2004. Special Issue on Computational Logic in Multi-Agent Systems.

9. H. Chen, T. Finin, and A. Joshi. The SOUPA Ontology for Pervasive Computing. In V. T. et al, editor, *Ontologies for Agents: Theory and Experiences*, pages 233–258. BirkHauser, 2005.

10. K. L. Clark and F. G. McCabe. Ontology schema for an agent belief store. *IJCIS*, 2006. To appear.

11. M. Dastani, M. B. van Riemsdijk, and J.-J. C. Meyer. Programming multi-agent systems in 3APL. In Bordini et al. [5], chapter 2.

12. J. de Bruijn, A. Polleres, and D. Fensel. Owl lite⁻. working draft, WSML delieverable D20 v0.1, WSML, 18th July 2004.
http://www.wsmo.org/2004/d20/v0.1/20040629/.

13. P. Gärdenfors. Conditionals and changes of belief. In I. Niiniluoto and R. Tuomela, editors, *The Logic and Epistemology of Scientific Change*, pages 381–404. North Holland, 1978.

14. P. Gärdenfors. *Knowledge in Flux: Modelling the Dynamics of Epistemic States*. The MIT Press, Cambridge, Mass., 1988.

15. I. Horrocks and P. F. Patel-Schneider. A proposal for an OWL rules language. In S. I. Feldman, M. Uretsky, M. Najork, and C. E. Wills, editors, *Proceedings of the 13th international conference on World Wide Web, WWW 2004*, pages 723–731. ACM, 2004.

16. D. Makinson. How to give it up: A survey of some formal aspects of the logic of theory change. *Synthese*, 62:347–363, 1985.

17. Á. F. Moreira, R. Vieira, and R. H. Bordini. Extending the operational semantics of a BDI agent-oriented programming language for introducing speech-act based communication. In J. Leite, A. Omicini, L. Sterling, and P. Torroni, editors, *Declarative Agent Languages and Technologies, Proc. of the First Int. Workshop (DALT-03), held with AAMAS-03, 15 July, 2003, Melbourne, Australia*, number 2990 in LNAI, pages 135–154, Berlin, 2004. Springer-Verlag.

18. A. F. Moreira, R. Vieira, R. H. Bordini, and J. Hübner. Agent-oriented programming with underlying ontological reasoning. In *Proceedings of the 3rd International Workshop on Declarative Agent Languages and Technologies (DALT 2005)*, number 3904 in LNCS, pages 155–170, Utrecht, the Netherlands, July 2005. Springer-Verlag.

19. B. Nebel. A knowledge level analysis of belief revision. In R. Brachman, H. J. Levesque, and R. Reiter, editors, *Principles of Knowledge Representation and Reasoning: Proceedings of the First International Conference*, pages 301–311, San Mateo, 1989. Morgan Kaufmann.

20. B. Nebel. Syntax-based approaches to belief revision. In P. Gärdenfors, editor, *Belief Revision*, volume 29, pages 52–88. Cambridge University Press, Cambridge, UK, 1992.

21. B. Nebel. Base revision operations and schemes: Representation, semantics and complexity. In A. G. Cohn, editor, *Proceedings of the Eleventh European Conference on Artificial Intelligence (ECAI'94)*, pages 341–345, Amsterdam, The Netherlands, August 1994. John Wiley and Sons.

22. A. S. Rao. AgentSpeak(L): BDI agents speak out in a logical computable language. In W. Van de Velde and J. Perram, editors, *Proceedings of the Seventh Workshop on Modelling Autonomous Agents in a Multi-Agent World (MAAMAW'96), 22–25 January, Eindhoven, The Netherlands*, number 1038 in Lecture Notes in Artificial Intelligence, pages 42–55, London, 1996. Springer-Verlag.

23. H. Rott. "Just Because": Taking belief bases seriously. In S. R. Buss, P. Hájaek, and P. Pudlák, editors, *Logic Colloquium '98—Proceedings of the 1998 ASL European Summer Meeting*, volume 13 of *Lecture Notes in Logic*, pages 387–408. Association for Symbolic Logic, 1998.

24. R. M. van Eijk, F. S. de Boer, W. van der Hoek, and J.-J. C. Meyer. Information-passing and belief revision in multi-agent systems. In J. P. Müller, M. P. Singh, and A. S. Rao, editors, *Intelligent Agents V — Agent Theories, Architectures, and Languages, 5th International Workshop, ATAL '98, Paris, France, July 4-7, 1998, Proceedings*, volume 1555 of *LNCS*, pages 29–45, Berlin, 1999. Springer-Verlag.

25. M.-A. Williams. Two operators for theory base change. In *Proceedings of the Fifth Australian Joint Conference on Artificial Intelligence*, pages 259–265. World Scientific, 1992.

26. M.-A. Williams. Iterated theory base change: A computational model. In *Proceedings of Fourteenth International Joint Conference on Artificial Intelligence (IJCAI-95)*, pages 1541–1549, San Mateo, 1995. Morgan Kaufmann.

27. M. Wooldridge. *Reasoning about Rational Agents*. The MIT Press, Cambridge, MA, 2000.

A Foundational Ontology of Organizations and Roles

Guido Boella[1] and Leendert van der Torre[2]

[1] Dipartimento di Informatica - Università di Torino - Italy
guido@di.unito.it
[2] University of Luxembourg
leendert@vandertorre.com

Abstract. In this paper we propose a foundational ontology of the social concepts of organization and role which structure institutions. We identify which axioms model social concepts like organization and roles and which properties distinguish them from other categories like objects and agents: the organizational structure of institutions and the relation between roles and organizations. All social concepts depend on descriptions defining them, which are collectively accepted, and the descriptions defining the components of organizations, including roles, are included in the description of the organizations they belong to. Thus, the relational dependence of roles means that they are defined in the organizations they belong to.

1 Introduction

In order to constrain the autonomy of agents and to control their emergent behavior in multiagent systems, the notion of organization has been applied [8,22]. According to Zambonelli *et al.* [22] "a multiagent system can be conceived in terms of an organized society of individuals in which each agent plays specific roles and interacts with other agents". For Zambonelli *et al.* [22] "an organization is more than simply a collection of roles [...] further organization-oriented abstractions need to be devised and placed in the context of a methodology [...] As soon as the complexity increases, modularity and encapsulation principles suggest dividing the system into different sub-organizations".

There is not yet a common agreement, however, on how to model organizations, sub-organizations and roles, and, in particular, which are the ontological assumptions behind them. For example, departments and roles are parts of an organization, but they do not exist without it. Can organizations be explained by means of agent based models? Or can they be better modelled with the object oriented paradigm?

Since the existence of institutions depends on what Searle [18] calls the construction of social reality, it is possible that institutions, organizations and roles have very different properties with respect to objects or agents. Searle [18] argues that social reality is constructed by means of so called "constitutive rules" which state what "counts as" institutional facts in the institution. Constitutive rules define institutions: they exist only because of the collective acceptance of constitutive rules by a community. Searle's construction of social reality does not explain all issues, in particular, the fact that some institutions have a structure in terms of sub-institutions and roles. We will call structured institutions organizations. Thus Searle's analysis is not sufficient starting point for a foundational ontology, that specifies which are the properties distinguishing organizations from objects and agents. We need to know the axioms which allow to

M. Baldoni and U. Endriss (Eds.): DALT 2006, LNAI 4327, pp. 78–88, 2006.

distinguish organizations from other concepts, rather than specifying all the properties of organizations, including those in common with agents. Thus the research questions of this paper are:

- How do organizations and roles differ from objects and agents?
- How can a foundational ontology of social entities like, organizations and roles be constructed?

We are inspired by [2,3] which study some properties of social entities. However, these works are based on a very specific multiagent framework, which uses the so called agent metaphor, i.e., the attribution of mental attitudes to social entities to explain them.

So in this paper we analyse organizations using a more abstract axiomatic ontology and we consider additional properties. The methodology we choose is to extend the ontology of Masolo *et al.* [15]. The main properties of their framework are three. First, it allows to express the fact that social concepts are defined by means of descriptions. Second, it explains the definitional dependence of a role from another concept and the relational nature of roles. Last, it offers a temporalized classification relation, used for modelling the fact that roles are anti-rigid.

We extend Masolo *et al.* [15]'s axiomatic ontology to model institutions and their organizational structure and to explain the asymmetry in the relations defining roles.

This paper is structured as follows. First, we consider the differences between social reality and objects and agents. In Section 3, we present Masolo *et al.* [15]'s model. In Section 4, starting from the limitations of [15] we extend it to define the foundational ontology. Conclusions end the paper.

2   The Properties of Organizations

The role of knowledge representation and software engineering is to provide models and techniques that make it easier to handle the complexity arising from the large number of interactions in a system [13]. Models and techniques allow expressing knowledge and to support the analysis and reasoning about a system to be developed. As the context and needs of software change, advances are needed to respond to changes. For example, today's systems and their environments are more varied and dynamic, and accommodate more local freedom and initiative [21].

For these reasons, agent orientation emerged as a new paradigm for designing and constructing software systems [13,21]. The agent oriented approach advocates decomposing problems in terms of autonomous agents that can engage in flexible, high-level interactions. Much like the concepts of activity and object that have played pivotal roles in earlier modelling paradigms - Yu [21] argues - the agent concept can be instrumental in bringing about a shift to a much richer, *socially-oriented ontology* that is needed to characterize and analyze today's systems and environments.

The notions of institution, organization and role are part of this socially-oriented ontology. It is not clear, however, if the ontological assumptions behind this kind of entities are the same which underlie objects and agents. Many approaches recognize as properties of social entities being the addressee of obligations [7], like agents are, the delegation mechanisms among roles [11], *etc*. Moreover, organizations are modelled as collections of agents, gathered in groups [8], playing roles [13,16] or regulated by organizational rules [22]. We focus instead on the distinguishing properties of the social concepts of organization and role.

Consider, for example, an organization which is composed by a direction area and a production area. The direction area is composed by the CEO and the board. The board is composed by a set of administrators. The production area is composed by two production units; each production unit by a set of workers. The direction area, the board, the production area and the production units are *sub-organizations*. In particular, the direction area and the production areas belong to the organization, the board to the direction area, *etc*. The CEO, the administrators and the members of the production units are *roles*, each one belonging to a sub-organization, e.g., the CEO is part of the direction area. This recursive decomposition terminates with roles: roles, unlike organizations and sub-organizations, are not composed by further social entities. Rather, roles are played by other agents, real agents who have to act as expected by their role.

Besides the decomposition structure, as [3] argue in organizations we have relations among the components of the organization which specify which are the powers of each component to modify the institutional properties of the other component institutions. This relation does not necessarily matches the decomposition hierarchy. For example, the senior board member has the power to command other members of the board to participate to a board meeting, even if it is at the same decomposition level of the other members. We do not consider yet this aspect in this paper.

Is it possible to model such structures in the object oriented paradigm? The object oriented paradigm is based on the idea that software design and implementation can be inspired by our commonsense view of the reality made of objects. For Booch [5] a basic property of objects is that they can be decomposed. Decomposition allows coping with complexity: "the most basic technique for tackling any large problem is to divide it into smaller, more manageable chunks each of which can then be dealt with in relative isolation". Isolation is the idea that code should be encapsulated in classes hiding the implementation of the objects' state; thus, other objects can access an object's state only via its public interface. Decomposition means that an object can include other objects which exist independently of it, like they were parts of the object.

In case of organizations, the situation is different. In the decomposition structure, the components of an organization do not exist independently from the organization itself. For example a department does not exist without the organization it belongs to. If an organization goes bankrupt its departments do not exist anymore and similarly the roles in them (there is no CEO nor employee anymore). Viceversa, an organization can close a department without necessarily giving up its identity.

One alternative could be to see whether organizations can be modelled as agents, but again some difficulties arise. Organizations can have organizations as their parts, while agents cannot have parts which are homogeneous with the whole. Moreover, agents can play roles but they cannot have roles as their parts.

However, some form of decomposition should be added to multiagent systems, as noticed by Zambonelli *et al.* [22]: agents alone, and also roles, are not sufficient to deal with the complexity of a system; an organizational structure added to a multiagent system fosters modularity and encapsulation.

3   Background

Masolo *et al.* [15] present a formal framework for developing axiomatical ontologies of socially constructed entities, and study the ontological nature of roles. Social entities and roles exist just because of social conventions, i.e., constitutive rules accepted by communities of agents: these can be social concepts like organization, nation, money, or social individuals like the ECAI Conference or the FIAT company.

In Masolo *et al.* [15] roles are 'properties' according the position defended by Sowa [19]: roles can be 'predicated' of different entities, i.e., different entities can play the same role, e.g., different persons can all be students. The basic properties of roles are the anti-rigidity (see Section 1) and being founded. According to Guarino and Welty [12] the definition of foundation is: "a property a is founded on a property b if, necessarily, for every instance x of a there exists an instance y of b which is not 'internal' to x". The notion of 'internalness' is complex: e.g., if x is a car, things internal to it can be parts of it (its wheels), but also constituents of it (the metal it is made of) or qualities of it (its color). To avoid all trivial cases, Fine [9] introduces another notion of dependence: "to say that an object x depends upon an F is to say that an F will be ineliminably involved in any definition of x".

This notion can be generalized to properties considering that a property a is *definitionally dependent* on a property b if, necessarily, any *definition* of a ineliminably involves b. To model this 'definitions' are explicitly introduced in the domain of discourse. [15] consider 'reified' social concepts and roles, as well as their descriptions, i.e, the constitutive rules that define them. This allows to formally characterize in a first-order theory the relationships among all these entities and to talk of roles as 'first-class citizens', similarly to more common entities like objects, events, *etc.*

Masolo *et al.* [15]'s approach is based on a distinction between the properties and relations in the ground ontology (like DOLCE [10]) and those at the object level representing the social reality. The former ones are represented as predicates and, therefore, assumed as static, rigid, extensional, and not explicitly defined or linked to a description (i.e., the primitive predicates of the theory). The latter ones (called "concepts") are reified and not necessarily static, rigid, and extensional, and for which it is possible to explicitly describe some aspects of the conventions that define them (called "descriptions").

Social concepts, denoted by $CN(x)$ are defined (DF) or used (US) by descriptions (DS) and they classify (CF) other individuals: $DF(x, y)$ stands for "the concept x is defined by the description y" to deal with the social, relational, and contextual nature of social concepts. $US(x, y)$ stands for "the concept x is used by the description y"; they introduce a temporalized classification relation to link concepts with the entities they classify, while accounting for the dynamic behavior of social roles: $CF(x, y, t)$ stands for "at the time t, x is classified by the concept y" or, more explicitly, "at the time t, x satisfies all the constraints stated in the description of y".

In the axioms defining [15]'s theory, $ED(x)$ stands for "x is an endurant", i.e., an entity that is wholly present at any time it is present, e.g., a book, Trento, a law, some metal, *etc.* $NASO(x)$ stands for "x is a non-agentive social object", i.e., an endurant that: (i) is not directly located in space and, has no direct spatial qualities; (ii) has no intentionality; (iii) depends on a community of intentional agents, e.g., a law, an organization, a currency, an asset *etc.*; $TL(x)$ stands for "x is a temporal location", i.e., a temporal interval or instant; $P(x, y)$ stands for "x is part-of y", for perdurants and temporal locations; $PRE(x, t)$ stands for "x is present at the time t".

We report here the most important axioms of their theory. Concepts, and descriptions as well, are non-agentive social objects; concepts are linked to descriptions by the relations used-by (US) and defined-by (DF). Theorem T2 below captures the fact that a concept must be defined by a single description. This is not true for the US relation: concepts can be used by different descriptions.

(A1) $DS(x) \supset NASO(x)$
(A2) $CN(x) \supset NASO(x)$
(A3) $DS(x) \supset \neg CN(x)$
(A4) $US(x, y) \supset (CN(x) \wedge DS(y))$
(A5) $DF(x, y) \supset US(x, y)$
(A8) $(DF(x, y) \wedge DF(x, z)) \supset y = z$
(T1) $DF(x, y) \supset (CN(x) \wedge DS(y))$
(T2) $CN(x) \supset \exists! y(DF(x, y))$
(A11) $CF(x, y, t) \supset (ED(x) \wedge CN(y) \wedge TL(t))$
(A14) $CF(x, y, t) \supset \neg CF(y, x, t)$
(A15) $(CF(x, y, t) \wedge CF(y, z, t)) \supset \neg CF(x, z, t)$

The properties of anti-rigidity (AR) and foundation (FD) for roles can be defined in this formalism. A concept is anti-rigid if, for any time an entity is classified under it, there exists a time at which the entity is present but not classified under the concept:

(D1) $AR(x) \equiv_{df} \forall y, t(CF(y, x, t) \supset \exists t'(PRE(y, t') \wedge \neg CF(y, x, t')))$

A concept x is founded if its definition involves (at least) another concept y (definitional dependence) such that for each entity classified by x, there is an external entity classified by y:

(D2) $FD(x) \equiv_{df}$
$$\exists y, d(DF(x, d) \wedge US(y, d) \wedge \forall z, t(CF(z, x, t) \supset$$
$$\exists z'(CF(z', y, t) \wedge \neg P(z, z', t) \wedge \neg P(z', z, t))))$$

Roles are anti-rigid and founded:

(D3) $RL(x) \equiv_{df} AR(x) \wedge FD(x)$

Masolo et al. [14] extend [15]'s framework introducing explicitly a relation between an institution and a role to express that a role like student is relationally dependent, e.g., for a person to be a student it requires the existence of another entity, namely a certain university, to which this person is related by an enrollment relation. As Steimann [20] shows, this view of roles as anti-rigid and relationally dependent predicates is supported by the vast majority of approaches in the conceptual modeling and object-modeling literature.

Roles can be defined on the basis of a relation whose arguments are characterized by specific properties. For example, the role of 'being a student' can be defined as: "a student is a person enrolled in a university". In this case, 'being a student' is defined on the basis of 'being enrolled in', 'being a person', and 'being a university'. Formally, considering the previous properties as predicates, this definition can be formulated as:

$$Student(x) \equiv_{df} Person(x) \land \exists y(enr(x, y) \land University(y))$$

But given a specific relation r of arity n, it is possible to define n different predicates r_m. For example, in the case of the relation $enr(x, y) \supset (Person(x) \land University(y))$, the predicate $EnrollingUni$ can be defined as:

$$EnrollingUni(x) \equiv_{df} \exists y(enr(y, x))$$

Hence the authors are aware that there is an asymmetry in the relation defining roles. $EnrollingUni$ has exactly the "same logical form" as $Student$, but this does not imply that $EnrollingUni$ is a role. Let us assume a theory containing an axiom stating that, necessarily, universities enroll at least one student, i.e., when a university loses all its students, it ceases to be a university. In this theory, 'being an enrolling university' is a rigid property of universities, and therefore it cannot be a role (assuming $University$ as rigid). In addition, the two predicates $EnrollingUni$ and $University$ coincide from an extensional point of view (since all universities are enrolling universities) and they cannot be distinguished by means of the theory. In this case, the predicate $EnrollingUni$ seems "redundant" with respect to the predicate $University$ because they are provably equivalent.

Bottazzi and Ferrario [6] start analysing organizations in [15]'s framework. They consider organizations as agentive entities, but they act in a very peculiar way, namely through the actions of some agents who, in virtue of the institutionalized ($INST$) roles (RL) they play (AFF), are delegated to act on their behalf (REP):

(B1) $AFF(x, y, t) \equiv_{df} AG(x) \land \exists z(RL(z) \land CF(x, z, t) \land INST(z, y))$

Moreover organizations are social individuals (SI), thus, differently from social concepts and roles, they don't classify particulars (like agents or physical objects):

(B2) $ORG(x) \supset SI(x)$

A necessary condition for social individual to be an organization (ORG) is the existence of at least one representative agent who is affiliated to it.

(B3) $ORG(x) \supset \exists y, z(AFF(y, x, t) \land REP(z, x))$

4   The Ontology of Organizations

Summarizing the discussion in Section 2, the basic properties of institutions, organizations and roles are, first, that organizations are institutions with an organizational structure in terms of sub-organizations and roles. Second, sub-organizations and roles are defined by the organizations they belong to. The decomposition hierarchy of the organizational structure, however, is not based on the part-of relation of objects. In particular, it is transitive (a role in a department is part of the organization the department belongs to), but the parts do not exist without and before the whole.

The formal framework of Masolo *et al.* [15] is the suitable starting point for defining a foundational ontology of organizations and roles. Our requirements, however, are not fully satisfied in their axiomatization.

First of all, they do not consider the structure of social entities. They do not define sub-organizations nor roles as parts of organizations. So an institution does not have a recursive decomposition structure. Roles have been recognized as depending on some other entity which is used in their definition, but they are not defined in the entity they depend on. Moreover, we need to extend this dependence relation to specify that also sub-organizations, and not only roles, depend on the organizations. The extended framework of [14] is a closer starting point for our axiomatization. The introduction of an explicit relation between an institution and a role explains the link between them. But still they do not capture the fact that a role is part of the institution and it is defined by it as we claim.

We will fulfill the above requirements in our ontology in the following way. The organizational structure of an institution is defined exploiting the fact that an institution is defined by a description. We say that a sub-organization or a role are defined by a description which is part of the description defining the institution they belong to. This explains also why the relations associating roles to institutions are asymmetric and why roles are part of the institution and not only involved in a relation with the institution.

In the ontology we define the following predicates used in the definitions below:

- The predicates social concept CN and description DS are borrowed from [15]. Non agentive social object ($NASO$), agent (AG), affiliate (AFF), representative (REP) and social individual (SI) are inspired by [6].
- The part-of relation P is extended to hold between descriptions: a description d of a concept c can use US other concepts, but it can also include the definition of another concept. We assume P is a transitive property and that a part (pre)exists independently of the whole:

$P(a,b) \supset \exists t(PRE(a,t) \wedge \neg PRE(b,t))$

- The relation defined-by of [15] relates concepts and descriptions $DF(c,d)$: the concept c ($CN(c)$) is defined by the description d ($DS(d)$). The defined-by relation is used also to define the relation *MDF* which identifies a minimal description of a concept c: a description which cannot be reduced without being unable to define the concept.

$MDF(c,d) \equiv_{df} DF(c,d) \wedge \neg \exists d' P(d',d) \wedge DF(c,d')$

Note that to have non-minimal descriptions we have to change Axiom A8 of [15] (and thus theorem T2), so that only minimal descriptions are unique:

(A8') $(MDF(x,y) \wedge MDF(x,z)) \supset y = z$

The first requirement of our foundational ontology is that organizations are institutions which have a structure. We do not introduce here a primitive part-of relation between organizations and suborganizations, nor we can use P since we need different properties, like the fact that the parts do not exist without the whole. Thus we introduce a new predicate *IP*. An organization c is institutionally part-of (*IP*) another organization c' if it is defined inside the minimal description defining the other one. Note that we need a minimal description, otherwise we could have a description d which is the union of two (minimal) descriptions d' and d'' defining two unrelated concepts. Requiring a minimal description thus means that the definition of c is essential to define c'.

$$IP(c, c') \equiv_{df} \exists d, d'\, MDF(c, d) \wedge MDF(c', d') \wedge P(d, d')$$

Since the P relation between descriptions is transitive, also the IP relation is transitive: a role which is part of a sub-organization of an organization, it is also part of the organization.

The following axiom states that if a sub-organization c is part of organization c' then the concept c' is used in the definition of c.

(C1) $IP(c, c') \supset \exists d\, MDF(c, d) \wedge US(c', d)$

We can use the IP predicate to define our notion of definitional foundation DFD for roles. Our definition is a revised version of the founded FD predicate of [15]. It captures the idea that a role is not only a concept which is part of (IP) another concept, but it requires the existence of an instance of such concept for each of its instances.

Definition 1 (Definitional foundation)

$DFD(x) \equiv_{df}$
    $\exists y\, IP(x, y) \wedge \forall z, t\, (CF(z, x, t) \supset \exists z'(CF(z', y, t) \neg P(z, z', t) \wedge \neg P(z', z, t)))$

We write also:

$DFD(x, y) \equiv_{df}$
    $IP(x, y) \wedge \forall z, t\, (CF(z, x, t) \supset \exists z'(CF(z', y, t) \wedge \neg P(z, z', t) \wedge \neg P(z', z, t)))$

The difference with respect to the FD predicate of [15] is that DFD requests that a concept is used in a definition of x, but also that this definition is part of the definition of another concept.

Which is the relation between the two definitions? The DFD property is stronger than FD since we assume Axiom C1.

Theorem 1

From Axiom C1 and from the fact that $MDF(x, d) \supset DF(x, d)$ we have:

$DFD(x) \supset$
    $[\exists y, d\, DF(x, d) \wedge US(y, d) \wedge$
    $\forall z, t\, (CF(z, x, t) \supset$
        $\exists z'\, (CF(z', y, t) \wedge \neg P(z, z', t) \wedge \neg P(z', z, t)))] \supset FD(x)$

We can introduce now our definition of institutions, organizations and roles. Extending [14] institutions (INS) are social individuals (SI, thus defined by descriptions) which act through their representatives (REP); organizations (ORG) are institutions which have affiliates, and thus may have sub-organizations and roles as their parts. Sub-organizations ($S\text{-}ORG$) are organizations which are part of some organization and roles are anti-rigid definitionally founded concepts, and there is no institution part of them.

Definition 2 (Institutions, organizations and roles)

$INS(x) \equiv_{df} SI(x) \wedge \exists y\, AG(y) \wedge REP(y, x)$
$ORG(x) \equiv_{df} INS(x) \wedge \exists y\, AFF(y, x)$

$$S\text{-}ORG(x) \equiv_{df} ORG(x) \wedge \exists y \, IP(x,y)$$
$$RL(x) \equiv_{df} AR(x) \wedge DFD(x) \wedge \neg \exists y \, IP(y,x)$$

where affiliation AFF is redefined in the following way since we do not have yet a notion of institutionalization and validity as [14]:

(C2) $AFF(x,y) \equiv_{df}$
$$AG(x) \wedge \exists z (RL(z) \wedge CF(x,z) \wedge IP(z,y))$$

As a consequence of this definition an organization must have at least a role. Since IP is transitive, it is possible that this role belongs to a sub-organization of the organization itself.

In the following example a simple organization composed by one institution with one role is illustrated:

Example 1
c_1 is an organization which is minimally defined by description d_1 (see Figure 1). Description d_1 includes also a subdescription d_2 which is the minimal description of the concept c_2, a role of c_1. c_2 classifies an agent a_1.

$DS(d_1), DS(d_2), SI(c_1), RL(c_2), AG(a_1)$
$MDF(c_1, d_1), MDF(c_2, d_2)$
$P(d_2, d_1), CF(a_1, c_2), REP(a_1, c_2)$

Thus, c_2 is a part of c_1: $IP(c_2, c_1)$, and c_1 is an organization $ORG(c_1)$, which is represented by its affiliate a_1.

Note that with respect to [14] we do not define roles in terms of relations. As discussed in Section 3, the limitation of their approach is that by defining roles based on relations, the asymmetry due to the definitional dependence of roles is lost. In our approach, instead, a relation like enrolment enr between the role $Student$ and $University$ is defined based on these two concepts: e.g.,

$$enr(x,y) \equiv_{def} Person(x) \wedge University(y) \wedge CF(x, Student) \wedge$$
$$IP(Student, University)$$

5   Conclusions

In knowledge representation, and more specifically in the field of description logics, the term 'role' is nowadays synonymous of an arbitrary binary relation used to characterize the structure of a concept. The concept 'person', for instance, may have the role 'likes', which represents the relationship between a person and what she likes best. But this is not what is meant by social roles.

In multi-agent systems (MAS) roles are generally viewed as descriptions of agent's acting and interacting, where agents include also societies or organizations of agents. The characterization of this kind of social roles (in the restricted sense) is founded on theories of action and behavior (involving tasks, goals, plans, *etc.*) and deontic notions. In [22] a role is viewed as an "abstract description of an entity's expected function" which is defined by four attributes: responsibilities (that determine the functionality

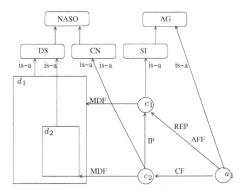

Fig. 1. An example of organization

of the role), permissions, activities, and protocols. Pacheco and Carmo [17] clearly distinguish roles from agents (agents can act, and roles cannot). But these descriptions do not tell much about what distinguish roles from objects or agents.

In object-oriented programming languages the focus has been on technical issues (multiple and dynamic classification, multiple inheritance, objects changing their attributes and behaviors, *etc.*), rather than what are the roles' distinguishing properties.

In this paper we propose a foundational ontology of organizations and roles which extend Masolo *et al.* [15]'s proposal. Institutions are social concepts which exist because of descriptions defining them, which are collectively accepted, and act through representatives. Organizations are institutions which have a structure in terms of sub-institutions. Sub-organizations are organizations which are parts of other organizations. Finally, roles are components which do not have further organizational structure and which can be played by agents.

This work can be seen as the ontological justification of other different approaches in the area of multiagent systems and also in programming languages.

For example, [3,4] study organizations composed of sub-organizations and roles using the so called agent metaphor. The agent metaphor allows to describe social entities, like normative systems, as they were agents, and thus attributing them mental attitudes like beliefs and goals. Since an organization is described as an agent, then it can attribute mental attitudes to other social entities, thus creating them. In this way, it can define sub-organizations and roles by describing them as agents, in a recursive way.

Moreover our ontology can be used to model organizations by means of standard object oriented representation languages, like UML. No new primitive in UML is needed, but just a pattern can be used, where, first, classes which are definitionally dependent on other classes are defined inside the class which they depend on; secondm each instance of the dependent class is related to an instance of the class it depends on. This pattern is used by Baldoni *et al.* [1] for extending object oriented programming languages like Java.

Future work is introducing the notion of power among the components of organizations. The difficulty is that powers access the institutional properties of the other components even if they are considered as private properties. Moreover, we do not distinguish descriptions from descriptions which are valid as [6] do.

References

1. M. Baldoni, G. Boella, and L. van der Torre, 'Powerjava: ontologically founded roles in object oriented programming language', in *Procs. of OOOPS Track of SAC'06*, (2006).
2. G. Boella and L. van der Torre, 'An agent oriented ontology of social reality', in *Procs. of FOIS'04*, pp. 199–209, Amsterdam, (2004). IOS Press.
3. G. Boella and L. van der Torre, 'Organizations as socially constructed agents in the agent oriented paradigm', in *LNAI n. 3451: Procs. of ESAW'04*, pp. 1–13, Berlin, (2004). Springer Verlag.
4. G. Boella and L. van der Torre, 'A game theoretic approach to contracts in multiagent systems', *IEEE Transactions on Systems, Man and Cybernetics - Part C*, (2006).
5. G. Booch, *Object-Oriented Analysis and Design with Applications*, Addison-Wesley, Reading (MA), 1988.
6. E. Bottazzi and R. Ferrario, 'A path to an ontology of organizations', in *Procs. of EDOC Int. Workshop on Vocabularies, Ontologies and Rules for The Enterprise (VORTE 2005)*, (2005).
7. M. Dastani, B. van Riemsdijk, J. Hulstijn, F. Dignum, and J-J. Meyer, 'Enacting and deacting roles in agent programming', in *Procs. of AOSE'04*, New York, (2004).
8. J. Ferber, O. Gutknecht, and F. Michel, 'From agents to organizations: an organizational view of multiagent systems', in *LNCS n. 2935: Procs. of AOSE'03*, pp. 214–230. Springer Verlag, (2003).
9. K. Fine, 'Ontological dependence', *Proceedings of the Aristotelian Society*, **95**, 269–290, (1995).
10. A. Gangemi, N. Guarino, C. Masolo, A. Oltramari, and L. Schneider, 'Sweetening ontologies with dolce', in *Proc. EKAW 2002*, Siguenza (SP), (2002).
11. D. Grossi, F. Dignum, M. Dastani, and L. Royakkers, 'Foundations of organizational structures in multiagent systems', in *Procs. of AAMAS'05*, (2005).
12. N. Guarino and C. Welty, 'Evaluating ontological decisions with ontoclean', *Communications of ACM*, **45(2)**, 61–65, (2002).
13. N. R. Jennings, 'On agent-based software engineering', *Artificial Intelligence*, **117(2)**, 277–296, (2000).
14. C. Masolo, G. Guizzardi, L. Vieu, E. Bottazzi, and R. Ferrario, 'Relational roles and qua-individuals', in *Procs. of AAAI Fall Symposium Roles'04*. AAAI Press, (2005).
15. C. Masolo, L. Vieu, E. Bottazzi, C. Catenacci, R. Ferrario, A. Gangemi, and N. Guarino, 'Social roles and their descriptions', in *Procs. of KR'04*, pp. 267–277. AAAI Press, (2004).
16. M. McCallum, T.J. Norman, and W.W. Vasconcelos, 'A formal model of organisations for engineering multi-agent systems', in *Procs. of CEAS Workshop at ECAI'04*, (2004).
17. O. Pacheco and J. Carmo, 'A role based model of normative specification of organized collective agency and agents interaction', *Autonomous Agents and Multiagent Systems*, **6**, 145–184, (2003).
18. J.R. Searle, *The Construction of Social Reality*, The Free Press, New York, 1995.
19. J.F. Sowa, *Knowledge Representation: Logical, Philosophical, and Computational Foundations*, Brooks/Cole, Pacific Growe (CA), 2000.
20. F. Steimann, 'On the representation of roles in object-oriented and conceptual modelling', *Data and Knowledge Engineering*, **35**, 83–848, (2000).
21. E. Yu, 'Agent orientation as a modelling paradigm', *Wirtschaftsinformatik*, **43(2)**, 123–132, (2001).
22. F. Zambonelli, N.R. Jennings, and M. Wooldridge, 'Developing multiagent systems: The Gaia methodology', *IEEE Transactions of Software Engineering and Methodology*, **12(3)**, 317–370, (2003).

When Agents Communicate Hypotheses in Critical Situations

Gauvain Bourgne, Nicolas Maudet, and Suzanne Pinson

LAMSADE, Université Paris-Dauphine
Paris 75775 Cedex 16, France
{bourgne,maudet,pinson}@lamsade.dauphine.fr

Abstract. This paper discusses the problem of *efficient propagation of uncertain information* in dynamic environments and critical situations. When a number of (distributed) agents have only partial access to information, the explanation(s) and conclusion(s) they can draw from their observations are inevitably uncertain. In this context, the efficient propagation of information is concerned with two interrelated aspects: spreading the information as quickly as possible, and refining the hypotheses at the same time. We describe a formal framework designed to investigate this class of problem, and we report on preliminary results and experiments using the described theory.

1 Introduction

Consider the following situation: witness of a threathening and unexpected event, say a fire in a building, Jeanne has to act promptly to both escape the danger and warn other people who might get caught in the same situation. However, there are no official signs or alarms indicating where the fire actually started. Given her partial knowledge of the situation, Jeanne may build some hypotheses explaining her observations (where the fire did start in the first place, maybe why), but the conclusions she may reach would remain *uncertain* (that is, uncertainty here lies on the fact that she has incomplete knowledge of the world, rather than untrusted perceptions of this world). In addition, there is no way for Jeanne to trigger an alarm. In other words, Jeanne will try to both circulate the information in order to spread the information to colleagues, and refine the hypotheses at the same time. Typically, Jeanne faces two questions:

- What information should I transmit?
- To whom should I transmit this information?

Clearly, these two questions are interrelated. Depending on the person Jeanne selected to communicate with, she may decide to transmit different messages: the objectives being to ensure that the transmitted information can be used efficiently in the next transmission, and so on. This defines, we believe, a problem of efficient propagation of uncertain information. The purpose of this paper is to put forward a formal framework expliciting both the reasoning and communicational aspects involved in these situations. We explore some preliminary

M. Baldoni and U. Endriss (Eds.): DALT 2006, LNAI 4327, pp. 89–104, 2006.

properties of the proposed framework and interaction protocol, and illustrate our approach with a case study experimented using the described theory.

The remainder of this paper is as follows. Section 2 presents the formal reasoning machinery that we shall use in the framework: it heavily builds upon Poole's Theorist system [14]. Section 3 details the communication module, and explores specifically some properties of a protocol designed to exchange hypotheses. Section 4 describes our case study example, instantiating the proposed framework. The situation involves a number of agents trying to escape from a burning building. We give the detail of a simple example, showing how critical, in this crisis context, can be the decisions taken by agents as to whether/what communicate. Section 5 draws connections to related works, and Section 6 concludes.

2   Agents' Reasoning

This section introduces the formal machinery involved in the agents reasoning process. The described situation suggests agents able to deal with partial perception of the world, to build hypotheses from observations they make, to draw conclusions from a set of explanations, and to communicate with each other in order to exchange pieces of information. Agents reasoning process builds on Poole's framework [14,15], which allows to elegantly combine both the explanation and the prediction processes, using a single axiomatization. In what follows, by formulae we mean well-formed formulae in a standard first order language. Each agent is (a slightly modified version of) an instance of a Theorist system [14]:

$$\langle \mathcal{F}, \mathcal{H}, \Delta, O, E, \leq \rangle$$

where

- $\mathcal{F}$ a set of *facts*, closed formulae taken as being true in the domain;
- Δ a set of *defaults*, formulae taken as being true without evidence of the contrary. They are used for prediction and can be part of an explanation;
- $\mathcal{H}$ a set of formulae which act as *conjectures*, possible hypotheses common to all agents, usually a set of *abducible predicates*;
- O is a set of grounded formulae representing the *observations* made so far by the agent. Each agent believes every observation in this set to be true;
- E is the set of *prefered explanations*, it is the set of all justifiable explanations of the observation set O;
- $\leq$ is the *preference relation*, a pre-order on the explanations common to all agents.

We first recall a number of basic definitions.

Definition 1 (Scenario [15]). *A scenario of $(\mathcal{F}, A)$ is a set $\theta \cup \mathcal{F}$ where θ is a set of ground instances of elements of A such that $\theta \cup \mathcal{F}$ is consistent. θ is called the assumption of the explanation.*

Definition 2 (Explanation of a closed formulae [15]). *If g is a closed formula, then an explanation of g from $(\mathcal{F}, A)$ is a scenario of $(\mathcal{F}, A)$ that implies g.*

We now introduce a couple of further notions that proved to be appropriate in our context. Events occuring in the world and observed by the agents may or may not be explained, or contradicted, by the agent model.

Definition 3 (Positive observation). *A positive observation of $(\mathcal{F}, \mathcal{H}, \Delta)$ is an observation o such that there exists an explanation of o from $(\mathcal{F}, \mathcal{H} \cup \Delta)$*

Definition 4 (Negative observation). *A negative observation of $(\mathcal{F}, \mathcal{H}, \Delta)$ is an observation $o \in O$ such that there exists an explanation of $\neg o$ from $(\mathcal{F}, \mathcal{H} \cup \Delta)$*

In the following, we shall note $P(O)$ to refer to the set of all positive observations of $(\mathcal{F}, \mathcal{H}, \Delta)$ in O, and $N(O)$ to refer to the set of all negative observations of $(\mathcal{F}, \mathcal{H}, \Delta)$ in O. Note that this is not necessarily a partition: some observations may have no explanation, while some others may have both positive and negative explanations.

Definition 5 (Explanation of an observation set). *If O is a set of observations, an explanation of O from $(\mathcal{F}, \mathcal{H} \cup \Delta)$ is an explanation ξ of $P(O)$ from $(\mathcal{F}, \mathcal{H} \cup \Delta)$ such that $\xi \cup N(O)$ is consistent (which implies the consistency of $\xi \cup O$).*
  That is: $\xi = P \cup D \cup \mathcal{F}$ where P is a set of ground instances of elements of $\mathcal{H}$, D is a set of ground instances of elements of Δ, $\xi \models P(O)$ and $P \cup D \cup \mathcal{F} \cup N(O)$ is consistent.

In the following, we shall also refer to the conjunction h of the elements of P as the *hypothesis* associated to this explanation.

Definition 6 (Justifiable explanation). *A justifiable explanation of O from $(\mathcal{F}, \mathcal{H})$ is an explanation such that if any element of its associated hypotheses set θ is removed from it, it is no longer an explanation of O. In other words, a justifiable explanation is an explanation that is minimal wrt. set inclusion.*

Based on this system, we also define, for each agent a_i:

1. H_i, the set of *prefered hypotheses* associated with E_i, the set of justifiable explanations. For a given set of observation O_i, $\mathcal{E}_{exp}$, the *explanation function* returns the set of all justifiable explanations of O_i from $(\mathcal{F}, \mathcal{H} \cup \Delta)$. $\mathcal{E}_{hyp}(O_i)$ gives the set of hypotheses associated with $\mathcal{E}_{exp}(O_i)$. We assume $\mathcal{E}_{exp}$ and $\mathcal{E}_{hyp}$ to be deterministic, and common to all agents.
2. h is the *favoured hypothesis* from E. The agent choses one favoured hypothesis among its own minimal hypotheses according to the preference relation.

In summary, for each agent we have:

- $E_i = \mathcal{E}_{exp}(O_i)$;
- $H_i = \mathcal{E}_{hyp}(O_i)$;
- $h_i \in min(H_i)$.

This ensures that h_i is associated with a minimal justifiable explanation for O_i, that is :

- h_i is consistent with O_i, that is $\not\exists o_i \in O_i$ s.t. $h_i \models \neg o_i$;
- h_i explains all elements of $P(O_i)$;
- h_i is justifiable from O_i, that is for each clause c_k of the conjunction h_i $(h_i = h'_i \wedge c_k)$, there is an element o of $P(O_i)$ such that $h_i \models o$ but $h'_i \not\models o$;
- h_i is minimal according to the preorder $\leq$.

Typically, as suggested by the aforementioned model, different explanations will exist for a given formula. What should be the preference relation between explanations? Clearly there can be many different ways to classify prefered explanations. In [14], different comparators are introduced. In our framework, we shall use variants of two of them:

1. *minimal explanation*— prefer the explanations that make the fewest (in terms of set inclusion) assumptions. This is what we have defined as *justifiable explanation* to avoid confusion with the minimal explanations according to the preference relation;
2. *least presumptive explanation*— an explanation is less presumptive than another explanation if it makes fewer assumptions in terms of what can be implied from this explanation. An explanation ξ_1 is less presumptive than another explanation ξ_2 iff $\forall g$ s.t. $\xi_1 \models g$, it is the case that $\xi_2 \models g$. Therefore, a least presumptive explanation is an explanation which is not less presumptive than any other explanation.

Now we need to see how these agents will evolve and interact in their environment. In our context, agents evolve in a dynamic environment, and we classicaly assume the following *system cycle*:

1. *Environment dynamics*: the environment evolves according to the defined rules of the system dynamics;
2. *Perception step* : agents get perceptions from the environment. These perceptions are typically partial (*e.g.* the agent can only see a portion of the map), but we assume that they are *certain*, in the sense that the sensors are assumed perfect;
3. *Reasoning step*: agents compare perception with predictions, seek explanations for (potential) difference(s), refine their hypotheses, draw new conclusions. More precisely, during this step, if the agent perception proves its hypothesis to be false, the agent computes the possible explanations for these new perception, given its previous perception. It makes use of Theorist for this task. It must then select the action to be executed in the next phase;
4. *Action step*: agents modify the environment by executing the action selected by the previous deliberation steps.

What remains to be described, of course, is the interaction module and the way agents will exchange hypotheses and observations.

3   Agents' Communication

In our system, observations are not only made directly by agents (by perceiving the environment): they can also result from communication between agents. The cycle is then augmented with an explicit *communication step*, which directly follows the *reasoning step*. During the *Communication step*, agents engage communication with other agents to warn of their observation and tune up their hypotheses. In a given round, a given agent can only communicate with *one* agent. If that agent is occupied talking to another agent, it must wait or choose a different agent to communicate with. We now describe the interaction protocol pictured in Fig. 1, together with agents' behaviour.

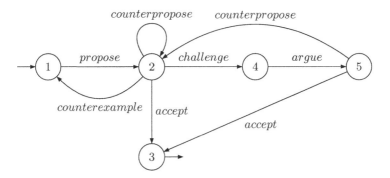

Fig. 1. Hypotheses Exchange Protocol

3.1   Description of the Interaction Protocol and Strategies

Upon receiving a hypothesis h_1 (*propose*(h_1) or *counterpropose*(h_1)) from a_1, agent a_2 is in state 2 and has the following possible replies:

- if $\exists o_2 \in N(O_2)$ s.t. $h_1 \models \neg o_2$, then the agent knows a counter-example that contradicts this hypothesis: he will communicate this counter-example and utter *counterexample*(o_2). We are back in state 1 of the protocol. Agent will then recompute his hypothesis with this new fact, and will propose h_1';
- if $\exists o_2 \in P(O_2)$ s.t. $h_1 \not\models o_2$, then the agent knows an example of positive observation that is *not* explained by this hypothesis: he will communicate this uncovered example and utter *counterexample*(o_2), as in the previous case.;
- otherwise, no observation made by a_2 contradicts h_1 and h_1 implies $P(O_2)$, that h_1 is the hypothesis associated with an explanation of O_2. We have then the following cases:
  - if the agent has no argument in favour of the hypothesis ($h_1 \notin H_2$ where H_i is the set of the hypothesis associated to agent a_i's prefered explanations), he will *challenge* a_1 in order to obtain some arguments supporting this hypothesis. Agent a_1 is then bound to communicate an argument

$(argue(arg))^1$, leading to state 5. Upon receiving this argument, a_2 re-computes his hypothesis by using this argument. If h_1 is obtained, he will *accept*, leading to the final state 3. Otherwise, a different hypothesis h'_2 is obtained and proposed, leading back to state 2;

- otherwise $h_1 \in H_2$: h_1 is a hypothesis associated to a justifiable explanation of O. We have then two possibilities:
  * if h_1 is not prefered to h_2 in the sense of the defined preference relation, then agent a_2 would *counterpropose*(h_2), leading to state 2 with inverted roles;
  * otherwise, h_1 is necessarily prefered to h_2: a_2 will then respond *accept*, concluding the conversation (state 3).

3.2 Local Properties of the Interaction Protocol

We first investigate locally the properties of the proposed protocol, that is, the outcome of a single dialogue governed by the rules and decision process described in the previous subsection, and involving only two agents.

Lemma 1. *Let* $c = |O_1 \cup O_2| - |O_1 \cap O_2|$. *If* $c = 0$ *then* $O_1 = O_2$ *and* $H_1 = H_2$.

Proof. Clearly, $O_1 \cap O_2 \subseteq O_1 \cup O_2$. If $c = 0$, $|O_1 \cup O_2| = |O_1 \cap O_2|$, hence $O_1 \cup O_2 = O_1 \cap O_2$. Now because $O_1 \cap O_2 \subseteq O_1 \subseteq O_1 \cup O_2$, (and symetrically for O_2), we have $O_1 = O_2$. By virtue of the determinism of the explanation function, we conclude that $H_1 = \mathcal{E}_{hyp}(O_1) = \mathcal{E}_{hyp}(O_2) = H_2$.   □

The first property that needs to be verified is the *termination*. We show that this algorithm enjoys this property.

Property 1 (Termination). Termination is guaranteed, and the length of the interaction process (in terms of the number of exchanged messages) is bounded by $4 \times c + |O_1 \cap O_2|$.

Proof. Let $c = |O_1 \cup O_2| - |O_1 \cap O_2|$. By Lemma 1, we know that in case $c = 0$, it follows that $O_1 = O_2$ and $H_1 = H_2$ (in which case we note $O = O_1 = O_2$ and $H = H_1 = H_2$). Then observe that, $H = \mathcal{E}_{hyp}(O)$, together with the fact that $h_1, h_2 \in H$, guarantees that h_1 and h_2 are the favoured hypotheses of the justifiable explanations of O. The following points then follow (i) $\not\exists o \in O$ s.t. $h_1 \models \neg o$ or $h_2 \models \neg o$, (ii) $\not\exists o \in P(O)$ s.t. $h_1 \not\models o$ or $h_2 \not\models o$, (iii) $h_1 \in H_2$ and $h_2 \in H_1$, and (iv) both $h_1, h_2 \in min(H)$, no hypothesis is then strictly prefered to the other one.

Given this, as soon as the system is in state 2, all termination conditions are met. But we also know that the message exchange between agents leads to state 2 every 3 messages at most. Termination is then guaranteed when $c = 0$.

We now need to prove that c will eventually reach the value 0. To do that, we will show that every 4 messages at most, it decreases of 1.

---

[1] Note that the agent keeps track of the communicated arguments, which allows him not to send twice the same argument to this agent during a communication step.

The first message leads to state 2. Without loss of generality, we assume that the last message is, say, from agent a_j to agent a_i (hypothesis h_j is then proposed to a_i). Following the agent's decision algorithm previously described, there are now four possibilities:

(i) $\exists o_i \in O_i$, s.t. $h_j \models \neg o_i$ or $\exists o_i \in P(O_i)$, s.t. $h_j \not\models o_i$, then a_i sends a counterexample o_i to a_j. In this case, $O'_j = O_j \cup \{o_i\}$ with $o_i \in O_i$ and $o_i \notin O_j$, which means that $|O'_j \cap O_i| = |O_j \cap O_i| + 1$, and $|O_j \cup O_i|$ remains unchanged. It follows that c is decreased by 1;

(ii) $\not\exists o_i \in O_i$ s.t. $h_j \models \neg o_i$ and $\forall o_i \in P(O_i)$, $h_j \models o_i$ and $h_j \notin H_i$, then a_i requires an argument and a_j provides o_j. In this case, $O'_i = O_i \cup \{o_j\}$. If $o_j \in O_i$, then a_i repeats its challenge until he gets an observation o_j he didn't know before. Since a_j keeps track of its messages, at most $|O_1 \cap O_2|$ such messages can be exchanged. We eventually reach o'_j such that $O'_i = O_i \cup \{o_{j'}\}$ where $o'_j \in O_j$ and $o'_j \notin O_i$;

(iii) $\not\exists o_i \in O_i$ s.t. $o_i \models \neg h_j$ and $\forall o_i \in P(O_i)$, $h_j \models o_i$ and $h_j \in H_i$ but $h_j \notin min(H_i)$, then a_i respond with $counterpropose(h_i)$. We are back in state 2, but now we are sure that $h_i \notin H_j$ (because $h_i \leq h_j$ and $h_j \in min(H_j)$, by definition), which means that we would be in case (i) or (ii);

(iv) $\not\exists o_i \in O_i$ s.t. $o_i \models \neg h_j$, and $\forall o_i \in P(O_i)$, $h_j \models o_i$, and $h_j \in min(H_i)$, but then a_i accepts and the protocol terminates.   □

Corollary 1. *After termination, the following properties are guaranteed:*

- *a_1 and a_2 are consistent;*
- *a_1 and a_2 have a hypothesis that explains both $P(O_1)$ and $P(O_2)$;*
- *a_1 and a_2 have a hypothesis that is justifiable from O_1 and O_2;*
- *a_1 and a_2 have a hypothesis that is minimal for O_1 and O_2 (that is $h_1 \in min(\mathcal{E}_{hyp}(O_2))$ and $h_2 \in min(\mathcal{E}_{hyp}(O_1)))$.*

3.3 Global Properties of the Communication Protocol

The properties previously described hold locally, when only two agents interact over one communication step. The next question is then to ask whether these properties can be guaranteed at a more global level. Clearly, many properties will not hold any longer when considered globally. One simple such property is the consistance, which cannot be transitive when only based on the bilateral hypotheses exchange protocol described. This can be observed by constructing an example where an agent a would first communicate a hypothesis to agent b, not revealing the full arguments supporting its position though. Now if b communicates in turn with a third agent, say c, it is clear that he may not be in a position to effectively defend this hypothesis, and may accept c's hypothesis. a and c would then not be consistent. This is formally stated as follows.

Property 2. The consistance property guaranteed by the communication protocol is not transitive.

Proof. We construct the following counterexample : agent a_1 can communicate with agent a_2 and a_3, but agents a_2 and a_3 cannot communicate with each other. We assume that they share the following facts $\{p(X) \rightarrow r(X), q(X) \rightarrow r(X), p(X) \rightarrow s(X)\}$, where $p(X)$ and $q(X)$ are hypotheses. We start with the following sets of observations $P_1 = \{r(a), \neg p(X)\}$, $P_2 = \{ \}$, and $P_3 = \{s(a)\}$. Agent a_1 communicates $q(A)$, which is challenged by a_2. a_1 then provides an explanation $(r(a))$. Now a_2 communicates with a_3 and proposes $q(a)$, but a_3 has an additional observation, namely $s(a)$. Upon receiving this hypothesis, a_3 challenges a_2 and a_2 provides the only argument he has in possession: $r(a)$. But a_3 knows the further observation that $s(a)$ which makes the hypothesis $p(a)$ prefered. a_3 makes this counterproposal, a_2 challenges and a_3 gives his argument $(s(a))$. Now a_2 will accept. At this point of the interaction though, a_1 holds $q(a)$ as favoured hypothesis, while a_3 prefers $p(a)$, which is not consistent with $\neg p(X) \in P_1$. □

What this suggests is that we will need much more elaborated synchronization techniques to guarantee that these desirable properties still hold at the global level. However, in our context where time is a critical factor, and where communication can be highly restricted, it will be interesting to investigate in which situations simple protocols, like the one described here, can still give promising result and ensure an average good efficiency of the information propagation. As a first step towards this objective, we give in the next section an instance of the proposed framework and show a critical situation where communication and hypotheses exchange proves to be efficient.

4   A Case Study: Crisis Management

This section presents an instance of the general framework introduced earlier. We first describe the different parameters used to instantiate the framework. A complete example is then detailed.

4.1   Description of the Situation

This experiment involves agents trying to escape from a burning building. The environment is described as a spatial grid with a set of walls and (thankfully) some exits. Time and space are considered discrete. Time is divided in rounds.

Agents are localised by their position on the spatial grid. These agents can move and communicate with other agents. In a round, an agent can move of one cell in any of the four cardinal directions, provided it is not blocked by a wall. In this application, agents communicate with any other agent (but, recall, a single one) given that this agent is in view, and that they have not yet exchanged their current favoured hypothesis. Note that this spatial constraint on agents' communication could be relaxed in other contexts (which would require, in turn, to apply a more elaborated recipient choice algorithm).

At time t_0, a fire erupts in these premises. From this moment, the fire propagates. Each round, for each cases where there is fire, the fire propagates in

the four directions. However, the fire cannot propagate through a wall. If the
fire propagates in a case where an agent is positioned, that agent burns and is
considered dead. It can of course no longer move nor communicate. If an agent
gets to an exit, it is considered saved, and can no longer be burned. It still can
communicate, but need not move.

Agents know the environment and the rules governing the dynamics of this
environment, that is, they know the map as well as the rules of fire propagation
previously described. They also locally perceive this environment, but cannot
see further than 3 cases away, in any direction. Walls also block the line of
view, preventing agents from seeing behind them. Within their sight, they can
see other agents and whether or not the cases they see are on fire. All these
perceptions are memorised.

In order to deliberate, agents maintain a list of their possible explanations E
(and a list of associated hypotheses H) explaining their observations about fire,
and a prediction of fire propagation based on their favoured hypothesis h. The
preference relation ($\leq$) is the following:

- the agent prefers the minimal explanation, taking into account only fire
  origins. In other words, an agent will prefer an explanation using an unique
  fire origin propagating over one using several sources;
- the agent prefer the least presumptive explanation, taking into account propagation and origins. In practice it means that the agent will favour an explanation considering the fire origin as closer to the observed manifestation.

Based on the reasoning described above, agents also maintain a list of possible
escape route, sorted by simply favouring the shortest paths to exits.

4.2   Sample of Agents Theories

We now give a snapshot of the declarative representation of agents' knowledge,
illustrating the different kind of rules involved in this example.

- Facts ($\mathcal{F}$), Defaults (Δ) allow to represent the static elements of the environment, as well as the general rules governing the dynamic of the environment.
  For instance, the following three rule state that there is indeed a vertical wall
  at location (0,1), that the fire can always be assumed to have started at the
  location it is observed, and eventually that the fire should propagate in four
  possible directions. This last one is an example of a rule justified in normal
  circumstances, but which may suffer exceptions: it is then represented as a
  default rule.

```
fact vwall(at(0,1)).
fact fire(T,at(X,Y)) <- origin(T,at(X,Y)).
default rule_propagates_L(T2,from(X2,Y)): fire(T,at(X,Y)) <-
        previous(X,X2), previous(T,T2), fire(T2,at(X2,Y)).
```

- Constraints prevent default rules from applying. They are considered as part
  of the Facts ((F)) For example, the landscape includes walls and doors which
  prevent the fire from propagating.

```
constraint not rule_propagates_L(T,from(X,Y)) <- vwall(at(X,Y))
```

- The possible hypotheses set $(\mathcal{H})$, in this example application, is the set of all conjunctions of possible fire origin(s).
- Observations (O) can either be of the form fire(T,at(X,Y)), or of the form nofire(T,at(X,Y)).

4.3   Example

We are now in a position to describe the steps of our illustrative example.

[Round t=0] A fire erupts at (6,6), but nobody can initially see it. It will propagate until t=3 before beeing seen.

[Round t=3]

Perception step. Agent a_1 sees fire at (3,6) (not expected), and agent a_3. Agent a_2 sees fire at (6,3) and (5,4) (not expected). Agent a_3 sees a_1.

Explanation step (a_1)**.** Having computed an explanation for fire(t=3, at (3,6)), a_1 gets 12 possible explanations, each one exhibiting a single origin. One such explanation, as provided by the Theorist system, states that the fire may have started at location (4,5), before propagating to the north (i.e. from south) and to the west.

```
Answer is fire(t3, at(3, 6))
Theory is
[rule_propagates_R(t2, from(4, 6)),
rule_propagates_D(t1, from(4, 5)),
origin(t1, at(4, 5))]
```

To classify these hypotheses, he first selects the minimal hypothesis considering only the origin. In this case, all the hypotheses suppose only one origin for the observed fire. Among those, he then selects the less presumptive hypothesis. In this case, the selected hypothesis is:

```
[origin(t3, at(3, 6))]
```

Explanation step (a_2)**.** Searching explanations for fire at (6,3) and (5,4), a_2 gets 6*6 possible explanations, such as :

```
Answer is fire(t3, at(6, 3)) and fire(t3, at(5, 4))
Theory is
[rule_propagates_R(t2, from(6, 4)),
origin(t2, at(6, 4)),
origin(t3, at(6, 3))]
```

Among those theories, only four of the explanations propose a common origin, and as such are minimal according to the origin criteria. Among those four, the less pre-emptive one is eventually:

```
[rule_propagates_R(t2, from(6, 4)),
rule_propagates_D(t2, from(6, 4)),
origin(t2, at(6, 4))].
```

Communication step. Agents a_1 and a_3 are the only agents seeing each other. Agent a_3 has no reason to initiate a communication, but a_1 has one: it has just changed its hypothesis and will try propagating and validating it. a_3 asks for arguments and a_1 sends it `fire(t=3,at(3,6))`. With this facts, Agent 3 recomputes its hypothesis and get the same favoured hypothesis. The hypothesis is confirmed and the communication stopped.

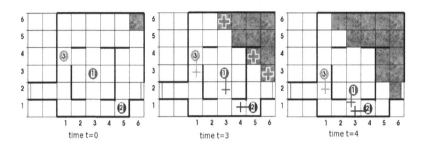

[Round t=4]

Action step. a_3 moves towards the west exit, which is the closest exit. a_1 moves towards the east exit, for the same reason. Although it is closer to the east exit, a_2 moves towards the west exit because it predicts that fire will arrive at the east exit before it can go out this way.

Perception step. Agent a_1 sees a_2 and conversely. All the fire seen by agents were predicted during this step.

Explanation step. No agents has been confronted to unpredicted events. They have no need for explanation and just trim their hypotheses list.

Communication step. Agents a_1 and a_2 will communicate. Agent a_1 sends its hypothesis (`origin(t=3,at(3,6))`). As this hypothesis is not invalidated by its perception but does not belong to its hypotheses list, a_2 asks for arguments. Agent a_1 sends argument (`fire(t=3,at(3,6))`), and a_2 then computes possible explanations for this and its perception, and gets 6*6*12 possible explanations. Among those, only one contains a common origin for the three observed fires:

```
[rule_propagates_R(t2, from(6, 4)),
rule_propagates_D(t2, from(6, 4)),
rule_propagates_D(t1, from(6, 5)),
rule_propagates_D(t0, from(6, 6)),
rule_propagates_R(t3, from(4, 6)),
rule_propagates_R(t1, from(5, 6)),
rule_propagates_R(t0, from(6, 6)),
origin(t0, at(6, 6))].
```

Agent a_2 then proposes this hypothesis to a_1, which in turn ask for arguments. Finally both agree upon this hypothesis.

Action step. Agent a_3 continues its escape towards the west exit. Agent a_2 confirms its chosen path with its new hypothesis, and keeps going towards the west door. Agent a_1, however, using its new hypothesis, discover that its escape route is bad. It changes its course to go towards the west exit.

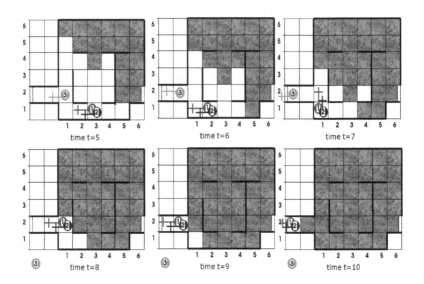

[Round t=5 to 10] From time t=5 to time t=10, agents a_1, a_2 and a_3 exit the building. Agents a_1 and a_2 are closely followed by the fire: one false move would have been fatal! If a_1 did not communicate with a_2 or a_3 it would not have been able to determine whether the fire was coming from left or right, and would have chosen the east exit and been trapped by the fire.

5   Related Work

Our approach has several facets that can be related to a number of related works. We now introduce some of these related works, starting with the studies of the notion of rumours in social science, that proved to be very inspiring for us.

Rumour in Social Sciences. Rumour is a complex phenomenon that has been the object of numerous studies in social science but is often seen as something that can only bring lies or diffamation. Studies of rumour in social science show, however, that there is more to rumour than just a routing or perception sharing system. Whereas the first studies, done during and after World War II, seem to consider rumour as something dangerous which should be avoided (rumours could lead to moral loss or information leak), more recent stances are somewhat more neutral or positive about it. J.N Kapferer [10] defines rumour as *"the emergence and circulation in the social body of information that either are not yet publicly confirmed by official sources or are denied by them".* As an unofficial information, it must use alternative ways to be distributed, such as individual communication (gossip, word-of-mouth). He precises that a rumour spreads very quickly because it has value, and because this value decreases over time. Moreover the rightness of the content has no importance. A true rumour spread exactly like a false rumour. The exactitude of the content is not a criteria to define rumour. However, one can choose to take a slightly different perspective on the rumouring process. Shibutani [20] defines rumour as improvised news resulting from a collective discussion process, usually originating from an important and ambiguous event. In his own words, rumour is *"common use of the group individual ressources to get a satisfying intepretation of an event"*. In this case, the rumour is seen as being both an (i) information routing process and (ii) an interpretation and comment adding process. Crucially, the distorsion of information that is often seen as characteristic of rumour is seen as an evolution of the content due to continual interpretation by the group. A crucial aspect of rumour, of course, is that it is a decentralized process. The information propagates without any official control. It is deeply linked with spatial or communication constraint, and can be an efficient way to convey information in spite of these. It is also expected that this process is quite robust to agent error or disparition.

Distributed Diagnosis. The problem of multiagent diagnosis has been studied by Roos and colleagues [16,17], where a number of distributed entities try to come up with a satisfying global diagnosis of the whole system. They show in particular that the number of messages required to establish this global diagnosis is bound to be prohibitive, unless the communication is enhanced with some suitable protocol. The main difference with our approach lies in the dynamic nature of our context, as well as in the constraints governing agents' interactions that we assume.

Argument-based Interaction. The idea of enhancing communication between agents by adding extra-information that may have the form of arguments has been influential over the last past years in the multiagent community [13]. However, although this approach has several clear advantages (*e.g.* improving expressivity, or facilitating conformance checking), its effectiveness regarding the speed and likelihood of fullfillment of the goal of the interaction has seldom been tested (exceptions are the work of [9], or [11], for instance).

Gossip Problem. Rumours and gossip first appeared within the distributed system community with the *gossip problem*: each agent has a distinct piece of information (called a rumour) to start with. The goal is to make every agent know all the rumours [19]. Some variation of it are the *rumour-spreading problem*, where the agent to communicate to is selected each round by an adversary [1], and the *collect problem*. In the last one, each of n processes in a shared memory system have several pieces of information, and all these processes must learn all the values of all others while making as few as possible primitive read or write operations [18]. It has also been used for reaching consensus [6]. This differs from our approach, mainly because we do not seek to necessarily converge towards a common knowledge of (initially distributed) informations. Also, in these approaches, agents do not modify informations they propagate.

Gossip-based protocols. Each agent has a determined number of neighbours it can communicate with. Each time an agent receives a rumour, it transmits it to to a number of agents chosen at random among its neighbours. Then in turn, each of these agents would do the same. This rumour spreading is analogous to the spreading of an epidemic, which have been the object of mathematical studies [2] and can spread exponentially fast. Such an information propagation system has first been used for replicated database consistency management [8]. It has been applied to unstructured peer-to-peer communities. Every time an agent detects a change in the system (that would be the rumour), it sends it to a random neighbour, and repeats this operation until it has contacted enough neighbour(s). Some anti-entropy mechanisms are sometimes used to ensure that every agent can get to know each change, even if the rumour has already died out [7]. Another application of these protocols is reliable multicast [3]. It aims at propagating an information from an agent to another agent without a centralised source or knowledge of the system topology, and with a lower cost than with a simple flooding. It is robust to agent deficiency, and very scalable. A variation of it uses weight to enhance the reliability in specific topology [12]. This approach is related to the "recipient selection" aspect of our problem. However, the transmitted information is, again, assumed to be unaffected by agents' reasoning.

Rumour routing. Another approach of rumour as an alternative to flooding is *rumour routing* [4]. In the context of sensor networks, there is a need to transmit queries to agents having observed an event. A fast route between an agent making a request and the agents observing the events might be needed. It can be found by flooding event notifications or queries, and creating a network-wide gradient field [21], but it is a costly approach. Braginsky and Estrin instead propose to use a kind of traceable rumour. Each time an agent observes a new event, it sends an event notification rumour to a random neighbour. This neighbour transmits it in turn to another neighbour, keeping trace of whom it received it from, and how many agent(s) have acted as relay(s), creating rumour paths. When an agent needs to make a query, it sends it to one of its neighbours. If it has heard of the event concerned before, it transmits the query to the agent who told it the rumour, else it transmits to a random neighbour. Eventually, the query will cross the rumour path and be led to the right source. As in the preceding cases, rumour routing propagates pure information, therefore the main studied aspects are the velocity and robustness of these processes.

Reputation Systems. Buchegger and Le Boudec, for instance, use the term of rumour in a reputation system [5]. Their agents can make decisions about the reliability of others agents according to their previously observed behaviour, but also according to what others agents tell about it. In this case, rumour is primarily intended to mean "second-hand information". In this case, agents can keep track of previous partners' behaviours, and also report their observations to other agents. However, these agents are not able to explicitly reason over the justifications governing their decisions.

6 Conclusion

This paper discusses the problem of *efficient propagation of uncertain information* in dynamic environments and critical situations. When a number of (distributed) agents have only partial access to information, the explanation(s) and conclusion(s) they can draw from their observations are inevitably uncertain. In this context, the efficient propagation of information is concerned with two interrelated aspects: spreading the information as quickly as possible, and refining the hypotheses at the same time. We describe a formal framework designed to investigate this class of problem, and propose a simple protocol allowing hypotheses exchange. We also prove some preliminary properties of the protocol and report on an experiment conducted using the described theory.

An obvious advantage of this process (that we observed on the described example) is that agents do not wait to collect all data before providing and propagating hypotheses. In our example this allows agents to escape a building before being caught by the fire. When exactly temporary hypotheses are good enough to be acted upon is to be determined, but this process definitely enable quicker reaction to events than a static centralized data analysis.

The problem is that, of course, it can give incomplete or wrong hypotheses, as the very preliminary analysis of the global properties of the framework suggests. More elaborated communication techniques may then be investigated, allowing agents to backtrack and further refine their hypotheses. In critical situations however, it is unlikely that agents will dispose of sufficient resources to fully synchronize their hypotheses and observations. In consequence, we believe the situations as the one described in our case study to be well suited to such an approach. Further studies are required, however, to determine when exactly this kind of communication would be beneficial, but we expect quickly evolving systems to provide interesting applications. Whereas this paper has mainly focused on agents' reasoning and content selection, we plan to investigate in future research the related problem of recipient selection. Finally, it would also be interesting to consider more complex cases, for instance where agents may have unreliable perceptions of the world, or where malicious propagators of information could adopt an uncooperative behaviour.

Acknowledgments. We would like to thank the anonymous reviewers whose detailed comments helped to greatly improve the paper.

References

1. J. Aspnes and W. Hurwood. Spreading rumors rapidly despite an adversary. In *Proc. 15th ACM Symposium on Principles of Distributed Computing*, pages 143–151, 1996.
2. N. Bailey. *The Mathematical Theory of Infectious Diseases*. Charles Griffin and Company, London, 1975.
3. K. Birman, M. Hayden, O. Ozkasap, Z. Xiao, M. Budiu, and Y. Minsky. Bimodal multicast. *ACM Transactions on Computer Systems*, 17(2), 1999.

4. D. Braginsky and D. Estrin. Rumor routing algorithm for sensor networks. In *Proceedings of the 1st ACM international workshop on Wireless sensor networks and applications*, 2002.
5. S. Buchegger and J. Le Boudec. The effect of rumor spreading in reputation systems for mobile ad-hoc networks. In *Proceedings of Modeling and Optimization in Mobile, Ad Hoc and Wireless Networks*, 2003.
6. B. Chlebus and D. Kowalski. Gossiping to reach consensus. In *Proceedings of the 14th ACM Symp. on Parallel Algorithms and Architectures*, pages 220–229, 2002.
7. F. M. Cuenca-Acuna, C. Peery, R. P. Martin, and T. D. Nguyen. PlanetP: Using Gossiping to Build Content Addressable Peer-to-Peer Information Sharing Communities. In *Twelfth IEEE International Symposium on High Performance Distributed Computing (HPDC-12)*, pages 236–246. IEEE Press, June 2003.
8. A. Demers, D. Greene, C. Hauser, W. Irish, J. Larson, S. Shenker, H. Sturgis, D. Swinehart, and D. Terry. Epidemic algorithms for replicated database maintenance. In *Proceedings of 6th ACM Symposium on Principles of Distributed Computing*, pages 1–12. Vancouver, British Columbia, Canada, 1987.
9. H. Jung and M. Tambe. Argumentation as distributed constraint satisfaction: Applications and results. In *Proceedings of the fifth international conference on Autonomous agents (AGENTS01)*, pages 324–331, 2001.
10. J.-N. Kapferer. *Rumeurs, le plus vieux média du monde*. Points Actuel, 1990.
11. N. C. Karunatillake and N. R. Jennings. Is it worth arguing? In *Proceedings of the First International Workshop on Argumentation in Multi-Agent Systems (ArgMAS 2004)*, pages 62–67, 2004.
12. M.-J. Lin and K. Marzullo. Directional gossip: Gossip in a wide area network. In *Proceedings of the Third European Dependable Computing Conference (EDCC-3)*, pages 364–379, 1999.
13. S. Parsons, C. Sierra, and N. R. Jennings. Agents that reason and negotiate by arguing. *Journal of Logic and Computation*, 8(3):261–292, 1998.
14. D. Poole. Explanation and prediction: An architecture for default and abductive reasoning. *Computational Intelligence*, 5(2):97–110, 1989.
15. D. Poole. A methodology for using a default and abductive reasoning system. *International Journal of Intelligent Systems*, 5:521–548, 1990.
16. N. Roos, A. ten Tije, and C. Witteveen. A protocol for multi-agent diagnosis with spatially distributed knowledge. In *Proceedings of the Second international joint conference on Autonomous Agents and Multi-Agent Systems (AAMAS03)*, pages 655–661, 2003.
17. N. Roos, A. ten Tije, and C. Witteveen. Reaching diagnostic agreement in multiagent diagnosis. In *Proceedings of the Third International joint conference on Autonomous Agents and Multi-Agent System (AAMAS04)*, pages 1254–1255, 2004.
18. M. Saks, N. Shavit, and H.Woll. Optimal time randomized consensus - making resilient algorithms fast in practice. In *Proceedings of the 2nd ACM-SIAM Symposium on Discrete Algorithms*, pages 351–362, 1991.
19. S.Even and B. Monien. On the number of rounds needed to disseminate information. In *Proceedings of the First Annual ACM Symposium on Parallel Algorithms and Architectures*, pages 318–327, 1989.
20. T. Shibutani. *Improvised News : A Sociological Study of Rumor*. Indianapolis and New york, 1966.
21. F. Ye, G. Zhong, S. Lu, and L. Zhang. Gradient broadcast: A robust data delivery protocol for large scale sensor networks. *ACM Wireless Networks*, 11(2), 2005.

A Fibred Tableau Calculus for Modal Logics of Agents[*]

Vineet Padmanabhan and Guido Governatori

School of Information Technology & Electrical Engineering
The University of Queensland, Queensland, Australia
{vnair,guido}@itee.uq.edu.au

Abstract. In [15,19] we showed how to combine propositional multimodal logics using Gabbay's *fibring* methodology. In this paper we extend the above mentioned works by providing a tableau-based proof technique for the combined/fibred logics. To achieve this end we first make a comparison between two types of tableau proof systems, (*graph* & *path*), with the help of a scenario (The Friend's Puzzle). Having done that we show how to uniformly construct a tableau calculus for the combined logic using Governatori's labelled tableau system **KEM**. We conclude with a discussion on **KEM**'s features.

1 Introduction

Modelling and reasoning about cognitive attitudes like knowledge, belief, desire, goals, intention etc. of agents is an active research area within the artificial intelligence community [6,23]. It is often the case that normal[1] multimodal logics are used to formalise these mental notions. Multimodal logics generalise modal logics allowing more than one modal operator to appear in formulae, i.e., a modal operator is named by means of a label, for instance $\Box_i$ which identifies it. Hence a formula like $\Box_i \varphi$ could be interpreted as φ *is known by the agent i or φ is believed by agent i etc.* representing respectively the knowledge and belief of an agent. In addition to the above representation, multimodal logics of agents (**MMA**) impose constraints between the different mental attitudes in the form of *interaction axioms*. For instance, if we consider **MMA**'s like BDI [20] then we can find interaction axioms of the form $\mathrm{INT}(\varphi) \rightarrow \mathrm{DES}(\varphi)$, $\mathrm{DES}(\varphi) \rightarrow \mathrm{BEL}(\varphi)$ denoting respectively intentions being stronger than desires and desires being stronger than beliefs. Moreover, these interaction axioms are *non-homogeneous* in the sense that every modal operator is not restricted to the same system, i.e., the underlying axiom systems for DES is **K** and **D** of modal logic whereas that of BEL is **KD45**. Hence the basic BDI logic $\mathbb{L}$ can be seen as a combination of different component logics plus the two interaction axioms as given below

$$\mathbb{L} \equiv (\otimes_{i=1}^{n} \mathbf{KD45}_{\mathrm{BEL}_i}) \otimes (\otimes_{i=1}^{n} \mathbf{KD}_{\mathrm{DES}_i}) \otimes (\otimes_{i=1}^{n} \mathbf{KD}_{\mathrm{INT}_i})$$
$$+ \{\mathrm{INT}_i \varphi \rightarrow \mathrm{DES}_i \varphi\} + \{\mathrm{DES}_i \varphi \rightarrow \mathrm{BEL}_i \varphi\} \tag{1}$$

---

[*] This work was supported by the Australian Research Council under Discovery Project DP0558854 on "A Formal Approach to Resource Allocation in Service Oriented Marketplaces".

[1] General modal systems with an arbitrary set of normal modal operators all characterised by the axiom **K**: $\Box(\varphi \rightarrow \psi) \rightarrow (\Box\varphi \rightarrow \Box\psi)$ and the necessitation rule. i.e., $\vdash \varphi / \vdash \Box\varphi$.

M. Baldoni and U. Endriss (Eds.): DALT 2006, LNAI 4327, pp. 105–122, 2006.

In a similar manner any **MMA** consists of a combined system of logic of knowledge, beliefs, desires, goals and intentions as mentioned above. They are basically well understood standard modal logics *combined together* to model different facets of the agents. A number of researchers have provided such combined systems for different reasons and different applications. However, investigations into a general methodology for combining the different logics involved has been mainly neglected to a large extent. Recently [15,19] it has been shown that *fibring/dovetailing* [8] can be adopted as a semantic methodology to characterise multimodal logics. But in that work we did not provide any proof techniques for the fibred logics. In this paper we extend our previous work so as to provide a tableau proof technique for the fibred logic which in turn is based on the labelled tableau system **KEM** [11,10,1].

The key feature of our tableau system is that it is neither based on resolution nor on standard sequent/tableau techniques. It combines linear tableau expansion rules with natural deduction rules and an analytic version of the cut rule. The tableau rules are supplemented with a powerful and flexible label algebra that allows the system to deal with a large class of intensional logics admitting possible world semantics (non-normal modal logic [14], multi-modal logics [11] and conditional logics [2]). The label algebra is intended to simulate the possible world semantics and it has a very strong relationship with fibring [10].

As far as the field of *combining logics* is concerned, it has been an active research area since some time now and powerful results about the preservation of important properties of the logics being combined has been obtained [16,4,22]. Also, investigations related to using fibring as a combining technique in various domains has produced a wealth of results as found in works like [8,24,21,5]. The novelty of combining logics is the aim to develop *general techniques* that allow us to produce combinations of *existing* and well understood logics. Such general techniques are needed for formalising complex systems in a systematic way. Such a methodology can help decompose the problem of designing a complex system into developing components (logics) and combining them.

One of the main advantages of using fibring as a semantic methodology for combining multimodal logics as compared to other combining techniques like *fusion* [2] is that the later has the problem of not being able to express interaction axioms, much needed for Multi-Agent-System (MAS) theories. Fibring is more powerful because of the possibility of adding conditions on the fibring function. These conditions could encode interactions between the two classes of models that are being combined and therefore could represent interaction axioms between the two logics. One such result was shown in [15]. Moreover, fibring does not require the logics to be normal. This allows fibring to be used to model combinations of epistemic logic without being forced to suffer from the logical omniscience problem. The drawbacks of other combining techniques like *embedding* and *independent combination* when compared to fibring have been discussed at length in [18]. Another advantage is that fibring makes it possible to combine logics at different levels, obtaining hierarchical modal logics, i.e., a logic with another logic embedded in it, or more precisely a logic with two modal operators such that

---

[2] Normal bimodal and polymodal logics without any interaction axioms are well studied as *fusions* of normal monomodal logics [16,22].

the first can occur in the scope of the other but not the other way around; see [9] for applications of hierarchical logics. For the second case it is possible to combine logic with different semantics. We can combine, let us say, a normal temporal logic whose semantics is given in terms of Kripke models and an epistemic non-normal modal logic with a neighbourhood semantics. This is not possible with other combining techniques where the semantics for the logics to be combined must be homogeneous. Finally the fibring methodology allows us to study the structure of the combined logic based on the structures of the component logics, and often it gives us conditions under which important meta-theoretical properties of the component logics (soundness, completeness, decidability and so on) are preserved by the combination.

The paper is structured as follows. The next section provides a brief introduction to the technique of fibring. Section 3 outlines the path-based and graph-based tableau procedures. Section 4 describes the **KEM** tableau system. The paper concludes with some final remarks.

2 Fibring Multimodal Logics

Consider the basic BDI logic $\mathbb{L}$ given in (1) which is defined from three component logics, viz., **KD45**$_n$ for belief, and **KD**$_n$ for desires and intentions. For sake of clarity, consider two of the component logics, $\blacktriangledown_1$(**KD45**) and $\blacktriangledown_2$(**KD**) and their corresponding languages $\mathscr{L}_{\blacktriangledown_1}, \mathscr{L}_{\blacktriangledown_2}$ built from the respective sets $\mathfrak{A}_1$ and $\mathfrak{A}_2$ of atoms having classes of models $\mathfrak{M}_{\blacktriangledown_1}, \mathfrak{M}_{\blacktriangledown_2}$ and satisfaction relations $\models_1$ and $\models_2$. Hence we are dealing with two different systems S_1 and S_2 characterised, respectively, by the class of Kripke models $\mathscr{K}_1$ and $\mathscr{K}_2$. For instance, we know how to evaluate $\square_1\varphi$ (BEL(φ)) in $\mathscr{K}_1$ (**KD45**) and $\square_2\varphi$ (DES(φ)) in $\mathscr{K}_2$ (**K D**). We need a method for evaluating $\square_1$ (resp. $\square_2$) with respect to $\mathscr{K}_2$ (resp. $\mathscr{K}_1$). In order to do so, we are to link (fibre), via a *fibring* function the model for $\blacktriangledown_1$ with a model for $\blacktriangledown_2$ and build a fibred model of the combination. The fibring function can evaluate (give a yes/no) answer with respect to a modality in S_2, being in S_1 and vice versa. The interpretation of a formula φ of the combined language in the fibred model at a state w can be given as

$$w \models \varphi \text{ if and only if } \boldsymbol{\mathfrak{f}}(w) \models^* \varphi$$

where $\boldsymbol{\mathfrak{f}}$ is a fibring function that maps a world to a model *suitable for interpreting φ* and $\models^*$ is the corresponding satisfaction relation ($\models_1$ for $\blacktriangledown_1$ or $\models_2$ for $\blacktriangledown_2$).

Example 1. Let $\blacktriangledown_1, \blacktriangledown_2$ be two modal logics as given above and let $\varphi = \square_1\lozenge_2\mathfrak{p}_0$ be a formula on a world w_0 of the fibred semantics. φ belongs to the language $\mathscr{L}_{(1,2)}$ as the outer connective ($\square_1$) belongs to the language $\mathscr{L}_1$ and the inner connective ($\lozenge_2$) belongs to the language $\mathscr{L}_2$.

By the standard definition we start evaluating $\square_1$ of $\square_1\lozenge_2$ at w_0. Hence according to the standard definition we have to check whether $\lozenge_2\mathfrak{p}_0$ is true at every w_1 accessible from w_0 since from the point of view of $\mathscr{L}_1$ this formula has the form $\square_1 p$ (where $p = \lozenge_2\mathfrak{p}_0$ is atomic). But at w_1 we cannot interpret the operator $\lozenge_2$, because we are in a model of $\blacktriangledown_1$, not of $\blacktriangledown_2$. In order to do this evaluation we need the fibring function $\boldsymbol{\mathfrak{f}}$ which at w_1 points to a world v_0, a world in a model suitable to interpret formulae from

▼$_2$. (Fig.1). Now all we have to check is whether $\diamond_2 \mathfrak{p}_0$, is true at v_0 in this last model and this can be done in the usual way. Hence the fibred semantics for the combined language $\mathscr{L}_{(1,2)}$ has models of the form $(\mathscr{F}_1, w_1, v_1, \mathfrak{f}_1)$, where $\mathscr{F}_1 = (W_1, R_1)$ is a frame, and $\mathfrak{f}_1$ is the fibring function which associates a model $\mathfrak{M}_w^2$ from $\mathscr{L}_2$ with w in $\mathscr{L}_1$ i.e. $\mathfrak{f}_1(w) = \mathfrak{M}_w^2$.

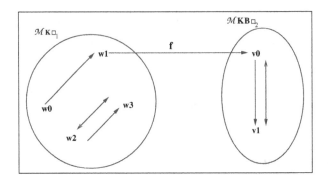

Fig. 1. An Example of Fibring

2.1   Fibring MMA

Let **I** be a set of labels representing the modal operators for the intentional states (belief, goal, intention) for a set of agents, and ▼$_i, i \in$ **I** be modal logics whose respective modalities are $\Box_i, i \in$ **I**.

Definition 1. *[8] A fibred model is a structure* $(W, S, R, \mathbf{a}, v, \tau, F)$ *where*

- W *is a set of possible worlds;*
- S *is a function giving for each w a set of possible worlds,* $S^w \subseteq W$;
- R *is a function giving for each w, a relation* $R^w \subseteq S^w \times S^w$;
- **a** *is a function giving the actual world* $\mathbf{a}^w$ *of the model labelled by w;*
- v *is an assignment function* $v^w(\mathfrak{q}_0) \subseteq S^w$, *for each atomic* $\mathfrak{q}_0$;
- τ *is the semantical identifying function* $\tau : W \to \mathbf{I}$. $\tau(w) = i$ *means that the model* $(S^w, R^w, \mathbf{a}^w, v^w)$ *is a model in* $\mathscr{K}_i$, *we use* W_i *to denote the set of worlds of type i;*
- **F**, *is the set of fibring functions* $\mathfrak{f} : I \times W \mapsto W$. *A fibring function* $\mathfrak{f}$ *is a function giving for each i and each* $w \in W$ *another point (actual world) in W as follows:*

$$\mathfrak{f}_i(w) = \begin{cases} w & \text{if } w \in S^{\mathfrak{M}} \text{ and } \mathfrak{M} \in \mathscr{K}_i \\ a \text{ value in } W_i, & \text{otherwise} \end{cases}$$

such that if $w \neq w'$ *then* $\mathfrak{f}_i(w) \neq \mathfrak{f}_i(w')$. *It should be noted that fibring happens when* $\tau(w) \neq i$. *Satisfaction is defined as follows with the usual truth tables for Boolean connectives:*

$$w \models \mathfrak{q}_0 \text{ iff } v(w, \mathfrak{q}_0) = 1, \text{ where } \mathfrak{q}_0 \text{ is an atom}$$

$$w \models \Box_i \varphi \text{ iff } \begin{cases} w \in \mathfrak{M} \text{ and } \mathfrak{M} \in \mathscr{K}_i \text{ and } \forall w' (w R w' \to w' \models \varphi), \text{or} \\ w \in \mathfrak{M}, \text{ and } \mathfrak{M} \notin \mathscr{K}_i \text{ and } \forall \mathfrak{f} \in \mathbf{F}, \mathfrak{f}_i(w) \models \Box_i \varphi. \end{cases}$$

We say the model satisfies φ *iff* $w_0 \models \varphi$.

A fibred model for $\blacktriangledown_{I}^{\mathfrak{f}}$ can be generated from fibring the semantics for the modal logics $\blacktriangledown_i, i \in \mathbf{I}$. The detailed construction is given in [19]. Also, to accommodate the interaction axioms specific constraints need to be given on the fibring function. In [15] we outline the specific conditions required on the fibring function to accommodate axiom schemas of the type $G^{a,b,c,d}$:[3]. We do not want to get into the details here as the main theme of this paper is with regard to tableau based proof techniques for fibred logics.

What we want to point out here, however, is that the fibring construction given in [15,19] works for normal (multi-)modal logics as well as non-normal modal logics.

3   Multimodal Tableaux

In the previous sections we showed that agent logics are usually normal multimodal logics with a set of interaction axioms and introduced general techniques like fibring to explain such combined systems. In this section, before getting into the details related to the constructs needed for a tableau calculus for a fibred/combined logic, we outline with an example two types of tableau systems (*graph* & *path*) that can be used to reason about the knowledge/beliefs of agents in a multi-agent setting. Having done that, in the next section, we describe how to uniformly construct a sound and complete tableau calculus for the combined logic from calculi for the component logics.

Example 2. (The Friends Puzzle) [3] Consider the agents Peter, John and Wendy with modalities $\Box_p, \Box_j,$ and $\Box_w$. John and Peter have an `appointment`. Suppose that Peter knows the `time` of appointment. Peter knows that John knows the `place` of their appointment. Wendy knows that if Peter knows the `time` of appointment, then John knows that too (since John and Peter are friends). Peter knows that if John knows the `place` and the `time` of their appointment, then John knows that he has an `appointment`. Peter and John satisfy the axioms T and 4. Also, if Wendy knows something then Peter knows the same thing (suppose Wendy is Peter's wife) and if Peter knows that John knows something then John knows that Peter knows the same thing.

The Knowledge/belief base for Example 2 can be formally given as follows;

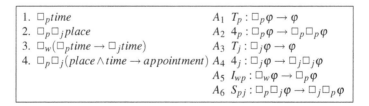

1. $\Box_p time$	A_1 $T_p : \Box_p \varphi \to \varphi$
2. $\Box_p \Box_j place$	A_2 $4_p : \Box_p \varphi \to \Box_p \Box_p \varphi$
3. $\Box_w(\Box_p time \to \Box_j time)$	A_3 $T_j : \Box_j \varphi \to \varphi$
4. $\Box_p \Box_j(place \wedge time \to appointment)$	A_4 $4_j : \Box_j \varphi \to \Box_j \Box_j \varphi$
	A_5 $I_{wp} : \Box_w \varphi \to \Box_p \varphi$
	A_6 $S_{pj} : \Box_p \Box_j \varphi \to \Box_j \Box_p \varphi$

Fig. 2. Knowledge base related to the Friend's puzzle

So we have a modal language consisting of three modalities $\Box_p, \Box_j$ and $\Box_w$ denoting respectively the agents Peter, John and Wendy and characterised by the set $A = \{A_i \mid i = 1,\dots,6\}$ of interaction axioms. Suppose now that one wants to show that each of

---

[3] $G^{a,b,c,d} \Diamond_a \Box_b \varphi \to \Box_c \Diamond_d \varphi.$

∧-rules	$\dfrac{\sigma\ \varphi\wedge\psi}{\sigma\ \varphi}$ $\sigma\ \psi$	$\dfrac{\sigma\ \neg(\varphi\vee\psi)}{\sigma\ \neg\varphi}$ $\sigma\ \neg\psi$	$\dfrac{\sigma\ \neg(\varphi\rightarrow\psi)}{\sigma\ \varphi}$ $\sigma\ \psi$	For any prefix σ
∨-rules	$\dfrac{\sigma\ \varphi\vee\psi}{\sigma\ \varphi\ \mid\ \sigma\ \psi}$	$\dfrac{\sigma\ \neg(\varphi\wedge\psi)}{\sigma\ \neg\varphi\ \mid\ \sigma\ \neg\psi}$	$\dfrac{\sigma\ \varphi\rightarrow\psi}{\sigma\ \neg\varphi\ \mid\ \sigma\ \neg\psi}$	For any prefix σ
¬¬-rules	$\dfrac{\sigma\neg\neg\varphi}{\sigma\varphi}$			For any prefix σ
◇-rules	$\dfrac{\sigma\ \Diamond_i\varphi}{\sigma.n_i\ \varphi}$	$\dfrac{\sigma\ \neg\Box_i\varphi}{\sigma.n_i\ \neg\varphi}$		if the prefix $\sigma.n_i$ is new to the branch ($i\in\{1,\dots,m\}$)
□-rules	$\dfrac{\sigma\ \Box_i\varphi}{\sigma.n_i\ \varphi}$	$\dfrac{\sigma\ \neg\Diamond_i\varphi}{\sigma.n_i\ \neg\varphi}$		If the prefix $\sigma.n_i$ already occurs on the branch ($i\in\{1,\dots,m\}$)
$T_p$rules:	$\dfrac{\sigma\ \Box_p\varphi}{\sigma\ \varphi}$	$\dfrac{\sigma\ \neg\Diamond_p\varphi}{\sigma\ \neg\varphi}$	$\dfrac{\sigma\ \varphi}{\sigma\ \Diamond_p\varphi}$	
$T_j$rules:	$\dfrac{\sigma\ \Box_j\varphi}{\sigma\ \varphi}$	$\dfrac{\sigma\ \neg\Diamond_j\varphi}{\sigma\ \neg\varphi}$	$\dfrac{\sigma\ \varphi}{\sigma\ \Diamond_j\varphi}$	
4_prules:	$\dfrac{\sigma\ \Box_p\varphi}{\sigma.n_p^*\Box_p\varphi}$	$\dfrac{\sigma\ \neg\Diamond_p\varphi}{\sigma.n_p^*\Box_p\neg\varphi}$	$\dfrac{\sigma.n_p\ \Diamond_p\varphi}{\sigma\ \Diamond_p\varphi}$	$\dfrac{\sigma.n_p\ \neg\Box_p\varphi}{\sigma\ \Diamond_p\neg\varphi}$
4_jrules:	$\dfrac{\sigma\ \Box_j\varphi}{\sigma.n_j^*\Box_j\varphi}$	$\dfrac{\sigma\ \neg\Diamond_j\varphi}{\sigma.n_j^*\Box_j\neg\varphi}$	$\dfrac{\sigma.n_j\ \Diamond_j\varphi}{\sigma\ \Diamond_j\neg\varphi}$	$\dfrac{\sigma.n_j\ \neg\Box_j\varphi}{\sigma\ \Diamond_j\neg\varphi}$
I_{wp}rules:	$\dfrac{\sigma\ \Box_w\varphi}{\sigma.n_p^*\varphi}$	$\dfrac{\sigma\ \neg\Diamond_w\varphi}{\sigma.n_p^*\neg\varphi}$	$\dfrac{\sigma.n_p\ \varphi}{\sigma\ \Diamond_w\varphi}$	
S_{pj}rules:	$\dfrac{\sigma\ \Box_p\Box_j\varphi}{\sigma.n_j^*\Box_p\varphi}$	$\dfrac{\sigma\ \neg\Diamond_p\Diamond_j\varphi}{\sigma.n_j^*\Box_p\neg\varphi}$	$\dfrac{\sigma.n_j\ \Diamond_p\varphi}{\sigma\ \Diamond_p\Diamond_j\varphi}$	$\dfrac{\sigma.n_j\ \neg\Box_p\varphi}{\sigma\ \Diamond_p\Diamond_j\neg\varphi}$

($*$) prefix already occurs on the branch

Fig. 3. Tableau rules corresponding to the Friend's Puzzle

the friends knows that the other one knows that he has an appointment, i.e., one wants to prove

$$\Box_j\Box_p appointment \wedge \Box_p\Box_j appointment \qquad (2)$$

is a theorem of the knowledge-base. The tableaux rules for a logic corresponding to the Friends puzzle are given in Fig.3 [17], and the tableaux proof for (2) is given in Fig.4 [17]. The tableaux in Fig.4. is a prefixed tableau [7] where the accessibility relations are encoded in the structure of the name of the worlds. Such a representation is often termed as a *path* representation. We show the proof of the first conjunct and the proof runs as follows. Item 1 is the negation of the formula to be proved; 2, 3, 4 and 5 are from Example 2; 6 is from 1 by a ◇-rule; 7 is from 6 by an S_{pj}-rule; 8 is from 7 by a ◇-rule; 9 is from 8 by a ◇-rule; 10 is from 5 by a □-rule; 11 is from 10 by a □-rule. 12 and 24 are from 11 by a ∨-rule; 13 and 16 are from 12 by a ∨-rule; 14 is from 3 by a □-rule; 15 is from 14 by a □-rule; the branch closes by 13 and 15; 17 is from 4 by an I_{wp}-rule; 18 and 22 are from 17 by a ∨-rule; 19 is from 18 by a ◇-rule; 20 is from 2 by

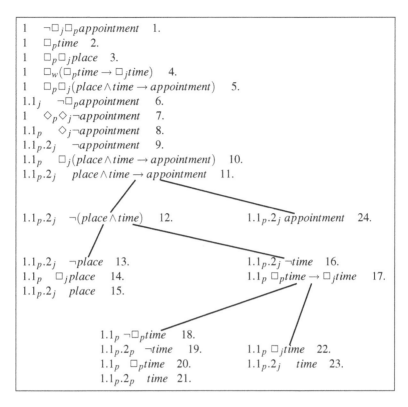

Fig. 4. Proof of $\Box_j\Box_p$ appointment using *path* representation

a 4_p-rule; 21 is from 20 by a $\Box$-rule; the branch closes by 19 and 21; 23 is from 22 by a $\Box$-rule; the branch closes by 16 and 23; by 9 and 24 the remaining branch too closes.

In a similar manner the tableaux proof for (2) using a *graph* representation where the accessibility relations are represented by means of an explicit and separate graph of named nodes is given in Fig.6. Each node is associated with a set of prefixed formulae and choice allows any inclusion axiom to be interpreted as a *rewriting rule* into the path structure of the graph. The proof uses the rules given in Fig.5. which is often referred to as the Smullyan-Fitting uniform notation. We will be using this notation in the next section for our **KEM** tableaux system. The proof for (2) as given in [3] runs as follows. Steps 1-4 are from Fig.2 and 5 is the first conjunct of (2). Using π-rule we get items 6 and 7 (from 5) and 8 and 9 (from 6). We get 10 from 7 using axiom A_6 in Fig.2 and ρ-rule in Fig.5. Similarly 11 is from 9 via A_6 and ρ-rule. By making use of the ν-rule in Fig.5 we get 12 (from 4 and 10) and 13 (from 12 and 11). 14a and 14b are from 13 using β-rule ("a" and "b" denote the two branches created by the application of β-rule). Branch "a" (14a) closes with 8. Applying β-rule again we get 15ba and 15bb from 14b ("ba" and "bb" denote the two branches created by the application of β-rule). Applying ν-rule we get 16ba (from 3 and 10) and 17ba (from 16ba and 11). Branch "ba" closes because of 15ba and 17ba. We get 16bb from 10 via axiom A_5 in Fig.2 and π-rule in Fig.5. Similarly from 2 and 16bb by using ν-rule we get 17bb. We get 18bba and 18bbb

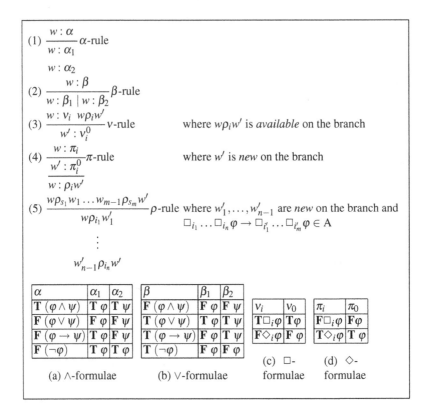

Fig. 5. Tableaux rules based on uniform notation for propositional inclusion modal logics [3]

from 17bb by applying the β-rule ("bba" and "bbb" denote the branches created by the β-rule). By using ν-rule we get 19bba (from 18bba and 11). Branch "bba" (19bba) closes with 15bb. From 18bbb using π-rule we get 19bbb and 20bbb. From 10 and 20bbb via axiom A_2 (in Fig.2) and ρ-rule (in Fig.5) we get 21bbb. By applying ν-rule to 1 and 21bbb we get 22bbb as a result of which the branch "bbb" closes (22bbb and 19bbb).

It should be noted that axiom schemas like $A_1, \ldots, A_6$ of Example 2 given in Fig. 2 belong to the class of axioms called *inclusion axioms*. In particular they belong to axiom sets of the form, $\Box_{i_1} \ldots \Box_{i_n} \rightarrow \Box_{i'_1} \ldots \Box_{i'_m}$ ($i_n > 0, i'_m \geq 0$), which in turn characterise the class of *normal modal logics* called *inclusion modal logics*. As shown in [3], for each axiom schema of the above type the corresponding *inclusion* property on the *accessibility relation* can be given as

$$R_{i_1} \circ R_{i_2} \circ \ldots R_{i_n} \supseteq R_{i'_1} \circ R_{i'_2} \ldots \circ R_{i'_m} \tag{3}$$

where "$\circ$" denotes the relation composition $R_{i_1} \circ R_{i_2} = \{(w, w'') \in W \times W \mid \exists w' \in W \text{ such that } (w, w') \in R_{i_1} \text{ and } (w', w'') \in R_{i_2}\}$. This inclusion property is used to rewrite items 7. ($w_0 R_{john} w_1$) and 9. ($w_1 R_{peter} w_2$) of the proof given in Fig.6 so as to derive a new

1.	$w_0 : \mathbf{T}\square_p time$	14b.	$w_2 : \mathbf{F}(place \wedge time)$
2.	$w_0 : \mathbf{T}\square_w(\square_p time \rightarrow \square_j time)$	15ba.	$w_2 : \mathbf{F}\ place$
3.	$w_0 : \mathbf{T}\square_p \square_j place$	16ba.	$w_3 : \mathbf{T}\square_j place$
4.	$w_0 : \mathbf{T}\square_p \square_j(place \wedge time \rightarrow appointment)$	17ba.	$w_2 : \mathbf{T}place$
5.	$w_0 : \mathbf{F}\square_j \square_p appointment$		$\times$
6.	$w_1 : \mathbf{F}\square_p appointment$	15bb.	$w_2 : \mathbf{F}time$
7.	$\quad w_0 \mathsf{R}_{john} w_1$	16bb.	$\quad w\mathsf{R}_{wife}w_3$
8.	$w_2 : \mathbf{F}\ appointment$	17bb.	$w_3 : \mathbf{T}(\square_p time \rightarrow \square_j time)$
9.	$\quad w_1 \mathsf{R}_{peter} w_2$	18bba.	$w_3 : \mathbf{T}\ \square_j time$
10.	$\quad w_0 \mathsf{R}_{peter} w_3$	19bba.	$w_2 : \mathbf{T}time$
11.	$\quad w_3 \mathsf{R}_{john} w_2$		$\times$
12.	$w_3 : \mathbf{T}\square_j(place \wedge time \rightarrow appointment)$	18bbb.	$w_3 : \mathbf{F}\square_p time$
13.	$w_2 : \mathbf{T}\ (place \wedge time \rightarrow appointment)$	19bbb.	$w_4 : \mathbf{F}time$
14a.	$w_2 : \mathbf{T}\ appointment$	20bbb	$\quad w_3 \mathsf{R}_{peter} w_4$
	$\times$	21bbb.	$\quad w_0 \mathsf{R}_{peter} w_4$
		22bbb.	$w_4 : \mathbf{T}\ time$
			$\times$

Fig. 6. Proof of $\square_j \square_p$ using *graph* representation

path $(w_0 \mathsf{R}_{peter} w_3)$ and $(w_3 \mathsf{R}_{john} w_2)$ as in items 10. and 11. The corresponding tableaux rule for this property is given as ρ-rule (5) in Fig.5. Also, the type of interaction axiom schemas of Example 2 involves the interaction between the *same mental attitude* of *different agents*. There is also another type where there is interaction between *different mental attitudes* of the *same agent*. The interaction axioms given in (1) is of the later type. In the coming sections we will show that the **KEM** tableau can deal with both types of interaction axioms.

As pointed out in [3], the main difference between the two types of tableaux, (graph and path), is in the use of ν-rule. In the case of *path* representation one needs to use a specific ν-rule for each logic as can be seen from Fig.3. These rules code the properties of the accessibility relations so as to express complex relations between prefixes depending on the logic. Whereas in the case of *graph* representation the accessibility relations are given explicitly. Also, it has been pointed out in [3] that the approach based on path representation can be used only for some subclasses of inclusion axioms and therefore difficult to extend the approach to the whole class of multi-modal systems.

4 Labelled Tableau for Fibred MMA Logic

In this section we show how to adapt **KEM**, a labelled modal tableaux system, to deal with the fibred combination of multimodal agent logics. In labelled tableaux systems, the object language is supplemented by labels meant to represent semantic structures (possible worlds in the case of modal logics). Thus the formulas of a labelled tableaux system are expressions of the form $A : i$, where A is a formula of the logic and i is a label. The interpretation of $A : i$ is that A is true at (the possible world(s) denoted by) i.

KEM's inferential engine is based on a combination of standard tableaux linear expansion rules and natural deduction rules supplemented by an analytic version of the cut rule. In addition it utilises a sophisticated but powerful label formalism that enables the logic to deal with a large class of modal and non-classical logics. Furthermore the label mechanism corresponds to fibring and thus it is possible to define tableaux systems for multi-modal logic by a seamless combination of the (sub)tableaux systems for the component logics of the combination.

It is not possible in this paper to give a full presentation of **KEM** for fully fledged multimodal agent logics supplemented with the interaction axioms given in Example 2. (for a comprehensive presentation see [10]). Accordingly we will limit ourselves to a single modal operator for each agent and we will show how to characterise the axioms and the interaction of example 2.

4.1   Label Formalism

KEM uses *Labelled Formulas* (*L*-formulas for short), where an *L*-formula is an expression of the form $A : i$, where A is a wff of the logic, and i is a label. For fibred **MMA** (from now on **FMMA**) we need to have labels for various modalities (belief, desire, intention) for each agent. However, as we have just explained we will consider only one modality and thus will have only labels for the agents.

The set of atomic labels, $\Im_1$, is then given as

$$\Im_1 = \bigcup_{i \in Agt} \Phi^i,$$

where *Agt* is the set of agents. Every Φ^i is partitioned into two (non-empty) sets of atomic labels: $\Phi^i_C = \{w^i_1, w^i_2, \ldots\}$ the set of constants of type *i*, and $\Phi^i_V = \{W^i_1, W^i_2, \ldots\}$ the set of variables of type *i*. We also add a set of auxiliary un indexed atomic labels Φ^A, again partitioned into variables $\Phi^A_V = \{W_1, W_2, \ldots\}$ and constants $\Phi^A_C = \{w_1, w_2, \ldots\}$, that will be used in unifications and proofs.

Definition 1 (labels). *A label $u \in \Im$ is either (i) an atomic label, i.e., $u \in \Im_1$ or (ii) a path term (u', u) where (iia) $u' \in \Phi_C \cup \Phi_V$ and (iib) $u \in \Phi_C$ or $u = (v', v)$ where (v', v) is a label.*

As an intuitive explanation, we may think of a label $u \in \Phi_C$ as denoting a world (a *given* one), and a label $u \in \Phi_V$ as denoting a set of worlds (*any* world) in some Kripke model. A label $u = (v', v)$ may be viewed as representing a path from v to a (set of) world(s) v' accessible from v (the world(s) denoted by v).

For any label $u = (v', v)$ we shall call v' the *head* of u, v the *body* of u, and denote them by $h(u)$ and $b(u)$ respectively. Notice that these notions are recursive (they correspond to projection functions): if $b(u)$ denotes the body of u, then $b(b(u))$ will denote the body of $b(u)$, and so on. We call each of $b(u)$, $b(b(u))$, etc., a *segment* of u. The length of a label u, $\ell(u)$, is the number of atomic labels in it. $s^n(u)$ will denote the segment of u of length n and we shall use $h^n(u)$ as an abbreviation for $h(s^n(u))$. Notice that $h(u) = h^{\ell(u)}(u)$. Let u be a label and u' an atomic label. We use $(u'; u)$ as a notation for the label (u', u) if $u' \neq h(u)$, or for u otherwise. For any label $u, \ell(u) > n$, we define the *counter-segment-n* of u, as follows (for $n < k < \ell(u)$):

$$c^n(u) = h(u) \times (\cdots \times (h^k(u) \times (\cdots \times (h^{n+1}(u), w_0))))$$

where w_0 is a dummy label, i.e., a label not appearing in u (the context in which such a notion occurs will tell us what w_0 stands for). The counter-segment-n defines what remains of a given label after having identified the segment of length n with a 'dummy' label w_0. The appropriate dummy label will be specified in the applications where such a notion is used. However, it can be viewed also as an independent atomic label. In the context of fibring w_0 can be thought of as denoting the actual world obtained via the fibring function from the world denoted by $s^n(u)$.

Example 3. Given the label $u = (w_4^i, (W_3^k, (w_3^j, (W_2^j, w_1^j))))$, according to the above definitions its length $\ell(u)$ is 5, the head $h(u)$ is w_4^i, the body $b(t)$ is $(W_3^k, (w_3^j, (W_2^j, w_1^j)))$, the segment of length 3 is $s^3(u) = (w_3^j, (W_2^j, w_1^j))$, and the relative counter-segment-3 is $c^3(u) = (w_4^i, (W_3^k, w_0))$, where $w_0 = s^3(u) = (w_3^j, (W_2^j, w_1^j))$.

To clarify the notion of counter-segment, which will be used frequently in the course of the present work, we present, in the following table the list of the segments of u in the left-hand column and the relative counter-segments in the right-hand column.

$$
\begin{aligned}
s^1(u) &= w_1 & c^1(u) &= (w_4^i, (W_3^k, (w_3^j, (W_2^j, w_0)))) \\
s^2(u) &= (W_2^j, w_1^j) & c^2(u) &= (w_4^i, (W_3^k, (w_3^j, w_0))) \\
s^3(u) &= (w_3^j, (W_2^j, w_1^j)) & c^3(u) &= (w_4^i, (W_3^k, w_0)) \\
s^4(u) &= (W_3^k, (w_3^j, (W_2^j, w_1^j))) & c^4(u) &= (w_4^i, w_0) \\
s^5(u) &= u & c^5(u) &= w_0
\end{aligned}
$$

So far we have provided definitions about the structure of the labels without regard to the elements they are made of. The following definitions will be concerned with the type of world symbols occurring in a label.

We say that a label u is *i-preferred* iff $h(u) \in \Phi^i$; a label u is *i-pure* iff each segment of u of length $n > 1$ is i-preferred. Thus when we consider the label u of Example 3 then u is i-preferred, $b(u)$ is k-preferred and $s^3(u)$ is j-pure and consequently k-preferred. We will use $\mathfrak{I}^i$, $i \in Agt$, for the set of i-pure labels.

4.2   Label Unifications

The basic mechanism of **KEM** is its logic dependent label unification. In the same way as each modal logic is characterised by a combination of modal axioms (or semantic conditions on the model), **KEM** defines a unification for each modality and axiom/semantic condition and then combines them in a recursive and modular way. In particular we use what we call unification to determine whether the denotation of two labels have a non empty intersection, or in other terms whether two labels can be mapped to the same possible world in the possible worlds semantics.

The second key issue is the ability to split labels and to work with parts of labels. The mechanism permits the encapsulation of operations on sub-labels. This is an important feature that, in the present context, allows us to correlate unifications and fibring functions. Given the modularity of the approach the first step of the construction is to define unifications (pattern matching for labels) corresponding to the single modality in the logic we want to study.

Every unification is built from a basic unification defined in terms of a substitution $\rho : \mathfrak{I}_1 \mapsto \mathfrak{I}$ such that:

$$\rho : \mathbf{1}_{\Phi_C}$$
$$\Phi_V^i \mapsto \mathfrak{I}^i \text{ for every } i \in Agt$$
$$\Phi_V^A \mapsto \mathfrak{I}$$

The substitution ρ is such that every constant is mapped to itself, while the mapping of variables depends on their types. For a variable of type i, $i \in Agt$, the variable is mapped to an arbitrary i-pure label, but this restriction is dropped for auxiliary variables, thus any label can be associated to an auxiliary variable.

Accordingly, we have that two atomic ("world") labels u and v σ-unify iff there is a substitution ρ such that $\rho(u) = \rho(v)$. We shall use $[u;v]\sigma$ both to indicate that there is a substitution ρ for u and v, and the result of the substitution. The σ-unification is extended to the case of composite labels (path labels) as follows:

$$[i;j]\sigma = k \text{ iff } \exists \rho : h(k) = \rho(h(i)) = \rho(h(j)) \text{ and } b(k) = [b(i);b(j)]\sigma$$

Clearly σ is symmetric, i.e., $[u;v]\sigma$ iff $[v;u]\sigma$. Moreover this definition offers a flexible and powerful mechanism: it allows for an independent computation of the elements of the result of the unification, and variables can be freely renamed without affecting the result of a unification, and the σ-unification of any two labels can be computed in linear time [13].

We are now ready to introduce the unifications corresponding to the modal operators at hand, i.e., $\square_w$, $\square_j$ and $\square_p$ characterised by the axioms in Figure 2. We can capture the relationship between $\square_w$ and $\square_p$ by extending the substitution ρ by allowing a variable of type w to be mapped to labels of the same type and of type p.

$$\rho^w(W^w) \in \mathfrak{I}^w \cup \mathfrak{I}^p$$

Then the unification σ^w is obtained from the basic unification σ by replacing ρ with the extended substitution ρ^w. This procedure must be applied to all pairs of modalities $\square_1, \square_2$ related by the interaction axiom $\square_1 \varphi \rightarrow \square_2 \varphi$.

For the unifications for $\square_p$ and $\square_j$ (σ^p and σ^j) we assume that the labels involved are i-pure. First we notice that these two modal operators are **S4** modalities thus we have to use the unification for this logic.

$$[u;v]\sigma^{S4} = \begin{cases} [u;v]\sigma^D \text{ if } \ell(u) = \ell(v) \\ [u;v]\sigma^T \text{ if } \ell(u) < \ell(v), h(u) \in \Phi_C \\ [u;v]\sigma^4 \text{ if } \ell(u) < \ell(v), h(u) \in \Phi_V \end{cases} \tag{4}$$

It is worth noting that the conditions on axiom unifications are needed in order to provide a deterministic unification procedure. The σ^T and σ^4 are defined as follows:

$$[u;v]\sigma^T = \begin{cases} [s^{\ell(v)}(u);v]\sigma \text{ if } \ell(u) > \ell(v), \text{ and} \\ \qquad \forall n \geq \ell(v), [h^n(u);h(v))]\sigma = [h(u);h(v)]\sigma \\ [u;s^{\ell(u)}(v)]\sigma \text{ if } \ell(u) > \ell(v), \text{ and} \\ \qquad \forall n \geq \ell(u), [h(u);h^n(v)]\sigma = [h(u);h(v)]\sigma \end{cases}$$

The above unification allows us to unify to labels such that the segment of the longest with the length of the other label and the other label unify, provided that all remaining elements of the longest have a common unification with the head of the shortest. This means that after a given point the head of the shortest is always included in its extension, and thus it is accessible from itself, and consequently we have reflexivity.

Example 4. For the notion of σ^T-unification, take for example the labels

$$u = (w_3^p, (W_1^p, w_1^p)) \qquad\qquad v = (w_3^p, (W_2^p, (w_2^p, w_1^p)))$$

Here $[W_2^p; w_3^p]\sigma = [w_3^p; w_3^p]\sigma$. Then the two labels σ^T-unify to $(w_3^p, (w_2^p, w_1^p))$. This intuitively means that the world w_3^p, accessible from a sub-path $s(v) = (W_2^p, (w_2^p, w_1^p))$, after the deletion of W_2^p from v, is accessible from any path u which turns out to denote the same world(s) as $s(u)$; in fact the step from w_2^p to W_2^p is irrelevant because of the reflexivity relation of the model.

$$[u;v]\sigma^4 = \begin{cases} c^{\ell(u)}(v) \text{ if } \ell(v) > \ell(u), h(u) \in \Phi_V \text{ and} \\ \qquad w_0 = [u; s^{\ell(u)}(v)]\sigma \\ c^{\ell(v)}(u) \text{ if } \ell(u) > \ell(v), h(v) \in \Phi_V \text{ and} \\ \qquad w_0 = [s^{\ell(v)}(u); v]\sigma \end{cases}$$

In this case we have that the shortest label unifies with the segment with the same length of the longest and that the head of the shortest is variable. A variable stands for all worlds accessible from the predecessor of it. Thus, given transitivity every element extending the segment with length of the shortest is accessible from this point.

Example 5. For the notion of σ^4-unification, take for example the labels

$$u = (W_3^j, (w_2^j, w_1^j)) \qquad\qquad v = (w_5^j, (w_4^j, (w_3^j, (W_2^j, w_1^j))))$$

Here $s^{\ell(u)}(v) = (w_3^j, (W_2^j, w_1^j))$. Then u and v σ^4-unify to $(w_5^j, (w_4^j, (w_3^j, (w_2^j, w_1^j))))$ since $[u; s^{\ell(u)}(v)]\sigma = [(W_3^j, (w_2^j, w_1^j)); (w_3^j, (W_2^j, w_1^j))]\sigma$. This intuitively means that all the worlds accessible from a sub-path $s^{\ell(u)}(v)$ of v are accessible from any path u which leads to the same world(s) denoted by $s^{\ell(u)}(v)$. Here W_3^j stands for the set of worlds accessible from w_2^j; Then w_3^j, after the unification of (w_2^j, w_1^j) and (W_2^j, w_1^j), is one of such worlds. w_4^j is accessible from w_3^j and, via transitivity, from w_2^j. The same for w_5^j.

Then a unification corresponding to axiom A6 from Example 2 is

$$[u;v]\sigma^{Sp,j} = \begin{cases} c^m(v) \text{ if } h(u) \in \Phi_V^j \text{ and } c^n(v) \text{ is } p\text{-pure, and} \\ \qquad h^{\ell(u)-1}(u) \in \Phi_V^p \text{ and } c^m(s^n(v)) \text{ is } j\text{-pure, and} \\ \qquad w_0 = [s^{\ell(u)-2}(u); s^m(v)]\sigma \\ c^m(u) \text{ if } h(v) \in \Phi_V^j \text{ and } c^n(u) \text{ is } p\text{-pure, and} \\ \qquad h^{\ell(v)-1}(v) \in \Phi_V^p \text{ and } c^m(s^n(u)) \text{ is } j\text{-pure and} \\ \qquad w_0 = [s^m(u); s^{\ell(v)-2}(v)]\sigma \end{cases}$$

This unification allows us to unify two labels such that in one we have a sequence of a variable of type p followed by a variable of type j and a label where we have a sequence of labels of type j followed by a sequence of labels of type p.

Example 6. As an example of $\sigma^{Sp,j}$-unification consider the labels

$$u = (W_2^j, (W_2^p, (w_2^p, w_1^w)))　　　　　v = (w_3^p, (W_4^j, (w_3^j, (W_1^p, w_1^w))))$$

Given the two labels u and v we have that the last two elements of u are, in this order, a variable of type j, $h(u) \in \Phi_V^j$, and a variable of type p, $h^3(u) \in \Phi_V^p$. Thus we have to check that there are two sequences of p-pure and j-pure labels in v. Clearly $c^4(v) = (w_3^p, w_0)$ is p-pure and $c^2(s^4(u)) = (W_4^j, (w_3^j, w_0))$ is j-pure. Thus the last thing to do is to verify whether $s^2(v)$ and $s^{\ell(u)-2}(u) = s^2(u)$ σ-unify; it is immediate to verify that $[s^2(u); s^2(v)]\sigma$. Thus $[u; v]\sigma^{Sp,j} = (w_3^p, (W_4^j, (w_3^j, (w_2^p, w_1^w))))$.

The unification for $\Box_p$ and $\Box_j$ are just the combination of the three unifications given above. Finally the unification for the logic **L** defined by the axioms A1–A6 is obtained from the following recursive unification

$$[u; v]\sigma_L = \begin{cases} [u; v]\sigma^{w,p,j} \\ [c^m(u); c^n(v)]\sigma^{w,p,j} \text{ where } w_0 = [s^m(u); s^n(v)]\sigma_L \end{cases}$$

$\sigma^{w,p,j}$ is the simple combination of the unifications for the three modal operators. Having accounted for the unification we now give the inference rules used in **KEM** proofs.

Example 7. To illustrate the σ_L-unification consider the labels

$$u = (w_3^j, (w_2^j, (W_1^j, (W_1^p, w_1^w))))　　　　　v = (W_2^j, (w_1^p, (w_1^j, w_1^w)))$$

A simple inspection of the label shows that none of the other unifications can be used here to unify the two labels. The only way is to split the labels in appropriate segments and counter-segments and then use the σ_L-unification. We split the labels as follows $c^3(u) = (w_3^j, (w_2^j, w_0))$ and $c^2(v) \doteq (W_2^j, w_0)$. Now it is easy to verify that $[c^3(u); c^{2(v)}]\sigma^4$. On the other hand we have that $s^3(u) = (W_1^j, (W_1^p, w_1^w))$ and $s^2(v) = (w_1^j, w_1^w)$, and $[s^3(u); s^2(u)]\sigma^{Sp,j}$. Thus we can identify w_0 with $[s^3(u); s^2(u)]\sigma^{Sp,j}$, and then $[u; v]\sigma_L$.

Notice that the unification mechanism, in particular the splitting of the labels into segments and counter-segments and the use of subunifications for them follows the same idea as fibring. As the fibring function takes us to a new model specific to the modal operator we evaluate, the decomposition of the unification allows us to reduce the unification of complex labels with atomic labels of multiple types to unifications of pure labels, where we can use the unifications for the component logics.

4.3 Inference Rules

For the inference rules we use the Smullyan-Fitting unifying notation [7].

$$\frac{\alpha : u}{\begin{array}{c} \alpha_1 : u \\ \alpha_2 : u \end{array}}(\alpha)　　　　　\frac{\begin{array}{c} \beta : u \\ \beta_i^c : v \end{array}}{\beta_{3-i} : [u; v]\sigma_L}(\beta) \quad (i = 1, 2)$$

The α-rules are just the familiar linear branch-expansion rules of the tableau method. The β-rules are nothing but natural inference patterns such as Modus Ponens, Modus

Tollens and Disjunctive syllogism generalised to the modal case. In order to apply such rules it is required that the labels of the premises unify and the label of the conclusion is the result of their unification.

$$\frac{v^i : u}{v_0^i : (W_n^i, u)}(v) \qquad\qquad \frac{\pi^i : u}{\pi_0^i : (w_n^i, u)}(\pi)$$

where W_n^i is a new label. The v and π rules are the normal expansion rule for modal operators of labelled tableaux with free variable. The intuition for the v rule is that if $\Box_i A$ is true at u, then A is true at all worlds accessible via R_i from u, and this is the interpretation of the label (W_n^i, u); similarly if $\Box_i A$ is false at u (i.e., $\neg\mathbf{B}A$ is true), then there must be a world, let us say w_n^i accessible from u, where $\neg A$ is true. A similar intuition holds when u is not i-preferred, but the only difference is that we have to make use of the fibring function instead of the accessibility relation

$$\frac{}{A : u \quad | \quad \neg A : u}(PB) \qquad\qquad \frac{\begin{array}{c}A : u \\ \neg A : v\end{array}}{\times}[\text{ if } [u;v]\sigma_L](PNC)$$

The *Principle of Bivalence* (PB) represents the semantic counterpart of the cut rule of the sequent calculus (intuitive meaning: a formula A is either true or false in any given world). PB is a zero-premise inference rule, so in its unrestricted version can be applied whenever we like. However, we impose a restriction on its application. PB can be only applied w.r.t. immediate sub-formulas of unanalysed β-formulas, that is β formulas for which we have no immediate sub-formulas with the appropriate labels in the tree. The *Principle of Non-Contradiction* (PNC) states that two labelled formulas are σ_L-complementary when the two formulas are complementary and their labels σ_L-unify.

It is possible to show that the resulting calculus is sound and complete for the class of (fibred) models corresponding to the (fibred) logic determined by the axiom in Fig. 2; see [10] for the techniques needed to prove the results. Notice that the Knowledge base of Fig 2 does not specify whether the modal operators are normal or not. While this could be a problem for other combination techniques and tableaux systems, this does not affect fibring, and **KEM**. It is possible to differentiate normal and non-normal modal logic in **KEM** based on additional conditions on the substitution function ρ, see [14].

4.4 Proof Search

Let $\Gamma = \{X_1, \ldots, X_m\}$ be a set of formulas. Then $\mathscr{T}$ is a **KEM**-*tree for* Γ if there exists a finite sequence $(\mathscr{T}_1, \mathscr{T}_2, \ldots, \mathscr{T}_n)$ such that (i) $\mathscr{T}_1$ is a 1-branch tree consisting of $\{X_1 : t_1, \ldots, X_m : t_m\}$; (ii) $\mathscr{T}_n = \mathscr{T}$, and (iii) for each $i < n$, $\mathscr{T}_{i+1}$ results from $\mathscr{T}_i$ by an application of a rule of **KEM**. A branch θ of a **KEM**-tree $\mathscr{T}$ of L-formulas is said to be σ_L-*closed* if it ends with an application of *PNC*, open otherwise. As usual with tableau methods, a set Γ of formulas is checked for consistency by constructing a **KEM**-tree for Γ. Moreover we say that a formula A is a **KEM**-*consequence of a set of formulas* $\Gamma = \{X_1, \ldots, X_n\}$ ($\Gamma \vdash_{\mathbf{KEM}(L)} A$) if a **KEM**-tree for $\{X_1 : u_1, \ldots, X_n : u_n, \neg A : v\}$ is closed using the unification for the logic L, where $v \in \Phi_C^A$, and $u_i \in \Phi_V^A$. The intuition behind this definition is that A is a consequence of Γ when we take Γ as a set of global assumptions [7], i.e., true in every world in a Kripke model.

We now describe a systematic procedure for **KEM** by defining the following notions. Given a branch θ of a **KEM**-tree, we call an L-formula $X : u$ *E-analysed in* θ if either (i) X is of type α and both $\alpha_1 : t$ and $\alpha_2 : u$ occur in θ; or (ii) X is of type β and one of the following conditions is satisfied: (a) if $\beta_1^C : v$ occurs in θ and $[u; v]\sigma$, then also $\beta_2 : [u; v]\sigma$ occurs in θ, (b) if $\beta_2^C : v$ occurs in θ and $[u; v]\sigma$, then also $\beta_1 : [u; v]\sigma$ occurs in θ; or (iii) X is of type μ and $\mu_0 : (u', u)$ occurs in θ for some appropriate u' of the right type, not previously occurring in θ. We call a branch θ of a **KEM**-tree *E-completed* if every L-formula in it is E-analysed and it contains no complementary formulas which are not $\sigma_\mathbf{L}$-complementary. We say a branch θ of a **KEM**-tree *completed* if it is E-completed and all the L-formulas of type β in it either are analysed or cannot be analysed. We call a **KEM**-tree *completed* if every branch is completed.

The following procedure starts from the 1-branch, 1-node tree consisting of $\{X_1 : u, \dots, X_m : v\}$ and applies the inference rules until the resulting **KEM**-tree is either closed or completed. At each stage of proof search (i) we choose an open non completed branch θ. If θ is not E-completed, then (ii) we apply the 1-premise rules until θ becomes E-completed. If the resulting branch θ' is neither closed nor completed, then (iii) we apply the 2-premise rules until θ becomes E-completed. If the resulting branch θ' is neither closed nor completed, then (iv) we choose an L-formula of type β which is not yet analysed in the branch and apply PB so that the resulting LS-formulas are $\beta_1 : u'$ and $\beta_1^C : u'$ (or, equivalently $\beta_2 : u'$ and $\beta_2^C : u'$), where $u = u'$ if u is restricted (and already occurring when $h(u) \in \Phi_C$), otherwise u' is obtained from u by instantiating $h(u)$ to a constant not occurring in u; (v) ("Modal PB") if the branch is not E-completed nor closed, because of complementary formulas which are not $\sigma_\mathbf{L}$-complementary, then we have to see whether a restricted label unifying with both the labels of the complementary formulas occurs previously in the branch; if such a label exists, or can be built using already existing labels and the unification rules, then the branch is closed, (vi) we repeat the procedure in each branch generated by PB.

It is possible to give termination conditions for **KEM**-trees resulting in canonical trees. Essentially a canonical tree will examine each combination of a formula and label only once, and it produces finitely many formulas and labels. Thus, if one proves that an unification for an axiom terminates and satisfies some reasonable algebraic properties, then the **KEM**-trees for that axiom terminate. Thus the proof search in a **KEM** tableau for a combination of logics $\mathbf{L}_1, \dots, \mathbf{L}_n$ terminates if each $\mathbf{L}_i$ has a terminating **KEM** search procedure, and connecting axioms have unifications satisfying some safe conditions. A thorough analysis of the termination conditions for **KEM** and fibring is beyond the scope of this paper and it is left for future research. In particular we want to study the extent of the termination conditions for canonical trees and label structures developed in [12].

Fig.7. shows a **KEM** tableaux proof using the inference rules in section 4.3 and following the proof search mentioned above to solve the first conjunct of (2). The proof goes as follows; 1. is the negation of the formula to be proved. The formulas in 2–5 are the global assumptions of the scenario and accordingly they must hold in every world of every model for it. Hence we label them with a variable W_0 that can unify with every other label. This is used to derive 12. from 11. and 5. using a β-rule, and for introducing 15.; 6. is from 1., and 7. from 6. by applying π rule. Similarly we get 8. from 2., 9. from 8. using ν rule. 10. comes from 9. and 7. through the use of modus tollens. Applying

1. $\mathbf{F}\square_j\square_p appt$	w_0	9. $\mathbf{T}(place \wedge time \rightarrow appt)$	(W_1^j, W_1^p, w_0)
2. $\mathbf{T}\square_p\square_j(place \wedge time \rightarrow appt)$	W_0	10. $\mathbf{F}place \wedge time$	(w_1^p, w_1^j, w_0)
3. $\mathbf{T}\square_w(\square_p time \rightarrow \square_j time)$	W_0	11. $\mathbf{T}\square_p time \rightarrow \square_j time$	(W_1^w, w_0)
4. $\mathbf{T}\square_p\square_j place$	W_0	12. $\mathbf{T}\square_j place$	(W_2^p, w_0)
5. $\mathbf{T}\square_p time$	W_0	13. $\mathbf{T}place$	(W_2^j, W_2^p, w_0)
6. $\mathbf{F}\square_p appt$	(w_1^j, w_0)	14. $\mathbf{F}time$	(w_1^p, w_1^j, w_0)
7. $\mathbf{F}appt$	(w_1^p, w_1^j, w_0)	15. $\mathbf{T}\square_p time$	(w_1^j, w_0)
8. $\mathbf{T}\square_j(place \wedge time \rightarrow appt)$	(W_1^p, w_0)	16. $\mathbf{T}time$	(W_3^p, w_1^j, w_0)
		$\times$	

Fig. 7. Proof of $\square_j\square_p$ using **KEM** representation

v rule twice we can derive 11. from 3. as well as 13. from 12. Through propositional reasoning we get 14. from 10. and by using v rule on 15. we get 16. (14. and 16.) are complementary formulas and this results in a closed tableaux because the labels in 14. and 16. unify, denoting that the contradiction holds *in the same world*.

5   Concluding Remarks

In this paper we have argued that multimodal logics of agents (**MMA**) can be explained in terms of fibring as combination of simpler modal logics. Then we have outlined three labelled tableaux systems (path, graph and unification). For each of the method we have seen how they can deal with the Friend's puzzle as a way to evaluate their features.

In the path approach, as mentioned earlier, we need to use specific v-rule for each logic whereas **KEM** uses only one v-rule and unification is logic dependent. The graph approach on the other hand does not require, in general, any new rule, since it uses the semantic structure to propagate formulas to the appropriate labels. It is then suitable for an approach based on fibring, since the relationships between two labels can be given in terms of fibring. But then the advantage of **KEM** over the graph approach is in the full flexibility of the application of the rules. In the graph based approach one need to apply the π-rules (or the ρ-rule) before the v-rules whereas in **KEM** no such restrictions exist. Also **KEM** is more suited for fibring because the mechanism it uses to check and manipulate labels during model generation is close to semantic fibring.

KEM, in general similar to the graph approach, does not need logic dependent rules, however, similar to the path approach, it needs logic dependent label unifications. We have seen that the label algebra can be seen as a form of fibring [10], thus simple fibring does not require special attention in **KEM**; therefore it allows for a seamless composition of (sub)tableaux for modal logics. The label algebra contrary to the graph reasoning mechanism is not based on first order logic and thus can deal with complex structure and is not limited to particular fragment. Indeed **KEM** has been proved able to deal with complex label schema for non-normal modal logics in a uniform way [14] as well as other intensional logics such as conditional logics [2]. For these reasons we believe that **KEM** offers a suitable framework for constructing decision procedures for multi-modal logic for multi-agent systems. As we only described the static fragment of

MMA logics, (no temporal evolution was considered), the future work is to extend the tableaux framework so as to accommodate temporal modalities.

References

1. A. Artosi, P. Benassi, G. Governatori, and A. Rotolo. Shakespearian modal logic: A labelled treatment of modal identity. In *Advances in Modal Logic*, volume 1. CSLI, 1998.
2. A. Artosi, G. Governatori, and A. Rotolo. Labelled tableaux for non-monotonic reasoning: Cumulative consequence relations. *Journal of Logic and Computation*, 12(6):1027–1060, 2002.
3. M. Baldoni. *Normal Multimodal Logics: Automatic Deduction and Logic Programming Extension*. PhD thesis, Universita degli Studi di Torino, Italy, 1998.
4. P. Blackburn and M. de Rijke. Zooming in, zooming out. *Journal of Logic, Language and Information*, 1996.
5. A. S. d' Avila Garcez and D. M. Gabbay. Fibring neural networks. In *AAAI-2004*, pages 342–347. AAAI/MIT Press, 2004.
6. R. Fagin, J. Y. Halpern, Y. Moses, and M. Y. Vardi. *Reasoning About Knowledge*. The MIT Press, 1995.
7. M. Fitting. *Proof Methods for Modal and Intuitionistic Logics*. Reidel, Dordrecht, 1983.
8. D. M. Gabbay. *Fibring Logics*. Oxford University Press, Oxford, 1999.
9. D. M. Gabbay and G. Governatori. Dealing with label dependent deontic modalities. In *Norms, Logics and Information Systems. New Studies in Deontic Logic*. IOS Press, 1998.
10. D. M. Gabbay and G. Governatori. Fibred modal tableaux. In *Labelled Deduction*. Kluwer academic Publishers, 2000.
11. G. Governatori. Labelled tableau for multi-modal logics. In *TABLEAUX*, volume 918, pages 79–94. Springer, 1995.
12. G. Governatori. *Un modello formale per il ragionamento giuridico*. PhD thesis, CIRSFID, University of Bologna, 1997.
13. G. Governatori. On the relative complexity of modal tableaux. *Electronic Notes in Theoretical Computer Science*, 78:36–53, 2003.
14. G. Governatori and A. Luppi. Labelled tableaux for non-normal modal logics. In *AI*IA 99: Advances in AI*, LNAI-1792, pages 119–130, Berlin, 2000. Springer.
15. G. Governatori, V. Padmanabhan, and A. Sattar. On Fibring Semantics for BDI Logics. In *Logics in Artificial Intelligence: (JELIA-02), Italy*, LNAI-2424. Springer, 2002.
16. M. Kracht and F. Wolter. Properties of independently axiomatizable bimodal logics. *The Journal of Symbolic Logic*, 56(4):1469–1485, 1991.
17. J. W. Llyod. Modal higher-order logic for agents. http://users.rsise.anu.edu.au/ jwl/beliefs.pdf, 2004.
18. A. Lomuscio. *Information Sharing Among Ideal Agents*. PhD thesis, School of Computer Science, University of Brimingham, 1999.
19. Vineet Padmanabhan. *On Extending BDI Logics*. PhD thesis, School of Information Technology, Griffith University, Brisbane, Australia, 2003.
20. A. S. Rao and M. P. Georgeff. Formal models and decision procedures for multi-agent systems. Technical note 61, Australian Artificial Intelligence Institute, 1995.
21. A. Sernadas, C. Sernadas, and A. Zanardo. Fibring modal first-order logics: Completeness preservation. *Logic Journal of the IGPL*, 10(4):413–451, 2002.
22. F. Wolter. Fusions of modal logics revisited. In *Advances in Modal Logic*, volume 1. CSLI Lecture notes 87, 1997.
23. M. Wooldridge. *Reasoning about Rational Agents*. The MIT Press, 2000.
24. A. Zanardo, A. Sernadas, and C. Sernadas. Fibring: Completeness preservation. *Journal of Symbolic Logic*, 66(1):414–439, 2001.

Programming Declarative Goals Using Plan Patterns

Jomi F. Hübner[1], Rafael H. Bordini[2], and Michael Wooldridge[3]

[1] University of Blumenau, Brazil
jomi@inf.furb.br
[2] University of Durham, UK
R.Bordini@durham.ac.uk
[3] University of Liverpool, UK
mjw@csc.liv.ac.uk

Abstract. AgentSpeak is a well-known language for programming intelligent agents which captures the key features of reactive planning systems in a simple framework with an elegant formal semantics. However, the original language is too abstract to be used as a programming language for developing multi-agent system. In this paper, we address one of the features that are essential for a pragmatical agent programming language. We show how certain *patterns* of AgentSpeak plans can be used to define various types of declarative goals. In order to do so, we first define informally how plan failure is handled in the extended version of AgentSpeak available in *Jason*, a Java-based interpreter; we also define special (internal) actions used for dropping intentions. We then present a number of *plan patterns* which correspond to elaborate forms of declarative goals. Finally, we give examples of the use of such types of declarative goals and describe how they are implemented in *Jason*.

1 Introduction

The AgentSpeak(L) language, introduced by Rao in 1996, provides a simple and elegant framework for intelligent action via the run-time interleaved selection and execution of plans. Since the original language was proposed, substantial progress has been made both on the theoretical foundations of the language (e.g., its formal semantics [6]), and on its use, via implementations of practical extensions of AgentSpeak [5]. However, one problem with the original AgentSpeak(L) language is that it lacks many of the features that might be expected by programmers in practical development. Our aim in this paper is to focus on the integration of one such features, namely the definition of declarative goals with the use of plan patters. Throughout the paper, we use AgentSpeak as a more general reference to AgentSpeak(L) and its extensions.

In this paper, we consider the use of *declarative goals* in AgentSpeak programming. By a declarative goal, we mean a goal that *explicitly* represents a state of affairs to be achieved, in the sense that, if an agent has a goal $p(t_1, \ldots, t_n)$, it expects to eventually believe $p(t_1, \ldots, t_n)$ (cf. [19]) and only then can the goal be considered achieved. Moreover, we are interested not only in goals representing states of affairs, but goals that may have complex temporal structures. Currently, although goals form a central component of AgentSpeak programming, they are only *implicit* in the plans defined by the agent programmer. For example, there is no explicit way of expressing that a goal

M. Baldoni and U. Endriss (Eds.): DALT 2006, LNAI 4327, pp. 123–140, 2006.

should be maintained until a certain condition holds; such temporal goal structures are defined implicitly, within the plans themselves, and by *ad hoc* efforts on the part of programmers.

While one possibility would be to extend the language and its formal semantics to introduce an explicit notion of declarative goal (as done in other languages, e.g., [19,7,22]), we show that this is unnecessary. We introduce a number of *plan patterns*, corresponding to common types of explicit temporal (declarative) goal structures, and show how these can be mapped into AgentSpeak code. Thus, a programmer or designer can conceive of a goal at the declarative level, and this goal will be expanded, via these patterns, into standard AgentSpeak code. We also show how such goal patterns can be used in *Jason*, a Java-based implementation of an extended version of AgentSpeak [4].

In order to present the plan patterns that can be used for defining certain types of declarative goals discussed in the literature, the *plan failure* handling mechanism implemented in *Jason*, and some pre-defined *internal actions* used for dropping goals, need to be presented. Being able to handle plan failure is useful more generally than simply in the context of defining plan patterns that can represent complex declarative goals. In most practical scenarios, plan failure is not only possible, it is commonplace: a key component of rational action in humans is the ability to handle such failures. After presenting these features of *Jason* that are important in controlling the execution of plans, we can then show the plan patterns that define more complex types of goals than has been claimed to be possible in AgentSpeak [7]. We present (declarative) maintenance as well as achievement goals, and we present different forms of commitments towards goal achievement/maintenance (e.g., the well-known blind, single-minded, and open-minded forms of commitment [18]). Finally, we discuss *Jason* implementations, using the defined patterns, of examples that appeared in the literature on declarative goals; the examples also help in showing why declarative goals with complex temporal structures are an essential feature in programming multi-agent systems.

2   Goals and Plans in AgentSpeak

In [17], Rao introduced the AgentSpeak(L) programming language: a logic-based language that provides an elegant abstract framework for programming BDI agents. In this paper, we only give a very brief introduction to AgentSpeak; see e.g. [6] for more details.

An AgentSpeak agent is created by the specification of a set of initial beliefs and a set of plans. A *belief atom* is simply a first-order predicate in the usual notation, and belief atoms or their negations are *belief literals*. The initial beliefs define the state of the belief base at the moment the agent starts running; the belief base is simply a collection of ground belief atoms (or, in *Jason*, literals).

AgentSpeak distinguishes two types of goals: *achievement goals* and *test goals*. Achievement goals are predicates (as for beliefs) prefixed with the '!' operator, while test goals are prefixed with the '?' operator. Achievement goals state that the agent wants to achieve a state of the world where the associated predicate is true. (In practice, these lead to the execution of other plans.) A *test goal* states that the agent wants to test whether the associated predicate is a belief (i.e., whether it can be unified with one of the agent's beliefs).

Next, the notion of a *triggering event* is introduced. It is a very important concept in this language, as triggering events define which events may initiate the execution of plans; the idea of *event*, both internal and external, will be made clear below. There are two types of triggering events: those related to the *addition* ('+') and *deletion* ('-') of mental attitudes (beliefs or goals).

Plans refer to the *basic actions* that an agent is able to perform on its environment. Such actions are also defined as first-order predicates, but with special predicate symbols (called *action symbols*) used to distinguish them. The actual syntax of AgentSpeak programs is based on the definition of plans, as follows. If e is a triggering event, $b_1, \ldots, b_m$ are belief literals, and $h_1, \ldots, h_n$ are goals or actions, then $e : b_1 \& \ldots \& b_m \leftarrow h_1 ; \ldots ; h_n$. is a *plan*.

An AgentSpeak(L) plan has a *head* (the expression to the left of the arrow), which is formed from a triggering event (denoting the purpose for that plan), and a conjunction of belief literals representing a *context* (separated from the triggering event by ':'). The conjunction of literals in the context must be satisfied if the plan is to be executed (the context must be a logical consequence of that agent's current beliefs). A plan also has a *body*, which is a sequence of basic actions or (sub)goals that the agent has to achieve (or test) when the plan is triggered.

Besides the belief base and the plan library, the AgentSpeak interpreter also manages a set of *events* and a set of *intentions*, and its functioning requires three *selection functions*. The event selection function selects a single event from the set of events; another selection function selects an "option" (i.e., an applicable plan) from a set of applicable plans; and a third selection function selects one particular intention from the set of intentions. The selection functions are supposed to be agent-specific, in the sense that they should make selections based on an agent's characteristics in an application-specific way. An event has the form $\langle te, i \rangle$, where te is a plan triggering event (as in the plan syntax described above) and i is that intention that generated the event or T for external events.

Intentions are particular courses of actions to which an agent has committed in order to handle certain events. Each intention is a stack of partially instantiated plans. Events, which may start the execution of plans that have relevant triggering events, can be *external*, when originating from perception of the agent's environment (i.e., addition and deletion of beliefs based on perception are external events); or *internal*, when generated from the agent's own execution of a plan (i.e., a subgoal in a plan generates an event of type "addition of achievement goal"). In the latter case, the event is accompanied with the intention which generated it (as the plan chosen for that event will be pushed on top of that intention). External events create new intentions, representing separate focuses of attention for the agent's acting within the environment.

3   Plan Failure

We identify three cases of plan failure. The first cause of failure is a *lack of relevant or applicable plans*, which can be understood as the agent "not knowing how to do something". This happens either because the agent simply does not have the know-how (in case it has no relevant plans) — this could happen through simple omission (the programmer did not provide any appropriate plans) — or because all known ways of achieving the goal cannot currently be used (there are known plans but whose contexts do not match the agent's current beliefs). The second is where a test goal fails; that is, where the agent "expected" to believe in a certain condition of the world, but in fact the condition did not hold. The third is where an action fails. There are two types of actions: internal actions can be compared to a "native method", and basic actions which effectively change the environment where the agent is situated. The former are boolean functions, whereas the latter represent the effectors within the agent architecture which are assumed to provide feedback to the interpreter stating whether the requested action was executed or not.

Regardless of the reason for a plan failing, the interpreter generates a goal deletion event (i.e., an event for "$-!g$") if the corresponding goal achievement ($+!g$) has failed. This paper introduces for the first time an (informal) semantics for the notion of goal deletion as used in *Jason*. In the original definition, Rao syntactically defined the possibility of goal deletions as triggering events for plans (i.e., triggering event with $-$! and $-$? prefixes), but did not discuss what they meant. Neither was goal deletion discussed in further attempts to formalise AgentSpeak or its ancestor dMars [12,11]. Our own choice was to use this as some kind of plan failure handling mechanism[1], as discussed below (even though this was probably not what they originally were intended for).

The idea is that a plan for a goal deletion is a "clean-up" plan, executed prior to (possibly) "backtracking" (i.e., attempting another plan to achieve the goal for which a plan failed). One of the things programmers might want to do within the goal deletion plan is to attempt again to achieve the goal for which the plan failed. In contrast to conventional logic programming languages, during the course of executing plans for subgoals, AgentSpeak programs generate a sequence of actions that the agent performs on the external environment so as to change it, the effects of which cannot be undone by simply backtracking (i.e., it may require further action in order to do so). Therefore, in certain circumstances, one would expect the agent to have to act so as to reverse the effects of certain actions taken before the plan failed, and only then attempting some alternative course of action to achieve that goal, and this is precisely the practical use of plans with goal deletions as triggering events.

It is important to observe that omitting possible goal deletion plans for existing goal additions implicitly denotes that such goal should never be backtracked, i.e., no alternative plan for it should be attempted in case one fails. To specify that backtracking should always be attempted (e.g., until special internal actions in the plan explicitly cause the intention to be dropped), all the programmer has to do is to specify a goal deletion plan (for a given goal g addition) with empty context and the same goal in the body, as in "$-!g$: true $\leftarrow$ $!g$.".

When a failure happens, the whole intention is dropped if the triggering event of the plan being executed was neither an achievement nor a test goal *addition*: only these can

---

[1] The notation $-!g$, i.e., "goal deletion" also makes sense for such plan failure mechanism; if a plan fails there is a possibility that the agent may need to drop the goal altogether, so it is to handle such event (of the possible need to drop a goal) that plans of the form '$-!g$: ...' are written.

be attempted to recover from failure using the goal deletion construct[2]. In cases other than goal aditions, a failed plan means that the whole intention cannot be achieved. If a plan for a goal addition $(+\,!\,g)$ fails, the intention i where that plan appears is suspended, and the respective goal deletion event $(\langle -\,!g, i\rangle)$ is included in the set of events. Eventually, this might lead to the goal addition being attempted again as part of the plan to handle the $-\,!\,g$ event. When the plan for $-\,!\,g$ finishes not only itself but also the failed $+\,!\,g$ plan below it[3] are removed from the intention. As it will be clear later, it is a programmer's decision to attempt the goal again or not, or even to drop the whole intention (possibly with special internal action constructs, whose informal semantics is given below), depending on the circumstances. What happens when a plan fails is shown in Figure 1.

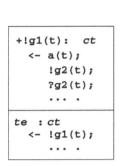

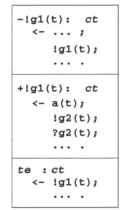

(a) An Intention before Plan Failure

(b) That Intention after Plan Failure

Fig. 1. Plan Failure

In the circumstance described in Figure 1(a) above, suppose $a(t)$ fails, or otherwise after that action succeeds an event for $+!g2(t)$ was created but there was no applicable plan to handle the event, or $?g2(t)$ is not is the belief base, nor there are applicable plans to handle a $+?g2(t)$ event. In any of those cases, the intention is suspended and an event for $-!g1(t)$ is generated. Assuming the programmer included a plan for $-!g1(t)$, and the plan is applicable at the time the event is selected, the intention will eventually look as in Figure 1(b). Otherwise the original goal addition event is reposted or the whole intention dropped, depending on a setting of the **Jason** interpreter that is configurable by programmers. (See [1] for an overview of how various BDI systems deal with the problem of there being no applicable plans.)

The reason why not providing goal deletion plans in case a goal is not to be backtracked works is because an event (with the whole suspended intention within it) is discarded in case there are no relevant plans for a generated goal deletion. In general, the lack of relevant plans for an event indicates that the perceived event is not significant for the agent in question, so they are simply ignored. An alternative approach for handling the lack of relevant plans is described in [2], where it is assumed that in some cases, explicitly specified by the programmer, the agent will want to ask other agents how to

---

[2] Note it is inappropriate to have a goal deletion event posted for a failure in a goal deletion plan, as this could easily cause a loop in an intention.

[3] The failed plan is left in the intention, for example, so that programmers could check which plan failed (e.g., by means of **Jason** internal actions).

handle such events. The mechanism for plan exchange between AgentSpeak agents presented in [2] allows the programmer to specify which triggering events should generate attempts to retrieve external plans, which plans an agent agrees to share with others, what to do once the plan has been used for handling that particular event instance, and so on.

In the next section, besides the plan failure handling mechanism, we also make use of a particular *standard* internal action. Standard internal actions, as opposed to user-defined internal actions, are those available with the *Jason* distribution; they are denoted by an action name starting with symbol '.'. Some of these pre-defined internal actions manipulate the implementation of the structures used in giving semantics to the AgentSpeak interpreter. For that reason, they need to be precisely defined. As the focus here is on the use of patterns for defining declarative goals, we will give only informal semantics to the internal action that will be used in the patterns given in the next section.

The particular internal action used in this paper is `.dropGoal`, which has two variants. The first is `.dropGoal(g,true)`, which is used when the agent realises the goal has already been achieved so whatever plan was being executed to achieve that goal does not need to be executed any longer. The second is `.dropGoal(g,false)`, which is used when the agent realises that the goal has become impossible to achieve, therefore the plan that required g being achieved as one of its subgoals has to fail. More specifically, when `.dropGoal(g,true)` is executed, any intention that has the goal g in the triggering event of any of its plans will be changed as follows. The plan with triggering event $+!g$ is removed and the plan below that in the stack of plans forming that intention carries on being executed at the point after goal g appeared. Goal g, as it appears in the `.dropGoal` internal action, is used to further instantiate the plan where the goal that was terminated early appears. With `.dropGoal(g,false)`, the plan for $+!g$ is also removed, but an event for the deletion of the goal whose plan body required g is generated instead: as there is no way of achieving g, the plan requiring g to be achieved has failed.

It is perhaps easier to understand how these actions work with reference to Figure 2. The figure shows the consequence of each of these internal actions being executed (the plan where the internal action appeared is not shown; it is likely to be within another intention). Note that the state of the intention, as shown in the figure, is not the immediate state resulting from the execution of one of these internal actions (i.e., not the state at the end of the reasoning cycle where the internal action was executed) but the most significant next state of the changed intention.

4   Declarative Goal Patterns

Although goals form a central component of the AgentSpeak conceptual framework, it is important to note that the language itself does not provide any explicit constructs for handling goals with complex temporal structure. For example, a system designer and programmer will often think in terms of goals such as "maintain P until Q becomes true", or "prevent P from becoming true". Creating AgentSpeak code to realise such complex goals has, to date, been largely an *ad hoc* process, dependent upon the experience of the programmer. Our aim in this section is firstly to define a number of

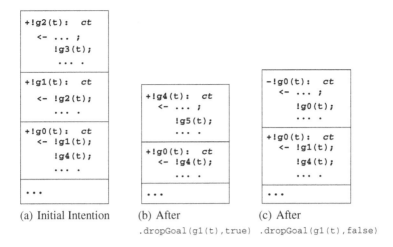

(a) Initial Intention   (b) After   (c) After
                     `.dropGoal(g1(t),true)`   `.dropGoal(g1(t),false)`

Fig. 2. Standard Internal Actions for Dropping Goals

declarative goal structures, and secondly to show how these can be realised in terms of *patterns* of AgentSpeak plans — that is, complex combinations of plan structures which are often useful in actual scenarios. As we shall see, such patterns can be used to implement, in a systematic way, not only complex types of declarative goals, but also the types of agent commitments that they can represent, as discussed for example by Cohen and Levesque [8].

As an initial motivational example for declarative goals, consider a robot agent with the goal of being at some location (represented by the predicate $l(X,Y)$) and the following plan to achieve this goal:

```
+!l(X,Y) : bc(B) & B > 0.2 ← go(X,Y).
```

where the predicate `bc/1` stands for "battery charge", and `go` identifies an action that the robot is able to perform in the environment.

At times, using an AgentSpeak plan as a procedure can be quite useful as a programming practice. Thus, in a way, it is important that the AgentSpeak interpreter does not enforce any declarative semantics to its only (syntactically defined) goal construct. However, in the plan above, $l(X,Y)$ is clearly meant as a declarative goal; that is, the programmer expects the robot to believe $l(X,Y)$ (by perceiving the environment) if the plan executes to completion. If it fails because, say, the environment is dynamic, the goal cannot be considered achieved and, normally, should be attempted again.

This type of situation is commonplace in multi-agent system, and this is why it is important to be able to define declarative goals in agent-oriented programming. However, in regards to AgentSpeak, this can be done without the need to change the language and/or its semantics. As similarly pointed out by van Riemsdijk *et al.* [19], we can easily transform the above procedural goal into a declarative goal by adding a corresponding *test goal* at the end of the plan's body, as follows:

```
+!l(X,Y) : bc(B) & B > 0.2 ← go(X,Y); ?l(X,Y).
```

This plan only succeeds if the goal is actually (believed to be) achieved; if the given (procedural) plan executes to completion (i.e., without failing) but the goal happens not to be achieved, the test goal at the end will fail. In this way, we have taken a simple *procedural* goal and transformed it into a *declarative* goal – the goal to achieve some state of affairs. We will see later that the plan failure mechanism in **Jason** can be used to for the various attitudes that agents can have due to a declarative goal not being achieved (e.g., because the test goal at the end of the plan failed).

The solution for defining simple declarative goals as given above forms a plan pattern, which can be applied to solve other similar problems that, as we mention above, are commonplace in agent programming. Our approach to include declarative goals in AgentSpeak programming is inspired by the successful adoption of design patterns in object oriented design [13]. To represent such patterns for AgentSpeak, we shall make use of skeleton programs with meta variables. For example, the general form of an AgentSpeak plan for a simple declarative goal, as the one used in the robot's location goal above, is as follows:

$$+!g: \ c \leftarrow p; \ ?g.$$

Here, g is a meta variable that represents the declarative goal, c is a meta variable that represents the context expression stating in which circumstances the plan is applicable, and p represents the procedural part of the plan body (i.e., a course of action to achieve g). Note that, with the introduction of the final test goal, this plan to achieve g finishes successfully only if the agent believes g after the execution of plan body p.

To simplify the use of the patterns, we also define pattern rules which rewrite a set of AgentSpeak plans into a new set of AgentSpeak plans according to a given pattern.[4] The following pattern rule, called **DG** (Declarative Goal), is used to transform procedural goals into declarative goals. The pattern rule name is followed by the parameters which need to be provided by the programmer, besides the actual code (i.e., a set of plans) on which the pattern will be applied.

$$+!g: \ c_1 \ \leftarrow \ p_1.$$
$$+!g: \ c_2 \ \leftarrow \ p_2.$$
$$\ldots$$
$$+!g: \ c_n \ \leftarrow \ p_n.$$

$$\rule{6cm}{0.4pt} \ \mathbf{DG}_g \ \ (n \geq 1)$$

$$+!g: \ g \ \leftarrow \ \texttt{true}.$$
$$+!g: \ c_1 \ \leftarrow \ p_1; \ ?g.$$
$$+!g: \ c_2 \ \leftarrow \ p_2; \ ?g.$$
$$\ldots$$
$$+!g: \ c_n \ \leftarrow \ p_n; \ ?g.$$
$$+g: \ \texttt{true} \ \leftarrow \ \texttt{.dropGoal}(g, \ \texttt{true}).$$

Essentially, this rule adds $?g$ at the end of each plan in the given set of plans which has $+!g$ as trigger event, and creates two extra plans (the first and the last plans above). The

---

[4] Note that some of the patterns presented in this paper require the atomic execution of certain plans, but we avoid including this in the patterns for clarity of presentation; this feature is available in **Jason** through a simple plan annotation.

first plan checks whether the goal g has already been achieved — in such case, there is nothing else to do. That last plan is triggered when the agent perceives that g has been achieved while it is executing any of the courses of action p_i ($1 \leq i \leq n$) which aim at achieving g; in this circumstance, the plan being executed in order to achieve g can be immediately terminated. The internal action `.dropGoal(g, true)` terminates such plan with success (as explained in Section 3).

In this pattern, when one of the plans to achieve g fails, the agent gives up achieving the goal altogether. However it could be the case that for such goal, the agent should try another plan to achieve it, as in the "backtracking" plan selection mechanism available in platforms such as JACK [21,14] and 3APL [10,9]. In those mechanisms, usually only when all available plans have been tried in turn and failed is the goal abandoned with failure, or left to be attempted again later on. The following rule, called **BDG** (Backtracking Declarative Goal), defines this pattern based on a set of conventional AgentSpeak plans $\mathcal{P}$ transformed by the **DG** pattern (each plan in $\mathcal{P}$ is of the form $+!g: c \leftarrow p$):

$$\frac{\mathcal{P}}{\begin{array}{l} \mathbf{DG}_g\,(\mathcal{P}) \\ \texttt{-!g: true} \leftarrow \texttt{!g.} \end{array}} \ \mathbf{BDG}_g$$

The last plan of the pattern catches a failure event, caused when a plan from $\mathcal{P}$ fails, and then tries to achieve that same goal g again. Notice that it is possible that the same plan is selected and fails again, causing a loop if the plan contexts have not been carefully programmed. Therefore, the programmer would need to specify the plan contexts in such a way that a plan is only applicable if it has a chance of succeeding regardless of it having been tried already (recently).

Instead of worrying about defining contexts in such complex way, in some cases it may be useful for the programmer to apply the following pattern, called **EBDG** (Exclusive BDG), which ensures that none of the given plans will be attempted twice before the goal is achieved:

$$\frac{\begin{array}{l} \texttt{+!g: } c_1 \ \leftarrow \ b_1. \\ \texttt{+!g: } c_2 \ \leftarrow \ b_2. \\ \cdots \\ \texttt{+!g: } c_n \ \leftarrow \ b_n. \end{array}}{\begin{array}{l} \texttt{+!g: } g \ \leftarrow \ \texttt{true.} \\ \texttt{+!g: not p1(g) \& } c_1 \ \leftarrow \ \texttt{+p1(g); } b_1. \\ \texttt{+!g: not p2(g) \& } c_2 \ \leftarrow \ \texttt{+p2(g); } b_2. \\ \cdots \\ \texttt{+!g: not pn(g) \& } c_n \ \leftarrow \ \texttt{+pn(g); } b_n. \\ \texttt{-!g: true} \ \leftarrow \ \texttt{!g.} \\ \texttt{+g: true} \ \leftarrow \ \texttt{-p1(g); -p2(g); } \cdots \ \texttt{.dropGoal(g, true).} \end{array}} \ \mathbf{EBDG}_g$$

In this pattern, each plan, when selected for execution, initially adds a belief $\texttt{p}i\,(\texttt{g})$; the goal g is used as an argument to p so as to avoid interference between various instances of the pattern for different goals. The belief is used as part of the plan contexts (note the use of `not pi` in the contexts of the plans in the pattern above) to state that the plan should not be applicable in a second attempt (of that same plan within a single adoption of goal g for that agent).

In the pattern above, despite the various alternative plans, the agent can still end up dropping the intention with the goal g unachieved, if all those plans become non-applicable. Conversely, in a *blind commitment goal* the agent can drop the goal only when it is achieved. This type of commitment towards the achievement of a declarative goal can thus be understood as *fanatical commitment* [18]. The $\mathbf{BCG}_{g,F}$ pattern below defines this type of commitment:

$$\frac{\mathcal{P}}{\begin{array}{l} \mathbf{F}(\mathcal{P}) \\ \texttt{+!}g\texttt{: true} \leftarrow \texttt{ !}g\texttt{.} \end{array}} \mathbf{BCG}_{g,F}$$

This pattern is based on another pattern rule, represented by the variable $\mathbf{F}$; $\mathbf{F}$ is often $\mathbf{BDG}$, although the programmer can chose any other pattern (e.g., $\mathbf{EBDG}$ if a plan should not be attempted twice). Finally, the last plan makes the agent attempt to achieve the goal even in case there is no applicable plan. It is assumed that the selection of plans is based on the order that the plans appear in the program and all events have equal chance of being chosen as the event to be handled in a reasoning cycle.

For most applications, $\mathbf{BCG}$-style fanatical commitment is too strong. For example, if a robot has the goal to be at some location, it is reasonable that it can drop this goal in case its battery charge is getting very low; in other words, the agent has realised that it has become impossible to achieve the goal, so it is useless to keep attempting it. This is very similar to the idea of a persistent goal in the work of Cohen and Levesque: a persistent goal is a goal that is maintained as long as it is believed not achieved, but still believed possible [8]. In [22] and [7], the "impossibility" condition is called "drop condition". The drop condition f (e.g., "low battery charge") is used in the Single-Minded Commitment ($\mathbf{SMC}$) pattern to allow the agent to drop a goal if it becomes impossible:

$$\frac{\mathcal{P}}{\begin{array}{l} \mathbf{BCG}_{g,BDG}(\mathcal{P}) \\ \texttt{+}f\texttt{: true} \leftarrow \texttt{ .dropGoal(}g\texttt{, false).} \end{array}} \mathbf{SMC}_{g,f}$$

This pattern extends the $\mathbf{BCG}$ pattern adding the drop condition represented by the literal f in the last plan. If the agent comes to believe f, it can drop goal g, signalling failure (refer to the semantics of the internal action `.dropGoal` in section 3). This effectively means that the plan in the intention where g appeared, which depended on g being achieved to then carry on the plan execution, must itself fail (as g is now impossible to achieve). However, there might be an alternative for that plan which does not depend on g, so that plan's failure handling may take care of such situation.

As we have a failure drop condition for a goal, we can also have a success drop condition, e.g., because the motivation to achieve the goal has ceased to exist. Suppose a robot has the goal of going to the fridge because its owner has asked it to fetch a beer from there; then, if the robot realises that its owner does not want a beer anymore, it should drop the goal [8]. The belief "my owner wants a beer" is the *motivation* m for the goal. The following pattern, called Relativised Commitment Goal (**RCG**) defines a goal that is relative to a motivation condition: the goal can be dropped with success if the agent no longer has the motivation for it.

$$\frac{\mathcal{P}}{\begin{array}{l}\mathbf{BCG}_{g,BDG}(\mathcal{P})\\ -m:\ \mathtt{true}\ \leftarrow\ \mathtt{.dropGoal(}g\mathtt{,\ true).}\end{array}}\ \mathbf{RCG}_{g,m}$$

Note that, in the particular combination of **RCG** and **BCG** above, if the attempt to achieve g ever terminates, it will always terminate with success, since the goal will be dropped only if either the agent believes it has been achieved achieved (by **BCG**) or m is removed from belief base.

Of course we can combine the last two patterns above to create a goal which can be dropped if it has been achieved, has become impossible to achieve, or the motivation to achieve it no longer exists, representing what is called an "open-minded commitment". The Open-Minded Commitment pattern (**OMC**) defines this type of goal:

$$\frac{\mathcal{P}}{\begin{array}{l}\mathbf{BCG}_{g,BDG}(\mathcal{P})\\ +f:\ \mathtt{true}\ \leftarrow\ \mathtt{.dropGoal(}g\mathtt{,\ false).}\\ -m:\ \mathtt{true}\ \leftarrow\ \mathtt{.dropGoal(}g\mathtt{,\ true).}\end{array}}\ \mathbf{OMC}_{g,f,m}$$

For example, an impossibility condition could be "no beer at location (X,Y)" (denoted below by $\neg\,\mathtt{b(X,Y)}$), and the motivation condition could be "my owner wants a beer" (denoted below by wb). Consider the plan below as representing the single known course of action to achieve goal $\mathtt{l(X,Y)}$:

```
+!l(X,Y): bc(B) & B > 0.2 ← go(X,Y).
```

When the pattern $\mathbf{OMC}_{l(X,Y),\neg b(X,Y),wb}$ is applied to the initial plan above, we get the following set of plans:

```
+!l(X,Y): l(X,Y) ← true.
+!l(X,Y): bc(B) & B > 0.2 ← go(X,Y); ?l(X,Y).
+!l(X,Y): true ← !l(X,Y).
-!l(X,Y): true ← !l(X,Y).
+¬b(X,Y): true ← .dropGoal(l(X,Y), false).
-wb: true ← .dropGoal(l(X,Y), true).
```

Another important type of goal in agent-based systems are *maintenance goals*, whereby an agent needs to ensure that the state of the world will always be such that g holds. Such agent will need plans to act on the events that indicate the maintenance goal may fail in the future. In realistic environments, however, agents will likely fail in preventing the maintenance goal from ever failing. Whenever the agent realises that g is no longer in its belief base (i.e., believed to be true), it will certainly attempt to bring about g again by having the respective (declarative) achievement goal. The pattern rule that defines a Maintenance Goal (**MG**), but particularly in the sense of realising the failure in a goal maintenance, is as follows:

$$\frac{\mathcal{P}}{\begin{array}{l} g. \\ -g: \ \texttt{true} \ \leftarrow \ !g. \\ \mathbf{F}(\mathcal{P}) \end{array}} \quad \mathbf{MG}_{g,F}$$

The first line of the pattern states that, initially (when the agent starts running) it will assume that g is true. (As soon as the interpreter obtains perception of the environment for the first time, the agent might already realise that such assumption was wrong.) The first plan is triggered when g is removed from the belief base, e.g. because g has not been perceived in the environment in a given reasoning cycle, and thus the maintenance goal g is no longer achieved. This plan then creates a declarative goal to achieve g. The type of commitment to achieving g if it happens not to be true is defined by $\mathbf{F}$, which would normally be **BCG** given that the goal should not be dropped in any circumstances unless it is has been achieved again. (Realistically, plans for the agent to attempt pro-actively to prevent this from ever happening would also be required, but the pattern is useful to make sure the agent will act appropriately in case things go wrong.)

We now show another useful pattern, called Sequenced Goal Adoption (**SGA**). This pattern should be used when various instances of a goal should not be adopted concur-rently (e.g., a robot should not try to clean two different places at the same time, even if it has perceived dirt in both places, which will lead to the adoption of goals to clean both places). To solve this problem, the **SGA** pattern adopts the first occurrence of the goal and records the remaining occurrences as pending goals by adding them as special beliefs. When one such goal occurrence is achieved, if any other occurrence is pending, it gets activated.

$$\frac{}{\begin{array}{l} t: \ \texttt{not fl(\_) \& } c \ \leftarrow \ !fg(g). \\ t: \ \texttt{fl(\_) \& } c \ \leftarrow \ +fl(g). \\ +!fg(g): \ \texttt{true} \ \leftarrow \ +fl(g); \ !g; \ -fl(g). \\ -!fg(g): \ \texttt{true} \ \leftarrow \ -fl(g). \\ -fl(\_): \ fl(g) \ \leftarrow \ !fg(g). \end{array}} \quad \mathbf{SGA}_{t,c,g}$$

In this pattern, t is the trigger leading to the adoption of a goal g; c is the context for the goal adoption; $\texttt{fl}(g)$ is the flag to control whether an instance of goal g is already active; and $\texttt{fg}(g)$ is a procedural goal that guarantees that $\texttt{fl}$ will be added to the belief base to record the fact that some occurrence of the goal has already been adopted, then adopts the goal $!g$, as well as it guarantees that $\texttt{fl}$ will be eventually removed whether $!g$ succeeds or not. The first plan is selected when g is not being pursued; it simply calls the $\texttt{fg}$ goal. The second plan is used if some other instance of that goal has already been adopted. All it does is to remember that this goal g was not immediately adopted by adding `f1 (g)` to the belief base. The last plan makes sure that whenever a goal adoption instance is finished (denoted by the removal of a `f1` belief), if there are any pending goal instances to be adopted, they will be activated through the `fg` call.

5 Using Patterns in *Jason*

Jason is an interpreter for an extended version of AgentSpeak and is available *Open Source* under GNU LGPL at `http://jason.sourceforge.net` [4]. It implements the operational semantics of AgentSpeak which first appeared in [6]. It also implements the plan failure mechanism and the pre-defined internal action[5] used in the patterns described in Section 4. Since these features are enough for programming declarative goals, *Jason* already supports this. However, it would be clearly not acceptable if the programmer had to apply the patterns by hand.

To simplify the programming of sophisticated goals by the use of patterns, we extended the language interpreted by *Jason* to include pre-processing directives. The syntax for pattern directives is:

```
directive ::=
  "{" "begin" <pattern-name>"("<parameters>")" "}"
     <agent-speak-program>
  "{" "end" "}"
```

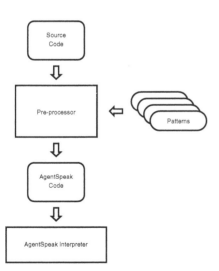

Fig. 3. *Jason* Pre-Processing and Patterns

We have implemented a pre-processor for *Jason* which also handles patterns as illustrated in Figure 3. Each pattern is implemented in a Java class that receives an AgentSpeak program and returns another program, transformed as defined by the respective pattern. This implementation allows us, and even users, to make new patterns available in a straightforward manner. One simply has to create a new Java class for the new pattern and register this class with the pre-processor[6].

In the remainder of this section, we will illustrate how the *Jason* pre-processing directives for the use of patterns can be used to program a cleaning robot for the scenario described in [7] (where the robot was implemented using

---

[5] The internal action used here is not yet available in the latest public release of *Jason*, but will be available in the next release.

[6] Note that this too will only be available in the next release of *Jason*.

Jadex [15,16]). The first goal of the robot is to maintain its battery charged: this is clearly a maintenance goal (**MG**). The agent should pursue this goal when its battery level goes below 20% and should remain pursuing it until the battery is completely charged. In the program below, based on the perception of the battery level, the belief battery_charged, which indicates that the goal is satisfied, is either removed or added to the belief base, signalling whether the corresponding achievement goal must be activated or not.

```
+battery_level(B): B < 0.2 ← -battery_charged.
+battery_level(B): B = 1.0 ← +battery_charged.

{ begin mg("battery_charged", bcg("battery_charged")) }
   +!battery_charged : not l(power_supply)
           go(power_supply).
   +!battery_charged: l(power_supply) ← plug_in.
{ end }
```

The first plan of the pattern for the battery_charged goal moves the agent to the place where there is a power supply, if it is not already there (according to its l(power_supply) belief). Otherwise, the second plan will plug the robot to the power supply. The plug_in action will charge the battery and thus change the robot's state that is perceived back through battery_level(B) percepts (which generate +battery_level(B) events).

The second goal the robot might adopt is to patrol the museum at night. This goal is therefore activated when the agent perceives sunset (represented by the event +night). Whenever activated, the goal can be dropped only if the agent perceives dawn (represented by the event -night). The following program defines patrol as this kind of goal using a **RCG** pattern with night as the motivation:

```
+night: true ← !patrol.

{ begin rcg("patrol", "night") }
   +!patrol: battery_charged ← wander.
{ end }
```

The agent will never have the belief patrol in its belief base, since no plan or perception of the environment will add this particular belief. The goal is, in some sense, deliberately unachievable, while RCG maintains the agent committed to the goal nevertheless. However, it is considered as achieved (finished with success) when the motivation condition is removed from the belief base. Note that the context for the !patrol plan is that the battery is charged, therefore while the maintenance goal battery_charged is active, the robot does not wander, but it resumes wandering as soon the battery becomes charged again. We are thus using this belief to create an *interference* between goals (i.e., charging the battery precludes patrolling).

The last goal the robot might adopt is to clean the museum during the day whenever it perceives waste around. Since the robot can perceive various different pieces of waste around, it would accordingly generate several concurrent instances of this goal. However these goals are mutually exclusive: they cannot be achieved simultaneously; trying to go in two different directions must be avoided, and expressing this at the declarative level avoids too much work on implementing application-specific intention selection functions (which are part of AgentSpeak interpreters). This is indeed another kind of interference between different goals. The **SGA** pattern is used in the program below to ensure that only one `clean` goal instance is being attempted at one moment in time. The event that triggers this goal is +waste(X,Y) (some waste being perceived at location ⟨X,Y⟩), and the context is not night:

```
{ begin sga("+waste(X,Y)", "not night", "clean(X,Y)")}
{ end }

{ begin omc("clean(X,Y)", "night", "waste(X,Y)")}
   +!clean(X,Y): l(X,Y) ← pick; go(bin); drop.
   +!clean(X,Y): not l(X,Y) ← go(X,Y).
{ end }
+battery_charged: true ← .suspend(clean(X,Y)).
-battery_charged: true ← .resume(clean(X,Y)).
```

In the program above, an open-minded commitment pattern (**OMC**) is used to create the clean(X,Y) goal with night as the failure condition (at sunset, the goal should be abandoned with failure) and waste(X,Y) as the motivation (if the agent cames to believe that there is no longer waste at that location, the goal can be dropped with success). The last two plans are used to suspend and resume the goal when the battery_charge goal is active. Of course we could add battery_charge in the context of the plans (as we did in the patrol goal); however, using the .suspend internal action is more efficient because the goal becomes actually suspended (until resumed with the respective .resume internal action) rather than being continuously attempted without any applicable plans.

6   Conclusions

In this paper we have shown that sophisticated types of goals discussed in the agents literature can be implemented in the AgentSpeak language with the extensions already available in *Jason*. In fact, this is done by combining AgentSpeak plans, forming certain patterns, for each type of goal and commitment towards goals that agents may have. Therefore, our approach is to take advantage of the simplicity and well-defined semantics of the AgentSpeak language, using only its well-known support for procedural goals plus the idea of "plan patterns" to support the use of declarative goals with complex temporal structures in AgentSpeak programming.

Besides the use of internal actions such as `.dropGoal` (that are available in *Jason* for general use, independently of this proposal for declarative goals), our proposal does not require either: (*i*) syntactical or semantical changes in the language (as done, for example, in [22,7]); nor (*ii*) the definition of a goal base (cf. [19]) which is also usual in other approaches. Van Riemsdijk *et at.* [20] also pointed out that declarative goals can be built based on the procedural goals available in 3APL, by simply checking if the corresponding belief is true at the end of the plan execution. What they proposed in that paper corresponds to our **BDG** pattern. In this work, we further define various other types of declarative goals, represented them as *patterns* of AgentSpeak programs, and we also presented an implementation in *Jason* (using a pre-processor) that facilitates this approach for declarative goals. Another advantage of our approach is that, as complex types of goals are mapped to plain AgentSpeak using pre-processing patterns, programmers can easily change existing patterns to fit their specific requirements, or indeed create new patterns if necessary.

In future work we intend to formalise our approach based on the existing operational semantics and to verify some properties of the programs generated by the patterns, including a comparison with approaches that use a goal base to introduce declarative goals. An example of an issue that might be of particular interest in such comparison is how the use of plan patters will affect other aspects of agent-based development such as debugging. In the future, we also plan to support conjunctive goals such as $p \wedge q$ (where both p and q should be satisfied at the same time, as done in [19]), possibly through the use of plan patterns as well. Furthermore, we plan to investigate other patterns that may useful in the practical development of large-scale multi-agent systems.

Acknowledgements

Many thanks to A.C. Rocha Costa for discussions on maintenance goals in AgentSpeak. Anonymous reviewers for this paper have made detailed comments which helped improve the paper. Rafael Bordini gratefully acknowledges the support of The Nuffield Foundation (grant number NAL/01065/G).

References

1. D. Ancona and V. Mascardi. Coo-BDI: Extending the BDI model with cooperativity. In J. Leite, A. Omicini, L. Sterling, and P. Torroni, editors, *Declarative Agent Languages and Technologies, Proc. of the First Int. Workshop (DALT-03), held with AAMAS-03, 15 July, 2003, Melbourne, Australia*, number 2990 in LNAI, pages 109–134, Berlin, 2004. Springer-Verlag.
2. D. Ancona, V. Mascardi, J. F. Hübner, and R. H. Bordini. Coo-AgentSpeak: Cooperation in AgentSpeak through plan exchange. In N. R. Jennings, C. Sierra, L. Sonenberg, and M. Tambe, editors, *Proc. of the Third Int. Joint Conference on Autonomous Agents and Multi-Agent Systems (AAMAS-2004), New York, NY, 19–23 July*, pages 698–705, New York, NY, 2004. ACM Press.
3. R. H. Bordini, M. Dastani, J. Dix, and A. El Fallah Seghrouchni, editors. *Multi-Agent Programming: Languages, Platforms, and Applications.* Number 15 in Multiagent Systems, Artificial Societies, and Simulated Organizations. Springer, 2005.

4. R. H. Bordini, J. F. Hübner, et al. *Jason: A Java-based AgentSpeak interpreter used with saci for multi-agent distribution over the net*, manual, release version 0.7 edition, Aug. 2005. `http://jason.sourceforge.net/`.
5. R. H. Bordini, J. F. Hübner, and R. Vieira. *Jason* and the Golden Fleece of agent-oriented programming. In Bordini et al. [3], chapter 1.
6. R. H. Bordini and Á. F. Moreira. Proving BDI properties of agent-oriented programming languages: The asymmetry thesis principles in AgentSpeak(L). *Annals of Mathematics and Artificial Intelligence*, 42(1–3):197–226, Sept. 2004. Special Issue on Computational Logic in Multi-Agent Systems.
7. L. Braubach, A. Pokahr, W. Lamersdorf, and D. Moldt. Goal representation for BDI agent systems. In R. H. Bordini, M. Dastani, J. Dix, and A. E. Fallah-Seghrouchni, editors, *Second Int. Workshop on Programming Multiagent Systems: Languages and Tools (ProMAS 2004)*, pages 9–20, 2004.
8. P. R. Cohen and H. J. Levesque. Intention is choice with commitment. *Artificial Intelligence*, 42(3):213–261, 1990.
9. M. Dastani, B. van Riemsdijk, F. Dignum, and J. Meyer. A programming language for cognitive agents: Goal directed 3APL. In *Proc. of the First Workshop on Programming Multiagent Systems: Languages, frameworks, techniques, and tools (ProMAS03)*, volume 3067 of *LNAI*, pages 111–130, Berlin, 2004. Springer.
10. M. Dastani, M. B. van Riemsdijk, and J.-J. C. Meyer. Programming multi-agent systems in 3APL. In Bordini et al. [3], chapter 2.
11. M. d'Inverno, D. Kinny, M. Luck, and M. Wooldridge. A formal specification of dMARS. In M. P. Singh, A. S. Rao, and M. Wooldridge, editors, *Intelligent Agents IV—Proceedings of the Fourth International Workshop on Agent Theories, Architectures, and Languages (ATAL-97), Providence, RI, 24–26 July, 1997*, number 1365 in LNAI, pages 155–176. Springer-Verlag, Berlin, 1998.
12. M. d'Inverno and M. Luck. Engineering AgentSpeak(L): A formal computational model. *Journal of Logic and Computation*, 8(3):1–27, 1998.
13. E. Gamma, R. Helm, R. Johnson, and J. Vlissides. *Design Patterns: Elements of Reusable Object-Oriented Software*. Addison-Wesley, 1995.
14. N. Howden, R. Rönnquist, A. Hodgson, and A. Lucas. JACK intelligent agents™ — summary of an agent infrastructure. In *Proceedings of Second International Workshop on Infrastructure for Agents, MAS, and Scalable MAS, held with the Fifth International Conference on Autonomous Agents (Agents 2001), 28 May – 1 June, Montreal, Canada*, 2001.
15. A. Pokahr, L. Braubach, and W. Lamersdorf. Jadex: A BDI reasoning engine. In Bordini et al. [3], chapter 6.
16. A. Pokahr, L. Braubach, and W. Lamersdorf. Jadex: A BDI reasoning engine. In Bordini et al. [3], chapter 6, pages 149–174.
17. A. S. Rao. AgentSpeak(L): BDI agents speak out in a logical computable language. In W. Van de Velde and J. Perram, editors, *Proc. of the Seventh Workshop on Modelling Autonomous Agents in a Multi-Agent World (MAAMAW'96), 22–25 January, Eindhoven, The Netherlands*, number 1038 in LNAI, pages 42–55, London, 1996. Springer-Verlag.
18. A. S. Rao and M. P. Georgeff. Modeling rational agents within a BDI-architecture. In J. Allen, R. Fikes, and E. Sandewall, editors, *Proceedings of the 2nd International Conference on Principles of Knowledge Representation and Reasoning (KR'91)*, pages 473–484. Morgan Kaufmann publishers Inc.: San Mateo, CA, USA, 1991.
19. B. van Riemsdijk, M. Dastani, and J.-J. C. Meyer. Semantics of declarative goals in agent programming. In F. Dignum, V. Dignum, S. Koenig, S. Kraus, M. P. Singh, and M. Wooldridge, editors, *Proceedings of the 4rd International Joint Conference on Autonomous Agents and Multiagent Systems (AAMAS 2005)*, pages 133–140. ACM, 2005.

20. M. B. van Riemsdijk, M. Dastani, and J.-J. C. Meyer. Subgoal semantics in agent programming. In C. Bento, A. Cardoso, and G. Dias, editors, *Proceedings of the 12th Portuguese Conference on Artificial Intelligence, EPIA 2005, Covilhã, Portugal, December 5-8, 2005*, volume 3808 of *LNCS*, pages 548–559, 2005.
21. M. Winikoff. JACK^{TM} intelligent agents: An industrial strength platform. In Bordini et al. [3], chapter 7, pages 175–193.
22. M. Winikoff, L. Padgham, J. Harland, and J. Thangarajah. Declarative and procedural goals in intelligent agent systems. In *Proceedings of the Eighth International Conference on Principles of Knowledge Representation and Reasoning*, 2002.

JADL – An Agent Description Language for Smart Agents

Thomas Konnerth, Benjamin Hirsch, and Sahin Albayrak

DAI Labor
Technische Universität Berlin
{Thomas.Konnerth,Benjamin.Hirsch,Sahin.Albayrak}@dai-labor.de

Abstract. In this paper, we describe the declarative agent programming language Jadl (JIAC Agent Description Language). Based on three-valued logic, it incorporates ontologies, FIPA-based speech acts, a (procedural) scripting part for (complex) actions, and allows to define protocols and service based communication. Rather than relying on a library of plans, the framework implementing Jadl allows agents to plan from first principles. We also describe the framework and some applications that have been implemented.

1 Introduction

The growth of interconnected devices, as well as the digitisation of content, has led to ever more complex applications running on ever more diverse devices. In recent years, the concept of service has become an important tool in coping with this development. Broadly speaking, services allow loosely coupled software entities to interact. Rather than providing a fixed and rigid set of interfaces, services provide means to adapt software to the ever faster changing environment of businesses. However, while the growing number of devices and networks poses a challenge to software engineering, it also opens the door to new application areas and offers possibilities to provide services on a new level of integration, context awareness, and interaction with the user.

In order to leverage the current and developing network and device technologies, a programming paradigm is needed that embraces distributed computing, open and dynamic environments, and autonomous behaviour.

Agent technology is such a paradigm. While there are many different areas and theories within the agent community, most work to make true the idea of an open, distributed, dynamic, and intelligent framework.

Without wanting to go into all the diverse subjects that research into agents encompasses, we want to point out some of the more prominent concepts and ideas here. On the level of single agents, BDI [1] has arguably been one of the most influential ideas. By assigning high level mentalistic notions to agents a new level of abstraction has been reached which allows to program agents in terms of goals rather than means. Agents contain not only functionality, but also the ability to plan (or alternatively a plan library) in order to achieve set goals. On

M. Baldoni and U. Endriss (Eds.): DALT 2006, LNAI 4327, pp. 141–155, 2006.

the other hand, reactive behaviour is often desirable within agents, and should be supported in some way.

Research into interaction between agents is another important field. Here, agent communication languages attach semantic information about the "state of mind" of the sending agent [2]. Also, in order to enable interaction between agents, they need to understand each other. Ontologies allow agents to use a shared vocabulary, and to de-couple syntax and interpretation.

Agent-based technologies provide one possible and much sought-after approach to containing the complexity of today's soft- and hardware environment. However, while agents have been the subject of research for more than a decade, there are hardly any applications in the industry. There are differing views as to the reason for the slow uptake. Some blame a lack of "killer applications", or the general disconnect between research community and industry players. Others say that there is no problem at all, because industry uptake only happens at a certain maturity level has been reached [3]. Another reason that agent technologies have not been so successful is the lack of dedicated programming languages that allow the programmer to map agent concepts directly onto language constructs, and frameworks that cater for the needs of enterprise applications, such as security and accounting.

In this paper, we present the agent programming language Jadl (JIAC Agent Description Language). The thrust of the paper is to give a rather broad overview over the language — a planned series of papers will go into the different areas and cover them in greater detail.

The structure of this paper is as follows. After a broad overview over the different elements of Jadl (Section 2), we will describe its different features in some detail. In particular, we highlight knowledge representation in Section 3, followed by Section 4 with some words about programming the agents using reactive and planning elements. Section 5 finalises this part with a discussion on high-level communication. After introducing the framework that implements Jadl in Section 6, we proceed by presenting some of the projects that have been implemented using the framework (Section 7), and wrap up with some conclusions in Section 8.

2   Jadl Overview

Before we delve into different aspects of the language, it is important to give a broad overview over the language, in order to allow the reader to place the different elements of the language within their respective context.

Jadl is an agent programming language developed during the last few years at the DAI Laboratory of the Technische Universität Berlin. It is the core of an extensive agent framework called JIAC, and has originally been proposed by Sesseler [4]. As JIAC has been developed in cooperation with the telecommunications industry, it has until now not been available to the general public (though this might change soon, so watch this space!). Its stated goal is to support the creation of complex service-based applications. In Sections 6 and 7 we describe the framework and some exemplary implementations based on JIAC.

Jadl is based on three-valued predicate logic [5], thereby providing an open world semantics. It comprises four main elements: *plan elements*, *rules*, *ontologies*, and *services*.

While the first three elements are perhaps not too surprising, we should say a word or two about the last part, services. While we go into details in Section 5, we note here that agents communicate via services. From the perspective of the agent execution engine, a service call is handled the same way internal (complex) actions are executed. This is possible as services have the same structure as actions, having pre- and post conditions, as well as a body that contains the actual code to be executed. Reducing (or extending) communication to only consist of service calls allows us to incorporate advanced features like security and accounting into our framework. Also, programming communication becomes easier as all messages are handled in a clearly defined frame of reference.

Agents consist of a set of ontologies, rules, plan elements, and initial goal states, as well as a set of so-called AgentBeans (which are Java classes implementing certain interfaces). The state of the world is represented within a so-called fact base which contains instantiations of categories (which are defined in ontologies). AgentBeans contain methods which can be called directly from within Jadl, allowing the agent to interact with the real world, via user interfaces, database access, robot control, and more.

In the following sections, we will detail some different areas of Jadl, namely knowledge representation, agent behaviour, and communications.

3   Knowledge Representation

The language Jadl was designed to specifically meet the needs of open and dynamic agent systems. In a dynamic system where agents and services may come and go any time, the validity period of local information is quite short. Therefore, any system that allows and supports dynamic behaviour needs to address the issue of synchronisation and sharing of information. One answer to this is addressed by research in the area of transaction management (e.g. [6]). Our approach, however is to incorporate the idea of uncertainty about bits of information into our knowledge representation and thus allow the programmer to actively deal with outdated, incomplete or wrong data. Even leaving aside for a moment that there are unsolved issues when it comes to transaction management in multi-agent systems, we felt there are many cases when a real transaction-management would have been too much and it is quite acceptable and probably even more effective to just identify the bits of information that are inconsistent and afterwards update those bits.

We realised the concept of uncertainty by using a situation calculus that features a three valued logic. The use of logic allows us to use powerful and well known AI-techniques within a single agent. The third truth value is added for predicates that cannot be evaluated, with the information available to a particular agent. Thus, a predicate can be explicitly evaluated as *unknown*. This is an integral part of the language, and the programmer is forced to handle uncertainty when developing a new agent. Consequently, JIAC allows to handle incomplete or wrong information explicitly.

Jadl allows to define knowledge bases which are the basis of most of the rest of the language. Every object that the language refers to needs to be defined in an ontology. Jadl implements strong typing, i.e. contrary to for example Prolog, variables range over categories, rather than the full universe of discourse.

Categories are represented in a tree-like structure. Each node represents a category, with attached a set of (typed) attributes. Categories "inherit" attributes of ancestors.

Categories are specified as follows:

```
CatDecl = (cat CatName (ext CatName+) AttributeDecl*), where
AttributeDecl = (AttName Type Keyword*)
```

Keywords encode meta-information about the attributes.

To note here is that we allow multiple inheritance. Categories inherit *all* attributes of all ancestors. As attribute names are silently expanded to include the category structure, naming conflicts are avoided.

In addition to categories, Jadl allows to define functions and comparisons (which essentially are functions with a boolean, or rather 3-valued return type). The interpretation of functions is given by operational semantics. In practise, functions are encoded in Java.

While Jadl uses its own language to describe ontologies, we have developed a OWL-light to Jadl translator which allows JIAC agents to use published OWL-based ontologies.

Complex actions, or plan elements, describe the functional abilities of the agent. They in turn might call Java-methods, or use the Jadl scripting language. There are different types of plan elements — (internal) actions, and protocols and service invocations. All of them though have the same global structure. They consist of three main elements (in addition to the action name):

```
(act ActName pre PreCond eff Effect Body)
```

Pre-condition and Effect are described using logical formulae, consisting of elements defined in associated ontologies. It should be noted here that Jadl does not always allow the full power of first order formulae. For example, pre-conditions and effects can only consist of conjuncts. Also, formulae have to be written in disjunctive normal form. The body of an action can be either a script, a service, or an inference. Once the exectuion of this body is finished, the results are written to the variables, and afterwards the effect-formula is evaluated with these results to determine whether the action was successful. This way JIAC ensures that the actual result of an action does match the specified effect. Furthermore, protocols usually inherit the effect of their associated service. They may however have their own precondition, as there may be multiple protocols for a service - not all of which have to be applicable at a certain state.

4   Agent Behaviour

4.1   Goals and Action Selection

As Jadl is meant to be interpreted in a BDI-like architecture, it includes the concept of achievement goals. These goals are implemented as simple formulae which an agent tries to fulfill once the goal is activated.

```
Goal = (goal Condition)
```

Once an agent has a goal, it tries to find an appropriate action that fulfills that goal. Such an action may either be a simple script or a service that is provided by another agent. For this selection, there is no difference between actions that can be executed locally and actions that are in fact services. The actual selection is done by comparing the formula stated in the goal (including the respective variable bindings) with the effects of all actions known to the agent. In this matching process, the literals of the formulae are compared, and if compatible, the values from the goal variables are bound to the corresponding variables of the action. After the action is completed, the results are writen to the original variables of the goal and the goal formula is evaluated to ensure that the goal is actually reached. If that is not the case, the agent is replanning its actions, and may try to reach the goal with other actions. One fact that should be mentioned here is that this matching of course considers the types of the variables. As these types may also include categories that come from ontologies, the matching process does also consider the semantic information that is present in those ontologies, e.g. inheritance.

4.2   Reactive Behaviour

Jadl allows to define *rules*. These rules are a means to realize the reactive behaviour of an angent. More specifically, a rule can give the agent a goal, whenever a certain event occurs. Rules are implemented in a rather straightforward fashion, consisting of a condition and two actions, one of which is executed when the condition becomes true, and the other when the condition becomes false.

```
Rule = (rule Condition Action Action)
```

Specifically, whenever an object is either added, removed, or changed in the fact base, the conditions that match the *object type* of the fact in question are tested against it, and execute the true or false action-part respectively. If the test yields unknown, no action is taken. The restriction of applicable rules to the matching object types is purely for efficiency purposes — if tested, rules whose condition does not match the fact will always yield **unknown**. Actions can themselves be either a new goal or a call to an AgentBean. In the former case, a new planning task for the agent is effectively created.

4.3 Planning

In the literature, there are numerous agent programming languages available. We can roughly classify them as logic based (such as AgentSpeak(L) [7,8], 3APL [9,10], Golog [11,12], and MetateM [13,14]) and Java based (such as Jack [15], Jade [16], Cougaar, [17] and MadKit [18]). The languages are mostly in the prototype stage, and provide high level concepts that implement some notion of BDI [19].

Generally, the concept of having beliefs, desires, and intentions, is "translated" into belief bases, goals, and a plan library. In particular, possibly with the exception of Golog and Cougaar, which allows for planning from first principles, all those languages assume a library of fully developed plans (modulo some parameters). A general execution cycle therefore maps internal and external states via some matching function to one or more plans, which are then (partially) executed.

While this approach certainly has its merits, in particular when it comes to execution speed, it is by no means clear that planning from first principles is not a viable alternative, certainly if approached with caution. The language we are presenting here has been used to implement numerous complex applications, showing that planning has its place and its uses in agent programming.

(Complex) Actions. Before we detail the execution algorithm, we need to introduce the plan elements which are combined to plans which then are executed by the agent.

Plan elements can take a number of different forms. These include *actions*, as well as *protocols*, and *services*, which we will detail in the next subsection.

Actions, rather than being atomic elements, can be scripts. Jadl script provides keywords for sequential and parallel execution, conditionals, calls to Agent-Beans, and even the creation of new goals, which then lead to new planning actions. It should be clear to the reader that extensive use of the scripting language, and especially the ability to trigger new plans, should be used with caution.

For a discussion on protocols and services, we refer the reader to Section 5.

While it is out of the scope of this paper to describe the action language in detail, we want to give the reader an impression in Figure 1. As Jadl is logic based, variables need to be bound and unbound to actual objects that are stored in the fact base. Also, formulae can be evaluated in order to ascertain their values. Sequential and parallel execution, as well as branching instructions can be used. Note further the keywords `iseq` and `seq` in the example. While the latter reflects a simple sequential execution of following elements, the former *iterates* through the given list (in this case a list of e-mail objects) and executes the sequence for each element. The `branch` statement executes the body if the test condition evaluates to true.

Plan Generation and Execution. While Jadl can be used to provide a library of fully developed plans, its execution environment allows for planning from first

```
(seq
    (unbind ?coredata)
    (unbind ?emailList)
    (unbind ?email)
    (eval (att coredata ?c ?coredata))
    (eval (att email ?coredata ?emailList))

    (bind ?haveIt false)

    (iseq ?emailList (var ?emailObj:EMailAddress)
        (seq
          (branch (isTrue (var ?haveIt))
            cont
            (par
              (eval (att email ?emailObj ?email))
              (bind ?haveIt true)
            )
            )
        )
    )
    (bind ?e ?email)
)
```

Fig. 1. Code Snippet of a complex script

principles. It employs the UCPOP algorithm [20], which generates a set of partial plans based on a goal state and a set of actions. The partial plans are then "flattened" by a scheduler to create a full plan.

In order to create partial plans, the system first tries to reach the goal state by using local plan elements only, as this is considered the fastest and cheapest way of reaching a goal. If no plan can be found, the directory facilitator (DF) of the agent platform is contacted, and all available services are downloaded to the planning agent. Then, a second planning cycle is run, this time with the services registered at the DF included in the search. To limit the search space as far as possible, the algorithm ever only considers plan elements (and therefore services) that are relevant. Here, relevancy is determined by using ontology information on pre-conditions. So, a plan elements written for cars will be considered when looking for a BMW, but plan elements dealing with houses will not be used to expand the plan.

4.4 Scheduling and Failure Handling

In order to arrive at a full plan, the partial plans need to be ordered in a consistent fashion. As scheduling can be computationally expensive, the algorithm does little optimisation, and mainly ensures that the causal links (i.e. the order of actions that depend on each other) are met. Actions that are executed in parallel are not checked for consistency.

The actual execution has fall-back mechanisms on several levels. As can be seen in Figure 2, the execution of a goal (which can be either a single goal, or one of a number of steps that have been computed by the planner) is approached as follows. First, the locally known plan elements are matched against the goal. If one is found, and its pre-conditions are met, it is executed. If the preconditions are not yet fulfilled, the planner tries to find further planelements, that may meet the preconditions recursively. If either the goal or some preconditions cannot be met with the locally known planelements, a request is sent to the directory facilitator (DF), and the goal is again matched against the received set of services. As mentioned before, elements that are atomic actions for the planner (and execution model) can be complex actions, and even service calls. We will describe service calls in details later, and want to mention only that in the case of service calls, unsuccessful service invocations are also repeated with different service providers before re-initiating the process of finding a new action. Also note that the re-initialisation only occurs once, as otherwise a loop could occur.

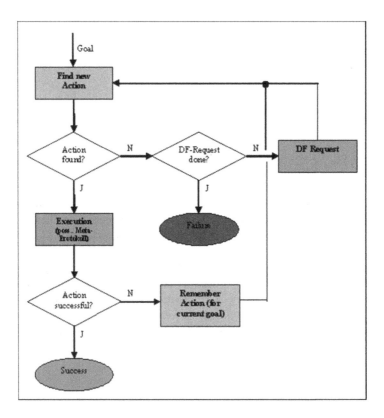

Fig. 2. Fulfilling a goal

5   High Level Communications

Protocols and services are used for communication purposes. In order to allow for an open system, agents solely communicate using service calls. Actual messages follow the FIPA ACL standard [21]. Rather than either exposing its whole functionality, or alternatively having an implicit representation of functionalities that might or might not be used by other agents, JIAC forces the programmer to define explicitly the functionalities that the agent exposes to the outside. This is done by explicitly configuring the list of services that are exposed to other agents. Each service has attached a number of protocols that can be executed during the service invocation, allowing for a conscious design of protocols. Figure 3 shows a small example which provides a time-synch service.

Figure 3 details a service definition. The example service is defined as an action (`act timeSyncService`) which has four elements. Firstly, a variable `?t` of type `TimeActualization` is declared. The type is defined in the `TimeSync` ontology. Second, we have the pre-conditions which must hold for the service to be executed. In our example, this is set to true, but can be any conjunctive formula (and can include *unkown* attributes as well. Thirdly, the effect of executing the service is described. The example service sets the attribute `locallySynchronized` of the object assigned to `?t` to `true`. Finally the actual service description starts.

A service consists of a service object, which is defined by a name, a set of protocols, and some ontologies. We should note here that the set of protocols includes protocols for negotiation as well as service provision. Figure 3 for example defines two protocols. The first describes the actual service protocol which implements the body of the service, while the `contractNet` protocol has the flag `multi true` which defines it as a one-to-many negotiation protocol that is used for provider-selection.

The actual linking of protocols to services happens during runtime. Whenever an agent decides to execute a service it looks up the corresponding protocols (which are identified by their names) an tries to negotiate the protocol with the service-partner. If they can find a common protocol, both protocol-sides are intiated, otherwise the service fails.

Channelling communication through services makes security much easier to implement. This is because agents can only interact through the clearly defined service invocation, rather than any sort of interaction. Secondly, services can define additional meta-data such as costs, AAA, or QoS in a clear and consistent manner, allowing agents (and their owners) to have clear policies concerning the provision of functionalities to third party contacts. Again, allowing for simple message exchanges makes accounting very complex.

The last two points, security and accounting, are important aspects of any industrial application of agent technology. Only if we can guarantee a certain level of security, and only if we can ensure that services offered can actually be accounted according to clear and definable policies can we ever hope to convince industry players to consider agent technology as a viable alternative to today's technologies.

```
(act timeSyncService
   (var ?t:TimeActualization)
   (pre true)
   (eff
     (att locallySynchronized ?t true)
   )
   (service
     (obj Service:DAI_1
       (name "timeSyncService")
       (protocols
         [Protocol:
           (obj Protocol
             (name "timeSyncServiceProtocol")
             (provider true)
           )
           (obj Protocol
             (name "contractNet")
             (multi true)
           )
         ]
       )
       (ontologies
         {string:
         "de.dailab.jiac.ontology.Service:DAI_1"
         "de.dailab.scb.ontology.TimeSync:DAI_1"
         }
       )
     )
   )
)
```

Fig. 3. Example of a service definition in Jadl

Meta-protocol

As mentioned before, service calls are wrapped by a meta-protocol in JIAC (see
Figure 4), which deals with session handling, security, accounting, provider and
transport selection, and error handling, leaving the programmer to concentrate
on the actual functionality and protocol interaction.

In order to trigger a service invocation, the agent must have failed to satisfy a
goal which using just actions that are available by the agent itself. This includes
services, that the agents provides by himself. If such a situation occurs, the agent
sends a request to the DF, which answers with a list of services that could fulfil
the goal. The agent then chooses one service, and notifies the DF, which again
sends back a list, but this time of agents that are providing the requested service.

As Figure 4 shows, a service invocation consists of three distinct phases. During the initiation phase, the user and provider(s) agree on a protocol to use. This
includes security negotiations, as well as accounting and QoS requirements.

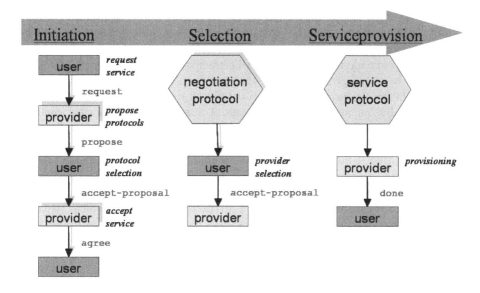

Fig. 4. Graphical representation of the meta-protocol

Once this is done, a (optional) negotiation protocol is triggered, during which the actual provider agent is chosen. Only then, the actual service is invoked.

To note here is that while a service provision is always a one-to-one communication, the actual service selection allows for one-to-many communication. If the negotiation protocol is empty, the first service provider is chosen. The meta protocol catches any errors that might occur during service provision (i.e. time outs, or cancel- and not-understood messages), and reacts accordingly. For example, in case of a failed service provisioning, it returns to the selection phase and chooses another agent that can provide the service. Only once no more agents are available does the service provisioning fail (from the point of view of the agent). In that case, a re-plan action is triggered.

For a more detailed description of the meta-protocol we refer the reader to [22].

6   JIAC

In the preceding sections we have described the Jadl language. Now, we describe the JIAC framework which implements Jadl.

JIAC consists of a (java-based) run-time environment, a methodology, tools that support the creation of agents, as well as numerous extensions, such as web-service-connectivity, accounting and management components, device independent interaction, an owl-to-Jadl translator, a OSGI-connector and more. An agent consists of a set of application specific java-classes, rules, plan elements, and ontologies. Strong migration is supported, i.e. agents can migrate from one platform to another during run-time. JIAC's component model allows to exchange, add, and remove components during run time. Standard components (which themselves can be exchanged as well) include a fact-base component, execution-component, rule-component, and more. A JIAC agent is defined within a property file which describes all elements that the agent consists of.

JIAC is the only agent-framework that has been awarded a common criteria EAL3 certificate, an internationally accepted and renowned security certificate.

Conceptually, an agent system consists of a number of platforms, each of which has its own directory facilitator and agent management system. The DF registers the agents on the platform, as well as the services that they offer. We have investigated a number of different techniques to connect different DF's, such as P2P and hierarchical approaches. On each platform, a number of agent "lives" at each moment. Agents themselves implement one or more agent roles. Each role consists of the components that are necessary to implement it. Usually, this will include plan elements, ontologies, rules, and AgentBeans. Here, Jadl and the elements that can be described using it come into play.

Currently we finalise a new version of the tool-suite which is based on Eclipse. Programming in Jadl, as well as creating and running JIAC agents is supported on different levels. Additional to text-based support elements such as syntax highlighting and code folding, most Jadl elements can be displayed and edited in a graphical interface, removing the sometimes awkward syntax as far as possible from the user, and allowing her to focus on functionality rather than syntax debugging.

In addition to the tools that support Jadl itself, we have created a number of additional tools. A security tool provides methods to manage certificates, and ensure secure communication between agents. An accounting tool provides the user with means to create and manage user databases and related elements such as tariff information. The Agent configurator allows to display and modify agent's components during run-time, and to change goals, plan elements, and so forth. We have also incorporated advanced testing and logging features, to facilitate debugging and the general quality of the produced code. Without wanting to go into details, we have extended the Unit-test approach to agents, thereby providing a test-environment where interactions of agents can be tested automatically, for example in conjunction with a cruise-control server.

While tools help to hide the inherent complexity, they can only partially support the programmer during the design phase of a project. Recognising this, JIAC provides users with a methodology which is rooted in the concepts of Jadl, and of JIAC. Here, we focus not only on design but also on practical needs of project management. The JIAC methodology describes the interaction between customer, designer, and project manager, and uses the agile programming approach [23]. Continuous integration is another important element of the methodology, and is supported by above described testing environment.

Both, the methodology and the tool-suite support re-use of components. On the tool side, we are currently implementing a repository which can can be accessed via the network, and which holds functionality that can be included in projects. On the methodology side, special care is taken to enable re-use during analysis, design, and implementation. It also encourages programmers to refine new functionality to a re-usable form towards the end of the project, facilitating further the re-use of components.

Most importantly, the service concept supports re-use of functionality by design. Each created service can be invoked by other agents, thereby offering the most natural re-use of functionality.

Another extension to JIAC is the IMASU (Intelligent Multi-Access Service Unit). With it, interfaces between agents and (human) users can be described abstractly. The unit creates an appropriate user interface for a number of devices, such as web-browsers (HTML), PDA's and mobile phones (WML), and telephone (VoiceXML) [24].

7   Implemented Applications

To give the reader an idea about the power of the framework, we present some of the projects that have been implemented.

BerlinTainment. This project is aimed at simplifying the provision of information over the internet. In order to provide cultural and leisure related functionality to visitors of Berlin, a personalised service based on the JIAC framework has been developed. Agents provide and integrate information from restaurants, route planners, public transport information, cinemas, theatres, and more. Using BerlinTainment, users can plan their day out, make reservations, be guided to the various locations, and be informed about touristic sites from one place, and with various devices [25].

PIA. (Personal Information Agent) concerns the collection, dissemination, and provision of personalised content. It employs agents on three layers. Firstly, extractor agents monitor sources of information and extract content provided in different formats, such as HTML pages, PDF, and Microsoft Word documents. Secondly, filter-agents analyse the content based on preferences of the users. Thirdly, presentation agents control the presentation and output of the filtered data, again based on the users preference and device. PIA is used internally in our institute to collect information concerning research projects and grants, as well as providing personalised news-letters [26].

8   Conclusion

In this paper we have presented the agent programming language Jadl. Based on three-valued logic, it provides constructs to describe ontologies, protocols and services, and complex actions. JIAC agents use a planner to construct plans from those actions. There, internal actions and service invocations are handled transparently to the planning component.

The Jadl language and its framework, JIAC, provide arguably all elements that are needed for a successful agent deployment. JIAC provides tools, a methodology, and a host of extensions that provide extensions like webservice-interaction,

OSGI-connectors, accounting, security, and network components that support the creation of complex services in commercial settings.

We do not claim to have created a language that the best choice for creating anything related with agents. However, we have tried to show that Jadl covers a host of issues that we think should be covered by agent programming languages. Using JIAC, several large implementations have been done, and shown to us the merits of the language.

Acknowledgements

Jadl and JIAC are based on work done by Sesseler [4] in the course of his doctoral thesis. JIAC has been developed with the kind support of Deutsche Telekom.

References

1. Rao, A.S., Georgeff, M.P.: Modeling rational agents within a BDI-architecture. In Allen, J., Fikes, R., Sandewall, E., eds.: Principles of Knowledge Representation and Reasoning: Proc. of the Second International Conference (KR'91). Morgan Kaufmann, San Mateo, CA (1991) 473–484
2. Labrou, Y., Finin, T., Peng, Y.: The current landscape of agent communication languages. IEEE Intelligent Systems **14** (1999) 45–52
3. Luck, M., McBurney, P., Shehory, O., Willmott, S.: Agent based computing - agent technology roadmap. Roadmap, AgentLink III (2005) Draft Version of July 2005.
4. Sesseler, R.: Eine modulare Architektur für dienstbasierte Interaktion zwischen Agenten. Doctocal thesis, Technische Universität Berlin (2002)
5. Kleene, S.C.: Introduction to Metamathematics. Wolters-Noordhoff Publishing and North-Holland Publishing Company (1971) Written in 1953.
6. Kotagiri, R., Bailey, J., Busetta, P.: Transaction oriented computational models for multi-agent systems. In: Proc. 13th IEEE International Conference on Tools with Artificial Intelligence (ICTAI 2001), IEEE Press (2001) 11–17
7. Rao, A.S.: AgentSpeak(L): BDI agents speak out in a logical computable language. In van Hoe, R., ed.: Agents Breaking Away, 7th European Workshop on Modelling Autonomous Agents in a Multi-Agent World, MAAMAW'96,. Volume 1038 of Lecture Notes in Computer Science., Eindhoven, The Netherlands, Springer Verlag (1996) 42–55
8. Bordini, R.H., Hübner, J.F., et al.: Jason: a Java Based AgentSpeak Interpreter Used with SACI for Multi-Agent Distribution over the Net. 5th edn. (2004)
9. Dastani, M.: 3APL Platform. Utrecht University. (2004)
10. Hindriks, K.V., Boer, F.S.D., der Hoek, W.V., Meyer, J.J.: Agent programming in 3apl. Autonomous Agents and Multi-Agent Systems **2** (1999) 357–401
11. Giacomo, G., Lesperance, Y., Levesque, H.: Congolog, a concurrent programming language based on the situation calculus: Foundations. Technical report, University of Toronto (1999)
12. Giacomo, G., Lesperance, Y., Levesque, H.: Congolog, a concurrent programming language based on the situation calculus: Language and implementation. Technical report, University of Toronto (1998)

13. Finger, M., Fisher, M., Owens, R.: Metatem at work: Modelling reactive systems using executable temporal logic. In: Proceedings of the International Conference on Industrial and Engeneering Applications of Artificial Intelligence, Gordon and Breach (1993)
14. Fisher, M., Ghidini, C., Hirsch, B.: Programming groups of rational agents. In Dix, J., Leite, J., eds.: CLIMA IV, Fourth International Workshop. Volume 2359 of LNAI. (2004) 16–33
15. Busetta, P., Rönnquist, R., Hodgson, A., Lucas, A.: JACK — components for intelligent agents in java. Technical report, Agent Oriented Software Pty, Ltd. (1999)
16. Bellifemine, F., Poggi, A., Rimassa, G.: JADE - a FIPA-compliant agent framework. Internal technical report, CSELT (1999) Part of this report has been also published in Proceedings of PAAM'99, London, April 1999, pp.97-108.
17. Helsinger, A., Thome, M., Wright, T.: Cougaar: A scalabe, distributed multi-agent architecture. In: IEEE SMC04. (2004)
18. Gutknecht, O., Ferber, J.: The MADKIT agent platform architecture. Technical Report R.R.LIRMM00xx, Laboratoire d'Informatique, de Robotqiue et de Microélectronique de Montpellier (2000)
19. Bratman, M.E.: Intentions, Plans, and Practical Reason. Havard University Press, Cambridge, MA (1987)
20. Penberthy, J.S., Weld, D.: UCPOP: A sound, complete, partial-order planner for ADL. In: Proceedings of Knowledge Review 92, Cambridge, MA (1992) 103–114
21. FIPA: Fipa acl message structure specification (2002)
22. Albayrak, S., Konnerth, T., Hirsch, B.: Ensuring security and accountability in agent communication. In Preparation (2005)
23. Lyons, K.: The agile approach. Technical report, Conoco Phillips Australia Pty Ltd. (2004)
24. Rieger, A., Cissée, R., Feuerstack, S., Wohltorf, J., Albayrak, S.: An agent-based architecture for ubiquituous multitmodal user interfaces. In: The 2005 International Conference in Active Media Technology. (2005)
25. Wohltorf, J., Cissée, R., Rieger, A.: BerlinTainment: An agent-based context-aware entertainment planning system. IEEE Communications Magazine **43** (2005) 102–109
26. Albayrak, S., Dragan, M.: Generic intelligent personal information agent. In: International Conference on Advances in Internet, Processing, Systems, and Interdisciplinary Research. (2004)

Agreeing on Defeasible Commitments

Ioan Alfred Letia and Adrian Groza

Technical University of Cluj-Napoca
Department of Computer Science
Baritiu 28, RO-3400 Cluj-Napoca, Romania
{letia,adrian}@cs-gw.utcluj.ro

Abstract. Social commitments are developed for multi-agent systems according to the current practice in law regarding contract formation and breach. Deafeasible commitments are used to provide a useful link between multi-agent systems and legal doctrines. The proposed model makes the commitments more expressive relative to contract law and it stresses the representational rather than the operational side of the commitment life cycle. As a consequence, the broader semantics helps in modeling different types of contracts (gratuitous promises, unilateral contracts, bilateral contracts, and forward contracts) and negotiation patterns. The semantics of higher-order commitments is useful in deciding whether to sign an agreement or not and to represent a larger variety of protocols and legal contracts.

1 Introduction

Artificial agents and the contracts they make are ubiquitous, while at the same time, there is a lack of application of the current practice in law to multi-agent systems (MAS). From the point of view of law, there is a philosophical debate regarding when to attach person-hood to artificial agents. The actual context of web services representing business entities and agents interacting with services implies legal responsibilities for each agent. From the engineering point of view, agents have to be built and synchronized with the norms and values of society.

Social commitments were introduced as a way to capture the public aspects of communication [1] and research has been focused on the development of agent communication languages and flexible interaction protocols [2,3]. As commitments appear to be sometimes too restrictive (deontic obligations) and sometimes too flexible, allowing unconstrained modification of commitments, social commitments should be more flexible than usual obligations but also more constrained than permissions [1]. On this line, we apply principles of contract law as an objective measure to decide on the flexibility of the operations on commitments, beginning with a commitment-based representation of different types of agreements from contract law. The main advantage of applying current practice in law to model commitments within multi-agents systems is that the principles of contract law are verified and polished during years of economical and judicial practice.

M. Baldoni and U. Endriss (Eds.): DALT 2006, LNAI 4327, pp. 156–173, 2006.
© Springer-Verlag Berlin Heidelberg 2006

Modeling agent communication implies several approaches: mental (BDI and modalities), social (which highlights the public and observable elements like social commitments that agents exchange when conversing), and argumentative (based on agent reasoning capabilities). When participating in an agreement, agents should use their mental states, share information and reason about new facts. We seek to synchronize the social commitments developed for MAS with existing legal doctrines, which the law applies in case of contract formation. We define a framework by using the temporalised normative positions in defeasible logic [4] to introduce defeasible commitments for representing contract laws [5] in the model of the life cycle of commitments.

2   Temporalised Normative Positions

For defining defeasible commitments, we are using the temporalised normative positions [4]. A theory in *normative defeasible logic* (NDL) is a structure $(F, R_K, R_I, R_A, R_O, \succ)$ where F is a finite set of facts, R_K R_I R_A R_O are respectively a finite set of persistent or transitive rules (strict, defeasible, and defeaters) for knowledge, intentions, actions, and obligations, and $\succ$ representing the superiority relation over the set of rules.

A rule in NDL is characterized by three orthogonal attributes: modality, persistence, strength. As for modality, R_K represents the agent's theory of the world, R_A encodes its actions, R_O the normative system or his obligations, while R_I and the superiority relation capture the agent's strategy or its policy. *A persistent rule* is a rule whose conclusion holds at all instants of time after the conclusion has been derived, unless a more powerful rule, according to the superiority relation, has derived the opposite conclusion. *A transient rule* establishes the conclusion only for a specific instance of time [4].

Strict rules are rules in the classical sense, that is whenever the premises are indisputable, then so is the conclusion, while *defeasible rules* are rules that can be defeated by contrary evidence. For "sending the goods means the goods were delivered", if we know that the goods were sent then they reach the destination, unless there is other, not inferior, rule suggesting the contrary. *Defeaters* are rules that cannot be used to draw any conclusions. Their only use is to prevent some conclusions, as in "if the customer is a regular one and he has a short delay for paying, we might not ask for penalties", they cannot be used to support a "not penalty" conclusion, but can prevent the derivation of the penalty conclusion.

We use the following notation: $\rightarrow^t_X$, $\Rightarrow^t_X$ and $\rightsquigarrow^t_X$ denote transitive rules (strict, defeasible, defeaters), while $\rightarrow^p_X$, $\Rightarrow^p_X$ and $\rightsquigarrow^p_X$ denote persistent rules (strict, defeasible, defeaters), where $X \in \{K, I, A, O\}$ represents the modality. A conclusion in NDL is a tagged literal where $+\Delta^\tau_X q{:}t$ means that q is definitely provable of modality X, at time t in NDL (figure 1); and $+\partial^\tau_X q{:}t$ means that q is defeasibly provable of modality X, at time t in NDL (figure 2). Here $\tau \in \{t, p\}$, t stands for transient, while p for a persistent derivation. A strict rule $r \in R_s$ is $\Delta_X - applicable$ if $r \in R_{s,X} \forall a : t_k \in A(r) : a_k : t_k$ is $\Delta_X - provable$. A strict rule $r \in R_s$ is $\Delta_X - discarded$ if $r \in R_{s,X} \exists a_k : t_k \in A(r) : a_k : t_k$ is $\Delta_X - rejected$, and similarly for ∂. The conditions for concluding whether a query is transient

$+\Delta_X^t$: If $P(i+1) = +\Delta_X^t q : t$ then
  $q : t \in F$, or
  $\exists r \in R_{s,X}^t[q : t]$ r is $\Delta_X - applicable$

$+\Delta_X^p$: If $P(i+1) = +\Delta_X^p q : t$ then
  $q : t \in F$, or
  $\exists r \in R_{s,X}^p[q : t]$ r is $\Delta_X - applicable$ or
  $\exists t' \in \Gamma : t' < t$ and $+\Delta_X^p q : t' \in P(1..i)$.

Fig. 1. Transient and persistent definite proof for modality X

or persistent, definitely provable is shown in the figure 1. For the transient case, at step $i + 1$ one can assert that q is definitely transient provable if there is a strict transient rule $r \in R_s^t$ with the consequent q and all the antecedents of r have been asserted to be definitely (transient or persistent) provable, in previous steps. For the persistent case, the persistence condition allows us to reiterate literals definitely proved at previous times. For showing that q is not persistent definitely provable, in addition to the condition we have for the transient case, we have to assure that, for all instances of time before now the persistent property has not been proved. According to the above conditions, in order to prove that q is definitely provable at time t we have to show that q is either transient, or persistent definitely provable [4]. Defeasible derivations have an argumentation

$+\partial_X^t$: If $P(i+1) = +\partial_X^t q : t$ then
  (1) $+\Delta_X q : t \in P(1..i)$ or
  (2) $-\Delta_X \sim q : t \in P(1..i)$ and
    (2.1) $\exists r \in R_{sd,X}[q : t]$: r is ∂_X-applicable and
    (2.2) $\forall s \in R[\sim q : t]$: s is ∂_X-discarded or
       $\exists w \in R(q : t)$: w is ∂_X-applicable or $w \succ s$

Fig. 2. Transient defeasible proof for modality X

like structure [4]: firstly, we choose a supported rule having the conclusions q we want to prove, secondly we consider all the possible counterarguments against q, and finally we rebut all the above counterarguments showing that, either some of their premises do not hold, or the rule used for its derivation is weaker than the rule supporting the initial conclusion q. A goal q which is not definitely provable is defeasibly transient provable if we can find a strict or defeasible transient rule for which all its antecedents are defeasibly provable, $\sim q$ is not definitely provable and for each rule having $\sim q$ as a consequent we can find an antecedent which does not satisfy the defeasible provable condition (figure 2). For the persistence case, an additional clause verifies if the literal $q : t$ has been persistent defeasibly proved before, and this conclusion remained valid all this time (there was no time t" when the contrary $\sim q$ was proved by firing the rule s, or the respective rule was no stronger than the one sustaining q).

3   Types of Commitments

The classical definition of a conditional commitment states that a commitment is a promise from a debtor x to a creditor y to bring about a particular sentence p under a condition q. Starting from this definition we provide a generalized commitment abstract data type.

Definition 1. *A commitment is a relation*

$$C_m^n(x, y, q^n : [t_{issue}], [\star]p^m : [t_{maturity}]) : [t_{expiration}]$$

with optional literals within square brackets, representing the promise p made by debtor x to creditor y in exchange of which the action q is requested, where the time of maturity $t_{maturity}$ shows the time remaining until the promise p^m is satisfied by the debtor x if the request q^n holds until time t_{issue} and $\star \in \{+\Delta, -\Delta, +\partial, -\partial\}$ is an optional tag used to express informing messages.

The parameters m and n help us to define meta commitments or higher-order commitments, providing a rich semantics used to express a large variety of contractual clauses and negotiation patterns: m is a measure of the promises made by the debtor to the creditor, while n is a measure of the requests made by the debtor to the crediror. We define two operators for the functional composition of commitments: $\circ_q$ which deals with requests and $\circ_p$ which deals with promises and one operator $\diamond$ for logical composition, used for aggregating commitments into contracts. We propose two main categories of high order commitments: contractual patterns which include contractual commitments and guarantee commitments and negotiation patterns as request commitments and informing commitments.

3.1   Contractual Commitments

When $m \in \{1, 3\}$ we name the resulting commitments contractual. Next, we discuss each type of contractual commitments from a legal point of view.

The example "I will give you the item g_1 in 5 days." is represented by $C_1^0(me, you, 1, g_1 : 5)$, defined by law as *gratuitous promise*.

Definition 2. *In a Gratuitous Promise (n=0, m=1) the debtor x promises the creditor y to bring about p until $t_{maturity}$ without requesting anything ($n = 0$).*

$$C_1^0(x, y, 1, p : t_{maturity})$$

The example "I will give you the item g_1 in 5 days after you will pay the price" will be represented by $C_1^1(me, you, pay(you) : t_{pay}, g_1 : t_{pay} + 5)$, where the condition is brought about by the creditor *you*. The law defines such a commitment a *unilateral contract*, involving an exchange of the offerer's promise p for the oferee's act q, with the completion of the act required to indicate acceptance.

Definition 3. *A Unilateral Contract (n=1, m=1) involves an exchange of the offerer's promise p for the oferee's act q, where the debtor x promises the creditor y to bring about p until $t_{maturity}$ if condition q holds at time t_{issue}.*

$$C_1^1(x, y, q : t_{issue}, p : t_{maturity})$$

Consider the example "I will give you the item g_1 no later than 5 days, if you promise me in maximum 1 day that you will pay the price no later than 3 days" represented as $C_3^1(me, you, C_1^0(you, me, 1, pay : 3) : 1, g_1 : 5)$.

Definition 4. *In a Bilateral Contract (n=1, m=3) both sides make promises, the debtor x promises the creditor y to bring about p if the creditor y promises x to bring about p_1.*

$$C_3^1(x, y, C_1^0(y, x, 1, p_1), p)$$

We note that a C_3^1 commitment is somehow weaker than a C_1^1 commitment. This fine grained mechanism opens the possibility of designing agents with different levels of attitude towards risk and it also refines the idea of leveled commitment contracts [6].

"I will give you the item g_1 no later than 5 days, if you promise me to pay the price no later than 3 days under the condition that oil price reaches 135\$; my offer expires in 10 days." is represented by $C_3^4(me, you, C_1^1(you, me, oilPrice = 135, pay : 3) : 10, g_1 : 5)$.

Definition 5. *In a Conditional Bilateral Contract (n=4, m=3) the debtor x promises the creditor y to bring about p if agent y promises x to bring about p_1 under condition q_1.*

$$C_3^4(x, y, C_1^1(y, x, q_1, p_1), p)$$

The above semantics includes a form of negotiation because, at the creation of the inner commitment, both C_3^4 and C_1^1 commitments are open offers (see section 4). Therefore, the agents are not committed to them[1] and they may be canceled anytime in this state, without considering it a breach.

"The supplier x commits to deliver an extra number of r items to the buyer y if the buyer orders that quantity no longer than 20 days" is represented by: $C_1^4(x, y, C_1^0(y, x, r, 1) : 20, deliver(r))$.

Definition 6. *In an Option Contract (n=4, m=1) the debtor x promises the creditor y to bring about p if the creditor y requests that p until $t_{expiration}$.*

$$C_1^4(x, y, C_1^0(y, x, p, 1) : t_{expiration}, p)$$

When an option contract is not exercised until $t_{expiration}$ it expires.

3.2   Guarantee Commitments

In these commitments ($m = 4$) the debtor promises that a specific commitment will exist in a given window of time.

For "I guarantee you that the bank will commit in maximum 7 days to give you the credit" we use the formula $C_1^0(me, you, 1, C_1^0(bank, you, 1, credit) : 7)$.

---

[1] A contract was not formed yet, from the contract law point of view, they are derived in this state as knowledge and not as obligations.

Definition 7. *In a Guarantee to Commit (n=0, m=4) the debtor x guarantees the creditor y that a special commitment will exist until $t_{expiration}$*

$$C_4^0(x, y, 1, C_1^0(z, y, 1, p_1) : t_{expiration})$$

obtainable from $C_1^0 \circ_p C_1^0$.

If $z = y$ the creditor manifests its own intention to commit or it guarantees that it will make the respective gratuitous promise no longer than $t_{expiration}$. It can be seen as a precommitment or an intention to commit.

Definition 8. *In a Forward Unilateral Contract (n=2, m=4) the debtor x guarantees the creditor y that a specific unilateral contract will exist until $t_{expiration}$.*

$$C_4^2(x, y, 1, C_1^1(z, y, q_1, p_1) : t_{expiration})$$

According to contract law, the particular case in which $z = x$ is a form of a *forward contract*, obtainable from $C_1^0 \circ_p C_1^1$. Applying the composition operators $\circ_q$ or $\circ_p$ we can also model *forward bilateral contracts* and *forward conditional bilateral contracts*.

3.3   Request Commitments

When $m \in \{0, 2\}$ the debtor does not promise anything directly, called request commitments. For both $m = 0$ and $n = 0$ we have a *free commitment* $C_0^0(x, y, 1, 1)$, while $n \neq 0$ gives the following types of requests.

"Please pay me the price in two days" is represented as a *request act* $C_0^1(me, you, price : 2, 1)^2$.

Definition 9. *In a Request Act (n=1, m=0) the debtor x requests the creditor y to bring about q until time t_{issue}.*

$$C_0^1(x, y, q : t_{issue}, 1)$$

The debtor does not promise anything, satisfying q leading to its acceptance. If the requested act is a negative sentence, it represents a *taboo* [7] or interdiction.

"Please promise me that you will pay for the item in 3 days" is represented as $C_2^1(me, you, C_1^0(you, me, 1, pay : 3), 1)$.

Definition 10. *A Request a Promise (n=1, m=2) is used by a debtor x to request the creditor y to promise until $t_{expiration}$ that it will bring about p_1 until $t_{maturity}$*

$$C_2^1(x, y, C_1^0(y, x, 1, p_1 : t_{maturity}) : t_{expiration}, 1)$$

obtainable from $C_0^1 \circ_q C_1^0$.

---

[2] With $n = 1$ we denote $q^1 = q$ and $p^0 = 1$.

Acceptance of the request is done by creating the inner commitment $C_1^0(y, x, 1, p_1 : t_{maturity})$ until the deadline $t_{expiration}$. When the time-out elapses the request commitment reaches the failed state. If the creditor wants to explicitly reject the request, it will respond by creating the negative commitment $\neg C_1^0(y, x, 1, pay : 3) : 5$, having the same deadline with the request commitment[3]. The meaning of the above rejection is "I will not commit to you to bring about p_1 in 3 days; I will reconsider your request after 5 days".

Definition 11. *In a Request a Unilateral Contract (n=4, m=2) the debtor x requests the creditor y to commit to bring about p_1 if the condition q_1 holds.*

$$C_2^4(x, y, C_1^1(y, z, q_1, p_1) : t_{expiration}, 1)$$

3.4   Informing Commitments

We see the informing act as a form of commitment in the sense that the agent who propagates some information guarantees its validity. In other words, it is committed to the creditor that the notified fact is true, based on the debtor's view of the world. Contract law names such type of statement *terms*. The truth of the term is guaranteed by the agent that made the statement. We use this type of commitment to allow information sharing between agents, a key-point in the coordination of multi-agent systems.

The situation "My partner informs me that he has already sent the money, while the bank says that the payment has not been made yet" is coded with $C_1^0(partner, me, 1, +\partial_K^p pay)$ and $C_1^0(bank, me, 1, -\partial_K^p pay)$. The agent me will fire both defeasible rules $r_1 : C_1^0(partner, me, 1, +\partial_K^p pay) \Rightarrow pay$ and $r_2 : C_1^0(bank, me, 1, -\partial_K^p pay) \Rightarrow \neg pay$, but it will give more credit to the statement of the bank $r_2 \succ r_1$.

Definition 12. *In a Fact Notification the debtor x informs creditor y if a specific sentence p is $+\Delta_X^\tau p$, $-\Delta_X^\tau p$, $+\partial_X^\tau p$, or $-\partial_X^\tau p$ according to its defeasible theory D.*

$$C_1^0(x, y, 1, \star p)$$

"I inform you that agent z has an active commitment for delivering to me the item g_1 within 3 days" is represented by $C_4^0(me, you, 1, +\Delta_O^p C_1^0(z, me, 1, g_1 : 3))$, which may help me in the negotiation process with you.

Definition 13. *In a Commitment Existence Notification the debtor x informs the creditor y about the existence of a specific commitment according to its defeasible theory D.*

$$C_4^0(x, y, 1, \star C_1^0(z, w, 1, p))$$

When the sentence is definitely provable ($\star = \pm\Delta$) we have a strong notification, while when it is deafeasibly provable ($\star = \pm\partial$) a weak notification, a revocable commitment[4].

---

[3] Otherwise a form of negotiation may arise.
[4] Similar to the FIPA ACL uncertainty operator.

4   Commitment Life Cycle

During its life cycle, a commitment may be in one of the following states: *open offer*, *active*, *released*, *breached*, *fulfilled*, *canceled*, or *failed* (figure 3), which are also useful to be considered from a legal perspective.

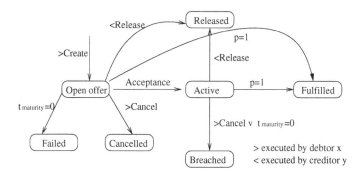

Fig. 3. Life cycle with acceptance dependent on the type of commitment

We consider first a gratuitous promise $C_1^0(x, y, 1, p : t_{maturity}) : t_{expiration}$. Under the donative-promise principle, a simple, unrelied-upon gratuitous commitment is unenforceable since there is no consideration [8] or no element of exchange. Therefore, the breach of a C_1^0 commitment attracts only social sanctions or trust sanctions. The use of normative foundation of trust attached to a C_1^0 commitment serves to promote business relations. In the case when the creditor y has relied on the commitment, one can make use of the doctrine of *promissory estoppel*. This doctrine comes from the equity part of the law and it prevents one party from withdrawing a promise made to a creditor, if that creditor has relied on that promise and acted upon it. The only remedy of contract law that can be applied in this case is *reliance damages* [8]. Also, the law stipulates that this reliance must be foreseeable. In the context of open agent systems we define a foreseeable fact as one which has been notified to the potential breacher. For instance, in a supply chain scenario, the creditor must notify the promiser that, based on the C_1^0 commitment, it has signed other contracts: "I inform you that, based on your gratuitous promise, I commit to deliver item g_1 to my client z within 3 days". This is represented by $C_4^0(me, you, 1, +\Delta_K^p C_1^0(me, z, 1, g_1 : 3))$. On the other hand, the estoppel is "a shield, not a sword". It cannot be used as the basis of an action on its own. Hence, we implement estoppel with defeaters.

In the case of the life cycle of a unilateral contract, the debtor x can revoke his commitment anytime before acceptance. When the condition q becomes true, the commitment becomes active. Until then, the debtor may cancel without considering this as a breach. Most courts now hold that creditor y must give notice of its acceptance after it has done the requested act. If it does not do that, the commitment that was formed by the act may be canceled without breach (of course, the debtor must return the money). Therefore, the acceptance of a C_1^1 commitment can be viewed as a composite operation: execution of q and a fact notification $C_1^0(x, y, 1, +\partial_K^p q)$. Due to the late activation of the C_1^1 commitment the promiser x has maximal protection. If acceptance is late ($t_{issue} < t_{acceptance} < t_{maturity}$), it becomes a counter-offer and it creates the power of acceptance for the initial debtor x.

Similar rules are defined for other types of commitments. The main idea is that the commitment is derived as knowledge in an open offer state and as obligation in an active state. The transition from the open offer state into the active state takes place when the acceptance of the proposed commitment occurs. The acceptance depends on the type of commitment and it is equivalent to: reliance in case of a gratuitous promise, accomplishment of q and notification about it in the case of a unilateral contract, creation of the required commitment in the case of a bilateral contract.

$$\rightarrow_I^t promise(p : t_m, y) : t_i$$
$$\Rightarrow_I^p riskProne : t_i$$
$$\rightarrow_K^p promissoryEstoppel : t_i$$
$$r_0 : promise(p : t_m, y) : t_i, riskProne : t_i \Rightarrow_A^t create(x, c) : t_i$$
$$r_1 : create(x, c) : t_i \rightarrow_K^p c : t_i$$
$$r_2 : c : t_i, t_m = t_i \rightarrow_K^p \neg c : t_i$$
$$r_3 : c : t_i, cancel(x, c) : t_i \Rightarrow_K^p \neg c : t_i$$
$$r_4 : c : t_i, release(y, c) : t_i \rightarrow_O^p \neg c : t_i$$
$$r_5 : breached : t_i \Rightarrow_O^p relianceDamages : t_{i+3}, \neg c : t_i$$
$$r_6 : specificPerformance : t_i \leadsto_O^p \neg c : t_i$$
$$r_7 : execute(p) : t_i \Rightarrow_K^p p : t_{i+2}$$
$$r_8 : assign(y, z, c) : t_i, c : t_i \Rightarrow_O^p \neg c : t_i, C_1^0(x, z, 1, p : t_m) : t_i$$
$$r_9 : delegate(x, z, c) : t_i, c : t_i \Rightarrow_O^p \neg c : t_i, C_1^0(z, y, 1, p : t_m) : t_i$$

Fig. 4. Sample of rules for commitment operations

Possible operations on commitments: create, cancel, release, assign, and delegate (figure 4) are discussed next, considering their legal effect on a gratuitous commitment $c = C_1^0(x, y, 1, p : t_m)$.

Create. Consider that agent x has the intention to satisfy sentence p for agent y, until deadline t_m. Its policy is risk prone, meaning that it creates the gratuitous commitment c, while it has no guarantee that its partner will give something in exchange. Moreover, the interaction is made under the doctrine of promissory estoppel. The above intentions drive the agent to create the commitment c (rule r_0, which being transitive, the *create* action is executed once). The creation of a commitment, an action typically undertaken by the debtor, is equivalent to an *open offer* in contract law. Therefore, it is derived only as persistence knowledge (rule r_1) and is not considered an obligation in this state.

Cancel. The debtor x may *cancel* a commitment with no penalties only if the commitment is an open offer (rule r_3). The *breached* state is reached when the time for accomplishing the promise elapses, activating the mechanism for computing reliance damages, which usually assumes the creation of another commitment or contrary-to-duty obligation. In some situations, a commitment may be active even after it is breached, allowed by defining rule r_5 as defeasible. Therefore, a normative agent may block the derivation of that conclusion in order to force the execution of a specific commitment c (rule r_6). When the time-out of an open offer commitment expires its state becomes *failed* (rule r_2).

Release. If the acceptance has been made, this operation releases the debtor from its gratuitous commitment (rule r_4). The agent x executes p, but the effect is expected to be seen after two time steps (rule r_7). The defeasible rule r_7 leaves space to treat some exceptions.

Assign. The *assign* operation, transferring the rights held by the creditor y to another party, the assignee z, may be executed only by the creditor y and the state of the commitment is preserved (rule r_8). Common law favors the freedom of assignment, unless there is an express prohibition against it, requiring that it must occur in the present, to assign in the future having no legal effect.

Delegate. The *delegate* operation, transferring the duties held by the debtor x to another party z, is executed only by the debtor x and the state of the commitment is preserved (rule r_9). The creditor must be informed of the act of delegation. In case z breaches, the creditor y may elect to treat this failure as a breach of the original commitment and to sue the debtor x or to choose the role of a third party beneficiary.

5   Using Higher-Order Commitments

5.1   English Auction

We illustrate the usage of commitments in the *English auction* (figure 5). According to contract law, when an item is put up for auction, this is usually not an offer, but rather a solicitation of offers (bids) or an invitation to treat. The English auction protocol uses the pattern "request a unilateral contract"[5]. Therefore, the auctioneer a has to compose a request commitment with a unilateral contract (f_1 in figure 6, where "-" is used to express existential quantification) for item g_1 with starting price 10\$, and bids expected for 3 time steps. If bids are accepted, a has to deliver g_1 at t_7, while b has to pay for it at t_9.

Suppose that two bids are received (f_2 and f_3) at t_2, both open offers. Hence, at this stage, both b and b' may cancel their C_1^1 commitments without breach, and a also may cancel its C_2^4 commitment, because the inner commitment is not active yet (according to current practice in law). The above commitments reach the *active* state and they become obligations only if a accepts them. The bidders have made offers according to the auctioneer request regarding the deadline for

---

[5] For the simplified Net bill protocol [9] which ignores the cryptography-related aspect and also the existence of a third party agent, unlike the complete version of the Net bill protocol [10] we would use the "request a conditional bilateral contract" $C_3^6(x, y, C_3^4(y, x, C_1^1(x, y, Deliver, EPO), receipt), 1)$.

$r_{21} : deliver(g_1) : t_3 \to_K^p C_1^0(b, a, 1, +\partial_K^p g_1 : t_7)) : t_3$
$r_{22} : deliver(g_1) : t_3 \Rightarrow_K^p g_1 : t_7$
$r_{23} : g_1 : t_3 \to_O^p C_1^0(b, a, 1, +\partial_K^p g_1 : t_7)) : t_3$
$r_{24} : pay : t_9 \to_A^t release(a, b, C_1^0(b, a, 1, 12 : t_9)) : t_9$

Fig. 5. Sample rules for English auction

$f_1 : \quad C_2^4(a, -, C_1^1(-, a, g_1 : t_7, bid > 10 : t_9) : 3, 1) : t_1$
$f_2 : \quad C_1^1(b, a, g_1 : t_7, 12 : t_9) : t_2$
$f_3 : \quad C_1^1(b', a, g_1 : t_7, 11 : t_9)) : t_2$
$f_4 : \quad C_4^2(a, b', 1, +\Delta_K^p \neg C_1^1(b', a, g_1 : t_7, 11 : t_9))) : t_3$
$f_5 : \quad C_4^2(a, b, 1, +\Delta_O^p C_1^1(b, a, g_1 : t_7, 12 : t_9))) : t_3$
$f_6 : \quad deliver(g_1) : t_3$
$f_7 : \quad C_1^0(a, b, 1, +\partial_K^p g_1 : t_7)) : t_3$
$f_8 : \quad C_1^0(b, a, 1, +\Delta_K^p g_1 : t_7)) : t_7$
$f_9 : \quad C_1^0(b, a, 1, +\partial_K^p 12 : t_9)) : t_7$

Fig. 6. A trace in English auction

sending bids and $t_{maturity}$. In other encounters they might react with different terms, which would be considered a counter-offer and a more complex form of negotiation would arise.

At t_3, when the deadline for receiving bids expires, a clears the auction, considering the bids that conform to the request and accepting the winning one (lower level aspects of coordination are not shown). It may explicitly reject one bid (f_4) and accept the other one (f_5). In a unilateral contract the completion of the requested act is necessary to indicate acceptance. Most courts now hold that creditor y must also give notice of its acceptance after it has done the requested act. Therefore, the acceptance of a C_1^1 commitment can be viewed as a composite operation: execution (f_6) and a commitment notification (f_7). At this time, the existence of the requested commitment C_1^1 in f_1 is verified and C_2^4 is discharged, leaving C_1^1.

The defeasible derivation rule r_{22} allows to treat some exceptions (e.g., due to an accident the item has not arrived). When the partner informs that the item has arrived (f_8), the strict rule r_{24} fires, C_1^1 becomes *active*, and when the item arrives after 4 time steps b_1 releases it. With the payment made, the auctioneer would release the debtor b from its commitment (rule r_{24}), otherwise the mechanism for treating exceptions should be activated according to a's policy.

5.2   Supply Chain Contract

Higher order commitments may be aggregated into contracts (figure 7) signed between agents. We illustrate the usage of commitments in the formal representation of supply chain contracts, traditionally governed by long time running contracts. The current trend consists in a reorientation towards more flexible contracts, at least regarding nonstrategic resources. The selection of the best alternative assumes a good estimation of the risk implied. The types of contractual clauses which include elements of risk management are: the total minimum quantity contract[6] (clause i), the periodical contract with options[7] (clauses ii, iii), or requirement contracts[8] (clause iv), illustrated in the following contract: (i) The supplier s commits to deliver the quantity of items needed by the buyer b at the price of 20$ per unit, if the buyer b guarantees that the respective quantity, in the orders made on June and July, consists of at least 100 items (r_{41} in figure 8). (ii) The supplier s commits to deliver daily the item g_1 to the buyer b at the price P=15$ (r_{44}, first part). (iii) The supplier s commits to deliver an extra number of r items to the buyer b for the price P=10$ if the buyer orders that quantity no longer than 20 days (r_{44}, second part). (iv) The buyer b commits to agent s not to order items from the competitor z, only if the delay in delivering the items is greater than 2 days (r_{46}). (v) The supplier s guarantees to notify the buyer b until 15 June if the rate of progress of the work is too slow to meet the time of maturity (r_{48} in figure 8).

We need two different commitments that are logically composed, in order to represent a periodical contract with options (r_{44} in figure 8). The periodicity is modeled by inferring the create operation with action modality. Hence, in each day a similar commitment will be created. This is logically composed with the commitment in which the seller promises to execute the option if the buyer exercises it before a future date. If we denote $C_0^1(b, s, p, 1) : Jun$ by C_i, $C_0^1(b, s, q, 1) : Jun$ by C_{ii}, $C_1^1(s, b, 15 : 1, 30 : 1) : 1$ by C_{iii}, $C_0^1(b, s, r, 1) : 20$ by C_{iv}, $C_0^1(b, z, g, 1)$ by C_v, and $C_1^0(s, b, 1, +\Delta tooSlow) : 15Jun)$ by C_{vi}, the static formal representation appears in figure 9.

5.3   Risk in the Supply Chain

A fundamental difference between human and agent societies is that humans, even if they are governed by laws during their interactions, demonstrate some heterogeneity in their interpretation of what a commitment represents. Allowing such a heterogeneity in agent societies is certainly not easy, but probably fundamental to deploy them in realistic applications, especially if they interact with

---

[6] The buyer guarantees that his cumulative orders for all periods in the contract horizon will exceed a specified minimum quantity. In return, the supplier offers price discounts. In practice, the supplier provides a menu of (per unit price, total minimum commitment) pairs from which the buyer chooses a commitment at the corresponding price (rules r_{42}, r_{43} in figure 8).

[7] At the beginning of the horizon, the buyer commits to purchase given quantities every period. The buyer has a limited flexibility to purchase options (at unit option price) from the supplier that allows him to buy additional units, by paying an exercise price. So, options permit the buyer to adjust order quantities to the observed demands.

[8] The supplier commits to deliver all the items that the buyer will order. The buyer commits not to order from another agent. Thus, the supplier takes the risk of demand fluctuations, while the buyer gives up its right of buying from another supplier. Therefore it can loose some future bargain opportunities. This contract assigns the seller a monopolistic power over its partner.

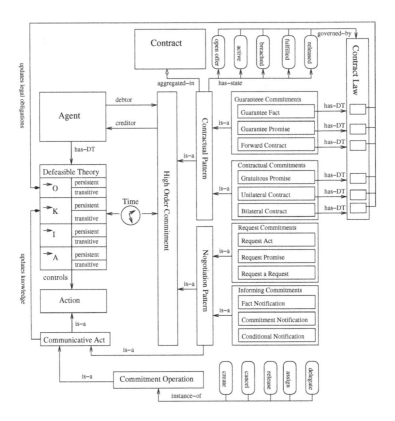

Fig. 7. Aggregation of contractual patterns into a contract

human users. Consider the contract between two agents *me* and *you*, with agent *me* having to deliver the item, while agent *you* having to pay for it.

There are more alternatives to represent this process, depending on the commitments signed between agents, identified here by five levels of risk attitudes (table 1)[9]. Assuming agent *me* has a risk prone strategy ($\Rightarrow^p_I riskProne : t_i$), it will create commitments $C^0_1(me, you, 1, deliver)$ and $C^4_0(me, you, C^0_1(you, me, 1, pay), 1)$. The acceptance of $C^0_1(me, you, 1, deliver)$ appears when agent *you* relies on it and it also notifies agent *me* about this reliance[10]. Once the acceptance occurred, the commitment reaches the active state ($\Rightarrow^p_O C^0_1(me, you, 1, deliver)$) and thus it becomes an obligation for agent *me*. On the other side, agent *you* has

---

[9] The agent's attitude towards risk has also consequences in choosing the type of remedy in case of breach. For instance, in case of a risk prone strategy, the gratuitous promise is governed by the reliance damages doctrine, while in the case of a moderate risk averse strategy the unilateral contract is preferred under the expectation damages theory.

[10] Such a notification may look like this: "I (agent *me*), based on a gratuitous promise, commit to deliver item g_1 to my client z within 3 days", represented by $C^0_4(you, me, 1, +\Delta^p_K C^0_1(you, z, 1, g_1 : 3))$.

$$r_{41} :\rightarrow_K^p C_5^3(s, b, C_3^0(b, s, 1, C_0^1(b, s, p, 1) : Jun \wedge C_0^1(b, s, q, 1) : Oct \wedge p + q > 100),$$
$$C_1^1(s, b, 20 * (p + q), p + q))$$
$$r_{42} :\rightarrow_K^p C_5^3(s, b, C_3^0(b, s, 1, C_0^1(b, s, p, 1) : Jun \wedge C_0^1(b, s, q, 1) : Oct \wedge p + q > 200),$$
$$C_1^1(s, b, 18 * (p + q), p + q))$$
$$r_{43} :\rightarrow_K^p C_5^3(s, b, C_3^0(b, s, 1, C_0^1(b, s, p, 1) : Jun \wedge C_0^1(b, s, q, 1) : Oct \wedge p + q > 300),$$
$$C_1^1(s, b, 16 * (p + q), p + q))$$
$$r_{44} :\rightarrow_A^p create(C_1^1(s, b, 15 : 1, g_1 : 1) : 1)\diamond$$
$$\rightarrow_K^p C_5^3(s, b, C_0^1(b, s, r, 1) : 20, C_1^1(s, b, 10 * r, r))$$
$$r_{46} :\rightarrow_K^p C_1^3(b, s, delay \leq 2, \neg C_0^0(b, z, g, 1))$$
$$r_{47} : C_0^1(b, z, g, 1)) \rightarrow_K^p breach$$
$$r_{48} :\rightarrow_K^p C_4^1(s, b, tooSlow : t_i \wedge t_i < 15 Jun, C_1^0(s, b, 1, +\Delta tooSlow) : 15 Jun)$$
$$r_{42} \succ r_{41}, r_{43} \succ r_{42}.$$

Fig. 8. Rules for generating a supply chain contract

$$\langle \{ [C_1^1(s, b) \circ_q (C_i \wedge C_{ii} \wedge p + q > 100) \circ_p (C_1^1(s, b) \circ_q 20 * (p + q) \circ_p p + q)] \vee$$
$$[C_1^1(s, b) \circ_q (C_i \wedge C_{ii} \wedge p + q > 200) \circ_p (C_1^1(s, b) \circ_q 18 * (p + q) \circ_p p + q)] \vee$$
$$[C_1^1(s, b) \circ_q (C_i \wedge C_{ii} \wedge p + q > 300) \circ_p (C_1^1(s, b) \circ_q 16 * (p + q) \circ_p p + q)] \} \wedge$$
$$\{ C_{iii} \diamond [C_1^1(s, b) \circ_q C_{iv} \circ_p (C_1^1(s, b) \circ_q 10 * r \circ_p r)] \} \wedge$$
$$C_1^1(b, s) \circ_q delay \leq 2 \circ_p C_v \wedge$$
$$C_1^1(s, b) \circ_q (tooSlow : t_i \wedge t_i \leq 15 Jun) \circ_p C_{vi} \rangle$$

Fig. 9. Representation of the contract

no obligation at all, knowing only that its partner has requested to promise to pay for the item[11]. In case of a risk neutral strategy, the acceptance occurs at the creation of the inner commitment ($\rightarrow_A^t create(you, C_1^0(you, me, 1, pay))$). Thus, each agent has one obligation: $\rightarrow_O^p C_1^0(me, you, 1, deliver)$ for agent me and $\rightarrow_O^p C_1^0(you, me, 1, pay)$ for agent you. In case of a risk averse strategy the acceptance of the unilateral contract is done by the completion of the requested act, in this case the payment. Therefore, agent me has the obligation to deliver the item only after it had received the payment ($pay \rightarrow_O^p C_1^0(me, you, 1, deliver)$).

Table 1. Risk attitudes between two agents

Risk	Commitments	Meaning
risk prone	$C_1^0(me, you, 1, deliver) \wedge$ $C_0^4(me, you, C_1^0(you, me, 1, pay), 1)$	I commit to deliver the item and I request you to commit to pay for it
moderate risk prone	$C_1^0(me, you, 1, deliver) \wedge$ $C_0^1(me, you, pay, 1)$	I commit to deliver the item and I request you to pay for it
risk neutral	$C_3^1(me, you, C_1^0(you, me, 1, pay),$ $deliver)$	I commit to deliver the item if you commit me to pay for it
moderate risk averse	$C_1^1(me, you, pay, deliver)$	I commit to deliver the item after you pay for it
risk averse	$C_4^1(me, you, pay, C_1^0(me, you, 1, deliver))$	I will commit to deliver the item if you pay me

---

[11] In the case of a moderate risk prone strategy, agent me requests agent you to effectively pay for the item and not only to promise to pay.

Table 2 illustrates a normal flow of the execution for both risk neutral and moderate risk averse agents. From another viewpoint, risk attitudes may be seen as different business interaction protocols used for executing the same task. Therefore, high order commitments can handle exceptions that might occur when

Table 2. Risk neutral and moderate risk averse behavior

	Moderate risk averse		
State	me	you	common information
t_1 open offer	$\to_A^t create(me, C_1^1(me,$ $you, pay, deliver))$		$\to_K^p C_1^1(me, you, pay, deliver)$
t_2 acceptance		$\to_A^t pay$	$\to_O^p C_1^1(me, you, 1, deliver)$
t_3 fulfilled	$\to_A^t deliver$		
	Risk neutral		
State	me	you	common information
t_1 open offer	$\to_A^t create(me, C_3^1(me, you,$ $C_1^0(you, me, 1, pay), deliver)$		$\to_K^p C_3^1(me, you, C_1^0(you, me,$ $1, pay), deliver)$
t_2 acceptance		$\to_A^t create(me,$ $C_1^0(you, me, 1, pay))$	$\to_O^p C_1^0(me, you, 1, deliver) \to_K^p C_1^0(you, me, 1, pay)$
t_3 fulfilled	$\to_A^t deliver$		$\to_O^p C_1^0(you, me, 1, pay)$
t_4		$\to_A^t pay$	

some actions might be executed in an unacceptable sequence, without the need to introduce preconditions for actions as in [9]. Note also, for the risk neutral scenario the *deliver* operation is equivalent to reliance on the contract and, based on the promissory estoppel principle, the commitment $C_1^0(you, me, 1, pay)$ is derived as obligation.

Now consider the situation when agent *me* is conditioned by its supplier *sup*. In order to deliver its output item, it has to obtain first its input item (table 3) with other possible attitudes towards risk. In table 3 agent *me* has the obligation

Table 3. Risk attitudes considering a third party

Risk	Commitments	Meaning
risk averse	$C_5^1(me, you, C_1^0(sup, me, 1, deliver'),$ $C_1^0(me, you, 1, deliver)$	If my supplier commits to deliver my input item, I commit to deliver my output item
risk neutral	$C_5^5(me, you, C_3^1(sup, me,$ $C_1^0(me, sup, 1, pay'), deliver'),$ $C_1^0(me, you, 1, deliver))$	If my supplier commits to deliver my input item if I promise him to pay, I commit to deliver my output item
risk prone	$C_5^5(me, you, C_1^1(sup, me, pay, deliver),$ $C_1^0(me, you, 1, deliver)$	If my supplier commits to deliver my input item if I pay it, I commit to deliver my output item

to deliver its output item only in case it has active contracts with its supplier regarding its input item. A similar risk averse strategy can be adopted on the other side of the flow within the supply chain. In this situation, the contracts with the suppliers become active only if demand exists for the items, a part of the market fluctuations being taken by the supplier instead of *me*.

We also advocate that defeasible logic is appropriate for the problem in hand. Consider the defeasible theory in figure 10 and the scenario in which

$badCreditCard$ appears after the agent has been inferred $C_0^1(me, you, 1, deliver : t_{i+2})$ as obligation. Traditionally two solutions exist: it is considered an exception, modeled as a protocol [9] which is attached to the initial flow that must be reconsidered or, in some deontic approaches, a rollback operator is used. The nonmonotonic property of defeasible logic allows the obligation to be defeated when an exception occurs.

$r_{51} :\to_K^p C_1^1(me, you, pay : t_i, deliver : t_{i+2})$
$r_{52} : pay : t_i \to_O^p C_0^1(me, you, 1, deliver : t_{i+2})$
$r_{53} : badCreditCard : t_i \rightsquigarrow_O^p C_0^1(me, you, 1, deliver : t_i)$
$r_{53} \succ r_{52}.$

Fig. 10. Dealing with new information

Another point is that defeasible logic simplifies the process of specifying preconditions for commitments in the spirit suggested by Winikoff et al. [9], who propose that preconditions be replaced by commitments to avoid certain actions, termed prohibitions. Thus, a prohibition of the form $P(x, a)$ states that agent x is prohibited from performing action a. At the communicative level, in our framework this is specified by $C_0^1(y, x, \neg a : t_{issue}, 1)$, in which agent y requests agent x not to execute action a at least until time t_{issue}. At the defeasible theory level, this prohibition is simply captured by defeaters: $\rightsquigarrow_A^p a : t_{issue}$. Following this idea, a conditional prohibition [9] of the form $P(x, a, p)$, stating that agent x is prohibited from performing action a if p holds, is specified as a communicative act by $C_2^4(y, x, C_1^1(x, y, p, \neg a) : t_{issue}, 1)$. Similarly, the correspondent rule at the logic level is $p \rightsquigarrow_A^p a : t_{issue}$. Additionally, we can specify exactly when the action is prohibited or if the prohibition is persistent.

6 Related Work and Conclusions

Ideas from legal reasoning have been applied to social commitments [1,7], but not using the contract law, although the rich semantics of higher-order commitments [7] introduces concepts like: ought, pledge, taboo, convention, collective commitment, obligation, claim, privilege, power, and immunity.

The declarative contracts in RuleML [11] use a semantic part for contracts and contracts have already been represented with defeasible logic and RuleML [12]. By introducing commitments, we offer a more flexible solution for contract monitoring and for agents reasoning on current actions.

Causal logic has been used [13] for protocol engineering, leading to a formal method for protocol design, and commitments can also be modeled in event calculus [14]. Our commitments are addressed in a more contractual style and the deadlines attached to commitments offer a realistic approach from a contractual point of view.

Commitments between a network of agents have also been analyzed [3], but without time constraints. Our higher-order commitments are closer to the leveled commitment contracts [6], with different attitudes toward risk.

Verdicchio and Collombetti [15] treat the semantics of communicative acts in terms of social commitments, instead of the classical approach, with a precommitment similar to our commitment having the *open offer* state derived from contract law. Our higher-order commitments have a similar semantics to the derivative communicative acts [15], but we also cover the completion of the requested act. In [16] a commitment-based architecture for contract enactment is proposed, where exceptions in the contract are handled by the virtual organization to which the agents belong. Our proposed commitments can model specific contracts that appear in real life scenarios and exceptions are caught using defeasible reasoning.

With defeasible commitments in the execution of contracts, we obtain two main advantages. On the one hand, agents can reason with incomplete information, including confidential contractual clauses. On the other hand, this framework is suitable for exceptions and legal reasoning: (i) concerning resolution of a dispute, strategies are explainable; (ii) skeptical mechanism; (iii) allows preferences; (iv) linear complexity; (v) fine-grained mechanism to deal with exceptions in the same manner for expected or unexpected ones.

Acknowledgments

We are grateful to the anonymous reviewers for useful comments. Part of this work was supported by the grant 27702-990 from the National Research Council of the Romanian Ministry for Education and Research.

References

1. Pasquier, P., Flores, R.A., Chaib-draa, B.: Modelling flexible social commitments and their enforcement. In Gleizes, M.P., Omicini, A., Zambonelli, F., eds.: Engineering Societies in the Agents World. LNAI 3451, Springer-Verlag (2005) 139–151
2. Mallya, A.U., Singh, M.P.: Modeling exceptions via commitment protocols. In: 4th International Joint Conference on Autonomous Agents and Multiagent Systems, Utrecht, Netherlands, ACM Press (2005) 122–129
3. Wan, F., Singh, M.: Formalizing and achieving multiparty agreements via commitments. In: 4th International Joint Conference on Autonomous Agents and Multiagent Systems, Utrecht, Netherlands, ACM Press (2005) 770–777
4. Governatori, G., Rotolo, A., Sartor, G.: Temporalised normative positions in defeasible logic. In: 10th International Conference on Artificial Inteligence and Law, Bologna, Italy (2005) 25–34
5. Letia, I.A., Groza, A.: Running contracts with defeasible commitments. In Moonis, A., Dapoigny, R., eds.: Advances in Applied Artificial Intelligence. LNCS 4031, Springer-Verlag (2006) 91–100
6. Sandholm, T., Lesser, W.: Leveled commitment contracts and strategic breach. Games and Economic Behavior **35** (2001) 212–270
7. Singh, M.P.: An ontology for commitments in multiagents systems: Toward a unification of normative concepts. Artificial Intelligence and Law **7** (1999) 97–113

8. Craswell, R.: Contract law: General theories. In Bouckaert, B., Geest, G.D., eds.: Encyclopedia of Law and Economics, Volume III. The Regulation of Contracts. Cheltenham (2000) 1–24

9. Winikoff, M., Liu, W., Harland, J.: Enhancing commitment machines. In: Declarative Agent Languages and Technologies. LNAI 3476, Springer-Verlag (2005) 198–220

10. Cox, B., Tygar, J., Sirbu, M.: Netbill security and transaction protocol. In: 1st USENIX Workshop on Electronic Commerce, New York (1995) 77–88

11. Grosof, B.: Representing E-Commerce rules via situated courteous logic programs in RuleML. Electronic Commerce Research and Applications 3(1) (2004) 2–20

12. Governatori, G.: Representing business contracts in RuleML. Journal of Cooperative Information Systems 14(2-3) (2005) 181–216

13. Chopra, A.K., Singh, M.P.: Contextualizing commitment protocols. In: 5th International Joint Conference on Autonomous Agents and Multiagent Systems, Hakodate, Japan, ACM Press (2006) 1345–1352

14. Yolum, P., Singh, M.P.: Reasoning about commitments in the event calculus: An approach for specifying and executing protocols. Annals of Mathematics and Artificial Intelligence 42(1-3) (2004) 227–253

15. Verdicchio, M., Colombetti, M.: A commitment-based communicative act library. In: 4th International Joint Conference on Autonomous Agents and Multiagent Systems, Utrecht, Netherlands, ACM Press (2005) 755–761

16. Udupi, Y.B., Singh, M.P.: Contract enactment in virtual organizations: A commitment-based approach. In: 21st National Conference on Artificial Intelligence, Boston, Massachusetts, AAAI Press (2006)

A Dynamic Logic Programming Based System for Agents with Declarative Goals

Vivek Nigam* and João Leite

CENTRIA, New University of Lisbon, Portugal
vivek.nigam@gmail.com,
jleite@di.fct.unl.pt

Abstract. Goals are used to define the behavior of (pro-active) agents. It is our view that the goals of an agent can be seen as a knowledge base of the situations that it wants to achieve. It is therefore in a natural way that we use Dynamic Logic Programming (DLP), an extension of Answer-Set Programming that allows for the representation of knowledge that changes with time, to represent the goals of the agent and their evolution, in a simple, declarative, fashion. In this paper, we represent agent's goals as a DLP, discuss and show how to represent some situations where the agent should adopt or drop goals, and investigate some properties that emerge from using such representation.

1 Introduction

It is widely accepted that *intelligent agents* must have some form of *pro-active* behavior [20]. This means that an intelligent agent will try to pursue some set of states, represented by its *goals*. Generally, to determine these states, agents must reason for example, with their beliefs, capabilities or with other goals. It is therefore our perspective that the goals of an agent can be seen as a *knowledge base* encoding the situations it wants to achieve. Consider the following program, containing one rule, as an example of an agent's *goal base*:

$$goal(write\_paper) \leftarrow not\ deadline\_over$$

the agent will consider to write a paper ($goal(write\_paper)$), if the deadline is believed not to be past ($not\ deadline\_over$).

Programming with a declarative knowledge representation has demonstrated several advantages over *classical programming*. For instance, explicitly encoded knowledge can easily be *revised* and *updated*. Recently, an increasing amount of research [19,7,14,17,18,16] has been devoted to the issue of programming agents with a declarative representation of goals. The declarative side of goals intimately related to the need to check if a goal has been achieved, if a goal is impossible, if a goal should be dropped, i.e., if the agent should stop pursuing a goal, if there is

* Supported by the Alβan Program, the European Union Programme of High Level Scholarships for Latin America, no. E04M040321BR.

M. Baldoni and U. Endriss (Eds.): DALT 2006, LNAI 4327, pp. 174–190, 2006.

interference between goals [19,16]; and also to the need to construct agents that are able to *communicate* goals with other agents [14]. In [19,16,14] the reader can find examples illustrating the need for a declarative aspect to goals.

Furthermore, agents, due to changes in the environment, have the need to *drop* goals (maybe because the goal has been achieved, or a failure condition is activated [19]), *adopt* new goals [6,17,16,19], or even change the way they reason to determine their goals. Consider, in the previous example, that the deadline to submit the paper has been postponed. Clearly, the previous rule is not valid, since the previous deadline in no longer a condition to drop the goal of writing the paper, hence the rule should be updated. This means that the goals of an agents are *dynamic knowledge bases*, where not only the *extensional part* (i.e., the set of facts) change, but also their *intentional part* (i.e., the set of rules).

In this paper, we will address the problem of representing and reasoning about dynamic declarative goals using *Dynamic Logic Programming (DLP)*.

In [13,9], the paradigm of *DLP* was introduced. According to *DLP*, knowledge is given by a series of theories, encoded as generalized logic programs[1], each representing distinct states of the world. Different states, sequentially ordered, can represent different time periods, thus allowing DLP to represent knowledge that undergoes successive updates. Since individual theories may comprise mutually contradictory as well as overlapping information, the role of *DLP* is to employ the mutual relationships among different states to determine the declarative semantics for the combined theory comprised of all individual theories at each state. Intuitively, one can add, at the end of the sequence, newer rules (arising from new or reacquired knowledge) leaving to *DLP* the task of ensuring that these rules are in force, and that previous ones are valid (by inertia) only so far as possible, i.e. that they are kept for as long as they are not in conflict with newly added ones, these always prevailing.

There has been, in the past years, an intense study of the properties of DLP to represent knowledge bases that evolve with time [2,9,12]. However, up to now, there hasn't been much investigation of how DLP could be used to represent, in a declarative manner, the goals of an agent. Since DLP allows for the specification of knowledge bases that undergo change, and enjoys the expressiveness provided by both strong and default negations, by dint of its foundation in answer-set programming, it seems a natural candidate to be used to represent and to reason about the declarative goals of an agent, and the way they change with time.

For our purpose, we will use a simple agent framework to be able to clearly demonstrate the properties obtained by using DLP. The agents in this framework are composed of data structures representing their beliefs (*definite logic program*), goals (*DLP*), and committed goals (*intentions*). The semantics of these agents are defined by a *transition system* composed of *reasoning rules*. We propose three types of reasoning rules: **1)** Intention Adoption Rules: used to *commit* to a goal by adopting plans to achieve it; **2)** Goal Update Rules: used to *update* an agent's goals using the DLP semantics; **3)** Intention Dropping Rules: used to *drop* previously committed goals. We show that agents in this frame-

---

[1] Logic programs with default and strong negation both in the body and head of rules.

work are able to express achievement and maintenance goals, represent failure conditions for goals, and are able to adopt, drop or change their goals.

The remainder of the paper is structured as follows: in the next Section we are going to present some preliminaries, introducing Dynamic Logic Programming. In Section 3, we introduce the agent framework we are going to use. Later in Section 4, we discuss some situations related to when to drop and adopt new goals, and how to use the DLP semantics to represent these situations. In Section 5, we give a *simple* example illustrating how DLP could be used to represent goals, to finally draw some conclusions and propose some further research topics in Section 6.

2   Preliminaries

In this section, we are going to give some preliminary definitions that will be used throughout the paper. We start by introducing the syntax and semantics of goal programs. Afterwards, we introduce the semantics of *Dynamic Logic Programming*.

2.1   Languages and Logic Programming

Let $\mathcal{K}$ be a set of propositional atoms. An *objective knowledge literal* is either an atom A or a strongly negated atom $\neg A$. The set of objective knowledge literals is denoted by $\mathcal{L}_{\mathcal{K}}^{-}$. If $\{L_1, \ldots, L_n\} \subseteq \mathcal{L}_{\mathcal{K}}^{-}$ then $goal\,(L_1, \ldots, L_n)$, $def\,(L_1, \ldots, L_n)$, $maintenance\,(L_1, \ldots, L_n) \in \mathcal{L}_{\mathcal{G}}{}^2$. We dub the element of $\mathcal{L}_{\mathcal{G}}$ *objective goal literals*. An *objective literal* is either an objective knowledge literal or an objective goal literal. A *default knowledge (resp. goal) literal* is an objective knowledge (resp. goal) literal preceded by *not*. A *default literal* is either a *default knowledge literal* or a *default goal literal*. A *goal literal* is either an objective goal literal or a default goal literal. A *knowledge literal* is either an objective knowledge literal or a default knowledge literal. A *literal* is either an objective literal or a default literal. We use $\mathcal{L}_{\mathcal{K}}^{-,not}$ to denote the set of knowledge literals and $\mathcal{L}_{\mathcal{G}}^{not}$ to denote the set of goal literals.

The set, $\mathcal{L}_{\mathcal{G}}$ also known as the goal language, uses a special symbol, *goal(.)* to represent the conjunction of achievement goals; the special symbol, *maintenance(.)*, to represent maintenance goals; the special symbol, *def(.)*, to represent defeasible goals.

A *goal rule* r (or simply a rule) is an ordered pair $Head\,(r) \leftarrow Body\,(r)$ where $Head\,(r)$ (dubbed the head of the rule) is a goal literal and $Body\,(r)$ (dubbed the body of the rule) is a set of literals. A rule with $Head\,(r) = L_0$ and $Body\,(r) = \{L_1, \ldots, L_n\}$ will simply be written as $L_0 \leftarrow L_1, \ldots, L_n$. A *goal program* (*GP*) P, is a finite or infinite set of rules. If $Head(r) = A$ (resp. $Head(r) = not\,A$) then $not\,Head(r) = not\,A$ (resp. $not\,Head(r) = A$). If $Head\,(r) = \neg A$ (resp.

---

[2] We will consider that there is a total order over the set of objective literals, $\mathcal{L}_{\mathcal{K}}^{-}$, and that the order in which the objective literals appear in the symbols of the goal language are based in this predefined ordering.

$Head(r) = A$), then $\neg Head(r) = A$ (resp. $\neg Head(r) = \neg A$). By the *expanded goal program* corresponding to the GP P, denoted by $\mathbf{P}$, we mean the GP obtained by augmenting P with a rule of the form $not \neg Head(r) \leftarrow Body(r)$ for every rule, in P, of the form $Head(r) \leftarrow Body(r)$, where $Head(r)$ is an objective goal literal[3]. Two rules r and r' are conflicting, denoted by $r \bowtie r'$, iff $Head(r) = not\, Head(r')$.

An *interpretation* M is a set of objective literals that is consistent i.e, M does not contain both:

- A and $\neg A$;
- $goal(L_1, \ldots, L, \ldots, L_n)$ and $goal(L_1, \ldots, \neg L, \ldots, L_n)$;
- $maintenance(L_1, \ldots, L, \ldots, L_n)$ and $maintenance(L_1, \ldots, \neg L, \ldots, L_n)$;
- $maintenance(L_1, \ldots, L, \ldots, L_n)$ and $goal(L_1, \ldots, \neg L, \ldots, L_n)$.

An objective literal L is true in M, denoted by $M \vDash L$, iff $L \in M$, and false otherwise. A default literal $not\, L$ is true in M, denoted by $M \vDash not\, L$, iff $L \notin M$, and false otherwise. A set of literals B is true in M, denoted by $M \vDash B$, iff each literal in B is true in M. Only inconsistent sets of objective literals (In), will entail the special symbol $\bot$ (denoted by $In \models \bot$). $\bot$ can be seen semantically equivalent to the formula $A \wedge \neg A$. An interpretation M is an *answer set* (or stable model) of a GP P iff $M' = least\,(\mathbf{P} \cup \{not\, A \mid A \notin M\})$, where $M' = M \cup \{not\_A \mid A \notin M\}$, A is an objective literal, and $least(.)$ denotes the least model of the definite program obtained from the argument program by replacing every default literal $not\, A$ by a new atom not_A.

For notational convenience, we will no longer explicitly state the alphabet $\mathcal{K}$. And as usual, we will consider all the variables appearing in the programs as a shorthand for the set of all their possible ground instantiations.

2.2 Dynamic Logic Programming

A *dynamic logic (goal) program* (DLP) is a sequence of goal programs. Let $\mathcal{P} = (P_1, ..., P_s)$ be a DLP and P' a GP. We use $\rho\,(\mathcal{P})$ to denote the multiset of all rules appearing in the programs $\mathbf{P}_1, ..., \mathbf{P}_s$, and $(\mathcal{P}, P')$ to denote $(P_1, ..., P_s, P')$.

The semantics of a DLP is specified as follows:

Definition 1 (Semantics of DLP). *[9,1] Let $\mathcal{P} = (P_1, \ldots, P_s)$ be a dynamic logic program A be an objective literal, $\rho\,(\mathcal{P})$, M' and $least(.)$ be as before. An interpretation M is a (goal dynamic) stable model of $\mathcal{P}$ iff*

$$M' = least\,([\rho\,(\mathcal{P}) - Rej(M, \mathcal{P})] \cup Def(M, \mathcal{P}))$$

Where:

$$Def(M, \mathcal{P}) = \{not\, A \mid \nexists r \in \rho(\mathcal{P}), Head(r) = A, M \vDash Body(r)\}$$
$$Rej(M, \mathcal{P}) = \{r \mid r \in \mathbf{P}_i, \exists r' \in \mathbf{P}_j, i \leq j \leq s, r \bowtie r', M \vDash Body(r')\}$$

---

[3] Expanded programs are defined to appropriately deal with strong negation in updates. For more on this issue, the reader is invited to read [10,9]. From now on, and unless otherwise stated, we will always consider generalized logic programs to be in their expanded versions.

We will denote by $SM(\mathcal{P})$ the set of stable models of the DLP $\mathcal{P}$. Further details and motivations concerning DLPs and its semantics can be found in [9].

The next example illustrates how a DLP could be used to represent the goals of an agent.

Example 1. Consider the goals of a young agent that reached a point in her life that she is interested in having a boyfriend. However, to find a boyfriend (as many know) may not be the easiest task, but she knows that being pretty helps to achieve it. We can represent this situation by the following program:

$$P_1 : goal(boyfriend) \leftarrow not\,boyfriend$$
$$goal(pretty) \leftarrow not\,pretty, goal(boyfriend)$$

As she is not pretty and doesn't have a boyfriend, her initial goals would be to have a boyfriend and to be pretty, represented by the unique stable model of P_1, $\{goal(boyfriend), goal(pretty)\}$. Her mother, noticing the desires of her daughter and as usual looking for the best for her child, immediately tells her that she should study. As the agent respects her mother, she updates her goals with the program P_2, stating the incompatibility between studying and having a boyfriend:

$$P_2 : not\,goal(boyfriend) \leftarrow goal(study)$$
$$goal(study) \leftarrow$$

Since, P_2 is a newer program than P_1, the rule $goal(boyfriend) \leftarrow not\,boyfriend$ will be rejected, according to the semantics of DLP, by the rule $not\,goal(boyfriend) \leftarrow goal(study)$. Furthermore, the goal of being pretty will no longer be supported. Hence, the DLP (P_1, P_2) has a unique stable model, $\{goal(study)\}$. After sometime, the agent grows and becomes more confident (to a point that she can question her mother). As she is tired of studying and attending the boring math classes, she decides that studying is no longer her objective. She then, updates her goals with the program P_3:

$$P_3 : not\,goal(study) \leftarrow$$

As a result, the rule $goal(study) \leftarrow$ will be rejected and she will once more have as a goal to find a boyfriend. The DLP (P_1, P_2, P_3) has the unique stable model $\{goal(boyfriend), goal(pretty)\}$. However, discussing with some of her friends (or maybe reading some women magazine), she discovers that to be pretty either she has to wear nice clothes (go to the shopping) or have a nice body (fitness), therefore she updates her goal with the program, P_4:

$$P_4 : goal(shopping) \leftarrow not\,shopping, goal(pretty), not\,goal(fitness)$$
$$goal(fitness) \leftarrow not\,fitness, goal(pretty), not\,goal(shopping)$$

The DLP (P_1, P_2, P_3, P_4) has two stable models, one representing that she has the goal of shopping $\{goal(boyfriend), goal(pretty), goal(shopping)\}$, and another of getting fit $\{goal(boyfriend), goal(pretty), goal(fitness)\}$.

As illustrated in the example above, a DLP can have more than one stable model. But then, how to deal with these stable models and how to represent the semantics of a DLP? This issue has been extensively discussed and three main approached are currently being considered [9]:

Skeptical - $\models_\cap$ According to this approach, the *intersection* of all stable models is used to determine the semantics of a DLP. Therefore, a formula φ is entailed by the DLP $\mathcal{P}$, denoted by $\mathcal{P} \models_\cap \varphi$, iff it is entailed by all the program's stable models;

Credulous - $\models_\cup$ According to this approach, the *union* of all stable models is used to determine the semantics of a DLP. Therefore, a formula φ is entailed by the DLP $\mathcal{P}$, denoted by $\mathcal{P} \models_\cup L$, iff it is entailed by one of the program's stable models;

Casuistic - $\models_\Omega$ According to this approach, one of the stable models is selected by a selection function Ω, to represent the semantics of the program. Since, the stable models can be seen as different consistent options, or possible worlds, by adopting this approach the agent would commit to one of these options. We use $\mathcal{P} \models_\Omega L$, to denote that formula φ is entailed by the stable model of the DLP $\mathcal{P}$, selected by Ω;

3   Agent Framework

In this Section, we define the agent framework[4] that we will use to demonstrate the properties obtained by using Dynamic Logic Programming to represent the goals of an agent. An agent in this framework is composed by a *belief base* representing what the agent believes the world is; a *goal base* representing the states the agent wants to achieve; a set of *reasoning rules*; and a set of *intentions* with two associated *plans* representing the goals that the agent is currently *committed* to achieve. We are considering that the agent has, at its disposal, a *plan library* represented by the set of plans *Plan*. A plan can be viewed as a *sequence of actions* that can modify the agent's beliefs or/and the environment surrounding it, and is used by the agent to *try* to achieve a committed goal, as well as to do the cleaning up actions.

The idea behind associating two plans to an agent's intention, is that one of the plans, $\pi_{achieve}$, will be used to try to achieve the intention, and the second plan, π_{clean}, is used to do all the *cleaning up* actions after the goal is dropped, or when there are no more actions to be performed in $\pi_{achieve}$. For example, if an agent's intention is to *bake a cake*, it would execute an appropriate plan to achieve its goal ($\pi_{achieve}$), gathering the ingredients, the utensils, and setting up the oven. After the cake is baked, the agent would still have to wash the utensils and throw the garbage away, these actions could be seen as clean up actions (π_{clean}).

---

[4] The agent framework defined in this section could be seen as a modified (simplified) version of the agent framework used in the 3APL multi-agent system [5].

Our main focus in this paper is to investigate the properties of representing the goal base as a Dynamic Logic Program. We are not going to give the *deserved* attention to the belief base. We consider the belief base as a simple definite logic program. However, a more complex belief base could be used. For example, we could represent the belief base also as a Dynamic Logic Program and have some mechanism such that the agent has an unique model for its beliefs[5]. Elsewhere, in [15], we explore the representation of 3APL agent's belief base as a DLP.

Since, the reasoning rules of an agent don't change, it is useful to define the concept of *agent configuration* to represent the variable state of an agent.

Definition 2 (Agent Configuration). *An agent configuration is a tuple* $\langle \sigma, \gamma,$ *$\Pi \rangle$, where σ is a definite logic program over $\mathcal{K}$, representing the agent's belief base, $\gamma = (P_1, \ldots, P_n)$ is a DLP representing it's goal base, such that every P_i is a goal program and that the DLP (γ, σ) has at least one stable model, and $\Pi \subseteq Plan \times Plan \times \mathcal{L_G}$ the intention base of the agent.*

As the goals of an agent might be dependent on its beliefs, to determine its goals it will be necessary to integrate the agent's belief base (σ) and its goal base (γ). We straightforwardly use the DLP semantics to do this integration by considering the DLP (γ, σ) to determine the agent's goals. Consider the following illustrative example:

Example 2. Consider an agent with a goal base, $\gamma = (P)$, consisting of the following program P, stating that the agent will try to have a girlfriend if it has money, and if it doesn't have the goal of saving money:

$$P : goal(girlfriend) \leftarrow have\_money, not\ goal(save\_money)$$

And with its belief base, σ, stating that the agent will have money if it has low expenses and a high income, and that currently this is the case:

$$\sigma : have\_money \leftarrow low\_expenses, high\_income$$
$$high\_income \leftarrow$$
$$low\_expenses \leftarrow$$

To determine if $goal(girlfriend)$ will be a goal of the agent we update γ with σ, and clearly having a girlfriend will be a goal of the agent, since $goal(girlfriend)$ will be entailed by the DLP (γ, σ). Note that since σ is a definite logic program, and goal rules in γ do not have knowledge literals in their heads, the update of γ with σ amounts to determine the unique model of σ and use it to perform a partial evaluation of γ.

Moreover, we only consider the agent configurations, $\langle \sigma, \gamma, \Pi \rangle$, where the DLP (γ, σ) has at least one model, since an agent without semantics for its goal base wouldn't be of much interest in this work.

---

[5] For example, a *belief model selector* that would select one of the stable models of the belief base to represent the agent's beliefs.

We assume that the semantics of the agents is defined by a *transition system*. A transition system is composed of a set of *transition rules* that transforms one agent configuration into another agent configuration, in one computation step. It may be possible that one or more transition rules are applicable in a certain agent configuration. In this case, the agent must decide which one to apply. This decision can be made through a *deliberation cycle*, for example, through a priority among the rules. In this paper, we won't specify a deliberation cycle. An unsatisfied reader can consider a *non-deterministic* selection of the rules.

We now introduce the *intention adoption rules*. These rules are used to adopt plans to try to achieve goals of the agent. Informally, if the agent has a goal, $goal(L_1, \ldots, L_n)$, that currently doesn't have plans in the agent's intention base (Π), the rule will adopt a couple of plans, $\pi_{achieve}, \pi_{clean}$, by adding the tuple $(\pi_{achieve}, \pi_{clean}, goal(L_1, \ldots, L_n))$ to the agent's intention base. However, as argued by Bratman in [4], agent's shouldn't pursue at the same time contradictory goals. Therefore, similarly as done in [18], we check if by adopting a new goal, the intentions of the agent are consistent.

Definition 3 (Intention Adoption Rules). *Let* $\langle \sigma, \gamma, \Pi \rangle$ *be an agent configuration and* $goal(L_1, \ldots, L_n) \in \mathcal{L}_{\mathcal{G}}$, *where*

$$\Pi = \{(\pi_{achieve}^1, \pi_{clean}^1, goal(L_1^1, ..., L_i^1)), ..., (\pi_{achieve}^m, \pi_{clean}^m, goal(L_1^m, ..., L_j^m))\}$$

such that $\{(\pi_{achieve}, \pi_{clean}, goal\,(L_1, \ldots, L_n))\} \nsubseteq \Pi$, *and* $x \in \{\cap, \cup, \Omega\}$.

$$\frac{[(\gamma, \sigma) \models_x goal\,(L_1, \ldots, L_n) \vee (\gamma, \sigma) \models_x maintenance\,(L_1, \ldots, L_n)] \wedge}{\{L_1^1, \ldots, L_i^1, \ldots, L_1^m, \ldots, L_j^m, L_1, \ldots, L_n\} \nvDash \bot}{\langle \sigma, \gamma, \Pi \rangle \longrightarrow \langle \sigma, \gamma, \Pi \cup \{(\pi_{achieve}, \pi_{clean}, goal\,(L_1, \ldots, L_n))\} \rangle}$$

Notice that the condition of consistency of the agent's intentions may not yet be the best option to avoid irrational actions. Winikoff et al. suggest, in [19], that it is necessary also to analyze the *plans* of the agent, as well as the *resources* available to achieve the intentions. However, this is out of the scope of this paper.

We have just introduced a rule to adopt new intentions. Considering that intentions are committed goals, if the goal that the intention represents is no longer pursued by the agent, it would make sense to drop it. Therefore, we introduce into our agent framework the *Intention Dropping Rule*. Informally, the semantics of this rule is to stop the execution of the plan used to achieve the goal $(\pi_{achieve})$, if the goal is no longer supported by the goal base of an agent, and start to execute the plan used to perform the cleaning up actions (π_{clean}). The next definition formalizes this idea.

Definition 4 (Intention Dropping Rule). *Let* $\langle \sigma, \gamma, \Pi \rangle$ *be an agent configuration,* $x \in \{\cap, \cup, \Omega\}$, *where* $\{(\pi_{achieve}, \pi_{clean}, \psi)\} \subseteq \Pi$, $\psi = goal\,(L_1, \ldots, L_n)$, *and* $\pi_{achieve} \neq \emptyset$. *Then:*

$$\frac{(\gamma, \sigma) \nvDash_x goal\,(L_1, \ldots, L_n) \wedge (\gamma, \sigma) \nvDash_x maintenance\,(L_1, \ldots, L_n)}{\langle \sigma, \gamma, \Pi \rangle \longrightarrow \langle \sigma, \gamma, \Pi \setminus \{(\pi_{achieve}, \pi_{clean}, \psi)\} \cup \{(\emptyset, \pi_{clean}, \psi)\} \rangle}$$

Since an agent's goal base is represented by a Dynamic Logic Program, an agent can easily update its goal base with a GP using the DLP semantics. As we will investigate in the next Section, updating a goal base with a GP will enable the agent to have dynamic goals, e.g. by goal adoption or goal dropping. For this purpose, we introduce a new type of reasoning rule to the system, namely the *Goal Update Rules*.

Definition 5 (Goal Update Rule). *The Goal Update Rule is a tuple* $\langle \Sigma_B, \Sigma_G, P \rangle$ *where* P *is a Goal Program, and* $\Sigma_B \subseteq \mathcal{L}^{\neg, not}$, *and* $\Sigma_G \subseteq \mathcal{L}_{\mathcal{G}}^{not}$. *We will call* Σ_B *and* Σ_G *the precondition of the goal update rule.*

Informally, the *semantics* of the goal update rule $\langle \Sigma_B, \Sigma_G, P \rangle$, is that when the precondition, Σ_B, Σ_G, is satisfied, respectively, by the agent's belief base and by its goal base, the goal base of an agent is updated by the goal program P. For example, consider the rule:

$$\langle \{tough\_competition\}, \{goal(go\_to\_school)\}, \{goal(good\_in\_math) \leftarrow\} \rangle$$

according to which the agent will only update its goal base with the goal of being good in math, if the agent believes that the competition will be tough ($tough\_competition$), and if it has the goal of going to school ($goal(go\_to\_school)$).

Definition 6 (Semantics of Goal Update Rules). *Let* $\langle \sigma, \gamma, \Pi \rangle$ *be an agent configuration, and* $x \in \{\sqcap, \sqcup, \Omega\}$. *The semantics of a Goal Update Rule,* $\langle \Sigma_B, \Sigma_G, P \rangle$ *is given by the transition rule:*

$$\frac{\sigma \models \Sigma_B \wedge (\gamma, \sigma) \models_x \Sigma_G}{\langle \sigma, \gamma, \Pi \rangle \longrightarrow \langle \sigma, (\gamma, P), \Pi \rangle}$$

In this framework, we will use the special symbols, $goal()$ and $maintenance()$ to be able to differentiate between *maintenance* and *achievement* goals. A maintenance goal represents a state of affairs that the agent wants to hold in all states. For example, a person doesn't want to get hurt. An achievement goal represents a state of affairs that, once *achieved*, is no longer pursued. For example, an agent that has as goal to write a paper for a congress, after it believes it has written the paper, it should no longer consider this as a goal.

We are going to use a *goal update operator* to drop the achievement goals that have been achieved. The idea is to apply the goal update operator whenever the belief base of the agent is changed (this could be done by a deliberation cycle).

Definition 7 (Goal Update Operator - Γ). *Let* $\langle \sigma, \gamma, \Pi \rangle \longrightarrow \langle \sigma', \gamma', \Pi' \rangle$ *be a transition in the transition system,* $x \in \{\sqcap, \sqcup, \Omega\}$, *where* $\langle \sigma, \gamma, \Pi \rangle$ *and* $\langle \sigma', \gamma', \Pi' \rangle$ *are agent configurations. We define the goal update operator,* Γ, *as follows:*

$$\Gamma(\gamma, \sigma') = \gamma' = (\gamma, \mu(\sigma', \gamma))$$

where:

$$\mu(\sigma', \gamma) = \{not\, goal(L_1, \ldots, L_m) \leftarrow\mid (\gamma, \sigma') \models_x goal(L_1, \ldots, L_m),$$
$$\sigma' \models \{L_1, \ldots, L_m\}\}$$

Notice that the agent will still consider maintenance goals as goals even if the goal is currently achieved.

As previously mentioned, the semantics of an individual agent is defined by the reasoning rules we just introduced. More specifically the meaning of individual agents consist of a set of so called computation runs.

Definition 8 (Computation Runs). *Given a transition system, a computation run, $CR(s_0)$, is a finite or infinite sequence, $s_0, \ldots, s_n, \ldots$, such that for all $i \geq 0$, s_i is an agent configuration, and $s_i \rightarrow s_{i+1}$ is a transition in the transition system.*

From the above definitions it is easy to see that a maintenance goal will remain entailed by the agent unless dropped by means of a goal update rule, or no longer supported due to some change in the agent's beliefs. Similar reasoning is applicable to achievement goals: if an achievement goal is not dropped using a goal update rule, and the beliefs of the agent do not change so as to no longer support it, it will remain entailed by an agent until it believes that the goal is achieved. We will investigate more about goal update rules in the next Section, when we discuss goal adoption and goal dropping.

4   Adopting and Dropping Goals

In this section we are going to investigate how to represent, in our system, situations where an agent has to adopt or drop goals. We begin, in Subsection 4.1, by discussing some possible motivations of why an agent should adopt a goal and also investigate how to represent these motivations in our agent framework. Later, in Subsection 4.2, we investigate how to represent failure conditions for goals and discuss some other situations to drop a goal. Finally in Subsection 4.3, we identify some further properties of our framework.

4.1   Goal Adoption

Agents often have to adopt new goals. The reasons for adopting new goals can be varied, the simplest one, when dealing with pro-active agents, could be because the agent doesn't have any goals and it is in an *idle* state.

We follow [17], and distinguish two motivations behind the adoption of a goal: *internal* and *external*. Goals that derive from the desires of an agent, represented by *abstract goals*, have an internal motivation to be adopted. External motivations, such as *norms*, *obligations*, and *impositions* from other agents, can also be a reason for the agent to adopt new goals. An example of a norm, in the daily life, is that a person should obey the law. Obligations could derive from a *negotiation* where an agent commits to give a service to another agent e.g. your internet provider should (is obliged to) provide the internet connection at your home. Agents usually have a *social point of view* e.g. a son usually respects his father more than a stranger, and it may be the case that an agent imposes another agent some specific goals e.g. a father telling the son to study.

To be able to commit to obligations, changes in norms, or changes in desires, an agent needs to be able to update its goal base during execution. For example, if a new deal is agreed to provide a service to another agent, the agent must entail this new obligation. By using the Goal Update Rule, an agent will be able to update its goal base and adopt new goals, as states the following proposition.

Proposition 1 (Goal Adoption Property). *Let $Goal \in \mathcal{L}_\mathcal{G}$, $\langle \sigma, \gamma, \Pi \rangle \longrightarrow \langle \sigma, \gamma', \Pi \rangle$ be the transition rule of the goal update rule $\langle \Sigma_B, \Sigma_G, P \rangle$, where r : $Goal \leftarrow\in P$ is not conflicting in P, and $x \in \{\cap, \cup, \Omega\}$. Then:*

$$(\gamma', \sigma) \models_x Goal$$

Proof: Since $Goal \leftarrow\in P$ is not conflicting in P. For all interpretations, r will not be rejected by any other rule in the goal base. Therefore, we have that $(\gamma', \sigma) \models_x Goal$.

Now, we discuss some situations where an agent has to adopt new goals.

Adopt New Concrete Goals - Dignum and Conte discuss in [6], that an agent may have some desires that can be represented by abstract goal κ that is usually not really achievable, but the agent believes that it can be approximated by some concrete goals $(\kappa_1, \ldots, \kappa_n)$. Consider that the agent learns that there is another concrete goal κ_l that, if achieved, can better approximate the abstract goal, κ. The agent can update its goal base using the following Goal Update Rule, $\langle \{concrete\_goal(\kappa_l, \kappa)\}, \{\}, \{goal(\kappa_l) \leftarrow goal(\kappa)\} \rangle$, as κ is a goal of the agent, it will activate the new rule, hence the new concrete goal, κ_l, will also be a goal of the agent. In example 1, the girl agent considers initially that a more concrete goal to have a boyfriend is of being pretty;

Norm Changes - Consider that the agent belongs to a *society* with some norms that have to be obeyed $(norm_1, \ldots, norm_n)$ and furthermore that there is a change in the norms. Specifically, the $norm_i$ is changed to $norm_i'$, hence the agent's goal base must change. We do this change straightforwardly, using the goal update rule, $\langle \{change(norm_i, norm_i')\}, \{\}, \{not\ goal(norm_i) \leftarrow; goal(norm_i') \leftarrow\} \rangle$. This update will force all the rules, r, with $Head(r) = goal(norm_i)$ to be rejected and $norm_i$ will no longer be a goal of the agent. Notice that there must be some coherence with the change in the norms. For example, the agent shouldn't believe that on $change(norm_i, norm_j)$ and at the same time on $change(norm_j, norm_i)$;

New Obligations - Agents are usually immersed with other agents in an environment and, to achieve certain goals, it might be necessary to negotiate with them. After a negotiation round, it is normal for agents to have an agreement that stipulates some conditions and obligations (e.g. in *Service Level Agreements* [8]). The agent can again easily use the goal update rules to incorporate new obligations, $\langle \{obligation(\phi)\}, \{\}, \{goal(\phi) \leftarrow\} \rangle$, as well as *dismiss* an obligation when an agreement is over, $\langle \{\neg obligation(\phi)\}, \{\}, \{not\ goal(\phi) \leftarrow\} \rangle$;

Impositions - Agents not only negotiate, but sometimes have to *cooperate* with or *obey* other superior agents. This sense of superiority is quite subjective and can be, for example, the obedience of an employee to his boss, or a provider towards his client. It will depend on the beliefs of the agent to decide if it should adopt a new goal or not, but this can be modeled using the goal update rule, $\langle \{received(achieve, \phi, agent_i), obey(agent_i)\}, \{\}, \{\ goal(\phi) \leftarrow \}\rangle$. Meaning that if it received a message from $agent_i$ to adopt a new goal ϕ, and the receiving agent believes it should obey $agent_i$, it will update its goal base. Notice that more complex hierarchy could be achieved by means of *preferences* between the agents. However, it would be necessary to elaborate a mechanism to solve possible *conflicts* (e.g by using Multi-Dimensional Dynamic Logic Programming [11]).

4.2   Goal Dropping

In this Subsection, we are going to investigate some situations where the agent must *drop a goal* and discuss how this could be done with our agent framework.

The next proposition, states that goal update rules can be used to drop achievement goals, as well as maintenance goals.

Proposition 2 (Goal Drop Property). *Let* $\langle \sigma, \gamma, \Pi \rangle \longrightarrow \langle \sigma, \gamma', \Pi \rangle$ *be the transition rule of the goal update rule* $\langle \Sigma_B, \Sigma_G, P \rangle$, *such that* $r : not\ Goal \leftarrow \in P$, *and* $x \in \{\cap, \cup, \Omega\}$, *where* $Goal \in \mathcal{L}_\mathcal{G}$. *Then:*

$$(\gamma', \sigma) \not\models_x Goal$$

Proof: Since $r \in P$ *and that the goal update rule semantics adds the program* P *to the end of the goal base.* r *will reject all the rules,* r', *in the goal base* γ, *with* $Head(r') = Goal$. *Therefore,* $(\gamma', \sigma) \not\models_x Goal$.

We already have discussed in the previous Subsection, some situations where the agent must drop a goal, for instance, when obligations with other agents are ended, or when there is change in the norms that the agent should obey. Another situation that could force an agent to drop a goal, is suggested by Winikoff et al. in [19], by defining *failure conditions*. The idea is that when the failure condition is true the goal should be dropped. We can easily define failure conditions for goals using Goal Update Rules. Consider the following example:

Example 3. Consider an agent that has to write a paper until a deadline of a conference. We could represent this situation using the following Goal Update Rule, $\langle \{deadline\_over\}, \emptyset, \{not\ goal(write\_paper) \leftarrow \}\rangle$. The agent will drop the goal of writing a paper if the deadline is over.

Agents should also drop achievement goals, whenever this goal is achieved. The agent framework will perform this by using the goal update operator whenever there is a change in the agent's beliefs. As the following proposition shows, this operator updates the agent's goal base in such a way that the agent will no longer consider as goals previous achievement goals that have been achieved.

Proposition 3 (Goal Update Operator Property). *Let* $\mathcal{A} = \langle \sigma, \gamma, \Pi \rangle$ *be an agent configuration such that* $\sigma \models \{L_1, \ldots, L_n\}$, *and* $(\gamma, \sigma) \models_x goal(L_1, \ldots, L_n)$, *and let* $\gamma' = \Gamma(\gamma, \sigma)$, *and* $x \in \{\cap, \cup, \Omega\}$. *Then for any belief base* σ_i:

$$(\gamma', \sigma_i) \not\models_x goal(L_1, \ldots, L_n)$$

Proof: Since $\sigma \models \{L_1, \ldots, L_n\}$, *and* $(\gamma, \sigma) \models_x goal(L_1, \ldots, L_n)$, *the goal update operator will update the goal base* γ *with a program* P *containing the rule* $not\, goal(L_1, \ldots, L_n) \leftarrow$, *that will reject all the rules in the goal base with head* $goal(L_1, \ldots, L_n)$. *Therefore, for any* σ_i *and* $x \in \{\cup, \cap, \Omega\}$, *we have that* $(\gamma', \sigma_i) \not\models_x goal(L_1, \ldots, L_n)$.

4.3 Further Properties

We still can identify some more properties that could be elegantly achieved by using the goal update rule:

Defining Maintenance and Achievement Goals - We can define a goal as a maintenance goal if a certain condition is satisfied. For example, an initially single male agent finds the woman agent of its life and marries it. After this is achieved, it might like to be married with this agent until the end of its life. This can be represented by the goal update rule $\langle\{married(girl)\}, \{\}, \{\ maintenance(married(girl)) \leftarrow\}\rangle$. The opposite can also be easily achieved, using the goal update rule. A goal that initially was a maintenance goal can be dropped or switched to an achievement goal. For example, consider that the previous agent had a fight with its agent wife and, after the divorce, it doesn't want to marry again. This can be represented by the goal update rule, $\langle\{divorce(girl)\}, \{\}, \{\ not\ goal(married(girl)) \leftarrow; not\ maintenance(married(girl)) \leftarrow\}\rangle$. We define a new achievement or modify a maintenance goal to an achievement by using the following goal update rule $\langle\{achieve(L)\}, \{\}, \{\ goal(L) \leftarrow; not\ maintenance(L) \leftarrow\}\rangle$;

    The next corollary guarantees the effectiveness of the change of one achievement goal to a maintenance goal. A similar result could be used to change one maintenance goal to an achievement goal.

Corollary 1 (Achievement to Maintenance Goal). *Let* $\langle \sigma, \gamma, \Pi \rangle \longrightarrow \langle \sigma, \gamma', \Pi \rangle$ *be the transition rule of the goal update rule* $\langle \Sigma_B, \Sigma_G, P \rangle$, *where* $P = \{maintenance(L_1, \ldots, L_n) \leftarrow; not\, goal(L_1, \ldots, L_n) \leftarrow\}$, *and* $x \in \{\cap, \cup, \Omega\}$. *Then:*

$$(\gamma', \sigma) \not\models_x goal(L_1, \ldots, L_n) \wedge (\gamma', \sigma) \models_x maintenance(L_1, \ldots, L_n)$$

Proof: Follows from propositions, 1 and 2.

Corollary 2 (Maintenance to Achievement Goal). *Let* $\langle \sigma, \gamma, \Pi \rangle \longrightarrow \langle \sigma, \gamma', \Pi \rangle$ *be the transition rule of the goal update rule* $\langle \Sigma_B, \Sigma_G, P \rangle$, *where*

$P = \{not\,maintenance(L_1,\ldots,L_n) \leftarrow; goal(L_1,\ldots,L_n) \leftarrow\}$, and $x \in \{\cap, \cup,$ $\Omega\}$. Then:

$$(\gamma',\sigma) \models_x goal(L_1,\ldots,L_n) \wedge (\gamma',\sigma) \not\models_x maintenance(L_1,\ldots,L_n)$$

Proof: Follows from propositions, 1 and 2.

Representing Defeasible Goals - We can use the special symbol $def(.)$ to represent *Defeasible Goals*, i.e. goals that with the current knowledge are considered as goals (or not), but if new knowledge is acquired, the goals are dropped (or adopted). We take the surgery example from Bacchus and Grove [3]. A person may prefer not having surgery over having surgery, but this preference might be reversed in the circumstances where surgery improves one's long term health. We can defeasibly infer that the person prefers no surgery only as long as it is known that surgery improves his or her long term health. This could be modeled by the following program:

$$maintenance(long\_life) \leftarrow$$
$$goal(\neg surgery) \leftarrow not\,goal(surgery), not\,def(\neg surgery)$$
$$goal(surgery) \leftarrow not\,goal(\neg surgery), not\,def(surgery)$$
$$def(\neg surgery) \leftarrow needs\_surgery, maintenance(long\_life)$$
$$def(surgery) \leftarrow not\,needs\_surgery$$

the agent will only have surgery as a goal if it needs surgery ($needs\_surgery$) and has the goal of living long.

5   Example

Consider the following situation. The *wife* agent of a recently married couple, invites her *mother-in-law* for dinner at her house. Since, the couple has recently been married, the *wife* is still very concerned of her relations with her mother-in-law (mother-in-law are famous for not being very fond of daughter-in-law). And as the daughter-in-law loves her husband, she doesn't want any problems with his mother. We can represent its initial goal base as $\gamma = (P_1)$, where P_1 is as follows:

$$P_1 : maintenance(husband's\_love) \leftarrow$$
$$goal(please\_motherInLaw) \leftarrow maintenance(husband's\_love)$$

P_1 states that she has as maintenance goal to have the love of her husband and hence, she has to please her mother-in-law, represented by its unique stable model, $\{maintenance(husband's\_love), goal(please\_motherInLaw)\}$. To please her mother-in-law is not a very easy task (probably, there is no plan to please a person, but there are plans to achieve more concrete goals). However, she knows that by making a good dinner, she will give her mother-in-law a very good impression. But not being a real master cook, the wife agent searches in the internet how to make a good dinner, and discovers that she should use *white wine* if serving *fish*, and *red wine* if serving *lamb*. Promptly, she updates her goals using the following goal update rule:

$$\langle \{norm(lamb, red\_wine), norm(fish, white\_wine)\}, \{goal(please\_\\motherInLaw)\}, P_2 \rangle$$

where:

$$P_2 : goal(lamb, red\_wine) \leftarrow not\, goal(fish, white\_wine)\\goal(fish, white\_wine) \leftarrow not\, goal(lamb, red\_wine)$$

The wife's goal base, (P_1, P_2) has two stable models, namely one where she has as goal to prepare fish with white wine ($\{maintenance(husband's\_love)$, $goal(please\_motherIn\ Law)$, $goal(fish, white\_wine)\}$) and another where she instead, would like to cook lamb with red wine ($\{maintenance(husband's\_love)$, $goal(please\_mother\ InLaw)$, $goal(lamb, red\_wine)\}$). She decides for some reason, that the lamb would be a better option. Notice that the agent in this example, is using the Casuistic approach to handle the multiple stable models (where the agent chooses one of the DLP's stable models to determine its semantics). However, she finds out that the red wine she reserved for a special occasion is mysteriously gone. Therefore, she cannot make lamb with red wine anymore (failure condition), updating its goal base with the following goal update rule, $\langle \{not\, red\_wine\}, \{\}, P_3 \rangle$, where:

$$P_3 : not\, goal(lamb, red\_wine) \leftarrow$$

After this update, the wife's goals will change, and she will have to prepare the fish with white wine. since the rule in P_3 will reject the rule with head $goal(lamb, red\_wine)$ in P_2. Hence, the DLP (P_1, P_2, P_3) will have one stable model, namely:

$$\{maintenance(husband's\_love), goal(please\_motherInLaw),\\goal(fish, white\_wine)\}.$$

After preparing the fish and collecting the white wine, the wife updates its goal base with the following program, P_4, obtained from the goal update operator:

$$P_4 : not\, goal(fish, white\_wine) \leftarrow$$

Since the rule $not\, goal(fish, white\_wine) \leftarrow$ in P_4 will reject the rule with head $goal(fish, white\_wine)$ in P_2, the goals of the agent will be again:

$$\{maintenance(husband's\_love), goal(please\_motherInLaw)\}$$

However, the wife agent still puzzled how the red wine mysteriously disappeared, tries to find it. Until a point that she looks inside the husband's closet, and finds a shirt stained with the wine and inside its pocket a paper with a love letter and a telephone. Immediately, she considers that her husband is cheating her with another women and updates her goals with the following goal update rule:

$$\langle \{cheating\_husband\}, \{\}, \{not\, maintenance(husband's\_love) \leftarrow\} \rangle$$

The rule in this new update will reject the rule $maintenance(husband's\_love) \leftarrow$ in P_1 and she won't consider as a goal to have the husband's love. Furthermore, the cheated wife will no longer consider as a goal to please her mother-in-law.

In this example, we illustrate several aspects of how an agent framework with a DLP representing its goal base, can be used. First, we can represent more concrete goals using logic rules, e.g., when the wife agent had the maintenance goal of having her husband's love, she had the more concrete goal of pleasing his mother. Second, representing the norms of society, e.g., when the agent investigated in the internet how the dinner should be, in this case, red wine with lamb and white wine with fish. Third, dropping goals, when the agent realized that the goal of preparing lamb with red wine is not achievable (since there is no red wine) the agent drops this goal, and when the agent prepared the fish and arranged the white wine the goal of making dinner was dropped. Fourth, knowledge updates, when the agent finds out that her husband is cheating her with another girl, she updates negatively the goal of having the love of her husband, and consequently, the goal of pleasing her mother-in-law is abandoned.

6   Conclusions

In this paper, we introduced a simple agent framework with the purpose of introducing the agent's goal base as a Dynamic Logic Program. We investigated some properties of this framework. We were able to express, in a simple manner, maintenance and achievement goals, as well as identify some situations where the agent would need to adopt and drop goals, and how this could be done in this framework.

Since the objective of this paper was to investigate the use of DLP as the goal base of an agent, we didn't investigate any additional properties we could have by also using the belief base as a DLP. We also didn't give an adequate solution for conflicting intentions, since it would probably be also necessary to analyze the plans of the agent as well as its resources [19] to be able to conclude which goals to commit to.

Further investigation could also be done to solve possible conflicts in the social point of view of the agent. For example, if the agent considers the opinion of his mother and father equally, it would be necessary to have a mechanism to solve the conflicts since the agent doesn't prefer any one of them more than the other. [11] introduces the concept of *Multi Dimensional Dynamic Logic Programming* (MDLP) that could represent an agent's social point of view. Further investigation could be made in trying to incorporate the social point of view of an agent as a MDLP in our agent framework.

References

1. J. J. Alferes, F. Banti, A. Brogi, and J. A. Leite. The refined extension principle for semantics of dynamic logic programming. *Studia Logica*, 79(1), 2005.
2. J. J. Alferes, J. Leite, L. M. Pereira, H. Przymusinska, and T. Przymusinski. Dynamic updates of non-monotonic knowledge bases. *Journal of Logic Programming*, 45(1-3):43–70, 2000.
3. Fahiem Bacchus and Adam J. Grove. Utility independence in a qualitative decision theory. In *KR*, pages 542–552, 1996.
4. M. Bratman. *Intentions, Plans and Practical Reason*. Harvard University Press, 1987.
5. M. Dastani, M. B. van Riemsdijk, and J.-J. Ch. Meyer. Programming multi-agent systems in 3APL. In *Multi-Agent Programming: Languages, Platforms and Applications*, chapter 2. Springer, 2005.
6. F. Dignum and R. Conte. Intentional agents and goal formation. In *Intelligent Agents IV*, volume 1365 of *LNAI*, pages 231–243, 1998.
7. K. V. Hindriks, F. S. de Boer, W. van der Hoek, and J.-J. Ch. Meyer. Agent programming with declarative goals. In *Intelligent Agents VII*, volume 1986 of *LNAI*, pages 228–243. Springer, 2000.
8. N. R. Jennings, T. J. Norman, P. Faratin, P. O'Brien, and B. Odgers. Autonomous agents for business process management. *Applied Artificial Intelligence*, 14(2):145–189, 2000.
9. J. Leite. *Evolving Knowledge Bases*. IOS press, 2003.
10. J. Leite. On some differences between semantics of logic program updates. In *IBERAMIA'04*, volume 3315 of *LNAI*, pages 375–385. Springer, 2004.
11. J. Leite, J. J. Alferes, and L. M. Pereira. On the use of multi-dimensional dynamic logic programming to represent societal agents' viewpoints. In *EPIA'01*, volume 2258 of *LNAI*, pages 276–289. Springer, 2001.
12. J. Leite, J. J. Alferes, and L. M. Pereira. Minerva - a dynamic logic programming agent architecture. In *Intelligent Agents VIII*, volume 2333 of *LNAI*. Springer, 2002.
13. J. Leite and L. M. Pereira. Generalizing updates: From models to programs. In *LPKR'97*, volume 1471 of *LNAI*, pages 224–246. Springer, 1998.
14. Á. F. Moreira, R. Vieira, and R. H. Bordini. Extending the operational semantics of a BDI agent-oriented programming language for introducing speech-act based communication. In *DALT'03*, volume 2990 of *LNAI*, pages 135–154. Springer, 2004.
15. V. Nigam and J. Leite. Incorporating knowledge updates in 3apl. In *PROMAS'06*, 2006.
16. J. Thangarajah, L. Padgham, and M. Winikoff. Detecting & avoiding interference between goals in intelligent agents. In *IJCAI'03*, pages 721–726. Morgan Kaufmann, 2003.
17. B. van Riemsdijk, M. Dastani, F. Dignum, and J.-J. Ch. Meyer. Dynamics of declarative goals in agent programming. In *DALT'04*, volume 3476 of *LNAI*, pages 1–18, 2004.
18. M. B. van Riemsdijk, M. Dastani, and J.-J. Ch. Meyer. Semantics of declarative goals in agent programming. In *AAMAS'05*. ACM Press, 2005.
19. M. Winikoff, L. Padgham, J. Harland, and J. Thangarajah. Declarative and procedural goals in intelligent agent systems. In *KR'02*. Morgan Kaufmann, 2002.
20. M. Wooldridge. *Multi-agent systems : an introduction*. Wiley, 2001.

A Collaborative Framework to Realize Virtual Enterprises Using 3APL

Gobinath Narayanasamy[1], Joe Cecil[2], and Tran Cao Son[1]

[1] Department of Computer Science
New Mexico State University, USA
{gonaraya,tson}@cs.nmsu.edu
[2] Department of Industrial Engineering
New Mexico State University, USA
jcecil@nmsu.edu

Abstract. In this paper, we propose a collaborative framework to realize a Virtual Enterprise (VE) for the domain of Micro Assembly. The framework is developed using 3APL technologies [7] and employs the idea of viewing WebService composition as a planning problem [8]. We describe the implementation of the framework and experiment with two micro assembly work cells.

1 Introduction

In today's business world, being innovative and withstanding competitive pressure from contemporary engineering partners are a key to success for any engineering partners. With dynamic nature of consumer demands, engineering partners often need a sophisticated mechanism to tap those momentous market demands. One such mechanism which will facilitate as well as satisfy the engineering partners need is the concept of a Virtual Enterprise (VE). A VE is a conglomeration of different engineering partners who are geographically distributed and are formed to meet the market demands; they share diverse resources and expertise. A resource can be a machine, a software program, a component, a service, etc. Each resource might have a cost associated with it. Furthermore, there might be one or several resources at various locations, which can be involved in one of the life cycle activities of a product (design, analysis, engineering, planning, assembly, service, etc.) of a product. However, the very diverse nature of a VE's resources (especially its software components) causes heterogeneity which slows down the process of forming and implementing collaborations among the engineering partners.

The goal of this research is to develop a framework that facilitates VE based collaborations and seamless flow of information exchange among the partners. We explore the design and implementation of such a framework using the agent technologies and address semantic interoperability issues.

To demonstrate our approach, a prototype VE was created using the proposed collaborative framework for an emerging domain called the assembly of micro devices. Micro Assembly is a domain where micron sized parts are assembled using computer enabled micro assembly work cells. We target this domain for the following reasons:

M. Baldoni and U. Endriss (Eds.): DALT 2006, LNAI 4327, pp. 191–206, 2006.

Micro Devices Assembly (MDA) is a technology alternative to Micro Electro Mechanical Systems (MEMS); when micron sized parts having varying material properties and complex shapes cannot be manufactured using MEMS methods, they have to be assembled. As MDA is an emerging industrial domain, many engineering partners do not possess the whole range of tools and resources to accomplish micro assembly related tasks such as micro assembly planning, simulation and actual physical implementation; this makes it necessary for such potential MDA partners to function as a VE. By coming together, the engineering partners and vendors can respond quickly to various customer requests.

As many parts in the Micro Assembly domain are assembled using computer programs within the context of an Internet based VE, we need a multi-agent devel-opment platform in which agents with various capabilities can be created to respond to various customer requests. Each agent should have their own belief, capabilities, goals, and rules for reasoning. This platform should also facilitate the agent commu-nication and collaboration. As 3APL [7] lends itself to addressing these issues, it was used for the design and implementation.

The paper is organized as follows: Section 2 provides a review of some past and recent developments of Virtual Enterprises using agent based approaches. Section 3 highlights the 3APL framework. Section 4 describes the collaborative system design. Section 5 discusses the development of collaborative framework using 3APL. Section 6 discusses VE formation for Micro Assembly domain using the proposed collaborative framework and Section 7 is the conclusions.

2   Literature Review

In this section, background information about virtual enterprises as well as a review of agent based systems is provided. Other issues such as agent communications, agent interaction protocols, and distributed problem solving approaches in agent based systems are also discussed.

In [3], the notion of a VE is outlined; a VE is a temporary consortium of companies where diverse resources in a working environment is used to manage all or part of different resources towards achieving a common goal. Common information definition and sharing problem while forming Virtual Enterprises are discussed in [6]. The paper also discusses the issues of interaction among the companies that will agree upon a contract to form virtual enterprise.

In [9], the concept of forming Virtual Enterprises using agent based systems is proposed. In this conceptualization, partners of a virtual enterprise are considered as software agents. This paper also discusses different agent communication protocols such as KQML and KIF. A significant agent communication protocol proposed by US Defense Advanced Research Projects Agency's (DARPA) Knowledge-Sharing Effort known as Knowledge Query Management Language (KQML) is presented in [11]. The language includes variety of primitives, assertives, and directives which allow agents to query other agents, subscribe to other agents services, or find other agents for distributed problem solving. KQML assumes that each agent is built with its own knowledge bases. This allows other agents to extract information from the knowledge base of that particular agent.

In [4], a language called Knowledge Interchange Format is discussed. KIF is a language for interchanging knowledge between heterogeneous programs. KIF has a declarative semantics which allows agents to understand a KIF representation without any interpreters. It allows expressing arbitrary sentences using first order predicate calculus. It has constructs to represent knowledge in the domain, represent non monotonic reasoning rules and define objects, functions and relations. KIF has been employed in the development of the Process Specification Language (PSL), a language specifically designed to facilitate correct and complex exchange of process information among manufacturing systems [5].

In [8], it is observed that web services markup will allow agent technologies to efficiently capture the 'meta' data associated with the services and reason about them. This paves way for agent technologies to perform automated web services discovery, execution, composition and interoperation. In automated web services discovery, the software agent automatically discovers the web services based on user constraints, which is performed manually in the current World Wide Web (WWW). In automated web services execution, the software agent discovers the web services based on user constraints, understands the requirements for the services, and executes them automatically. In automated web services composition and interoperation, the software agent selects the required web services, compose and interoperate them to accomplish the requested complex task.

In [13], a need is identified to automate the process of discovering, executing, composing, and monitoring services. Automation refers to no human intervention and allows for the use of software agents. For a software agent to automatically process and execute a service, a machine understandable description of the service is required. One such language which provides descriptions that are machine understandable is OWL-S which is evolved as a collaborative work of BBN Technologies, Carnegie Mellon University, Nokia, Stanford University, SRI International, and Yale University.

In [2], the importance of using ontologies in manufacturing domain is explained. The paper emphasis on the need for developing richer ontological structures especially to the manufacturing domain so that more sophisticated intelligent applications can be developed.

3   3APL Language

An Abstract Agent Programming Language (3APL) developed at Universiteit Utrecht is a new agent oriented programming language for developing agents with cognitive capability, as given in [7]. The language comes with programming constructs that allows developing agents with complex mental states. An 3APL agent developed using this language is given by a tuple

$$\langle B, G, P, A \rangle$$

where

- B is Belief base,
- G is Goal base,

– P is a set of Practical reasoning rules and
– A is an Action base.

A discussion of each of these components follows

3.1   Belief Base

A belief base encodes the agent knowledge about its operating environment and is a set of first order sentences. For example, a belief that $Robot$ is at room A is reprensented by the atom $at(Robot, RoomA)$; other belief that a robot is not at the room x then it is at the room next to x is rexpressed by the sentence $\forall x, y(\neg at(Robot, x) \wedge nextto(x, y) \Rightarrow at(Robot, y))$. Notice that a belief base can contain non-grounded sentences.

3.2   Goal Base

A goal base consists of *goals-to-do* goals. 3APL considers goals of procedural type. Under this view, a goal can be considered as an imperative program. A goal defines a plan of actions for an agent to execute. The language allows for the definition of simple and complex goals. Simple goals (also called basic goals) are of three types: basic action, test goal, and achievement goal. For example, a simple goal like *inquireUDDI()* allows an agent to inquire the UDDI registry. Complex goals (also called composite goals) are composed from basic goals and are used to specify complex actions such as sequences of actions, disjunctive goals, or non-deterministic choices, etc. Conventional programming constructs such as ';' and '+' are used to create complex goals. For example, "$goal_1; goal_2$" defines a sequence of goals and "$goal_1 + goal_2$" defines a disjunctive goal.

3.3   Practical Reasoning Rules

A 3APL agent can manipulate its goals by using a set of practical reasoning rules. These reasoning rules define a plan of action for an agent to execute its goals. Using these rules, an agent can monitor as well as revise its goals in the goal base. A type of reasoning called Means-End reasoning is followed, which means that if there is an agent which believes that an assembly plan, say plan_1, is qualified enough to accomplish its goal, then it will conclude to follow that plan. A practical reasoning rule has head, body, guard, global and local variables as its components which is symbolically given by

$$\pi \leftarrow \varphi | \pi',$$

where

– π is the head of a given rule,
– φ is the guard of the given rule and
– π' is the body of the rule,

Global variables are free first order variables in the head of a rule, and local variables are non global first order variables in the body of a rule.

A practical rule $\pi \leftarrow \varphi | \pi'$ says that if the agent adopts some goal or plan π and believes that φ is true, then it may consider adopting π' as a new goal.

3.4   Action Base

Action base defines the set of primitive actions (or basic actions) that an agent can execute. This set of basic actions defines the capabilities of an agent with which an agent can change its mental state of belief about its working environment.

4   Framework Design

We follow the idea behind the design of this system follows the model proposed in [9,10]. We view each partner in a VE as an agent who has its own knowledge about the environment, its actions (basic and complex), its set of practical rules, and its own goals. A VE is a collection of agents who collaborate to achieve a common goal. As we have discussed above, most activities in the Micro Assembly domain are controlled by computer programs. As such, each partner is implemented as a software agent who can offer their services (or actions) to others. Our framework facilitates the communication between agents and allows users of the system to simulate the VE. The overall design of our framework is depicted in Figure 1.

Central to our system is a central manager agent which is a 3APL agent. This agent facilitates the communication between different agents and creating solutions for users' requests.

An agent can advertise its services in a service directory, which is implemented as a part of our system. A 3APL service directory agent provides other agents in the system the capability to find service provider(s) that can satisfy their needs. This agent communicates with other agents through the agent manager. In our implementation, each service is specified by its inputs and its execution method.

One issue in a collaborative framework is the semantically differences between different agents. This is also an issue in our framework. We follow others by addressing this issue using ontologies and develop ontologies for the Micro Assembly domain. To incorporate ontologies into our system, a 3APL agent is developed. This agent also communicates with other agents through the agent manager. We call this the meta-information of services.

We note that in [1], design and development of ontologies for physical devices are explained.

5   Framework Implementation

This section discusses the implementation of the collaborative framework as shown in Figure 1. It consists of following agents

1. User Agent
2. Virtual Enterprise Agent (or Enterprise Agent Manager)
3. Ontology Agent
4. Service Directory Agent and
5. Service Provider Agents

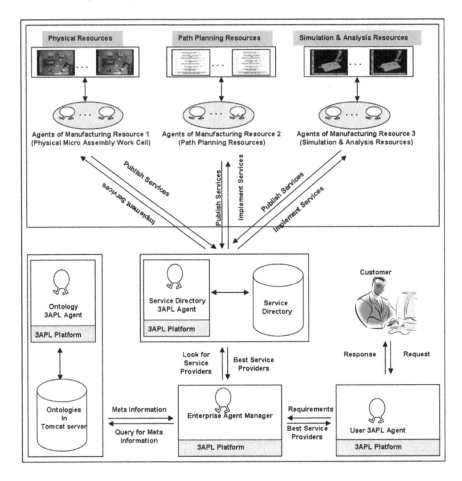

Fig. 1. Collaborative System for Virtual Enterprise

All these agents are implemented using 3APL and they run in 3APL platform. Plug-in programming construct is provided by 3APL platform so that agents can use the plug-in as their working environments and access the methods available in them. With the help of plug-ins, agents in 3APL platform can access the external JAVA methods, virtually allowing an agent to execute a service provided by another agent. For each agent in the our system, an associated plug-in is developed to assist the formation of Virtual Enterprise in real time. Detailed descriptions of 3APL agents used in the collaborative system are given below.

5.1   User Agent

User Agent provides the user interface to the collaborative system. This agent is probably the simplest agent in the system. It acts on behalf of real world entities such as human users, software applications, or even other business vendors who may need to accomplish a task.

5.2   Virtual Enterprise Agent

The Virtual Enterprise Agent coordinates the various activities in the collaborative framework. It is responsible for processing users' requests (from the user agent) and providing an initial solution (i.e. plan) for these requests. In the course of find-ing this solution, it queries the Ontology agent for meta-information and uses this information to find a list of best available service providers by querying the Service Directory agent.

The Virtual Enterprise Agent also serves as a search engine for other agents who need to find service providers for their own needs. Figure 2 shows a view of collaborative framework implemented in 3APL platform with developed plug-ins and participating software agents

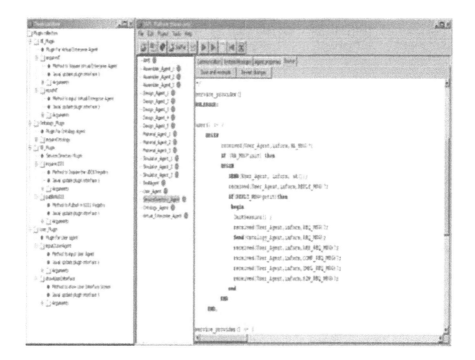

Fig. 2. Collaborative System for VE using 3APL

5.3   Ontology Agent

The Ontology Agent in the collaborative system provides the necessary meta-information for the VE agent to further process the input from the user agent. For demonstration purpose, some sample ontologies are created using Stanford's Protege editor. Figure 3 displays a part of the ontology developed for the Micro Assembly domain.

The ontologies developed for the collaborative system are deployed in a Tomcat web server. Any modifications to the existing ontologies are done through the ontology

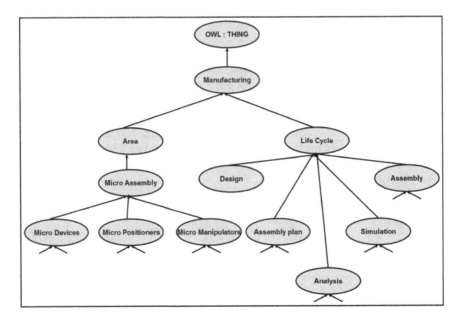

Fig. 3. Sample Ontology

agent. This is achieved by means of a Ontology plug-in developed to assist the ontology agent. Ontology plug-in contains some basic functions for querying and modifying existing ontologies.

5.4   Service Directory Agent

The Service Directory Agent in the collaborative system is used to maintain a service directory where service provider agents will publish their services. This will facilitate other agents in the collaborative system, especially VE agents, to access the available services and use them to process the user agent's input. Oracle UDDI registry is used as the service directory in this collaborative system. Oracle UDDI registry comes along with the Oracle Application Server 10g. In this UDDI registry, instead of saving normal WSDL descriptions for services, OWL-S descriptions of services are saved. Requests from other agents for available services in the UDDI registry are made through this service directory agent. A service directory plug-in is developed for the agent to accomplish this task. The plug-in is developed with methods to connect to the service directory, publish OWL-S services in the service directory and inquire for available services.

5.5   Service Provider Agent

The engineering services in the collaborative system are provided by the service provider agents. Services provided by these agents range from software resources to actual physical implementation. Along with describing the service capabilities, the configurations of actual physical implementations are also described using OWL. This allows the Virtual Enterprise agent to know more about the actual hardware implementation of devices. The collaborative system contains multiple service pro-viders who will serve the needs of a user agent. Publication of services by these agents is accomplished through the service directory plugin, which provides methods for publishing the services into the UDDI registry.

6   Example Scenario

In this section, an example scenario is provided from the Micro Assembly domain for the collaborative framework implemented. In this application scenario, a user agent wants to assemble various micron sized parts (for eg. cams) on micron sized pins. Here, the goals of user agent are identification and formation of partnerships with potential engineering partners and their subsequent execution of associated services.

Possible interactions that will happen in this collaborative framework are listed below (refer to Figure 4) and are elaborated subsequently.

1. Interactions between Service Directory Agent and Service Provider Agents.
2. Interactions between Virtual Enterprise Agent and Ontology Agent.

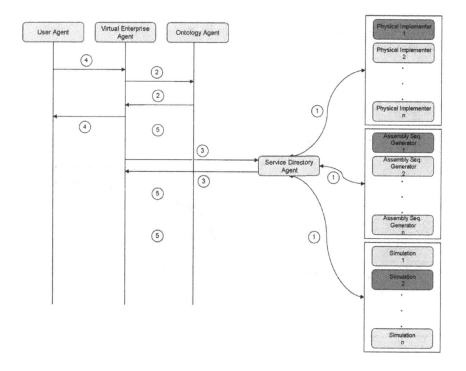

Fig. 4. Interactions among the agents in the collaborative system

3. Interactions between Virtual Enterprise Agent and Service Directory Agent.
4. Interactions between User Agent and Virtual Enterprise Agent.
5. Interactions between Service Provider Agents and User Agent.

6.1 Service Directory Agent and Service Provider Agents

To demonstrate this interaction, a set of service provider agents have been designed and implemented. These include service directory agents capable of providing

1. Services based on software applications such as assembly sequence generators, 3D path planners and virtual prototyping and analysis Environments.
2. Services based on actual physical resources such as micro assembly work cells.

A brief description of some of these resources is provided along with their OWL and OWL-S descriptions.

In order to assemble micron sized parts on micron sized pins, various micro assembly work cells with different assembling capabilities can be used. An ontology is developed to describe the capabilities in terms of work cell specifications. For example, a physical work cell as shown in the left hand side of Figure 5 is developed with gripper having the capability of assembling pins and cams in the size range of 100-200 microns (diameter) and a few millimeters in length. Due to the page limit, all OWL descriptions and grounding files necessary for the operation of the example are omitted. They are accessible from http://web.nmsu.edu/~gobinath/file.htm. The maximum and minimum gripping force exerted by the gripper on its target object and its operating conditions are also described by an OWL element.

The assembly services of the micro assembly work cells are made available as web services. As the assembly service requires physical components (cams and pins in this case) to be assembled, a software validation program is developed to validate the dimensions of input components with the capability of the respective micro assembly work cell. For example, in micro assembly work cell as shown in Figure 5, the validation

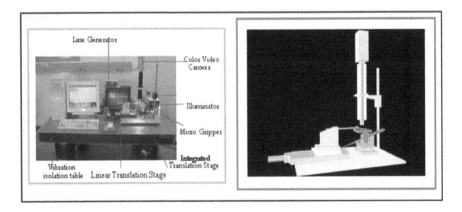

Fig. 5. Micro Assembly Work Cells (Left: Physical Work Cell , Right: Virtual Work Cell)

program validates the input by comparing the dimensions of the gripper and the parts to be assembled. If the validation program returns the positive results, further steps will be taken to ship the parts to the respective work cell location. This validation program is also made available as web services whose grounding information in OWL-S format is given in the above mentioned URL.

Apart from the work cells, virtual prototyping environments have been developed which form part of the VE resources. Right hand side of Figure 5 shows a snapshot of the virtual environment (which depicts work cell), which can be used to study alternates assembly and path plans, etc.

The virtual environment is also accessible via web services. Service grounding information for one of the these VE partners is described in OWL-S format and is available at `http://web.nmsu.edu/~gobinath/file.htm`.

Some of the software resources within the collaborative framework include micro assembly sequence generators as well as 3D path planners.

6.2   Genetic Algorithm Based Assembly Sequence Generator Agent

Assembly sequence generators are used to determine the order in which parts have to be assembled to form a final product. In this research, a genetic algorithm based assembly sequence generator is used to determine the order in which pins have to be picked and placed during micro assembly. This module is developed specific to the micro assembly work cell and it takes initial and final part positions and Gripper home position as its input.

6.3   Path Planning Agent

Path planning service provider agent is used to determine a shortest collision free path for each candidate assembly sequence in a given virtual micro assembly work cell configuration (otherwise known as state). At any given time instance, the configuration of a virtual micro assembly work cell is defined by positions of all four translation stages and open or closed nature of gripper. For a given configuration, the positions of components such as micro pins, obstacles and destination holes/cams in work piece platen are updated in order to maintain their positional relativity with the translation stages. Countless number of configurations are possible for a given micro assembly work cell and all are not useful in determining the path for the gripper. Therefore, the configurations are categorized into two types:

1. Feasible configuration
2. Infeasible configuration

A Feasible configuration is defined as the one for which the positions of four translation stages are not in their limiting zones. If position of any one of the translation stage is in the limiting zone for a configuration, then it is infeasible.

In this project, two path planners based on genetic algorithm and A* are implemented. The input information to these path planners are information that can be obtained about the presence of obstacles and other work cell components; the output from the path planner can be used as inputs to a virtual reality based simulation environment, which can be used to compare various path planning alternatives provided by path planning agents in the VE. It should be noted that a variety of path planning agents which are based on various approaches such as Dijkstra's algorithm and heuristics can also be incorporated; while other approaches have been implemented, they are not included in the discussion for purposes of brevity. An overview of A* based path planning agent is provided below.

6.4   A* Based Path Planner

This path planning agent first generates a grid structure based on position of obstacles and other work components in the virtual micro assembly work cell. After generating the grid structure, except the pin that needs to be picked, it marks out other pins in the grid as obstacles. The position of the pin that needs to be picked first in the grid becomes the initial node for the agent. From the initial node, the agent starts to explore adjacent grid cells by deciding upon which translation stages (X, Y or Z) need to be moved. It uses Manhattan Distance method to estimate the distance from the current node to the goal node (destination hole / cam). The agent stops exploring grid cells once it reaches the destination hole / cam without any collisions. If it wouldn't determine the path to the destination hole/cam, it queries the sequence generator agent for another candidate assembly sequence. Below steps provide an overall idea about its implementation.

- Inputs:
  - Positions of Linear, X, Y and Z translation stages before assembly
  - Positions of pins (1 n), obstacles (1m) and holes/cams (1n), where m is the number of obstacles and n is the number of pins and cams
- Output:
  - A shortest collision free path

STEPS:

1. From the configuration space of the virtual micro assembly work cell, select a feasible configuration
2. Generate the grid structure to the selected feasible configuration with grid element size equal to the bounding box size of the gripper
3. Restructure the grid by calculating the number of units Y translation stage needs to be moved
4. Save the Y translation stage movements in a global PATH variable
5. Using assembly sequence, find the pin that needs to be picked first. Mark other pins as obstacles in the grid
6. Depending upon the pin that needs to be picked, update PATH variable with X / Z translation stage movements
7. Create a search graph with the position of the pin (P) that needs to be picked as its starting node. Put the starting pin position on the OPEN list

8. Create another list called CLOSE to mark the positions that are already visited by the gripper in the grid. Initially this will be empty
9. If the OPEN list is empty, then exit with failure
10. Select the first pin position from the OPEN list. If pin position is same as destination hole / cam position, we have a path and save it in PATHTEMP list. If they are not same, save it in PATHTEMP list
11. Identify the adjacent gird element positions for the first pin position from OPEN list. Save those grid element positions in OPEN list. Also save those positions in CLOSE list and mark them as visited. If the adjacent grid element position is already marked for visited, then it cannot be saved in the CLOSE list
12. Calculate the distance ($f(n)$) for each adjacent grid element position in OPEN list. Distance calculation is done by $f(n) = g(n) + h(n)$, where $g(n)$ is number of units moved by X / Z translation stages and $h(n)$ is the heuristic estimation.Manhattan Distance method is used in this implementation and the value of $h(n)$ is calculated by $[(Cx - Gx) + (Cy - Gy) + (Cz - Gz)]*DISTANCE$, where where Cx, Cy, Cz = Position of pin in the grid, Gx, Gy, Gz = Position of destination hole/cam in the grid and DISTANCE = Number of units needs to be moved in X or Z translation stage
13. Sort OPEN list with adjacent element close to destination position
14. Repeat steps from 10 to 14 until destination position is reached. Now PATHTEMP list contains the path with grid element positions
15. Update the PATH variable with PATHTEMP variable to get the final path
16. Repeat steps from 5 to 15 for other pins in the assembly sequence
17. If path cannot be found for any one of the pins in the assembly sequence, go to step 1 to choose another feasible configuration

The Virtual Reality based environment is considered as a simulation agent in the VE. It uses a scene graph for internal representation and management of various objects of interest. The VR environment is built using COIN3D (which is the open source version of OpenGL Inventor). The scenegraph contains CAD models of physical micro assembly work cells in its nodes. The scenegraph is further rendered as a virtual reality environment by the COIN3D graphical engine.

After receiving messages from the service provider agent, the service directory agent publishes the service in the Oracle UDDI registry.

6.5 User Agent and Virtual Enterprise Agent

In this interaction, the user agent sends the input requirements to the virtual enterprise agent. Below are some sample input requirements to the VE agent:

```
Send (VE_Agent, inform, domain (Micro_Assembly))
Send (VE_Agent, inform, input ())
Send (VE_Agent, inform, radius (pin1, 0.5))
Send (VE_Agent, inform, radius (pin2, 0.5))
Send (VE_Agent, inform, radius (pin3, 0.5))
Send (VE_Agent, inform, radius (cam1, 0.6))
```

```
Send (VE_Agent, inform, radius (cam2, 0.6))
Send (VE_Agent, inform, radius (cam3, 0.6))
Send (VE_Agent, inform, goal ())
Send (VE_Agent, inform, on (cam1, pin1))
Send (VE_Agent, inform, on (cam2, pin2))
Send (VE_Agent, inform, on (cam3, pin3))
```

This sequence of message states that the user would like to assemble three pins $(pin1, pin2, pin3)$ of radius 0.5 into three cams of radius 0.6 by placing $pin1$ on $cam1$, $pin2$ on $cam2$, and $pin3$ on $cam3$.

6.6   Virtual Enterprise Agent and Ontology Agent

For the VE agent to process users' request, it needs to create a plan for doing it and who can provide the necessary services required to execute this plan. This information is available in the meta-information managed by the Ontology agent. The VE agent first queries the Ontology agent for meta-information about the services available in the system and devises a plan to achieve the goals of the users (as done in[8]).

In our experimental scenario, ontology for the micro assembly domain is developed and deployed in a Tomcat Application Server. Some sample 3APL messages for this interaction are given below.

```
Send (Ontology_Agent, inform,
                queryForMeta (Micro_Assembly))
Send (Ontology_Agent, inform, whatis (pin1))
Send (Ontology_Agent, inform, whatis (cam1))
```

Once the Ontology Agent receives the input from the VE agent, the Ontology Agent processes the input to find the corresponding ontology (in this case the ontology of Micro Assembly domain) and queries the ontology to find possible relationships between the input and the concepts it contained using the ontology plug-in. For sample input messages from VE agent, the ontology agent responds by sending the following messages,

```
Send(VE_Agent, inform, metaInfo (Micro_Assembly))
Send(VE_Agent, inform, steps ())
Send(VE_Agent, inform, physical_implementation ())
Send(VE_Agent, inform, planning ())
Send(VE_Agent, inform, simulation ())
Send(VE_Agent, inform, isObject (pin1, true))
Send(VE_ Agent, inform, isObject (cam1, true))
```

6.7   Virtual Enterprise Agent and Service Directory Agent

With the meta information and the original input, the VE agent now requests the service directory agent for service providers. The sample messages of this interaction are given below.

```
Send(SD_Agent, inform,
     serviceProviderfor(physical_implementation))
Send(SD_Agent, inform, serviceProviderfor(planning))
Send(SD_Agent, inform, serviceProviderfor(simulation))
```

After receiving these messages, the service directory agent searches the UDDI registry for available service providers. In a UDDI registry, there may be more than one service provider who can serve the user agent's input request. Those service providers are known as potential partners in VE context. From the list of potential service providers, the service directory agent should choose one best service provider for the user agent. Before the selection of a best service provider, the Service direc-tory agent will check for the requirements for each of the potential service providers. The requirements for a service provider may be correct inputs or even some services from other service providers. If all the requirements of a service provider are satis-fied and it also satisfies the requirements of user agent, the service directory agent will announce the service provider as best partner. If user agent's requirement does not match with the service providers' requirements, then service directory agent will announce the unavailability of service providers. After finding the service providers, the service directory agent re-turns the access point URLs of each of the identified business vendors to the VE agent. Message transfers during this interaction are

```
Send(VE_Agent, inform, accessPointURL
(http://128.123.245.156:9090/ontology/Implementer.owl))
Send(VE_Agent, inform, accessPointURL
(http://128.123.245.156:9090/ontology/planning.owl))
Send(VE_Agent, inform, accessPointURL
(http://128.123.245.156:9090/ontology/simulator.owl))
```

The resulting access point URLs are then sent to User Agent for execution.

6.8   Service Directory Agent and User Agent

After obtaining the access point URLs of service provider agents, the User agent executes the services available at the service provider sites.

7   Conclusion

In this paper, a collaborative system is developed to form a Virtual Enterprise for the domain of Micro Assembly. 3APL language is used to develop the agents which constitute the collaborative system. Ontology for Micro Assembly domain is developed to provide a common ground to share the information contained in it among the agents. Although it is still an ad-hoc development, this prototypical system demonstrates that agent technologies can be very useful in VE development, a rather new area to agent researchers. In the future, we would like to study and develop methodologies for a systematic development of VE in the Micro Assembly domain.

References

1. Bandara, A., Payne, T., Roure, D., Clemo, G. An Ontological Framework for Semantic Description of Devices. Third International Semantic Web Conference (ISWC 2004), Poster Session, Hiroshima, Japan, 7 - 11 Nov 2004.
2. Borgo, S., P. Leitäo. The Role of Foundational Ontologies in Manufacturing Domain Applications. In R. Meersman, Z. Tari et al. (eds.) OTM Confederated International Conferences, ODBASE 2004, Ayia Napa, Cyprus, October 29, 2004, LNCS 3290, Proceedings Part 10, Springer Verlag, pp. 670-688.
3. Camarinha-Matos, L. M., Asfarmanesh, H. Virtual Enterprise Modeling and Support Infrastructures: Applying Multi-Agent System Approaches in Multi-agent Systems and Applications. In M. Luck, V. Marik, O. Stpankova, R. Trappl (eds.), LNAI 2086, Springer, July 2001.
4. Genesereth, M. R., Fikes, R. E. Knowledge Interchange Format (KIF) Version 3.0, Reference Manual.
5. Gruninger, M. and Menzel, C. The Process Specification Language (PSL) Theory and Applications, AAAI Magazi, 63-74, Fall 2000.
6. Hardwick, M., Spooner, D. L., Rando, T., and Morris, K. C. Sharing manufacturing information in virtual enterprises.   Commun. ACM 39, 2 (Feb. 1996), 46-54. http://doi.acm.org/10.1145/230798.230803
7. Hindriks, K. V., De Boer, F., Van Der Hoek, W., Ch. Meyer, J. J. Agent Programming in 3APL. Autonomous Agents and Multi-Agent Systems, ACM, Volume 2 , Issue 4 (November 1999) Pages: 357 - 401
8. McIlraith, S. A., Son, T. C., Zeng, H. Semantic Web Services. IEEE Intelligent Systems, vol. 16, no. 2, pp. 46-53, March/April, 2001.
9. Petersen, S. A., Gruninger, M. An Agent-based Model to Support the Formation of Virtual Enterprises. Int. ICSC Symposium on Mobile Agents and Multi-Agent in Virtual Organizations and E-Commerce (MAMA '2000), in Wollongong, Australia, 11-13 Dec. 2000.
10. Petersen, S. A., Rao, J., Matskin, M. AGORA Multi-agent Architecture for Implementing Virtual Enterprises. Norsk Informatikkonferanse NIK2003, Oslo, Norway, November 2003.
11. Singh, M. P. Agent Communication Languages: Rethinking the Principles. Computer, vol. 31, no. 12, pp. 40-47, December, 1998.
12. Wilbur, S. Computer Support for Co-operative Teams: Applications in Concurrent Engineering. IEEE Colloqium on Current Development in Concurrent Engineering Methodologies and Tools, June 1994.
13. The OWL Services Coalition.   OWL-S: Semantic Markup for Web Services http://www.daml.org/services/owl-s/1.0/owl-s.html.

A Modeling Framework for Generic Agent Interaction Protocols

José Ghislain Quenum[2], Samir Aknine[1], Jean-Pierre Briot[1], and Shinichi Honiden[2]

[1] Laboratoire d'Informatique de Paris 6,
8 rue du Capitaine Scott, 75015 Paris, France
{Samir.Aknine,Jean-Pierre.Briot}@lip6.fr
[2] National Institute of Informatics
2-1-2 Hitotsubashi, Tokyo 101-8430, Japan
{joque,honiden}@nii.ac.jp

Abstract. Agent-UML (AUML) extended UML in order to facilitate the modeling process for agent based systems. It offers several graphical notations, including protocol diagrams which represent agent interaction protocols. In this paper, we describe an AUML-based framework to specify generic protocols. We call generic protocols, agent interaction protocols where only a general behavior of the interacting entities can be described. From AUML protocol diagrams, we identified five fundamental concepts on top of which we defined formal specifications of generic protocols. Through our specifications, we addressed a lack in generic protocol representation by emphasizing the description of actions performed in the course of interactions based on such protocols. The framework we developed is formal, expressive and of practical use. It helps decouple interaction concerns from the rest of an agent's architecture. As an application, we used this framework to publish the specifications of generic protocols for agent interactions in several multi-agent system applications we developed. Additionally, the framework helped us address two issues faced in the design of agent interactions based on generic protocols, protocol configuration and their dynamic selection.

1 Introduction

Interaction is one of the key aspects in agent-oriented design. It allows agents to put together the necessary actions in order to perform complex tasks collaboratively. The coordination mechanisms needed for a safe performance of these actions are often represented as a sequence of message exchanges, called interaction protocols. Usually, only a general description of the behavior required of agents partaking in these interactions is provided. Such protocols are called generic protocols. The description of generic protocols, especially with respect to their correct interpretation is a critical issue in open and heterogeneous multi-agent systems (MAS). A subsequent issue is the need to decouple interaction concerns from the other components of an agent, whatever architecture is adopted for that agent.

To date, there has been some endeavor to develop new protocol specification formalisms. The formalisms developed thus far have several drawbacks. They usually focus on data exchange through a communication channel (Promela/SPIN [10]). Some

M. Baldoni and U. Endriss (Eds.): DALT 2006, LNAI 4327, pp. 207–224, 2006.

others are either informal (or semi-formal) (e.g., AUML [2]) or demand advanced knowledge in logics (e.g., the formal notations defined by Paurobally et al [13], Alberti et al [1] and Giordano et al [8]). Therefore, there is an obvious need for a formal, yet practical and expressive generic protocol representation framework. Additionally, such a framework should provide the building blocks to help fix the separation issue between interaction aspects and the other elements of the architecture adopted for an agent. We address this need in this paper.

The solution we developed is a framework to specify generic protocols. It conforms to the principles established for conversation policies by Greaves et al [9]. Our protocol notation is based on Agent-UML (AUML), a popular agent interaction representation formalism. But, we address (in our framework) the lacks and incompleteness which limit AUML. As commonly witnessed in several protocol representation formalisms, AUML only stresses the sequence of message exchanges. However, some actions are needed to produce these messages and handle them when received. Even, as we will see later, some actions which neither send messages nor handle them, might be executed during an interaction. Thus, in addition to the description of message exchange, our framework introduces the description of actions needed in the course of an interaction. This provides us with the ability to describe the behavior agents will exhibit while playing a role in a protocol. A particular aspect in our framework is our focus on generic protocols, which keeps us from providing a complete representation for actions. Hence, we introduced action categories to fix this weakness.

Our framework offers several advantages. It builds on the graphical representation of protocol diagrams in AUML, which offers the (human) designers a better message exchange perception. In addition, it offers the means to depict what happens beyond the message exchange layer, in the course of an interaction. The framework is expressive, formal and of practical use for protocol representation. Particularly, we offer at least the same expressiveness as in AUML (and its extensions) without introducing new constructs (sequence, loop and other control flows). Rather, we efficiently exploit event description to cover all these possibilities. Also, protocols in our framework are easily implemented following a XML format. As a concrete application, we used our framework to publish the specifications of generic protocols agent interactions are based on in several MAS applications we developed. Moreover, we used this framework to address two issues in agent interaction design for open and heterogeneous MAS: (1) an automatic derivation of agent interaction model from generic protocol specifications, in order to address the issue of consistency during interactions based on generic protocols in an heterogeneous MAS; and (2) an analysis of generic protocol specifications in order to enable agents to dynamically select protocols when they have to perform tasks in collaboration.

The remainder of this paper is organized as follows. Section 2 discusses some related work. Section 3 introduces the fundamental concepts we use in the framework and presents both the specifications and their semantics. Section 4 discusses some properties one can check for a protocol represented following this framework. Finally, section 5 concludes the paper.

2   Related Work

Several formalisms have been developed to represent interaction protocols. We discuss some of them in this section.

AUML [2] and its extensions are graphical frameworks for protocol diagram representation. These frameworks, though practical and easy to use, do not emphasize the representation of actions performed in the context of an interaction. It is then hard to reason about the behavior agents, playing a role in a protocol, should be required of beyond the message exchange layer. As well, the graphical representation is useful only for human designers; it remains unreadable for computers. Casella and Mascardi [3] addressed this limitation by automating the translation process from AUML to a textual description, which is more machine readable. Winikoff [18] puts this textual representation of AUML protocol diagrams a step further. The work proposed a textual notation which defines a syntax for AUML protocol diagram specifications. The notation is accompanied by a tool that helps view the graphical representation corresponding to a textual specification. The advantage of relating a textual notation to AUML (whether automatically or not), though undebatable, is weakened by many other AUML's original limitations, f.i., the lack of emphasis on the description of (generic) actions in protocol representation, and the ambiguity about the formal semantics for protocols as well.

Some formal frameworks have been proposed for protocol representation. For example, Walton [17] defined a framework using concepts similar to ours. However, this framework directly introduces the notion of agent in protocol representation. This does not help separate the interaction concerns from the other parts of the architecture of an agent. In our opinion, this association between agents and roles should result from a configuration and instantiation process of protocols. Paurobally et al [13] made significant advances in the area of protocol representation for agent interaction. This work developed a formal framework which combines Propositional Dynamic Logic and belief and intention modalities (PDL-BI). The framework covers a broad spectrum of issues related to agent interactions. However, it requires advanced knowledge in logics. In our opinion, logics is useful to define the semantics and check some properties for protocols. But due to the complexity it may introduce, we strongly believe that it should be hidden at the specification stage, as usually done in programming languages. Additionally, PDL-BI focuses on message exchanges. But, as we showed above, agent interaction protocols demand more than message exchange. Alberti et al [1] and Giordano et al [8] also developed formal protocol representation notations based on temporal logic. These formalisms are too theoretical, and thus cannot gain wide adoption in the area of protocol representation. Also, they suit commitment protocols, which aim at describing the social states the agents share during an interaction, instead of their mental states. The main difference between these two formalisms and ours is the different (representation and) interpretation of actions and messages.

IOM/T [5] is another recent language for agent interaction representation. Our work, though sharing some similarities with IOM/T, departs from it in the following points. Firstly, we focus on generic protocols, where we consider generic actions. Secondly, the behavior of agents in IOM/T (the actions they perform) is not associated with the events which occur in the MAS. Thirdly, the language is Java-like. However, we believe that a protocol description language is supposedly a declarative one. Especially for open and heterogeneous MAS. We address this need in this paper by developing a formal framework for generic protocol representation. Our framework proposes an expressive declarative language which offers ease of use.

3   The Framework

We introduce the fundamental concepts our framework is based on. Then, we present the specifications and the semantics of these concepts.

3.1   Fundamental Concepts

Our framework is based on the AUML protocol diagram. From AUML, we identified five fundamental concepts: *protocol*, *role*, *event*, *action* and *phase*. A graphical illustration of these concepts is given in Fig. 1.

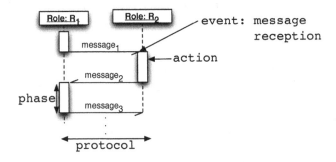

Fig. 1. Graphical illustration of concepts in generic protocols

Definition 1. (Protocol) *A protocol is a sequence of message exchanges between at least two roles. The exchanged messages are described following an Agent Communication Language (ACL) e.g., FIPA ACL [7], KQML [12], the commitment-based ACL introduced in [4].*

More formally, a protocol consists of a collection of roles **R**, *which interact with one another through message exchanges. The messages belong to a collection* **M** *and the exchange takes place following a sequence,* Ω. *A protocol can also have some intrinsic properties* Θ *(attributes and keywords) which are propositional contents (actually predicates) that provide a context for a further interpretation of the protocol. We note* $p \stackrel{def}{=} < \Theta, \mathbf{R}, \mathbf{M}, \Omega >$.

In Ω, the message exchange sequence, each element is denoted by $r_i \xrightarrow[a_\alpha, m_{k-1}]{m_k} r_j$, to be interpreted as "the role r_i sends the message m_k to r_j, and that m_k is generated after action a_α's execution and the prior exchange of m_{k-1}".

Definition 2. (Generic Protocol) *A generic protocol is a protocol wherein the actions which are taken, to handle, produce the contents of exchanged messages, etc. are not*

thoroughly specified. A complete description of these actions depends on the architecture of each agent playing a role in the protocol.

Each of the communicating entities is called a role. Roles are understood as standardized patterns of behavior required of all agents playing a part in a given functional relationship in the context of an organization [6].

Definition 3. (Role) *In our framework, a role consists of a collection of phases. As we will see later (Section 3.2), a role may also have global actions (which are not bound to any phase) and some data other than message content,* variables.

$\forall r \in \mathbf{R}, r \stackrel{\text{def}}{=} < \Theta_r, \Pi, \mathbf{A_g}, \mathbf{V} >$, where Θ_r corresponds to the role's intrinsic properties (e.g., cardinality) which are propositional contents that help further interpret the role, Π the set of phases, $\mathbf{A_g}$ the set of global actions and $\mathbf{V}$ the set of variables. In our framework, roles can be of two types: (1) *initiator*, the unique role of the protocol in charge of starting[1] its execution; (2) *participant*, any role partaking in an interaction based on the protocol.

The behavior of a role is governed by events. An event is an atomic change which occurs during the interaction. An informal description of the types of event we consider in our framework is given in Table 1. A formal interpretation of these events is discussed in Section 3.3. The behavior a role adopts once an event occurs is described in terms of actions.

Table 1. Event Types

Event Type	Description
Change	The content of a variable has been changed.
Endphase	The current phase has completed.
Endprotocol	The end of the protocol is reached.
Messagecontent	The content of a message has been constructed.
Reception	A new message has been received.
Variablecontent	The content of a variable has been constructed.
Custom	Particular event (error control or causality).

Definition 4. (Action) *An action is an operation a role performs during its execution. This operation transforms the whole environment or the internal state of the agent currently playing this role. An action has a category ν, a signature Σ and a set of events it reacts to or produces. We note $a \stackrel{\text{def}}{=} < \nu, \Sigma, E >$.*

Since our framework focuses on generic protocols, we can only provide a general[2] description for the actions which are executed in these protocols. Hence, we introduced action categories to define the semantics of these actions. Table 2 contains an informal description of these categories. We discuss their semantics in Section 3.3.

---

[1] Starting a protocol demands more than sending its initial message.

[2] The term general here is used in the sense of describing the skeleton of these actions.

Table 2. Action Categories

Action Category	Description
Append	Adds a value to a collection.
Remove	Removes a value from a collection.
Send	Sends a newly generated message.
Set	Sets a value to a variable.
Update	Updates the value of a variable.
Compute	Computes a new information.

Definition 5. (Phase) *Successive actions sharing direct links can be grouped together. Each group is called a phase. Two actions a_i and a_j share a direct link, if the input arguments (or only a part of the input) of a_j are generated by (the output result of) a_i.*

3.2   Formal Specifications

The formal specifications are defined through an EBNF grammar. Only essential parts of this grammar are discussed in this section. A thorough description of this grammar is given in Appendix A. In sake of easy implementation of generic protocols, we represent them in XML in our framework. However, as XML is too verbose, a simpler (bracket-based) representation will be used for illustration in this paper.

Running Example. We will use the Contract Net Protocol (CNP) [16] to illustrate our specification formalism. The sequence diagram (protocol diagram in AUML) of this protocol is given in Fig. 2. Note that the labels placed on the message exchange arrows in the figure are not performatives, but message identifiers.

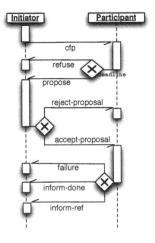

Fig. 2. The Contract Net Protocol

The rationale of CNP consists in an initiator having some participants perform some processing on its behalf. But beforehand, the participants which will perform the processing are selected on the basis of the bids they proposed, in-reply to the initiator's call for proposals. When the selected participants are done with their processing, each of them notifies the initiator agent of the correct execution (or error occurrence) of the part it committed to performing.

Protocol. The following production rules define a protocol. In As one can see from these rules, the exchange sequence Ω contrary to Definition 1, is not explicitly specified. Actually, it is located in the definition of roles, and precisely in the *send* actions of these roles.

$$< protocol > := < protproperties >< roles >< messagepatterns >$$
$$< protproperties > := < protdesc >< protattributes >< protkeywords? >$$
$$< protdesc > := < identifier >< title >< location >$$
$$< protattributes > := < class >< participantcount >$$
$$< protkeywords > := < protkeyword+ >$$
$$< protkeyword > := "Incremental Resolution"| \ldots$$

Example 1, we exemplified the use of these rules to specify CNP.

```
(protocol
 (protproperties
  (protdesc :ident cnpprot :title ContractNet :location Cnp.xml)
  (protocolattributes :class Request :participantcount 1)
  (protkeywords ''containsMultipleInstanceRole''))
 (roles ...)
 (messagepatterns ...))
```

Example 1. Specifying CNP

The properties of a protocol consist of descriptors (identifier, title and location), keywords and attributes, which we identified from the experiments we carried out with our framework. The keywords are propositional contents which help further characterize the protocols. Currently, we consider the following keywords: (1) *ContainsMultipleInstanceRole* which means that there can be several instances of a participant role in this protocol; (2) *ContainsIterativeProcess*, which means that a sequence of actions can be repeatedly executed in the protocol; (3) *IncrementalResolution*, which means that an anytime algorithm can lie behind the execution of the protocol; (4) *ContainsDividableProcessing* which means that the processing associated with this protocol can be divided for several participants; (5) *SubscriptionRequired*, which means that the processing associated with this protocol requires a prior subscription; (6) *AlterableCommitment* which means that the commitments are not indefeasible.

Concerning the attributes, they are functions which we use to refine the description of a protocol. The current version of our framework allows two attributes to be set: (1) *class*, which indicates what kind of processing is implied by the protocol, (2) *participantcount*, which indicates how many types of participant roles does the protocol contain.

Role. Protocol diagrams only show the communication flow between roles. However, there may be some information beyond the communication layer. For example, in CNP, the action an initiator executes, in order to make a decision upon the bids the participants issued, is hidden behind the communication flow. Actually, this action exploits information from different participants of the protocol. Moreover, information like the deadline for bidding, cannot be extracted from any message content. We introduced a global area for each role where we describe actions which are beyond the communication flow, as well as data which cannot be extracted from any message content. Note that actions relevant to the global area are not tied up with any phase. The production rules hereafter define a role.

$$< roles > := < role >< role > \,|\, < roles >< role >$$
$$< role > := < roleprop >< variables? >< actions? >< phases >$$
$$< roleprop > := < roledesc >< roleattributes >< rolekeywords? >$$
$$< roledesc > := < identifier >< name >$$
$$< roleattributes > := < cardinality >$$
$$< variables > := < variable+ >$$
$$< variable > := < ident >< type >$$
$$< actions > := < action+ >$$

Each role is described through its intrinsic properties (f.i., cardinality), its variables, its global actions and phases. From Example 2, the *initiator* role of CNP has three variables: `deadline`, `bidsCol` and `deliberations`. `deadline` informs of the moment when bidding should stop. `bidsCol` is a collection where bids issued by participants are stored. `deliberations` contains the decision (accept or reject) the initiator made upon each bid. Each variable has an identifier and the type of data it contains. The content of a variable is characterized using some abstract data types. We also use these data types to represent message content and action signature. String, Number and Char are some examples of the data types we use in our framework. The description of these types is out of the scope of this paper. The only global action in this role is named `Deliberate`. Through this action, the initiator makes a decision upon the participants' bids. Global actions are described in the same way as local (located in a phase) ones: category (see Table 3.1), signature (input and output data types) and events (input and output). Note that each part (input and output) of the signature as well as the events is composite. We introduce three types of connector (*and, or, xor*, with their usual meanings) to assemble the elements of these parts. `Deliberate` is a *compute* action. It takes a *date* and a *collection* as input arguments (*:dir in*) and a *Map* as output result. `Deliberate` is executed when the value of `deadline` changes (*change* event) and that at least one bid has been stored in `bidsCol`. Once executed it changes the value of `deliberations`. The reserved word *eventref* is used here to refer to an event defined elsewhere (*change* event which occurred against the `bidsCol` variable). As we will see later, this special word sometimes helps define causality between actions.

```
(role :ident initiator
 (roleprop (roledesc :ident initiator :name Initiator)
  (roleattributes :cardinality 1))
 (variables (variable :ident bidsCol :type collection)
  (variable :ident deliberations :type map)
  (variable :ident deadline :type date))
 (actions(action :category compute :description Deliberate
   (signature (arg :type date :dir in)
    (arg :type collection :dir in)(arg :type map :dir out))
   (events (event :type change :dir in :object deadline :ident evt0)
    (eventref :dir in :ident evt5)
    (event :type change :dir out :object deliberations :ident evt1))))
 (phases ...))
```

Example 2. Specifying the initiator role of CNP

Phase. As stated above, each phase is a group of actions that share direct links. We use the following rules to define a phase.

$$< phases > := < phase+ >$$
$$< phase > := < actions >$$
$$< action > := < category >< description? >< signature >< events >$$

For example, in the initiator role of CNP, the first phase consists of producing and sending the `cfp` message. This phase contains two actions: `prepareCFP` and `sendCFP`. `prepareCFP` produces the `cfp` message. It is followed by `sendCFP` which sends the message to each identified participant. The description of this phase is given in Example 3.

```
(phase :ident phs1
 (actions (action :category compute :description prepareCFP
  (signature(arg :type date :dir in)(arg :type any :dir out))
  (events (event :type variablecontent :dir in :object deadline)
   (event :type messagecontent :dir out :object cfp :ident evt2)))
  (action :category send :description sendCFP
  (signature (message :ident cfp))
  (events(eventref :dir in :ident evt2)
   (eventref :type custom :dir out :ident cus01)
   (event :type endphase :dir out :ident evt3)))))
```

Example 3. Specifying the first phase of the initiator role of CNP

Message. Though we did not define messages as a concept, we use them in the formal specifications because they contain part of the information manipulated during interactions. The concept of message is well known in ACL, and their semantics is defined accordingly. We propose an abstract representation of messages, which we call *message patterns*. A message pattern is composed of the performative and the content type of the message. We also offer the possibility to define the content pattern, a UNIX-like regular expression which depicts the shape of the content. Note that at runtime, these messages will be represented with all the fields as required by the adopted ACL. In our framework, we represent all the message patterns once in a block and refer to them in the course of the interaction when needed. In our opinion, it sounds that only one ACL be used all along a single protocol description. The following rules define message patterns. Example 4 describes the message patterns used in CNP.

$$< messagepatterns > := < acl >< messagepattern+ >$$
$$< acl > := 'fipa'|'kqml'$$
$$< messagepattern > := < performative >< identifier >< content >$$
$$< content > := < type >< pattern? >$$

```
(messagepatterns :acl Kqml
 (messagepattern :performative achieve :ident achmsg
  (content :type any :pattern ...))
 (messagepattern :performative sorry :ident refuse
  (content :type null :pattern ...))
 (messagepattern :performative tell :ident propose
  (content :type any :pattern ...))
 (messagepattern :performative deny :ident reject
  (content :type null :pattern ...))
 (messagepattern :performative tell :ident accept
  (content :type string :pattern ...)) ...)
```

Example 4. Specifying message patterns in CNP

Design Guideline. As a guideline for protocol design and specifications in our framework, we recommend several design rules. Following these rules ensures that the resulting protocol specifications are wellformed and correct (ambiguity and inconsistency-proof). In the future, we envision to devise some algorithms (and a tool) which automate the process of checking whether a protocol specification complies with our guidelines. We introduce these guidelines here.

Proposition 1. *For each role of a protocol, there should be at least one action which drives into the terminal state. Every such action should be reachable from the role's initial state.*

Corollary 1. *From their semantics, roles can be represented as graphs. And for every path in this graph, there should be an action which drives to a terminal state.*

Proposition 2. *For every message m_i of the message set $\mathbf{M}$ of a protocol, there is at least one send action of a role in the protocol, which sends m_i.*

Proposition 3. *When two distinct actions can be executed at a point in a role definition, the set of events which fire each action, though intersect-able, should be distinguishable.*

Proposition 4. *When an action produces a message, it should be immediately followed by a* send *action, which will be responsible for sending the message.*

3.3   Semantics of the Concepts

Event. As we saw, an event informs of an atomic change. This change may have to do with the notified role's internal state. But usually, the notification is about other roles' internal state. Therefore, events are the grounds for role coordination. In this section, we briefly discuss the semantics of some events used in our framework. When needed in the definition of the semantics of our concepts, we introduce some expressions in a meta-language, which we call primitives.

change: this event type notifies of a change of the variable's value. Let v be a variable, *change(v)* denotes the event. We introduce the *value* primitive, which returns the value of a data at a given time point. Let d and t be a data and a time point respectively, $Value(d, t)$ denotes this function. $Value(d, t) = \emptyset$ means that the data d does not exist yet at time point t. We interpret the *change* event as follows:

$$\exists\, t_1, t_2(t_1 < t_2) \wedge (\mathrm{Value}(v, t_1) \neq \emptyset) \wedge (\mathrm{Value}(v, t_1) \neq \mathrm{Value}(v, t_2))$$

endprotocol: this event type notifies of the end of the current interaction. The phases in each role, have either completed or are unreachable. Also any global action of each role is either already executed or unreachable. A phase is unreachable if none of its actions is reachable. Actually, if the initial action is unreachable, the phase it belongs to will also be unreachable. We introduced three new primitives: *Follow*, *Executed* and *Unreachable*. *Follow* is a function which returns all the immediate successors of a phase. Let π_1 and π_2 be two phases, π_2 immediately follows π_1, if any of the input events of the initial action of π_2 refers to a prior event generated by one of the actions (usually the last one) of π_1. *Unreachable* is a predicate which means that the required conditions for the execution of an action do not hold, therefore preventing this action from being executed. Finally, *Executed* is a predicate which means that an action has already been executed. Let Π be the set of phases for a role r and A_π the set of executable actions for a phase π in r. Let also A_{G_r} be the set of global actions of r. We interpret the *endprotocol* event as follows:

$$\forall r \in \mathcal{R}, \forall a_\alpha \in A_{G_r}, (\mathrm{Unreachable}(a_\alpha) \vee \mathrm{Executed}(a_\alpha)) \wedge (\forall \pi \in \Pi, (\mathrm{Follow}(\pi){=}\emptyset)$$
$$\vee(\forall a_i \in A_\pi, \mathrm{Unreachable}(a_i)))$$

reception: this event type notifies of the reception of a new message. Let m' denote the received message, we interpret this event as follows (notation being *reception(m')*):

$$\exists\, t_1, t_2(t_1 < t_2) \wedge (\mathrm{m'} \notin_{t_1} \mathfrak{M}') \wedge (\mathrm{m'} \in_{t_2} \mathfrak{M}')$$

The symbol $\in_t$ (resp. $\notin_t$) means *belongs* (resp. *does not belong*) at time point t. $\mathfrak{M}'$ is the set of messages an agent received during an interaction.

variablecontent: this event notifies of the (fresh) construction of the content of a variable. Let v be a variable, *variablecontent(v)* denotes the event, which we interpret as follows:

$$\exists\, t_1, t_2 (t_1 < t_2) \wedge (\text{Value}(v, t_1) = \emptyset) \wedge (\text{Value}(v, t_2) \neq \emptyset)$$

Action. Actions are executed when events occur. And once executed, they may generate new events. Events are therefore considered as *Pre* and *Post* conditions for actions' execution. Here again, we only discuss the semantics of some action categories: *append*, *set*, *compute* and *send*. Let $\mathbf{E}$ be the set of all the event types we consider in our framework and $\mathbf{E}' = \mathbf{E} - \{endphase, endprotocol\}$.

append: this action adds a data to a collection. Let a_i be such an action. In the following we introduce two primitives: *isElement()* and *Arguments()*. *isElement()* is a predicate which returns true when a data belongs to a collection at a given time point. *Arguments()* returns the input arguments of an action.

$\text{Pre} = \{e_j, e_j \in \mathbf{E}'\}$
$\text{Post} = \{e_j, \exists k\ e_k = change \ \wedge (\exists t_1, t_2, d, v \in \text{Arguments}(a_i), (t_1 < t_2) \wedge$
$(\text{isElement}(v, d, t_1) = false) \wedge (\text{isElement}(v, d, t_2) = true))\}$

send: this action sends a message. It is effective both at the sender and the receiver sides. Let a_i be such an action. We interpret it as follows:
at the sender side:

$\text{Pre} = \{e_j, \forall m_j \in \text{Arguments}(a_i), \exists\, k, e_k = messagecontent(m_j)\}$
$\text{Post} = \{Trans(m_j) = true\}$

at the receiver side:

$\text{Pre} = \emptyset$
$\text{Post} = \{e_j, \forall m_j \in \text{Arguments}(a_i), \exists!\, k, e_k = reception(m_j)\}$

set: this action sets the value of a data. Let a_i be such an action,

$\text{Pre} = \{e_j, e_j \in \mathbf{E}'\}$
$\text{Post} = \{e_j, \forall v_j \in \text{Arguments}(a_i), \exists!\, e_j, e_j = variablecontent(v_j)\}$

compute: this action computes some information. Let a_i be such an action,

$$\text{Pre} = \{e_j, e_j \in \mathbf{E}'\}$$
$$\text{Post} = \{e_j, e_j \in \mathbf{E}' - \{reception\}\}$$

ACL usually define the semantics of their performatives by considering the belief and intention of the agents exchanging (sender and receiver) these performatives. This approach is useful to show the effect of a message exchange both at the sender and the receiver sides. In our framework, we adopt a similar approach when an action produces or handles a message. We use the knowledge the agent performing this action has with respect to the message. Hence, we introduce a new predicate, $Know(\phi, a_g)$, which we set to true when the agent a_g has the knowledge ϕ. $Know$ is added to the post conditions of the action when the latter produces a message. It is rather added to the pre conditions of the action when it handles a message. Note that ϕ is the content of the message. In the future, we wish to extend the interpretation of this predicate and enable agents to share some social states. Thus, our specification formalism could cover the commitment protocols.

Moreover, when an action ends up a phase or the whole protocol, its Post condition is extended with *endphase* and *endprotocol*, respectively.

Phase. The semantics of a phase is that of a collection of actions sharing some causality relation. The direct links between actions of a phase are augmented with a causality relation introduced by events. We note $\pi \stackrel{\text{def}}{=} < \mathbf{A}_\pi, \prec >$, where $\mathbf{A}_\pi$ is a set of actions and $\prec$ a causality relation which we define as follows:

$$\forall \mathbf{a}_i, \mathbf{a}_j \in \mathbf{A}_\pi, \mathbf{a}_i \prec \mathbf{a}_j \Longleftrightarrow \exists e \in Post(\mathbf{a}_i), e \in Pre(\mathbf{a}_j).$$

Proposition 5. *Let $\mathbf{a}_i$ and $\mathbf{a}_j$ be actions of a phase π, such that $\mathbf{a}_i$ always precedes $\mathbf{a}_j$,*

$$(\mathbf{a}_i \prec \mathbf{a}_j) \vee (\exists \mathbf{a}_p, \dots, \mathbf{a}_k, \mathbf{a}_i \prec \mathbf{a}_p \dots \prec \mathbf{a}_k \prec \mathbf{a}_j)$$

Role. The causality relation between actions of phases can be extended to interpret roles. Indeed, an event generated at the end of a phase can be referred to in other phases. On this basis, we defined an operational semantics for roles. The inference rules behind this semantics cover sequences, loops, alternatives, etc. In these inference rules, defined as usually, the statements are replaced by actions. We do not discuss these rules in this paper due to space constraint. Thanks to the operational semantics, we interpret a role is a labeled transition system with some intrinsic properties. $\mathbf{r} =< \mathbf{\Theta_r}, \mathbf{S}, \mathbf{\Lambda}, \longrightarrow >$ where $\mathbf{\Theta_r}$ are the intrinsic properties of the role, $\mathbf{S}$ is a finite set of states, $\mathbf{\Lambda}$ contains transitions labels (these are the actions the role performs while running), and $\longrightarrow \subseteq \mathbf{S} \times \mathbf{\Lambda} \times \mathbf{S}$ is a transition function. As an illustration, we give the semantics of the initiator role of CNP, which we call $\mathbf{r_0}$. Note that the messages associated with the send actions are numbered following their position in Fig. 2. $\mathbf{r_0} =< \mathbf{\Theta_{r_0}}, \mathbf{S}, \mathbf{\Lambda}, \longrightarrow > \mathbf{\Theta_{r_0}} = \{"cardinality = 1" \wedge "isInitiator = true"\} \mathbf{S} = \{\mathbf{S_0}, \mathbf{S_1}, \mathbf{S_2}, \mathbf{S_3}, \mathbf{S_4}, \mathbf{S_5}, \mathbf{S_6}, \mathbf{S_7}, \mathbf{S_8}, \mathbf{S_9}, \mathbf{S_{10}}, \mathbf{S_{11}}, \mathbf{S_{12}}\} \ \mathbf{\Lambda} = \{\mathbf{a_0}, \mathbf{a_1}, \mathbf{a_2}, \mathbf{a_3}, \mathbf{a_4}, \mathbf{a_5}, \mathbf{a_6}, \mathbf{a_7}, \mathbf{a_{11}}\} \longrightarrow = \{(\mathbf{S_0}, \mathbf{a_0}, \mathbf{S_1}), (\mathbf{S_1}, \text{send}_{[\mathbf{m_0}]}, \mathbf{S_2}), (\mathbf{S_2}, \mathbf{a_1}, \mathbf{S_7}), (\mathbf{S_2}, \mathbf{a_2}, \mathbf{S_3}), (\mathbf{S_3}, \mathbf{a_4}, \mathbf{S_4}), (\mathbf{S_4}, \mathbf{a_3}, \mathbf{S_5}), (\mathbf{S_5}, \text{send}_{[\mathbf{m_3}]}, \mathbf{S_{11}}), (\mathbf{S_5}, \text{send}_{[\mathbf{m_4}]}, \mathbf{S_6}), (\mathbf{S_6}, \mathbf{a_5}, \mathbf{S_8}), (\mathbf{S_6}, \mathbf{a_6}, \mathbf{S_9}), (\mathbf{S_6}, \mathbf{a_7}, \mathbf{S_{10}}), (\mathbf{S_2}, \mathbf{a_{11}}, \mathbf{S_{12}})\}.$

Protocol. The semantics of a protocol is that of a collection of interacting graphs (the roles) which coordinate their execution following the message exchange sequence Ω. This collection also has some intrinsic properties, some propositional contents which are true in the environment of the MAS. Nevertheless, some limitations subsist in this way of interpreting generic protocols. Usually *a priori* semantics is proposed for protocols. However, *a priori* semantics is not sufficient to interpret a generic protocol. Two main reasons account for such an insufficiency. Firstly, the message exchange sequence can be mapped to a graph of possibilities in the regard of exchanged messages. Therefore, the semantics of an interaction based on this protocol corresponds to a path in this graph. Secondly, the semantics of communicative acts defined in ACL is not enough to define the semantics of a protocol. The semantics of the executed actions should be included too. However, except send actions, all the other actions can only have general interpretation before the execution of the interaction, or its configuration for an agent. A more precise semantics of these actions can only be known at runtime (or sometimes the design time for agents). To this end, we introduce *a posteriori* semantics for protocols in our framework. Particularly, we draw on *Protocol Operational Semantics (POS)* developed by Koning and Oudeyer [11]. In our framework, this additional interpretation feature consists in refining the path followed in each graph corresponding to the roles involved in the interaction. Also, the semantics of the actions is enriched by that of the methods executed in place.

As an illustration, let us assume that the semantics of each role of CNP is known, we define that of the whole protocol as follows. $\mathbf{p} = <\Theta, \mathbf{R}, \mathbf{M}, \Omega>$, where $\mathbf{R} = \{r_0, r_1\}$ and $\mathbf{M} = \{m_0, m_1, \ldots m_8\}$. $\Omega = < r_0 \xrightarrow[a_0]{m_0} r_1, r_1 \xrightarrow[a_7, m_0]{m_1 | m_2 | m_8} r_0, r_0 \xrightarrow[a_3, m_2]{m_3 | m_4}$

$r_1, r_1 \xrightarrow[a_{10}, m_4]{m_5 | m_6 | m_7} r_0 >$.

4 Properties

When one designs a generic protocol, it is mandatory to formally prove its properties, in order to ease a wide adoption of this protocol. In this section we discuss some general properties for protocols designed in our framework. Here, we focus on two properties, liveness and safety, related to the correctness of protocols specified following our framework. Finally, we discuss the termination property, which one of the critical ones, for generic protocols. Note that we assume that the design guidelines discussed in Section 3.2 are respected. There are other properties specific to generic protocols, *equivalence, compliance, similarity*, which we do not discuss in this paper.

4.1 Liveness

Definition 6. *Liveness A role of a protocol is alive when it still has a sequence of actions to perform before reaching its terminal state. As a consequence, a protocol is alive when at least one of its roles is still alive.*

Proposition 6. *For every role of a protocol, events will always occur and fire some transition until the concerned role enters a terminal state.*

Proof. We prove this property only on a design standpoint, i.e. we do not assume anything about what actually happens in the MAS at runtime. Each role is considered a transition system; and from the description of transition systems, unless a faulty situation is encountered, an event will always occur and require to fire a transition until the role enters a terminal state, where the execution stops.

4.2 Safety

Definition 7. (Safety) *A safe protocol is one where nothing inconsistent happens during its execution. Particularly, we focus on two aspects of safety: (1)* consistent message exchange, *which means that each sent message is received and handled by at least one role; (2)* Unambiguous execution, *which explicitly requires some clear conditions to hold every time a role has to take an action.*

Proposition 7. (Consistent message exchange) *The message exchange sequence of a protocol, designed in our framework and which respects our design guidelines, is consistent. Precisely, any message a role sends is received and handled at least by one role. By the same token, any message a role receives has a sender (generally another role).*

Proof. From Proposition 2, each message in $\mathbf{M}$ is sent at least by one *send* action. On the other hand, every *reception* event in any role is related to a received message which belongs to $\mathbf{M}$ too. Thus, every received message has been generated and automatically sent (see Proposition 4) by a *send* action, supposedly of a different role.

Proposition 8. (Unambiguous protocol execution) *For each action a role can take, there is an unambiguous set of events which fire its execution.*

Proof. Let a_i be an action of a role r and E_{a_i} be the set of events which fire the execution of a_i. If a_i is the unique action that can be performed at the current execution point of r, the proposition is straightforward. Let's now assume that there exists another action a_j which can be executed at the same point as a_i. If $E_{a_i} \cap E_{a_j} = \emptyset$, then the proposition is also straightforward. In the case where $E_{a_i} \cap E_{a_j} \neq \emptyset$, from Proposition 3 we know that $E_{a_i} \neq E_{a_j}$. Thus, for a_i to be performed events in $E_{a_i} - E_{a_j}$ should occur. And $E_{a_i} - E_{a_j}$ is a unambiguous subset of E_{a_i}.

4.3 Termination

Proposition 9. (Termination) *Each role of a protocol represented in our framework always terminates.*

Proof. From Proposition 1, each role has a sequence of actions which bring that role to a terminal state. Once this terminal state is reached, the interaction stops for the concerned role. When all the roles enter a terminal state, the whole interaction definitely stops. However, this proof is insufficient when there are several alternatives or loops in the protocol. Corollary 1 addresses this case. Actually, only one path of the graph (with respect to the transition system) corresponding to the current role will be explored. And as this path ends up with an action driving to a terminal state, the role will terminate.

5 Conclusion

We believe that a special care is needed for the specifications of generic protocols, since only partial information can be provided for them. Therefore, we developed a framework to represent generic protocols for agent interactions. Our framework puts forth the description of the actions performed by the agents during interactions, and hence highlights the behavior required of them during the execution of protocols. In this, we depart from the usual protocol representation formalisms which only focus on the description of exchanged messages. Our framework is based on a graphical formalism, AUML. It is formal, at least as expressive as AUML (and its extensions) and of practical use. As we discussed in the paper, this framework has been used to address various issues in agent interaction design.

Since actions in generic protocols can be described only in a general way, a more precise description of these actions is dependent on the architecture of the agent that will perform them in the context of an interaction. This is usually done by hand by agent designers when they have to set up agent interaction models. Doing such a configuration by hand may lead to inconsistent message exchange in an heterogeneous MAS. We address this issue by developing an automatic generic protocol configuration mechanism (see [15]). This mechanism consist in looking for similarities between the functionalities in the architecture of an agent and actions of generic protocols.

Protocol selection is another issue we faced while designing agent interactions based on generic protocols. Usually, agent designers select the protocols their agents will use to interact during the performance of collaborative tasks. However, this static protocol selection severely limits interaction execution in open and heterogeneous MAS. Thus, we developed a dynamic protocol selection mechanism (see [14]) to address these limitations. During the dynamic protocol selection, agents reason about the specifications of the protocols known to them and the specification of the task to perform. Again, we used this framework, since it enables us to accomplish the reasoning about the mandatory coordination mechanisms for the performance of collaborative tasks.

References

1. M. Alberti, D. Daolio, and P. Torroni. Specification and Verification of Agent Interaction Protocols in a Logic-based System. In *ACM Symposium on Applied Computing (SAC)*, pages 72–78. ACM Press, 2004.
2. B. Bauer and J. Odell. UML 2.0 and Agents: how to build agent-based systems with the new UML standard. *Journal of Engineering Applications of Artificial Intelligence*, 18:141–157, 2005.
3. G. Casella and V. Mascardi. From AUML to WS-BPEL. Technical report, Computer Science Department, University of Genova, Italy, 2001.
4. M. Colombetti, N. Fornara, and M. Verdicchio. A Social Approach to Communication in Multiagent Systems. In J. A. Leite, A. Omicini, L. Sterling, and P. Torroni, editors, *Declarative Agent Languages and Technologies (DALT)*, number LNCS 2990, pages 191–220, Australia, Melbourne, 2003. Springer.
5. T. Doi, Y. Tahara, and S. Honiden. IOM/T: An Interaction Description Language for Multiagent Systems. In *Proceedings of the International Conference on Autonomous Agents and Multiagent Systems (AAMAS)*, pages 778–785, 2005.
6. M. Esteva, J. A. Rodriguez, C. Sierra, P. Garcia, and J. L. Arcos. On the Formal Specification of Electronic Institutions. In *Agent-mediated Electronic Commerce (The European AgentLink Perspective)*. 2001.

7. FIPA. FIPA Communicative Act Library Specification. Technical report, Foundation for Intelligent Physical Agents, 2001.

8. L. Giordano, A. Martelli, and C. Schwind. Specifications and Verification of Interaction Protocols in a Temporal Action Logic. In *Journal of Applied Logic (Special Issue on Logic-based Agent Verification)*, 2005.

9. M. Greaves, H. Holmback, and J. Bradshaw. What is a Conversation Policy? In *Proceedings of the Workshop on Specifying and Implementing Conversation Policies, Autonomous Agents 1999*, 1999.

10. G.J. Holzmann. The model checker spin. *IEEE Transactions on Software Engineering*, 23:279–295, 1997.

11. J-L Koning and P-Y Oudeyer. Introduction to POS: A Protocol Operational Semantics. *International Journal on Cooperative Information Systems*, 10(1 2):101–123, 2001. Special Double Issue on Intelligent Information Agents: Theory and Applications.

12. Y. Labrou and T. Finin. A proposal for a new KQML specification. Technical report, University of Maryland Baltimore County (UMBC), 1997.

13. S. Paurobally, J. Cunningham, and N. R. Jennings. A Formal Framework for Agent Interaction Semantics. In *Proceedings. 4th International Joint Conference on autonomous Agents and Multi-Agent Systems*, pages 91–98, Utrecht, The Netherlands, 2005.

14. J. G. Quenum and S. Aknine. A Dynamic Joint Protocols Selection Method to Perform Collaborative Tasks. In P. Petta M. Pechoucek and L.Z. Varga, editors, *4th International Central and Eastern European Conference on Multi-Agent Systems (CEEMAS 2005)*, LNAI 3690, pages 11–20, Budapest, Hungary, September 2005. Springer Verlag.

15. J. G. Quenum, A. Slodzian, and S. Aknine. Automatic Derivation of Agent Interaction Model from Generic Interaction Protocols. In P. Giorgini, J. P. Muller, and J. Odell, editors, *Proceedings of the Fourth International Workshop on Agent-Oriented Software Engineering*. Springer Verlag, 2003.

16. G. Smith. The Contract Net Protocol: High-level Communication and Control in a Distributed Problem Solver. *IEEE Trans. on Computers*, 29(12):1104–1113, 1980.

17. C. Walton. Multi-agent Dialogue Protocols. In *Proceedings of the Eight Int. Symposium on Artificial Intelligence and Mathematics*, 2004.

18. M. Winikoff. Towards making agent UML practical: A textual notation and tool. In *Proc. of the First Int. Workshop on Integration of Software Engineering and Agent Technology (ISEAT)*, 2005.

A   EBNF Grammar

$$< protocol > := < protproperties >< roles >< messagepatterns >$$
$$< protdescriptors > := < protdescriptors >< protattributes >< protkeywords? >$$
$$< protattributes > := < class >< participantcount >$$
$$< protocolkeyword > := "containsconcurrentroles"|"iterativeprocess"|\ldots$$
$$< roles > := < role >< role > \mid < roles >< role >$$
$$< messagepatterns > := < acl >< messagepattern+ >$$
$$< role > := < roleproperties >< variables? >< actions? >< phases >$$
$$< roledescriptors > := < roledescriptors >< roleattributes >< rolekeywords? >$$
$$< roleattributes > := < cardinality >< concurrentparticipants? >$$
$$< rolekeywords > := < rolekeyword+ >$$
$$< cardinality > := < digit+ > \mid "n"$$
$$< variables > := < variable+ >$$
$$< variable > := < identifier >< type >$$
$$< type > := "number"|"string"|"char"|"boolean"|\ldots$$
$$< actions > := < action+ >$$
$$< phases > := < phase+ >$$
$$< phase > := < identifier >< actions >$$
$$< action > := < category >< description? >< signature? >< events >$$
$$< category > := "append"|"custom"|"remove"|"send"|"set"|"update"$$
$$< signature > := < arguments > \mid < messages >$$
$$< arguments > := (< argset > \mid < argdesc >) +$$
$$< argset > := < settype > (< argset > \mid < argdesc >) +$$
$$< argdesc > := < identifier >< type >< direction >$$
$$< messages > := (< message > \mid < messageset >) +$$
$$< message > := < identifier >$$
$$< messageset > := < settype > (< messageset > \mid < message >) +$$
$$< settype > := "and"|"or"|"xor"$$
$$< events > := (< event > \mid < eventref > \mid < eventset >) +$$
$$< eventset > := < settype > (< event > \mid < eventref > \mid < eventset >) +$$
$$< event > := < identifier? >< eventtype >< object >$$
$$< eventtype > := "change"|"custom"|"endphase"|\ldots$$
$$< object > := < message > \mid < variableid >$$
$$< eventref > := < identifier >$$
$$< messagepattern > := < identifier >< performative >< content >$$
$$< performative > := < fipaperformative > \mid < kqmlperformative >$$
$$< content > := < type >< pattern? >$$

Plan Generation and Plan Execution in Agent Programming

M. Birna van Riemsdijk and Mehdi Dastani

Institute of Information and Computing Sciences
Utrecht University
The Netherlands
{birna,mehdi}@cs.uu.nl

Abstract. This paper presents two approaches for generating and executing the plans of cognitive agents. They can be used to define the semantics of programming languages for cognitive agents. The first approach generates plans before executing them while the second approach interleaves the generation and execution of plans. Both approaches are presented formally and their relation is investigated.

1 Introduction

Various programming languages have been proposed to implement cognitive agents [14,2,8,6,9,12,5,7,11]. These languages provide data structures to represent the agent's mental attitudes such as beliefs, goals and plans. Beliefs describe the state of the world the agent is in, goals describe the state the agent wants to reach and plans are the means to achieve these goals.

Most of these programming languages can be viewed as inspired in some way by the Procedural Reasoning System (PRS) [6]. This system was proposed as an alternative to the traditional planning systems [13], in which plans to get from a certain state to a goal state are constructed by reasoning about the results of primitive actions. PRS and most of today's cognitive agent programming languages, by contrast, use a library of pre-specified plans.[1] The goals for the achievement of which these plans can be selected, are part of the plan specification. Further, plans might not consist of primitive actions only, but they can also contain subgoals. If a subgoal is encountered during the execution of a plan, a plan for achieving this subgoal should be selected from the plan library, after which it can be executed. An agent can for example have the plan to take the bus into town, to achieve the subgoal of having bought a birthday cake, and then to eat the cake.[2] This subgoal of buying a birthday cake will have to be fulfilled by selecting and executing in turn an appropriate plan of for example which shops to go to, paying for the cake, etc., before the agent can execute

---

[1] The language ConGolog [7], in which the agent reasons about the result of the execution of its actions, is an exception.

[2] Assuming that both taking the bus into town and eating cake are primitive actions that can be executed directly.

M. Baldoni and U. Endriss (Eds.): DALT 2006, LNAI 4327, pp. 225–238, 2006.

the action of eating the cake. Plans containing subgoals are called *partial* plans, while plans containing only primitive actions are called *total*.

An important advantage of PRS and similar systems over traditional planning systems is that they do not require search through potentially large search spaces. A disadvantage of PRS-like systems has to do with the fact that most of these systems allow for multiple plans to be executed concurrently, i.e., the agent may pursue multiple goals simultaneously. These plans can conflict, as they, for example, can require the same resources. In PRS-like systems, in which plans for subgoals are selected during execution of the plan, it is difficult to predict whether plans will conflict. If a plan containing subgoals is selected, it is not yet known how the subgoals of this plan will be achieved. It is therefore difficult to assess whether this plan will conflict with other plans of the agent.

One way to approach this issue, is to use a representation of plans that contains information that can be used to detect possible conflicts among plans, as proposed by Thangarajah et al. [16,15]. Once these conflicts are detected, plans can be scheduled in such a way that conflicts do not occur during execution of the plans.

In this paper, we take a slightly different approach. That is, in order to be able to compare an approach in which information about conflicting plans is taken into account with an approach of *plan execution* in the PRS style, we take an operational approach to the former, which we call *plan generation*. The idea of plan generation is to use pre-specified partial plans to generate total plans offline, i.e., before the plans are executed. Since conflicts among plans generally depend on the primitive actions within the plans, the generation of total plans provides for the possibility to check whether plans are conflicting. We assume that a specification of conflicts among plans is given, e.g., in a way comparable with the work of Thangarajah et al.

In order to compare plan generation with plan execution, we first introduce a framework for plan generation (Section 2). This framework defines how non-conflicting sets of plans can be generated on the basis of a plan library (i.e., rules for selecting plans to achieve (sub)goals), a set of top-level goals, and a set of initial partial plans. These definitions are inspired by default logic. In default logic, various so-called extensions, which consist of consistent sets of first-order formulas, can be derived on the basis of possibly conflicting default rules, and an initial set of facts. The fact that default rules might conflict, gives rise to the possibility of deriving multiple extensions on the basis of a single default theory. We adapt the notion of extension as used in default logic, to the context of conflicting plans. An extension then consists of a set of non-conflicting plans. The idea of adapting the notion of extension as used in default logic to the context of plans, is inspired by the BOID framework [2]. It was however not worked out in detail in the cited paper.

The language we use as an example of a PRS style framework, is a simplified version of the cognitive agent programming language 3APL [8,3], and is presented in Section 3. We assume that a specification of conflicts among plans is given. Ways of specifying conflicts have been investigated in the literature (see, e.g., [16]), and further research along these lines is beyond the scope of this paper. We show in Section 4 that, for any total plan in an extension of a so-called plan generation agent, there is a corresponding initial plan in the execution setting, which has the same semantics. If one would assume that in an offline plan generation context, a single extension is chosen for execution, one could say that the behavior of a plan generation agent is "included" in the behavior of a plan execution agent. This is intuitive, since the incorporation of a notion of conflict among plans *restricts* the set of plans which can be executed concurrently.

2   Plan Generation

In this section, we present a framework for plan generation that is based on [2]. In that paper, a non-standard approach to planning is taken, in which rules are used to specify which plan can be adopted for a certain goal. This is in contrast with planning from first principles, in which action specifications are taken as the basis, and a sequence of actions is sought that realizes a certain goal state according to the action specifications, given an initial situation. In [2] and in the current paper, it is the job of the agent *programmer* to specify which (composed) plan (or plan recipe) is appropriate for which goal.

Throughout this paper, we assume a language of propositional logic $\mathcal{L}$ with negation and conjunction, with typical element ϕ. The symbol $\models$ will be used to denote the standard entailment relation for $\mathcal{L}$.

Below, we define the language of plans. A plan is a sequence of basic actions and $achieve(\phi)$ statements, the latter representing that the goal ϕ is to be achieved. In correspondence with the semantics of 3APL, basic actions change an agents beliefs when executed. This will be defined formally in Section 3. One could add a test statement and non-deterministic choice, but we leave these out for reasons of simplicity. A total plan is a plan containing only basic actions.

Definition 1. *(plans)* Let BasicAction with typical element a be a set of basic actions and let $\phi \in \mathcal{L}$. The set of plans Plan with typical element π is then defined as follows.

$$\pi ::= a \mid achieve(\phi) \mid \pi_1; \pi_2$$

The set of total plans TotalPlan is the subset of Plan containing no $achieve(\phi)$ statements. We use ϵ to denote the empty plan and identify $\epsilon; \pi$ and $\pi; \epsilon$ with π.

Before we define the notion of an agent, we define the rules that represent which plan can be adopted to achieve a certain goal. These plan generation rules have a propositional formula as the head, representing the goal, and a plan as the body. In principle, plan generation rules can be extended to include a belief condition in the head, indicating that the plan in the body can be adopted if the agent has a certain goal *and* a certain belief. The belief condition could then be viewed as the precondition of the plan. For reasons of simplicity, we however define rules as having only a condition on goals.

Definition 2. *(plan generation rule)* The set of plan generation rules $\mathcal{R}_{PG}$ is defined as follows: $\mathcal{R}_{PG} = \{\phi \Rightarrow \pi \mid \phi \in \mathcal{L}, \pi \in \text{Plan}\}$.

A plan generation agent is a tuple consisting of a belief base, a goal base, a plan base and a rule base. The belief base and goal base are consistent. The rule base consists of a set of plan generation rules and may not contain multiple rules for the same goal. This prevents that multiple plans for the same goal can be adopted, which could be considered undesirable. The plans base contains the initial set of plans of the agent.

Definition 3. *(plan generation agent)* A plan generation agent[3], typically denoted by $\mathcal{A}$, is a tuple $\langle \sigma, \gamma, \Pi, \mathsf{PG} \rangle$ where $\sigma \subseteq \mathcal{L}$ is the belief base, $\gamma \subseteq \mathcal{L}$ is the goal base, $\Pi \subseteq \mathsf{Plan}$ is the plan base and $\mathsf{PG} \subseteq \mathcal{R}_{\mathsf{PG}}$ is a set of rules. Further, $\sigma \not\models \bot$ and $\gamma \not\models \bot$ and all sets σ, γ, Π and PG are finite. Finally, PG does not contain multiple rules with an equivalent head, i.e., if $\phi \Rightarrow \pi \in \mathsf{PG}$, there is not a rule $\phi' \Rightarrow \pi' \in \mathsf{PG}$ such that $\phi \equiv \phi'$.

When generating plans, we want to take into account conflicts, for example with respect to resources, that may arise among plans. For this, we assume a notion of coherency of plans. A plan π being coherent with a set of plans Π will be denoted by $coherent(\pi, \Pi)$. We assume that once a (partial) plan is incoherent with a set of plans, this plan cannot become coherent again by refining the plan, i.e., by replacing a subgoal with a more concrete plan.

We are now in a position to define how a coherent set of plans is generated on the basis of an agent $\langle \sigma, \gamma, \Pi, \mathsf{PG} \rangle$. A natural way in which to define this plan generation process, is an approach inspired by default logic. In default logic, consistent sets of formulas or *extensions* are generated on the basis of a possibly conflicting set of default rules, and a set of formulas representing factual world knowledge. Here, we generate sets of coherent plans on the basis of an initial set of plans Π, a goal base γ, and a set of plan generation rules PG.

The idea is that we take the plan base Π of the agent, which may contain partial plans, as the starting point. These partial plans in Π are refined by means of applying plan generation rules from PG. If $\pi_1; achieve(\phi); \pi_2$ is a plan in Π and $\phi \Rightarrow \pi$ is a rule in PG, then this rule can be applied, yielding the plan $\pi_1; \pi; \pi_2$. This process can continue, until total plans are obtained. Further, a plan generation rule $\phi \Rightarrow \pi$ can be applied if ϕ follows from the goal base γ. In that case, a new plan π is added to the existing set of plans, which can in turn be refined through rule applications.

The plans that are generated in this way should however be mutually coherent. A plan can thus only be added to the existing set of plans through refinement or plan addition, if this plan is coherent with already existing ones. Different choices of which plan to refine or to add may thus have different outcomes in terms of the resulting set of coherent plans: the addition of a plan may prevent the addition of other plans that are incoherent with this plan.

Differing from [2], we define the notion of an extension in the context of plans through the notion of a *process*. This is based on the concept of a process as used in [1] to define extensions in the context of default logic. A process is a sequence of sets of plans, such that each consecutive set is obtained from the previous by

---

[3] In this section we take the term "agent" to mean "plan generation agent".

applying a plan generation rule. A process can formally be defined in terms of a transition system which is a set of transition rules that indicate the transitions between consecutive sets of plans.

Given a set of plans E_i and an agent $\langle \sigma, \gamma, \Pi, \mathsf{PG} \rangle$, a rule $\phi \Rightarrow \pi \in \mathsf{PG}$ can be applied if ϕ follows from γ. The plan π is then added to E_i, that is, if $\pi \notin E_i$ and $coherent(\pi, E_i)$. This rule can also be applied if there is a plan of the form $\pi_1; achieve(\phi); \pi_2$ in E_i.[4] In that case, the plan $\pi_1; \pi; \pi_2$ is added to E_i, again only if the plan is not already in E_i and it is coherent with E_i. One could also remove the original plan $\pi_1; achieve(\phi); \pi_2$ from E_i, but addition of the refined plan is more in line with the definition of processes and extensions in default logic. It would be more useful if a plan of the form $\pi_1; achieve(\phi); \pi_2$ could be refined by a rule $\phi' \Rightarrow \pi$ if $\phi \equiv \phi'$, but we omit this extra clause to simplify our definitions. The first element of a process of an agent is the plan base Π of the agent.

Definition 4. *(process)* Let $\mathcal{A} = \langle \sigma, \gamma, \Pi, \mathsf{PG} \rangle$ be an agent. A sequence of sets $E_0, \ldots, E_n$ with $E_i \subseteq \mathsf{Plan}$ is a process of $\mathcal{A}$ iff $E_0 = \Pi$ and it holds for all E_i with $0 \leq i \leq n - 1$ that $E_i \rightarrow E_{i+1}$ is a transition that can be derived in the transition system below. Let $\phi \Rightarrow \pi \in \mathsf{PG}$ be a plan generation rule. The transition rule for *plan addition* is then defined as follows:

$$\frac{\gamma \models \phi \qquad \pi \notin E \qquad coherent(\pi, E)}{E \rightarrow E'}$$

where $E' = E \cup \{\pi\}$. The transition rule for *plan refinement* is defined as follows:

$$\frac{\pi_1; achieve(\phi); \pi_2 \in E \qquad \pi_1; \pi; \pi_2 \notin E}{coherent(\pi_1; \pi; \pi_2, E)}$$
$$\frac{}{E \rightarrow E'}$$

where $\pi_1, \pi_2 \in \mathsf{Plan}$ and $E' = E \cup \{\pi_1; \pi; \pi_2\}$.

We assume that the plan generation rules of an agent are such that no infinite processes can be constructed on the basis of the corresponding transition system.

The notion of an extension is defined in terms of the notion of a closed process. A process is closed iff no rules are applicable to the last element of the process. This is formalized in the definitions below. Note that not all processes are closed. A closed process can be viewed as a process that has terminated, i.e., there are no transitions possible from the last element in the process. It is however the case that we assume that any process can become a closed process.

Definition 5. *(applicability)* A plan generation rule $\phi \Rightarrow \pi$ is applicable to a set $E \subseteq \mathsf{Plan}$ iff a transition $E \rightarrow E'$ can be derived in the transition system above on the basis of this rule.

---

[4] Note that, for example, a plan $achieve(\phi)$ is also of this form, as π_1 and π_2 can be the empty plan ϵ (see Definition 1).

Definition 6. *(closed process)* process $E_0, \ldots, E_n$ of an agent $\mathcal{A} = \langle \sigma, \gamma, \Pi, \mathsf{PG} \rangle$ is closed iff there is not a plan generation rule $\delta \in \mathsf{PG}$ such that δ is applicable to E_n.

Definition 7. *(extension)* A set $E \subseteq \mathsf{Plan}$ is an extension of $\mathcal{A} = \langle \sigma, \gamma, \Pi, \mathsf{PG} \rangle$ iff there is a closed process $E_0, \ldots, E_n$ of $\mathcal{A}$ such that $E = E_n$.

The execution of a plan generation agent is as follows. An extension of the agent is generated. This extension is a coherent set of partial and total plans. The total plans can then be executed according to the semantics of execution of basic actions as will be provided in Section 3.

3   Plan Execution

In this section, we present a variant of the agent programming language 3APL, which suits our purpose of comparing the language with the plan generation framework of the previous section. An important component of 3APL agents that we need in this paper, is the so-called plan revision rules which have a plan as the head and as the body. During execution of a plan, a plan revision rule can be used to replace a prefix of the plan, which is identical to the head of the rule, by the plan in the body. If the agent for example executes a plan $a; b; c$ and has a plan revision rule $a; b \Rightarrow d$, it can apply this rule, yielding the plan $d; c$.

Here we do not need the general plan revision rules that can have a composed plan as the head. We only need rules with statements of the form $achieve(\phi)$ as the head and a plan as the body.

Definition 8. *(plan revision rule)* The set of plan revision rules $\mathcal{R}_{\mathsf{PR}}$ is defined as follows: $\mathcal{R}_{\mathsf{PR}} = \{achieve(\phi) \Rightarrow \pi \mid \phi \in \mathcal{L}, \pi \in \mathsf{Plan}\}$.

An agent in this context is similar to the plan generation agent of Definition 3, with a rule base consisting of a set of plan revision rules. The rule base may not contain multiple rules for the same $achieve(\phi)$ statement. We also introduce a function $\mathcal{T}$ that takes a belief base σ and a basic action a and yields the belief base resulting from executing a in σ. This function is needed in order to define the semantics of plan execution. We use $\Sigma = \wp(\mathcal{L})$ to denote the set of belief bases.

Definition 9. *(plan execution agent)* Let $\mathcal{T} : (\mathsf{BasicAction} \times \Sigma) \to \Sigma$ be a function specifying the belief update resulting from the execution of basic actions. A plan execution agent, typically denoted by $\mathcal{A}'$, is a tuple $\langle \sigma, \gamma, \Pi, \mathsf{PR}, \mathcal{T} \rangle$, where $\sigma \subseteq \mathcal{L}$ is the belief base, $\gamma \subseteq \mathcal{L}$ is the goal base, $\Pi \subseteq \mathsf{Plan}$ is the plan base and $\mathsf{PR} \subseteq \mathcal{R}_{\mathsf{PR}}$ is a set of plan revision rules. Further, $\sigma \not\models \perp$ and $\gamma \not\models \perp$ and all sets σ, γ, Π and PR are finite. The rule base PR does not contain multiple rules with an equivalent head, i.e., if $achieve(\phi) \Rightarrow \pi \in \mathsf{PR}$, there is not a rule $achieve(\phi') \Rightarrow \pi' \in \mathsf{PR}$ such that $\phi \equiv \phi'$.

We can now move on to defining the semantics of plan execution. As it will become clear, we only need the semantics of individual plans for the relation between plan generation and plan execution that we will establish in Section 4. The semantics of executing a plan base containing a set of plans can be defined by interleaving the semantics of individual plans (see [8]).

The semantics of a programming language can be defined as a function taking a statement (plan) and a state (beliefbase), and yielding the set of states resulting from executing the initial statement in the initial state. In this way, a statement can be viewed as a transformation function on states. There are various ways of defining a semantic function and in this paper we are concerned with the so-called *operational* semantics [4].

The operational semantics of a language is usually defined using transition systems [10]. A transition system for a programming language consists of a set of axioms and derivation rules for deriving transitions for this language. A transition is a transformation of one configuration into another and it corresponds to a single computation step. A configuration is here a tuple $\langle \pi, \sigma \rangle$, consisting of a plan π and a belief base σ. Below, we give the transition system $\mathsf{Trans}_{\mathcal{A}'}$ that defines the semantics of plan execution. This transition system is specific to agent $\mathcal{A}'$.

There are two kinds of transitions, i.e., transitions describing the execution of basic actions and those describing the application of a plan revision rule. The transitions are labelled to denote the kind of transition. A basic action at the head of a plan can be executed in a configuration if the function $\mathcal{T}$ is defined for this action and the belief base in the configuration. The execution results in a change of belief base as specified through $\mathcal{T}$ and the action is removed from the plan.

Definition 10. *(Trans$_{\mathcal{A}'}$)* Let $\mathcal{A}'$ be a plan execution agent with a set of plan revision rules PR and a belief update function $\mathcal{T}$. The transition system $\mathsf{Trans}_{\mathcal{A}'}$, consisting of a transition rule for action execution and one for rule application, is defined as follows. Let $a \in \mathsf{BasicAction}$.

$$\frac{\mathcal{T}(a, \sigma) = \sigma'}{\langle a; \pi, \sigma \rangle \rightarrow_{exec} \langle \pi, \sigma' \rangle}$$

Let $achieve(\phi) \Rightarrow \pi \in \mathsf{PR}$.

$$\langle achieve(\phi); \pi', \sigma \rangle \rightarrow_{apply} \langle \pi; \pi', \sigma \rangle$$

Note that the goal base is not used in this semantics. Based on this transition system, we define the operational semantic function below. This function takes an initial plan and belief base. It yields the belief base resulting from executing the plan on the initial belief base, as specified through the transition system.

Definition 11. *(operational semantics)* Let $x_i \in \{exec, apply\}$ for $1 \leq i \leq n$. The operational semantic function $\mathcal{O}^{\mathcal{A}'} : \mathsf{Plan} \rightarrow (\Sigma \rightarrow \Sigma)$ is a partial function that is defined as follows.

$$\mathcal{O}^{\mathcal{A}'}(\pi)(\sigma) = \begin{cases} \sigma_n & \text{if } \langle \pi, \sigma \rangle \rightarrow_{x_1} \ldots \rightarrow_{x_n} \langle \epsilon, \sigma_n \rangle \text{ is a finite sequence of} \\ & \text{transitions in } \mathsf{Trans}_{\mathcal{A}'} \\ \text{undefined otherwise} \end{cases}$$

The result of executing a plan is a single belief base, as plan execution as defined in this paper is deterministic: in any configuration, there is only one possible next configuration (or none). See for example [17] for a specification of the semantics of plan execution in case of non-determinism.

4   Relation Between Plan Generation and Plan Execution

In this section, we will investigate how these two are related. In order to do this, we first define a function f, which transforms plan generation rules into plan revision rules of a similar form.

Definition 12. *(plan generation rules to plan revision rules)*   The function $f : \wp(\mathcal{R}_{PG}) \to \wp(\mathcal{R}_{PR})$, transforming plan generation rules into plan revision rules, is defined as follows: $f(PG) = \{achieve(\phi) \Rightarrow \pi \mid \phi \Rightarrow \pi \in PG\}$.

The theorem we prove, relates the operational semantics of the total plans of an extension of a plan generation agent, to the plans in the initial plan base of a corresponding plan execution agent. It says that for any total plan α in the extension, there is a plan π in the plan base of the plan execution agent, such that the operational semantics of α and π are equivalent. The plan α is a plan from the plan generation agent and we have not defined an operational semantics in this context. We however take for the operational semantics of α the operational semantics for plans as defined in the context of plan execution agents. Note though that, for the semantics of α, only the *exec* transition of the transition system on which the operational semantics is based, is relevant.[5]

The intuition as to why this relation would hold, is the following. The generation of a total plan α from a partial plan π under a set of plan generation rules PG, corresponds with the execution of π, under a set of plan revision rules $f(PG)$. The plan revision rules applied during execution of π have a plan generation counterpart that is applied during generation of α. Further, the basic actions that are executed during the execution of π, are precisely the basic actions of α (in the same order). Because of this, the operational semantics of α and π are equivalent, as the execution of basic actions completely determines the changes to the initial belief base, and therefore the belief base at the end of the execution.

If $\mathcal{A} = \langle \sigma, \gamma, \Pi, PG \rangle$ is a plan generation agent, the rule base of the corresponding plan execution agent $\mathcal{A}'$ should thus be $f(PG)$. For the belief base and goal base of $\mathcal{A}'$, we take σ and γ, respectively. As for the plan base of $\mathcal{A}'$, we cannot just take Π, for the following reason. A total plan α in an extension of $\mathcal{A}$ can be generated either from a partial plan π that was already in Π, or from a plan π that has been added by applying a plan generation rule to the goal base (through a plan addition transition in the process). If the latter is the case, we

---

[5] We could have defined a new transition system for total plans, only containing the *exec* transition of the system of Definition 10, and a corresponding operational semantics. This is straightforward, so we omit this.

have to make sure that π is in the plan base of $\mathcal{A}'$, as this is the plan of which the semantics is equivalent with α. We thus define that the plan base of $\mathcal{A}'$ is $\Pi \cup \{\pi \mid achieve(\phi) \Rightarrow \pi \in f(\mathsf{PG}), \gamma \models \phi\}$. We now have the following theorem.

Theorem 1. Let $\mathcal{A} = \langle \sigma, \gamma, \Pi, \mathsf{PG} \rangle$ be an agent and let E be an extension of $\mathcal{A}$. Let $\mathcal{A}' = \langle \sigma, \gamma, \Pi', f(\mathsf{PG}), \mathcal{T} \rangle$ where $\Pi' = \Pi \cup \{\pi \mid achieve(\phi) \Rightarrow \pi \in f(\mathsf{PG}), \gamma \models \phi\}$ and let $\alpha \in \mathsf{TotalPlan}$. We then have the following.

$$\forall \alpha \in E : \exists \pi \in \Pi' : \mathcal{O}^{\mathcal{A}'}(\alpha)(\sigma) = \mathcal{O}^{\mathcal{A}'}(\pi)(\sigma)$$

In order to prove this theorem, we need a number of auxiliary definitions and lemmas. The first is the notion of an extended process. The idea is, that we want to derive from a given process p and a given total plan α in the extension corresponding with p, those steps in p that lead from some initial partial plan π to α. For this, we give each plan in the plan base of the agent a unique number. Then, we associate with each step in the process the number of the plan that is being refined. If a plan is added through a plan addition transition, we give this new plan a unique number and associate this number with the transition step.

The elements of the sets of an extended process are thus pairs from $\mathsf{Plan} \times \mathbb{N}$. A pair $(\pi, i) \in (\mathsf{Plan} \times \mathbb{N})$ will be denoted by π^i. We use the notion of a natural number i being fresh in E to indicate uniqueness of i in E: i is fresh in E if there is not a plan π^i in E.[6] Further, a rule $\phi \Rightarrow \pi$ can only be applied to refine a plan $\pi_1; achieve(\phi); \pi_2$, if $achieve(\phi)$ is the leftmost $achieve$ statement of the plan, i.e., if π_1 is a total plan. This corresponds more closely with the application of plan revision rules in plan execution, as during execution always the first (or leftmost) $achieve$ statement of a plan is rewritten.

Definition 13. (extended process) Let $\mathcal{A} = \langle \sigma, \gamma, \Pi, \mathsf{PG} \rangle$ be a plan generation agent and let $I(\Pi)$ be Π where each plan in Π is assigned a unique natural number. A sequence of sets, alternated with natural numbers, $E_0, i_1, E_1, \ldots, i_n, E_n$ with $E_i \subseteq \mathsf{Plan}$ and $i_j \in \mathbb{N}$ with $1 \leq j \leq n$ is an extended process of $\mathcal{A}$ iff $E_0 = I(\Pi)$ and it holds for all triples E_k, i, E_{k+1} in this sequence that $E_k \rightarrow_i E_{k+1}$ is a transition that can be derived in the transition system below.

Let $\phi \Rightarrow \pi \in \mathsf{PG}$ be a plan generation rule. The transition rule for *plan addition* is then defined as follows:

$$\frac{\gamma \models \phi \qquad \pi \notin E \qquad coherent(\pi, E)}{E \rightarrow_i E'}$$

where $E' = E \cup \{\pi^i\}$ with i fresh in E. The transition rule for *plan refinement* is defined as follows:

$$\frac{(\alpha_1; achieve(\phi); \pi_2)^i \in E \qquad (\alpha_1; \pi; \pi_2)^i \notin E}{E \rightarrow_i E'} \\ coherent(\alpha_1; \pi; \pi_2, E)$$

where $\alpha_1 \in \mathsf{TotalPlan}$, $\pi_2 \in \mathsf{Plan}$ and $E' = E \cup \{(\alpha_1; \pi; \pi_2)^i\}$.

---

[6] We refer to the pairs π^i as plans and we will from now on take the set Plan as including both ordinary plans π and pairs π^i.

The notion of a closed process (Definition 6) as defined for processes in Definition 4, is applied analogously to extended processes.

We will prove theorem 1 using the notion of an extended process. Theorem 1 is however defined in terms of an extension, which is defined in terms of ordinary processes, rather than extended processes. We thus have to show that extended processes and processes are equivalent in some sense. We show that for any closed process there is a closed extended process that has the same final set of plans, with respect to the total plans in this set. We only provide a brief sketch of the proof.

Lemma 1. *(process equivalence)*   Let $\mathcal{A}$ be a plan generation agent and let $t : \wp(\mathsf{Plan}) \to \wp(\mathsf{TotalPlan})$ be a function yielding the total plans of a set of plans. The following then holds: there is a closed process $E_0, \ldots, E_n$ of $\mathcal{A}$, iff there is a closed extended process $E_0', i_1, E_1', \ldots, i_n, E_n'$ of $\mathcal{A}$ such that $t(E_n) = t(E_n')$ (modulo superscripts of plans).

Sketch of proof: ($\Leftarrow$) If a transition $E \to_i E'$ can be derived in the transition system of Definition 13, then a transition $E \to E'$ can be derived in the system of Definition 4 (modulo superscripts). ($\Rightarrow$) This is proven by viewing the plan generation rules as the production rules of a grammar and the total plans that can be generated by these rules as the language of this grammar. The formulas ϕ and the statements $achieve(\phi)$ are considered the non-terminals of the grammar and the set of basic actions $\mathsf{BasicAction}$ the terminals. The plans of the first element of an (extended) process can be viewed as the start symbols of the grammar, together with those plans that are added through the transition rule for plan addition.

It is the case that for any derivation of a string (or total plan) in the grammar, an equivalent leftmost derivation, in which at each derivation step the leftmost non-terminal is rewritten, can be constructed. Derivations in an extended process correspond with leftmost derivations, from which the desired result can be concluded.   □

Given a closed extended process p with E_n as its final element, and a total plan $\alpha^i \in E_n$, we are interested in those steps of p that lead to the derivation of α^i. In other words, we are interested in those steps that are labelled with i. For this, we define the notion of an i-process of an extended process. This consists of a sequence of pairs of sets of plans, where each pair corresponds with a derivation step that is labelled with i, in the original extended process.

Given the i-process p_i of an extended process p, we define the notion of the i-derivation of p_i. The i-derivation of p_i is the sequence of singleton sets of plans,[7] that is yielded by subtracting for each pair (E, E') occurring in p_i, the set E from the set E'. An i-derivation is thus a sequence $\pi_1^i, \pi_2^i, \ldots, \pi_m^i$,[8] in which

---

[7] It is a sequence of *singleton* sets, as each pair in an i-process corresponds with a derivation step in the original process. In a derivation step from E to E', exactly one plan is added to E.

[8] We omit curly brackets.

each plan is labelled with i. The sequence can be viewed as the derivation of the plan π_m^i from the initial plan π_1^i, as each step from π_j^i to π_{j+1}^i in this sequence corresponds with the application of a plan generation rule to π_j^i, yielding π_{j+1}^i.

Definition 14. *(i-derivation)* Let $\mathcal{A} = \langle \sigma, \gamma, \Pi, \mathsf{PG} \rangle$ be a plan generation agent and let $p = E_0, i_1, E_1, \ldots, i_n, E_n$ be a closed extended process of $\mathcal{A}$. The i-process p_i of p is then defined as a sequence of pairs $(E_0', E_1'), \ldots, (E_{m-1}', E_m')$ such that the following holds: (E, E') occurs in p_i iff E, i, E' occurs in p and for any two consecutive pairs $(E_j, E_{j+1}), (E_{j+2}, E_{j+3})$ occurring in p_i it should hold that $E_{j+1} \subseteq E_{j+2}$.

Let $p_i = (E_0, E_1), \ldots, (E_{m-1}, E_m)$ be the i-process of a closed extended process p. The i-derivation of p_i is then defined as follows: $(E_1 \backslash E_0), \ldots, (E_m \backslash E_{m-1})$.

We want to associate the semantics of a total plan α in some extension of a plan generation agent, with the semantics of a corresponding plan π in the initial plan base of a plan execution agent. We do this by showing that the basic actions executed during the execution of π, correspond exactly with the basic actions of α. For this, we define a variant of the transition system of Definition 10, in which the configurations are extended with a third element. This element, which is a total plan, represents the basic actions that have been executed so far in the execution. Further, we define the execution of a sequence of basic actions in one transition step. This is convenient when proving lemma 2.

Definition 15. *(Trans$'_{\mathcal{A}'}$)* Let $\mathcal{A}'$ be a plan execution agent with a set of plan revision rules PR and a belief update function $\mathcal{T}$. The transition system Trans$'_{\mathcal{A}'}$, consisting of a transition rule for action execution and one for rule application, is defined as follows.

Let $\alpha \in \mathsf{TotalPlan}$ be a sequence of basic actions and let $\mathcal{T}' : (\mathsf{TotalPlan} \times \Sigma) \to \Sigma$ be the lifting of $\mathcal{T}$ to sequences of actions, i.e., $\mathcal{T}'(a; \alpha)(\sigma) = \mathcal{T}'(\alpha)(\mathcal{T}(a)(\sigma))$. Further, let $\alpha' \in \mathsf{TotalPlan}$ be a sequence of basic actions, representing the actions that have already been executed.

$$\frac{\mathcal{T}'(\alpha, \sigma) = \sigma'}{\langle \alpha; \pi, \sigma, \alpha' \rangle \to_{exec} \langle \pi, \sigma', \alpha'; \alpha \rangle}$$

Let $achieve(\phi) \Rightarrow \pi \in \mathsf{PR}$.

$$\langle achieve(\phi); \pi', \sigma, \alpha \rangle \to_{apply} \langle \pi; \pi', \sigma, \alpha \rangle$$

It is easy to see that an operational semantics $\mathcal{O}'$ can be defined[9] on the basis of this transition system that is equivalent with the operational semantics of Definition 11, i.e., such that $\mathcal{O}'(\pi)(\sigma) = \mathcal{O}(\pi)(\sigma)$ for any plan π and belief base σ. The initial configuration of any transition sequence in Trans$'_{\mathcal{A}'}$ should be of the form $\langle \pi, \sigma, \epsilon \rangle$, as the third element represents the sequence of actions that have been executed, which are none in the initial configuration.

In the proof of lemma 2, we use the notion of a maximum prefix of a plan.

---

[9] We omit superscript $\mathcal{A}'$.

Definition 16. *(maximum prefix)* Let $\alpha \in \mathsf{TotalPlan}$ and let $\pi \in \mathsf{Plan}$. We then say that α is a maximum prefix of π iff $\alpha = \pi$ or $\pi = \alpha; achieve(\phi); \pi'$. Note that π' can be ϵ.

Lemma 2 says the following. Let α^i be a total plan in a closed extended process of a plan generation agent, and let π_1^i be the first plan of the i-derivation of α^i. It is then the case that the actions executed during the execution of π_1 (given an appropriate set of plan revision rules), are exactly the actions of α (in the same order).

Lemma 2. Let $\mathcal{A} = \langle \sigma, \gamma, \Pi, \mathsf{PG} \rangle$ be a plan generation agent and let $p = E_0, i_1, E_1, \ldots, i_n, E_n$ be a closed extended process of $\mathcal{A}$. Let $\alpha^i \in E_n$ where $\alpha \in \mathsf{TotalPlan}$. Further, let $\pi_1^i, \ldots, \alpha^i$ be the i-derivation of the i-process p_i of p. Let $\mathcal{A}' = \langle \sigma, \gamma, \Pi', f(\mathsf{PG}), \mathcal{T} \rangle$ be a plan execution agent where $\Pi' = \Pi \cup \{ \pi \mid achieve(\phi) \Rightarrow \pi \in f(\mathsf{PG}), \gamma \models \phi \}$. Further, let $\mathcal{T}'(\alpha)(\sigma)$ be defined and let $x_i \in \{exec, apply\}$ for $1 \leq i \leq m - 1$. The following then holds.

A transition sequence of the form

$$\langle \pi_1, \sigma, \epsilon \rangle \to_{x_1} \cdots \to_{x_{m-1}} \langle \epsilon, \sigma_m, \alpha \rangle$$

$$\text{can be derived in } \mathsf{Trans}'_{\mathcal{A}'}. \quad (4.1)$$

Sketch of proof: We say that a plan π^i corresponds with a configuration $\langle \pi', \sigma, \alpha \rangle$ iff $\pi = \alpha; \pi'$. Let π_k^i and π_{k+1}^i be two consecutive plans in the i-derivation of p_i, where π_k^i is of the form $\alpha_2; achieve(\phi_2); \pi_2$ and π_{k+1}^i is of the form $\alpha_2; \pi; \pi_2$. This corresponds with the application of plan generation rule $\phi_2 \Rightarrow \pi$. Let π be of the form $\alpha_3; achieve(\phi_3); \pi_3$. We then have that the following transition sequence can be derived in $\mathsf{Trans}'_{\mathcal{A}'}$.

$$\langle achieve(\phi_2); \pi_2, \sigma, \alpha_2 \rangle \to_{apply}$$
$$\langle \alpha_3; achieve(\phi_3); \pi_3; \pi_2, \sigma, \alpha_2 \rangle \to_{exec}$$
$$\langle achieve(\phi_3); \pi_3; \pi_2, \sigma', \alpha_2; \alpha_3 \rangle \quad (4.2)$$

This pair of transitions is correspondence and maximum prefix preserving. If π_1 (transition sequence (4.1)) is of the form $\alpha_1; achieve(\phi_1); \pi$, we can derive a transition in which α_1 is executed. This yields a configuration of the form $\langle achieve(\phi_1); \pi, \sigma', \alpha_1 \rangle$, which corresponds with π_1^i and for which it holds that α_1 is a maximum prefix of π_1. From this configuration, a sequence of *apply* and *exec* transitions can be derived, given that we have (4.2) for every pair π_k^i and π_{k+1}^i occurring in the i-derivation. From the fact that this sequence of transitions is correspondence and maximum prefix preserving, we can conclude that the final configuration $\langle \pi_m, \sigma_m, \alpha_m \rangle$ of the sequence must be of the form $\langle \epsilon, \sigma_m, \alpha \rangle$ (observe that α_i is the final plan of the i-derivation, which should correspond with $\langle \pi_m, \sigma_m, \alpha_m \rangle$).   □

We are now in a position to prove theorem 1.

Proof of theorem 1 (sketch):   We do not repeat the premises of the theorem. Let $\alpha \in E$ be a total plan in E. By lemma 1, we then have that there is a closed extended process with a final set E_n such that $\alpha^i \in E_n$ for some natural number i. Let $\pi_1^i, \ldots, \alpha^i$ be the corresponding i-derivation. The plan π_1 was either added in the process through a plan addition transition, or it was already in Π. From this we can conclude that $\pi_1 \in \Pi'$.

If $T'(\alpha)(\sigma)$ is defined, we have by lemma 2 that a transition sequence of the form $\langle \pi_1, \sigma, \epsilon \rangle \rightarrow_{x_1} \ldots \rightarrow_{x_{m-1}} \langle \epsilon, \sigma_m, \alpha \rangle$ can be derived in $\mathsf{Trans}'_{\mathcal{A}'}$. We thus have $\mathcal{O}^{\mathcal{A}}(\pi_1)(\sigma) = \sigma_m$. From the fact that only action executions may change the belief base, and the fact that α are the actions executed over the transition sequence, we can then conclude that $\mathcal{O}^{\mathcal{A}}(\alpha)(\sigma) = \sigma_m$. A similar line of reasoning can be followed if $T'(\alpha)(\sigma)$ is not defined. $\qquad \square$

5   Conclusion and Future Research

In this paper, we presented two formal approaches for generating and executing the plans of cognitive agents and discussed their characteristics. We explained how these approaches can be used to define the semantics of programming languages for cognitive agents in terms of operational semantics. The relation between these approaches is investigated and formally established as a theorem. The presented theorem shows that the behavior of plan generation agents is "included" in the behavior of plan execution agents.

However, for reasons simplicity, many simplifying assumptions have been introduced which make the presented approaches too limited to be applied to real cognitive agent programming languages. Future research will thus concern extending the results to more elaborate versions of the presented agent programming frameworks. Also, the characteristics of special cases will have to be investigated such as the case where there is only one extension of a plan generation agent. Finally, the notion of coherence between plans is not explored and left for future research.

References

1. G. Antoniou. *Nonmonotonic Reasoning*. Artificial Intelligence. The MIT Press, Cambridge, Massachusetts, 1997.
2. M. Dastani and L. van der Torre. Programming BOID-Plan agents: deliberating about conflicts among defeasible mental attitudes and plans. In *Proceedings of the Third Conference on Autonomous Agents and Multi-agent Systems (AAMAS'04)*, pages 706–713, New York, USA, 2004.
3. M. Dastani, M. B. van Riemsdijk, F. Dignum, and J.-J. Ch. Meyer. A programming language for cognitive agents: goal directed 3APL. In *Programming multiagent systems, first international workshop (ProMAS'03)*, volume 3067 of *LNAI*, pages 111–130. Springer, Berlin, 2004.
4. J. de Bakker. *Mathematical Theory of Program Correctness*. Series in Computer Science. Prentice-Hall International, London, 1980.

5. M. d'Inverno, D. Kinny, M. Luck, and M. Wooldridge. A formal specification of dMARS. In *ATAL '97: Proceedings of the 4th International Workshop on Intelligent Agents IV, Agent Theories, Architectures, and Languages*, pages 155–176, London, UK, 1998. Springer-Verlag.
6. M. Georgeff and A. Lansky. Reactive reasoning and planning. In *Proceedings of the Sixth National Conference on Artificial Intelligence (AAAI-87)*, pages 677–682, 1987.
7. G. d. Giacomo, Y. Lespérance, and H. Levesque. *ConGolog*, a Concurrent Programming Language Based on the Situation Calculus. *Artificial Intelligence*, 121(1-2):109–169, 2000.
8. K. V. Hindriks, F. S. de Boer, W. van der Hoek, and J.-J. Ch. Meyer. Agent programming in 3APL. *Int. J. of Autonomous Agents and Multi-Agent Systems*, 2(4):357–401, 1999.
9. F. F. Ingrand, M. P. Georgeff, and A. S. Rao. An architecture for real-time reasoning and system control. *IEEE Expert*, 7(6):34–44, 1992.
10. G. D. Plotkin. A Structural Approach to Operational Semantics. Technical Report DAIMI FN-19, University of Aarhus, 1981.
11. A. Pokahr, L. Braubach, and W. Lamersdorf. Jadex: a BDI reasoning engine. In R. H. Bordini, M. Dastani, J. Dix, and A. El Fallah Seghrouchni, editors, *Multi-Agent Programming: Languages, Platforms and Applications*. Springer, Berlin, 2005.
12. A. S. Rao. AgentSpeak(L): BDI agents speak out in a logical computable language. In W. van der Velde and J. Perram, editors, *Agents Breaking Away (LNAI 1038)*, pages 42–55. Springer-Verlag, 1996.
13. R.E.Fikes and N.J.Nilsson. STRIPS: A new approach to the application of theorem proving to problem solving. *Artificial Intelligence*, 2:189–208, 1971.
14. Y. Shoham. Agent-oriented programming. *Artificial Intelligence*, 60:51–92, 1993.
15. J. Thangarajah, L. Padgham, and M. Winikoff. Detecting and avoiding interference between goals in intelligent agents. In *Proceedings of the 18th International Joint Conference on Artificial Intelligence (IJCAI 2003)*, 2003.
16. J. Thangarajah, M. Winikoff, L. Padgham, and K. Fischer. Avoiding resource conflicts in intelligent agents. In F. van Harmelen, editor, *Proceedings of the 15th European Conference on Artifical Intelligence 2002 (ECAI 2002)*, Lyon, France, 2002.
17. M. B. van Riemsdijk, F. S. de Boer, and J.-J. Ch. Meyer. Dynamic logic for plan revision in intelligent agents. In J. A. Leite and P. Torroni, editors, *Computational logic in multi-agent systems: fifth international workshop (CLIMA'04)*, volume 3487 of *LNAI*, pages 16–32, 2005.

A Functional Program for Agents, Actions, and Deontic Specifications*

Adam Zachary Wyner

King's College London
London, UK
adam@wyner.info

Abstract. We outline the *Abstract Contract Calculator*, a prototype language implemented in Haskell (a declarative programming language) in which we model agents executing abstract actions relative to deontic concepts derived from Standard Deontic Logic and Dynamic Deontic Logic. The concepts of abstract actions are derived from Dynamic Logic. The logics are declarative, while the implementation is operational. Actions have explicit action preconditions and postconditions. We have deontic specification of complex actions. We implement a *Contrary-to-Duty Obligations* case. We distinguish *Contrary-to-Duty Obligations* from obligations on sequences, which has not previously been accounted for in the literature. The central innovation is the expression of complex violation and fulfillment markers. The language can be used to express a range of alternative notions of actions and deontic specification.

1 Introduction

We present an overview of key elements of the *Abstract Contract Calculator* (ACC) written in Haskell, which is a functional programming language (see Wyner (2006a) for the code and documentation for the ACC). The ACC processes the deontic notions of *prohibition, permission,* and *obligation* applied to complex, abstract actions. As an intuitive example, suppose *Bill is obligated to leave the room.* The *deontic specification* "obligated" applies to an *agentive action* "Bill's leaving the room". Were Bill to remain in the room, he would violate the obligation. He may then be obligated to pay a fine. An example with a complex action is *Bill is obligated to leave the room, and after having left the room, to going downstairs.* Bill can violate this obligation by first leaving the room, but not then going downstairs. The objective of the implementation is to abstractly model such reasoning patterns.

The scope of the paper is restricted in several ways. Actions and deontic notions have been extensively discussed in the Deontic Logic and Dynamic Logic literature (Lomuscio and Nute 2004; Jones and Sergot 1993; Sergot 1991; Royakkers 1996; d'Altan, Meyer, and Wieringa 1996; Wieringa and Meyer 1993b;

---

* The author thanks Tom Maibaum, Andrew Jones, and reviewers for comments, and Hewlett-Packard Research Labs, Bristol, UK for financial support. Errors rest with the author.

M. Baldoni and U. Endriss (Eds.): DALT 2006, LNAI 4327, pp. 239–256, 2006.

Harel 2000; Meyer 1988; and Khosla and Maibaum 1987). We do not have space to present these logics. We cannot presume the reader is an expert in this literature. Therefore, we discuss only what is useful for our presentation. As a tool to investigate alternative formal representations of the concepts, the implementation contributes to clarifying the issues around the logics.

A second restriction is that while we use intuitive concepts to *guide* the implementation, the implementation applies to *abstractions*. Though we discuss intuitions of obligations on an action such as *leaving a room*, he implementation only applies to abstract actions such as `Action6`. We work with abstractions because we can fully define the abstract actions, how functions apply to them, and how the deontic notions apply to them. It is hard define how the functions could apply to intuitive notions such as *leave the room*. Furthermore, the intuitive actions divert from the core issues of the implementation which are deontic specifications on abstract simple and complex actions, contract states, contract modification, and an agent's execution of an action relative to a contract. We believe it is valuable to study these abstract issues, which can then be applied in more concrete examples.

The outline of the paper is as follows. In the first section, we informally discuss the key issues which motivate the implementation. In the second section, we present an overview of the implementation conceptually along with relevant fragments of Haskell code. In the final two sections, we touch on other proposals for implementing deontic notions, weakness of the implementation, several aspects of the implementation which were not discussed in this paper, and issues for future research.

2   Driving Issues

The implementation is driven by four interlocking issues: compositional and productive flags which signal violation or fulfillment of a deontic specification; negation of an action as *antonym* or *opposite*; complex actions, particularly sequences; and the Contrary-to-Duty paradox. In the following, we briefly outline the motivations which guide the implementation.

2.1   Violability

We adopt the view that *violability* is the central notion of the deontic specification. For example, if *Bill is obligated to leave the room* and does not, then we want to represent that Bill has *violated* his obligation, which we may do here with the proposition *Bill has violated his obligation to leave the room*. Consequences may follow from this violation. In this way, bad behavior is *marked* and *reasoned with* rather than ruled out (Anderson and Moore 1967; Meyer 1988; and Khosla and Maibaum 1987). We do not adopt the approach of recent proposals which use the deontic notions to *filter out* or to *prioritize* actions (Garcia-Camino et. al. 2005; Aldewereld et. al. 2005).

In Standard Deontic Logic (Carmo and Jones 2002) or Dynamic Deontic Logic (Khosla and Maibaum 1987; Meyer 1988), a distinguished *proposition* marks that a deontic specification has been violated. However, this implies that all violations are alike. Yet, it is clear that a single violation marker is not sufficient. Jill's violation of an obligation to leave the room may have different consequences from Bill's violation of an obligation to walk down the stairs. The richer the structure of the marker, the subtler the ways it can be used (van den Meyden 1996; Wieringa and Meyer 1993a; and Kent, Maibaum, and Quirk 1993).

Wyner (2006b) has argued that the markers for violation markers have to be productively and compositionally derived from the agent, the deontic specification, the input actions, and the mode of combination of the actions. Productivity here means that from a finite lexicon and a finite set of well-formedness rules on simple and complex expressions, we can generate novel expressions. Compositionality means that the meaning of a complex expression is determined by the meanings of the component expressions and the mode of combination. Propositional and predicate logic are productive and compositional. For example, we want to distinguish between the violation markers relative to *Bill is obligated to leave the room* and *Jill is obligated to go downstairs*. In the former, the violation marker should be *Bill has violated his obligation to leave the room*, while in the latter it should be *Jill has violated her obligation to go downstairs*. Clearly, these two propositions are distinct, and distinct consequences may follow from each. In addition, the violation markers are derived from the obligation expression. Therefore, just as the obligation expressions are formed from productive and compositional rules, so too should be the related violation markers.

2.2   Action Opposition and Deontic Specification

Another component of our analysis is the calculation of actions in opposition. Suppose *Bill is obligated to deliver pizzas for an hour*. It is intuitively clear that *some* actions count toward fulfilling the obligation and *some other* actions count towards violating the obligation. Furthermore, *not just any activity which is not itself an action of delivering pizzas counts toward a violation*. Indeed, some actions which Bill executes are *deontically underspecified*. If this were not the case, then *anything* Bill does other than delivering pizzas leads to a violation. More formally, set-theoretic complementation is not the appropriate notion for action negation *in our domain of application*, for it would imply that at any one time, the agent can either violate the obligation or fulfill it. There would be no actions which are deontically underspecified, which is unreasonable. Instead, we need some means to calculate the *opposite actions* with respect to the particular input action, leaving other actions underspecified.

In general, we want to be able to calculate the *relevant* opposite of an action, if there is one (a restriction discussed below). Though action opposition in natural language is unclear, we can define it clearly on *abstract actions*. Suppose α, β, and γ are abstract actions. For an action, say α, from the domain of actions, we provide the means to calculate the opposite action, say it is β. We can say that

γ is not in any relation of opposition to either α or β. Thus, if it is obligatory to do α, one violates this obligation by doing β. If one had done γ, no violation or fulfillment would be implied.

The function from an action to its opposites is *partial*; it need not be the case that every action has an opposite. For our purposes, we observe that an obligation on an action is only semantically meaningful where there is an opposite of the action as well. For example, suppose that *Bill is obligated to leave the room*. If the action descriptions of *leaving the room* and *remaining in the room* are both provided in the model, then the obligation appears to be well-formed and meaningful. However, if for any reason, *leaving the room* is not available (say Bill is unable to move), then the obligation appears vacuous. We only allow obligations which can be fulfilled by one action or violated by another.

2.3   Contrary-to-Duty Obligations

Contrary-to-Duty (CTD) Obligations have been a central problem in Deontic Logic (Carmo and Jones 2002). Thus, an implementation ought to provide for it. One example of a CTD problem is as follows:

Example 1.   [a.]   It is obligatory that Bill leave the room.
[b.]   If Bill leaves the room,
    then it is obligatory that Bill goes downstairs.
[c.]   If Bill doesn't leave the room,
    then it is obligatory that Bill looks out the window.
[d.]   Bill doesn't leave the room.

We conclude from (d) and (a) that Bill has violated the obligation to leave the room. Furthermore, from (c) and (d), we conclude that it is obligatory that Bill look out the window. Though this is a toy example, legal reasoning often follows such patterns where one obligation together with a fact implies another obligation (Carmo and Jones 2002).

Wyner (2006b) argues that violation and fulfillment markers are key to an analysis of CTD cases; that is, rather than reasoning from propositional antecedents in (b) and (c), we reason from violation and fulfillment markers relative to the primary obligation as follows:

Example 2.   [a.]   It is obligatory that Bill leave the room.
[b.]   If Bill fulfills his obligation to leave the room,
    then it is obligatory that Bill goes downstairs.
[c.]   If Bill violates his obligation to leave the room,
    then it is obligatory that look out the window.
[d.]   Bill doesn't leave the room.

Given (d) and (a), it is implied that Bill has violated his obligation to leave the room. In turn, this violation and (c) imply that it is obligatory for Bill to look out the window.

The advantage to this alternative analysis is that it creates a tight link between the initial obligation (a), restricted conditions of violation (d), and the implied obligations (b) or (c). It blocks unwanted inferences in other cases (Wyner 2006b), which we do not have space to demonstrate here.

2.4   Obligations on Sequences Versus Sequences of Obligations

Wyner (2006b) argues that obligations on sequences and sequences of obligations are not equivalent, contra Meyer (1988), who conflates them, and Khosla and Maibaum (1987), who mention the distinction, but do not elaborate. For example, suppose two actions *leaving the room* and *going downstairs*. We can put them together as a sequence *leave the room, and having left the room, go downstairs*. We can impose an obligation on the sequence: *It is obligatory for Bill to leave the room, and having left the room, to go downstairs*. Alternatively, we can make a sequence of obligations, where one obligation follows another: *It is obligatory for Bill to leave the room, and having left the room, it is obligatory for him to go downstairs*. In the first, Bill can fulfull the obligation *only after* executing both actions in the proper order. Bill can violate the obligation on the sequence by failing to execute one action or by executing the actions out of turn. In the sequence of obligations case, there are *two* obligations. Bill can fulfill the first obligation, and yet violate the second. This shows that the obligation on the sequence and the sequence of obligations are not equivalent.

In addition, the violations which are marked are distinct: in an obligation on a sequence, the violation must mark that it is a violation on a sequence *leaving the room, and having left the room, going down stairs* per se. In a sequence of obligations, the violations only mark violations of particular actions *leaving the room* and *going down stairs.*

A key objective of the implementation is to support a language which can distinguish obligations on sequences and sequences of obligations. The language should also generate distinct violation markers for each so as to allow different inferences to follow.

In general, we have to be able to productively and compositionally calculate the opposite of any action as well as the violation marker for any action. This is crucial since it is not feasible to have a listing of every possible complex action and its opposite, nor the violation markers for every possible complex action. Productivity and compositionality are also crucial to handle *novel actions*, which are new basic actions that we introduce to a particular system. For instance, if our total inventory of basic actions is *leaving the room* and *going downstairs*, we could apply a function to a *list* to determine the opposites as well as the violation markers. That is, the opposition of *leaving the room* is listed as *remaining in the room* and the violation marker for *It is obligatory for Bill to leave the room* is *Bill has violated the obligation to leave the room*. But, if our functions need to apply to an action not otherwise on the list, say *jumping up and down*, no output would be produced and the system would hang. We do not want reasoning and action execution to hang when it is fed novel input.

So far as we know, the importance of productivity, compositionality, lexical semantic opposition, or the calculation of complex violation markers have not been recognized in the Deontic Logic or Dynamic Logic literature.

To this point, we have sketched some of the key conceptual issues which drive the structure of the implementation.

3   An Overview of the Implementation

We have implemented our system in Haskell, which is a functional programming language. Speaking broadly, functional programming languages implement the *Lambda Calculus*. It is a programming language which is particularly well suited to computational semantics (Doets and van Eijck 2004; van Eijck 2004).

In the following subsections, we present highlights of the prototype implementation. It is a *programming tool* in that provides a language in which alternative notions of deontic specification on agentive actions can be systematically examined and animated. One enters at the command line an agentive action in a context, and the program calculates whether the agent has violated or fulfilled a particular contract as well as any ways this induces contract modification. The result of the calculation is output.

We present the implementation starting from the simplest. *States of Affairs* are lists of atomic propositions along with indices for worlds and times. *Basic Actions* are essentially functions from States of Affairs to States of Affairs. *Lexical Semantic Functions* allow us to *calculate* actions in specified lexical semantic relations such as *opposite*. These functions help us define the consequences of deontically specified actions. *Deontic Operators* apply to actions to specify what actions lead to States of Affairs in which fulfillment or violation is marked relative to the action and agent. We call such a specification a *Contract Flag State*. We implement reasoning for *Contrary-to-Duty Obligations* by modifying contract states relative to violation or fulfillment *flags*. Code snippets and input/output examples are given in numbered **Code** and **Data** samples.

3.1   States of Affairs

We construct many of our expressions from basic Haskell types for strings `String`, integers `Int`, and records, which are labels associated with values of a given type. In terms of these, we have several derived types.

```
Code 1.    type PropList =  [String]
           type World    =  Int
           type Time     =  Int
           type SOA      =  Rec (properties :: PropList,
                                 time :: Time, world :: World)
           type DBSoas   =  [SOA]
```

Our atomic propositions are of type `String` such as `prop1` and `prop2`. Prefixing a string with `neg-` forms the negation of a proposition, and we have a *double negation elimination* rule. Lists of propositions, of type `PropList`, form the properties which define the properties which hold of a state of affairs. We can filter the lists for consistency. This means that we remove from the model any list of properties which has a proposition and its negation such as [`prop1`, `neg-prop1`]. Filtering serves to *constrain* the logical space of models under consideration and used for processing. For our purposes, we do not have complex propositions other than negation. Nor do we address inference from propositions at the level of contexts.

States-of-Affairs, which are of type `SOA`, are records comprised of a list of properties along with indices for world and time. An example SOA is:

Data 1.   (properties = [prop1, prop7, prop5, neg-prop3],
           time = 2, world = 4)

Lists of expressions of type `SOA` are of type `DBSoas`. These can be understood as *alternative states of affairs* or *possible worlds*.

3.2   Basic Actions

An *action* is of a record of type `Action`, which has fields for a `label` of type `String`, preconditions `xcond` of type `PropList`, and postconditions `ycond` of type `PropList`. An action is used to express *state transitions* from SOAs where the preconditions hold to SOAs where the postconditions hold. An action with an agent is of type `AgentiveAction`, which is a record with fields for an action and an `Agent` of type `String`. A list of agentive actions is of type `DBAgentiveAction`.

Code 2.

```
type Action          = Rec (label :: String,
                            xcond :: PropList,
                            ycond :: PropList)
type DBAction        = [Action]
type Agent           = String
type AgentiveAction  = Rec (action :: Action,
                            agent :: Agent)
type DBAgentiveAction = [AgentiveAction]
```

An example of an agentive action is:

Data 2.   (action = (label = Action6,
            xcond = [prop1, prop7, prop5],
            ycond = [prop3, neg-prop4, neg-prop6]),
        agent = Jill)

This represents an *abstract agentive action*, which contrasts with agentive actions found in natural language such as *Jill leaves*. We work exclusively with abstract agentive actions since we can explicitly work with the properties which exhaustively define them. It is harder to do so with natural language expressions since it is not clear that we can either explicitly or exhaustively define them in terms of component properties. Nonetheless, we can refer to the natural language examples where useful.

The function `doAgentiveAction` in **Code 3** takes expressions of type `SOA` and `AgentiveAction` and outputs an expression of type `SOA`.

Code 3.   type doAgentiveAction :: SOA $\rightarrow$ AgentiveAction $\rightarrow$ SOA

In the definition of the function (not provided), an action can be executed so long as the preconditions of the action are a subset of the properties of the `SOA` with respect to which the action is to be executed. Following execution of the action, the postconditions of the action hold in the subsequent context, and the time index of the resultant `SOA` is incrementally updated (in this paper, we do not manipulate the world index). Further constraints on the execution of the well-formed transitions are that the properties of the resultant `SOA` must be *consistent* (no contradictions) and *non-redundant* (no repeat propositions). In addition, we *inertially maintain* any properties of the input `SOA` which are not otherwise changed by the execution of the action. In **Data 3**, we have an example.

Data 3.   input> doAgentiveAction
          (properties = [prop1, neg-prop3, prop5, prop7],
            time = 2, world = 4)
          (action = (label = Action6,
            xcond = [prop1, prop5, prop7],
            ycond = [prop3, neg-prop4, neg-prop6]),
            agent = Jill)
        output> (properties = [prop1, prop3, neg-prop4,
          prop5, neg-prop6, prop7],
          time = 3, world = 4)

3.3 Lexical Semantic Functions

For the purposes of deontic specification on agentive actions, we define lexical semantic functions. These functions allow us to *functionally* (in the mathematical sense) determine actions in specified relationships. This is especially important for the definition of *obligation*, where we want to determine which *specific alternatives* of a given action induce violation. One observation we want to account for is the following. Informally, if it is obligatory for Jill to leave the room, then Jill would violate the obligation by remaining in the room. On the other hand, if it is obligatory for Jill to remain in the room, then Jill would violate the obligation by leaving the room. In other words, we see a *reciprocal* relationship between actions in opposition. Furthermore, notice that if Jill's leaving the room is obligatory, then the action which fulfills the obligation and the action which violates the obligation *must both be executable* in the same SOA. This means that the actions have *the same precondition properties*. While the natural language case provides the intuitions behind the functions, we implement them with respect to our abstract actions. We only provide a sample of the lexical semantic functions (see Wyner (2006a) for further discussion).

Let us suppose a (partial) lexical semantic function `findOpposites`, which is a function from `Action` to `Action`. For processing, it takes a lexicon and some constraints. For example, suppose `findOpposites` applied to the action labelled `Action6` yields `Action7` and vice versa. While there are many potential implementations of action opposition, we have defined the function `findOpposites` such that it outputs an action which is the same as the input action but for the negation of one of the postcondition propositions. This closely models the natural language example of the opposition between *leave* and *remain*. As an illustration, we have the following:

Data 4.   input> findOpposites (label = Action6,
        xcond = [prop1, prop7, prop5],
        ycond = [prop3, neg-prop4, neg-prop6])
    output> (label = Action7, xcond = [prop1, prop7, prop5],
        ycond = [prop3, neg-prop4, prop6])

Three things are important about the function `actionOpposites` for our purposes. First, we can calculate *specific alternative actions* which give rise to violations. As discussed earlier, it is unintuitive that just *any action* other than the obligated action should give rise to violation. Second, as a calculation, we can find an opposite for any action *where the lexical structure allows one*. For the purposes of deontic specification, it need *not* be the case that every action *has* an antonym (although one could define a function and lexical space to allow this). Crucially, this holds for atomic as well as complex actions. And finally, the function `actionOpposites` is defined so as to provide reciprocal actions; that is, the opposite of `Action6` is `Action7` and vice versa. Thus, the function closely models the natural language case discussed above.

3.4   Deontic Specifications

The previous three subsections are components of deontic specifications on actions, which we model on the following intuition. Suppose an agent *Jill* is obligated to delivery a pizza. This implies that were she to deliver the pizza, in the context after the delivery of the pizza, we would want to indicate that *Jill* has delivered the pizza. Moreover, by doing so, she has fulfilled her obligation *with respect to her obligation to deliver the pizza*. On the other hand, suppose *Jill* were not to deliver the pizza, which is the opposite of delivering the pizza. In this case, we should indicate in the subsequent context that Jill that has not delivered the pizza. Furthermore, by doing so, she has *violated her obligation with respect to delivering the pizza*. We assume there are *deontically underspecified* actions as well. For example, if *Jill* eats an apple, which she could do concurrently over the course of delivering the pizza or not delivering the pizza, it may be that she does not incur a violation or fulfillment flag relative to that action. While it is possible that we use a *fixed* list for some cases to determine when violation markers arise, this will not work for complex actions or novel actions, which are those actions that are not already prelisted in a lexicon.

To define the deontic specifications, we provide a type `ContractFlag`. This type is a record having fields for: the action which is executed (indicated by the label), the deontic specification on the action (i.e. *obligated*, *permitted*, or *prohibited*), the action which is deontically specified (indicated by the label and which can be distinct from the action that is executed), whether execution of the action flags for violation or fulfillment, and the agent which executes the action. Lists of contract flags are of type *ContractFlagState*.

Code 4.
```
type ContractFlag = Rec (actionDone::String,
          deonticSpec::String, onSpec:: String,
          valueFlag::String, agent::Agent)
type ContractFlagState = [ContractFlag]
```

The violation and fulfillment flags, which are `String` types that are values of `valueFlag`, are key in reasoning what follows from a particular flag. In other words, that an agent has violated an obligation on an action may imply that the agent *incurs* an additional obligation. Indeed, such reasoning is central to legal reasoning. This is further developed in the section below on *Contrary-to-Duty Obligations*.

A deontic specifier is a function from an `AgentiveAction` to a list of results in a `ContractFlagState`. A list of actions `DBAction` and propositions `PropList` are also input for the purposes of code development.

Code 5.
```
type obligatedCompFlag :: AgentiveAction →
          DBAction → [PropList] → ContractFlagState
```

In **Code 6**, a `ContractStateFlag` is calculated relative to an input agentive action `inAgentiveAction` (along with a lexicon and compatibility constraints). Expressions of the form `#label list` return the *value* associated with given the *label* found in the *list*. Expressions of the form [x | x ← P] are *list comprehensions* in Haskell; they are analogous to the set-builder notation of set theory, where for S = {x + 2 | x ∈ {1,...,5} ∧ odd(x)}, the result is S = {3, 5, 7}. List comprehension works much the same way, but using lists rather than sets.

We discuss the code relative to the line numbers in **Code 6**. Lines 1-2 constitute a *guard* on the function: if the action from the input agentive action *has* an opposite (i.e. is a non-empty list), only then do we return a non-empty `ContractStateFlag` list. Otherwise, we return the empty list (line 14). This reflects the conceptual point that there can only be obligations on an action where the obligation can be violated (Wyner 2006a). Thus, where we return a non-empty list, there is some action in opposition to the input action. In lines 3-7, we create a list of type `ContractState` which represents the *fulfillment* of the obligation on the action. In lines 7-13, we find the opposite to the input action and use it to create a list of type `ContractState` which represents the *violation* of the action. We use ++ to conjoin these to lists to produce a list of type `ContractFlagState`.

Code 6.
```
          obligatedCompFlag inAgentiveAction inDBAction inComp
1            | ((findOpposites (#action inAgentiveAction)
2               inDBAction inComp) /= []) =
3                 ([[(actionDone=(#label (#action inAgentiveAction)),
4                    deonticSpec="Obligated",
5                    onSpec=(#label (#action inAgentiveAction)),
6                    valueFlag="Fulfilled",
7                    agent=(#agent inAgentiveAction))] ++
8                  [(actionDone=(#label x), deonticSpec="Obligated",
9                    onSpec=(#label (#action inAgentiveAction)),
10                   valueFlag="Violated",
11                   agent=(#agent inAgentiveAction))
12                     | x ← (findOpposites
13                       (#action inAgentiveAction) inDBAction [])])
14            | otherwise = []
```

To illustrate, let us assume that when we apply `obligatedCompFlag` to an agentive action labelled `Action6` with agent `Jill`. The output is:

Data 5.
```
          [(actionDone = Action6, agent = Jill,
             deonticSpec = Obligated, onSpec = Action6,
             valueFlag = Fulfilled),
           (actionDone = Action7, agent = Jill,
             deonticSpec = Obligated, onSpec = Action6,
             valueFlag = Violated)]
```

This is of type `ContractStateFlag`. It indicates that were `Jill` to execute `Action6`, then `Jill` would have fulfilled her obligation on `Action6`. On the other hand, were `Jill` to execute `Action7`, then `Jill` would have violated her obligation on `Action6`.

As lists of records, we can manipulate them. For example, we can add to or subtract from contract states. For example, the following represents Jill's obligation with respect to `Action6` and Bill's prohibition with respect to `Action9`.

Data 6.
```
          [(actionDone = Action6, agent = Jill,
               deonticSpec = Obligated, onSpec = Action6,
               valueFlag = Fulfilled),
           (actionDone = Action7, agent = Jill,
               deonticSpec = Obligated, onSpec = Action6,
               valueFlag = Violated),
           (actionDone = Action9, agent = Bill,
               deonticSpec = Prohibited, onSpec = Action9,
               valueFlag = Violated)]
```

Manipulations of `ContractStateFlag` expressions are crucial for *modelling* contract change, which is key to the analysis and implementation of Contrary-to-Duty Obligations.

3.5 Contrary-to-Duty Obligations

To model reasoning for CTDs, we enrich our States-Of-Affairs to include expressions of type `contractFlagState` as well as *histories* of type `history`. Histories are lists of records of what was done, when, by whom, and whether it counts as a fulfillment or violation relative to a deontic specification. Such records are of type `HistoryFlag`. They are much like `ContractState` expressions, but record the world and time at which the action is executed. An important difference between `HistoryFlag` and `ContractStateFlag` expressions is in *how they are processed*. This is further developed below.

```
Code 7.    type HistoryFlag = Rec (actionDone::String,
              deonticSpec::String, onSpec:: String,
              valueFlag::String, agent::Agent,
              world::World, time::Time)
           type History = [HistoryFlag]
```

Our SOAs are enriched with both a `ContractFlagState` and a `History`.

```
Code 8.    type SOAHistorical = Rec (properties::PropList,
              actionDone::String, history::History,
              contractFlagState::ContractFlagState,
              world::World, time::Time)
```

Actions are executed with `doAgentiveActionSOAHist`, which is function from `SOAHistorical` to `SOAHistorical`. We illustrate this informally below. Suppose the following input `SOAHistorical` to `doAgentiveActionSOAHist`. Notice that the history is empty, which means that there is no evidence that an action has been executed.

```
Data 7.    (contractFlagState =
              [(actionDone = Action6, agent = Jill,
                deonticSpec = Obligated, onSpec = Action6,
                valueFlag = Fulfilled),
               (actionDone = Action7, agent = Jill,
                deonticSpec = Obligated, onSpec = Action6,
                valueFlag = Violated),
               (actionDone = Action9, agent = Bill,
                deonticSpec = Prohibited, onSpec = Action9,
                valueFlag = Violated)],
           history = [],
           properties = [prop1, prop7, prop5, neg-prop4,
              neg-prop6], time = 2, world = 7)
```

Suppose that Jill does execute `Action7` with respect to this `SOAHistorical`. This means that we should indicate that Jill has violated her obligation. Thus, in the *history* of the subsequent `SOAHistorical`, we record that Jill executed `Action7`. We also record that this action violates Jill's obligation to execute

Action6, as well as the world and time stamp where the violation occurred. We also see that the time of the SOAHistorical is updated. The properties are updated as well.

Data 8.   (contractFlagState =
      [(actionDone = Action6, agent = Jill,
        deonticSpec = Obligated, onSpec = Action6,
        valueFlag = Fulfilled),
      (actionDone = Action7, agent = Jill,
        deonticSpec = Obligated, onSpec = Action6,
        valueFlag = Violated),
      (actionDone = Action9, agent = Bill,
        deonticSpec = Prohibited, onSpec = Action9,
        valueFlag = Violated)],
    history = [(actionDone = Action7, agent = Jill,
      deonticSpec = obligated, onSpec = Action6,
      time = 2, valueFlag = Violated, world = 7)],
    properties = [prop1, prop7, prop5, prop3, neg-prop4,
      prop6], time = 3, world = 7)

The next step in the implementation of CTDs is to allow contract state modification *relative to actions which have been executed in the history*. Recall from the discussion of CTDs that we only want a secondary obligation to arise *in a context where some other obligation has been violated*. In other words, if a particular violation of an obligation is marked in the History, we want a secondary obligation to be introduced into (or subtracted from) the ContractStateFlag of the SOAHistorical. For example, suppose Jill is obligated to leave the room. If Jill violates this obligation (by remaining in the room), then she incurs a secondary obligation to pay £5 to Bill. On the other hand, if Jill fulfills her obligation, then she incurs a secondary permission to eat an ice cream. The secondary obligations or permissions only arise in cases where a primary obligation has been violated or fulfilled.

To implement this, we have to examine whether a particular violation marker appears in the history. Second, we have to make that violation marker *trigger* ContractStateFlag modification. For instance, suppose that it is marked in the *History* that Jill has violated her obligation to do Action6 by doing Action7. As a consequence of that, we modify the current contract state by removing her previous obligation and introducing an obligation on Action11. In such an operation, only the ContractStateFlag is modified. This gives the appearance of inference in a state, for there is no state change marked by temporal updating.

We have a function doRDS, which implements action execution for *relativized deontic specifications*; it is a function from AgentiveActions and SOAHistorical to SOAHistorical. It incorporates modification of the ContractStateFlag. Where we assume the steps just outlined are applied to the ContractStateFlag in **Data 7**, a result is along the following lines:

Data 9.   (contractFlagState =
          [(actionDone = Action11, agent = Jill,
             deonticSpec = Obligated, onSpec = Action11,
             valueFlag = Fulfilled),
           (actionDone = Action15, agent = Jill,
             deonticSpec = Obligated, onSpec = Action11,
             valueFlag = Violated),
           (actionDone = Action9, agent = Bill,
             deonticSpec = Prohibited, onSpec = Action9,
             valueFlag = Violated)],
       history = [(actionDone = Action7, agent = Jill,
             deonticSpec = obligated, onSpec = Action6,
             time = 2, valueFlag = Violated, world = 7)],
       properties = [prop1, prop7, prop5, prop3, neg-prop4,
             prop6], time = 3, world = 7)

The implementation captures the essence of the CTD problem. It models how the execution of an action relative to a ContractFlagState induces a modification of the ContractFlagState.

3.6 Deontic Specification on Complex Actions

Earlier, we argued that we want to provide richer markers for deontic specification on complex actions. In order to construct these richer markers, we represent a sequence such as $\alpha;\beta$ with a richer structure which distinguishes the input actions α and β, the resultant action (suppose) γ, and the mode of formation such as the sequence operator. The deontic specifiers can then access different component *parts* of the complex action representation. This allows us to define a range of deontic specifications, as discussed below.

We implement complex actions as records. Complex Actions have fields for the input actions, the complex action operator, and the result of the application of the operator to the input actions. We discuss here only the sequence operator, as it raises the more complex and interesting problems for deontic specification. We represent sequences schematically as follows.

Data 10. (inActionA = ActionA, inActionB = ActionB,
             operator = SEQ, outAction = ActionC)

The *outAction* is, in this case, *function composition* of the input actions (*pace* several restrictions on well-formedness and alternative formulations): the preconditions of *ActionC* are the preconditions of *ActionA*; the postconditions of *ActionC* are those of *ActionB* together with those of *ActionA* which remain by *inertia*; the preconditions of *ActionB* must be a subset of the postcondition properties of *ActionA*; and the postcondition properties of *ActionC* must otherwise be consistent. Our decomposition of actions into explicit preconditions and postconditions as well as our explicit construction of complex actions relative to those conditions distinguishes our approach from Dynamic Logic approaches, where there are basic actions.

In Meyer (1988), obligations on sequences are reduced to sequences of obligations on the component actions. In Khosla and Maibaum (1987), obligations on sequences are irreducible to sequences of obligations, but rather are obligations on the sequence *per se*. In Wyner (2006a), we have further discussion of the significance of the difference, particularly the CTD problem. Here, we simply point out that the implementation provides ways to articulate these differences. For example, suppose *Jill* is the agent of the sequence and *ActionD* is the opposite of *ActionA* and *ActionE* is the opposite of *ActionB*. To provide the distributive interpretation of obligation in Meyer (1988), Obl_{dist}, we need two components. First, we have an initial contract state for the obligation on the first action:

Data 11.   [(actionDone = ActionA, agent = Jill, deonticSpec =
           Obligated, onSpec = ActionA, valueFlag = Fulfilled),
         (actionDone = ActionD, agent = Jill, deonticSpec =
           Obligated, onSpec = ActionA, valueFlag = Violated)]

In addition, we have a ContractStateModTrigger record which specifies that in the context where the first action has been executed (checked in the history), then the obligation on the second action of the sequence is introduced. This results in the following contract state, which specifies the fulfillment and violation cases for each of the *component* actions:

Data 12.   [(actionDone = ActionA, agent = Jill, deonticSpec =
           Obligated, onSpec = ActionA, valueFlag = Fulfilled),
         (actionDone = ActionD, agent = Jill, deonticSpec =
           Obligated, onSpec = ActionA, valueFlag = Violated),
         (actionDone = ActionB, agent = Jill, deonticSpec =
           Obligated, onSpec = ActionB, valueFlag = Fulfilled),
         (actionDone = ActionE, agent = Jill, deonticSpec =
           Obligated, onSpec = ActionB, valueFlag = Violated)]

We might say that the obligated sequence has been fulfilled where the obligations on each action have been fulfilled and in the right order.

In contrast, we could represent Khosla and Maibaum's (1987) interpretation by applying the operator to *ActionC* with a collective interpretation of obligation, Obl_{coll}. We suppose that *ActionF* is the opposite of *ActionC*:

Data 13.   [(actionDone = ActionC, agent = Jill, deonticSpec =
           Obligated, onSpec = ActionC, valueFlag = Fulfilled),
         (actionDone = ActionF, agent = Jill, deonticSpec =
           Obligated, onSpec = ActionC, valueFlag = Violated),

The most interesting case is the interruptable notion of obligation on a sequence. In this case, there is a violation and fulfillment flag with respect to the *whole sequence*, and the actions must apply in a given order. We assume the following initial contract state, where we emphasize that the marker for violation is relative to the complex action *per se* and there is no marker for fulfillment of the sequence:

Data 14. [(actionDone = ActionD, agent = Jill, deonticSpec =
           Obligated, onSpec = ActionC, valueFlag = Violated),

The second component is the ContractStateModTrigger, which specifies that *after* execution of the first action ActionA, an obligation to execute the second action arises such that fulfillment of this obligation marks fulfillment of the obligation of the sequence, while violation of this obligation marks violation of the obligation on the sequence. The resulting contract state looks like:

Data 15. [(actionDone = ActionD, agent = Jill, deonticSpec =
           Obligated, onSpec = ActionC, valueFlag = Violated),
        (actionDone = ActionB, agent = Jill, deonticSpec =
           onSpec = ActionC, valueFlag = Fulfilled),
        Obligated, (actionDone = ActionE, agent = Jill,
           deonticSpec = Obligated, onSpec = ActionC,
           valueFlag = Violated),

It is in such cases that a productive and compositional analysis comes to the fore.

We see that we can define deontic specifications on complex actions in different ways, which may be designed to suit particular purposes and interpretations. The language is thus very expressive and can be used to implement different notions of values applied to actions for the purposes of simulation in a multi-agent system. Further discussion appears in Wyner (2006a).

4   Some Comparisons

There have been several recent efforts to operationalize deontic specifications. Some we have already discussed. For example, Garcia-Camino et. al. (2005) and Aldewereld et. al. (2005) appear to use deontic specifications to filter out or sort actions. We do not believe that this represents the essence of the deontic notions. Sergot (2004) uses the event calculus and only considers permissions. While we may eventually want to integrate deontic specifications into an event calculus, we would want to be clear about deontic specifications themselves; it does not seem necessary to add the additional and potentially obscuring components of the event calculus. In addition, Sergot (2004) has neither complex actions nor an analysis of the CTD problem. Boella and van der Torre (2006) present an architecture for normative systems which is similar in that deontic specifications *add* information to basic information. However, it is unclear how they implement their design, integrate complex actions, or account for the CTD problem.

5   Conclusion

We have sketched the issues and implementation of the *Abstract Contract Calculator*. We have pointed out the key role of calculating *action opposition* and *violation and fulfillment* markers for complex actions. We have shown the importance of violation and fulfillment markers for reasoning with the CTD case. We sketched the implmentation in a Haskell program. The language allows the expression of alternative concepts of the deontic notions. One can input an agentive action, whether simple or complex, and determine, relative to a contract, whether that action violates or fulfills an obligation.

The main strength of the approach is that it allows alternative definitions of actions and deontic notions to be represented and animated. One can select which, out of those alternatives, most accurately represent one's intuitions. However, the program is a language, not a logic, even if logic-based. It needs to be expressed in an explicit logic. Along these lines, we can consider the various databases or registers (i.e. `contractFlagState`, `history`, and `properties`) as abstract objects which are input to functions that provide output such as we find in the database. Actions are then made to be functions on assignment functions on values to variables, capturing the dynamic aspect. As the implementation uses abstract actions and has no temporal operators, it has limited application.

One key aspect of the implementation which we have not discussed here are *consistency* constraints and *implicational* relations between deontic specifications. For this, we define a notion of the *negation* of a deontic specification. We also introduce lexical relations between positive and negative deontic specifications. Further discussion appears in Wyner (2006a).

We plan to enrich the structure of agents to give them some capacity to *reason* with respect to their goals, preferences, and relationships to other agents. As we want to model organizational behavior, we want to add *roles*, *powers*, a *counts as* relation between actions, and *organizational struture* to the implementation. The jural relations of *rights* and *duties* can also be incorporated into the language.

References

Huib Aldewereld, Davide Grossi, Javier Vazquez-Salceda, and Frank Dignum. Designing normative behaviour by the use of landmarks. In G. Lindeman, S. Ossowski, J. Padget, and J. Vzquez-Salceda, editors, *Proceedings of AAMAS-05, Fourth International Workshop on Agents, Norms and Institution for Regulated Multi Agent Systems*, pages 5–18, Utrecht, 2005.

Alan Anderson and Omar Moore. The formal analysis of normative concepts. *The American Sociological Review*, 22(1):9–17, 1957. Reprinted in: I.M. Copi and J.A. Gould (eds). 1967. *Contemporary Readings in Logical Theory*. MacMillan, New York.

Guido Boella and Leon van der Torre. An architecture of a normative system. In *Proceedings of AAMAS'06*, 2006.

Jose Carmo and Andrew Jones. Deontic logic and contrary-to-duties. In Dov Gabbay and Franz Guenthner, editors, *Handbook of Philosophical Logic. 2nd Edition*, pages 265–343. Kluwer Academic Publishers, Dordrecht, 2002.

Piero d'Altan, John-Jules Meyer, and Roel Wieringa. An integrated framework for ought–to–be and ought–to–do constraints. *Artificial Intelligence and Law*, 2(4):77–111, 1996. Revised version, dated 1998 at website; page references to download.

Kees Doets and Jan van Eijck. *The Haskell Road to Logic, Maths and Programming*. King's College Publications, 2004.

Andrés García-Camino, Juan Rodríguez-Aguilar, Carles Sierra, and Wamberto Weber Vasconcelos. A distributed architecture for norm-aware agent societies. In Matteo Baldoni, Ulle Endriss, Andrea Omicini, and Paolo Torroni, editors, *Declarative Agent Languages and Technologies III, Third InternationalWorkshop, DALT 2005*, Utrecht, The Netherlands, July, 2005 2006. Springer-Verlag.

David Harel, Dexter Kozen, and Jerzy Tiuryn. *Dynamic Logic*. The MIT Press, 2000.

Andrew Jones and Marek Sergot. On the characterisation of law and computer systems: the normative systems perspective. In J.-J.Ch. Meyer and R.J. Wieringa, editors, *Deontic Logic in Computer Science – Normative System Specification*, pages 275–307. Wiley, 1993.

Stuart Kent, Tom Maibaum, and William Quirk. Formally specifying temporal contraints and error recovery. In *Proceedings of the IEEE International Symposium on Requirements Engineering*, pages 208–215. IEEE C.S. Press, 1993.

Samit Khosla and Tom Maibaum. The prescription and description of state-based systems. In B. Banieqbal, H. Barringer, and A. Pneuli, editors, *Temporal Logic in Specification*, pages 243–294. Springer-Verlag, 1987.

Alessio Lomuscio and Donald Nute, editors. *Deontic Logic in Computer Science: Proceedings of the 7th International Workshop on Deontic Logic in Computer Science*, London, 2004. Springer-Verlag.

John-Jules Meyer. A different approach to deontic logic: Deontic logic viewed as a variant of dynamic logic. *Notre Dame Journal of Formal Logic*, 29(1):109–136, 1988.

Lamber Royakkers. *Representing Legal Rules in Deontic Logic*. PhD thesis, Katholieke Universiteit Brabant, Tilburg, 1996.

Marek Sergot. $(c+)^{++}$: An action language for modelling norms and institutions. http://www.doc.ic.ac.uk/research/technicalreports/2004/ DTR04-8.pdf.

Marek Sergot. The representation of law in computer programs. In T.J.M. Bench-Capon, editor, *Knowledge-Based Systems and Legal Applications*, pages 3–67. Academic Press, 1991.

Ron van der Meyden. The dynamic logic of permission. *Journal of Logic and Computation*, 6(3):465–479, 1996.

Jan van Eijck. Computational semantics and type theory. Website download, 2004.

Roel Wieringa and John-Jules Meyer. Actors, actions, and initiative in normative system specification. *Annals of Mathematics and Artificial Intelligence*, pages 289–346, 1993.

Roel Wieringa and John-Jules Meyer, editors. *Deontic Logic in Computer Science: Normative System Specification*. John Wiley and Sons, 1993.

Adam Zachary Wyner. *Violations and Fulfillments in the Formal Representation of Contracts*. PhD thesis, Department of Computer Science, King's College London, 2006. In preparation.

Adam Zachary Wyner. Sequences, obligations, and the contrary-to-duty paradox. In Lou Goble and John-Jules Meyer, editors, *Deontic Logic and Artificial Normative Systems: Proceedings of the 8th International Workshop on Deontic Logic in Computer Science*, pages 255–271, Berlin, 2006. Springer-Verlag.

Author Index

Lecture Notes in Artificial Intelligence (LNAI)

Vol. 4133: J. Gratch, M. Young, R. Aylett, D. Ballin, P. Olivier (Eds.), Intelligent Virtual Agents. XIV, 472 pages. 2006.

Vol. 4130: U. Furbach, N. Shankar (Eds.), Automated Reasoning. XV, 680 pages. 2006.

Vol. 4120: J. Calmet, T. Ida, D. Wang (Eds.), Artificial Intelligence and Symbolic Computation. XIII, 269 pages. 2006.

Vol. 4118: Z. Despotovic, S. Joseph, C. Sartori (Eds.), Agents and Peer-to-Peer Computing. XIV, 173 pages. 2006.

Vol. 4114: D.-S. Huang, K. Li, G.W. Irwin (Eds.), Computational Intelligence, Part II. XXVII, 1337 pages. 2006.

Vol. 4108: J.M. Borwein, W.M. Farmer (Eds.), Mathematical Knowledge Management. VIII, 295 pages. 2006.

Vol. 4106: T.R. Roth-Berghofer, M.H. Göker, H.A. Güvenir (Eds.), Advances in Case-Based Reasoning. XIV, 566 pages. 2006.

Vol. 4099: Q. Yang, G. Webb (Eds.), PRICAI 2006: Trends in Artificial Intelligence. XXVIII, 1263 pages. 2006.

Vol. 4095: S. Nolfi, G. Baldassarre, R. Calabretta, J.C.T. Hallam, D. Marocco, J.-A. Meyer, O. Miglino, D. Parisi (Eds.), From Animals to Animats 9. XV, 869 pages. 2006.

Vol. 4093: X. Li, O.R. Zaïane, Z. Li (Eds.), Advanced Data Mining and Applications. XXI, 1110 pages. 2006.

Vol. 4092: J. Lang, F. Lin, J. Wang (Eds.), Knowledge Science, Engineering and Management. XV, 664 pages. 2006.

Vol. 4088: Z.-Z. Shi, R. Sadananda (Eds.), Agent Computing and Multi-Agent Systems. XVII, 827 pages. 2006.

Vol. 4087: F. Schwenker, S. Marinai (Eds.), Artificial Neural Networks in Pattern Recognition. IX, 299 pages. 2006.

Vol. 4068: H. Schärfe, P. Hitzler, P. Øhrstrøm (Eds.), Conceptual Structures: Inspiration and Application. XI, 455 pages. 2006.

Vol. 4065: P. Perner (Ed.), Advances in Data Mining. XI, 592 pages. 2006.

Vol. 4062: G.-Y. Wang, J.F. Peters, A. Skowron, Y. Yao (Eds.), Rough Sets and Knowledge Technology. XX, 810 pages. 2006.

Vol. 4049: S. Parsons, N. Maudet, P. Moraitis, I. Rahwan (Eds.), Argumentation in Multi-Agent Systems. XIV, 313 pages. 2006.

Vol. 4048: L. Goble, J.-J.C.. Meyer (Eds.), Deontic Logic and Artificial Normative Systems. X, 273 pages. 2006.

Vol. 4045: D. Barker-Plummer, R. Cox, N. Swoboda (Eds.), Diagrammatic Representation and Inference. XII, 301 pages. 2006.

Vol. 4031: M. Ali, R. Dapoigny (Eds.), Advances in Applied Artificial Intelligence. XXIII, 1353 pages. 2006.

Vol. 4029: L. Rutkowski, R. Tadeusiewicz, L.A. Zadeh, J.M. Zurada (Eds.), Artificial Intelligence and Soft Computing – ICAISC 2006. XXI, 1235 pages. 2006.

Vol. 4027: H.L. Larsen, G. Pasi, D. Ortiz-Arroyo, T. Andreasen, H. Christiansen (Eds.), Flexible Query Answering Systems. XVIII, 714 pages. 2006.

Vol. 4021: E. André, L. Dybkjær, W. Minker, H. Neumann, M. Weber (Eds.), Perception and Interactive Technologies. XI, 217 pages. 2006.

Vol. 4020: A. Bredenfeld, A. Jacoff, I. Noda, Y. Takahashi (Eds.), RoboCup 2005: Robot Soccer World Cup IX. XVII, 727 pages. 2006.

Vol. 4013: L. Lamontagne, M. Marchand (Eds.), Advances in Artificial Intelligence. XIII, 564 pages. 2006.

Vol. 4012: T. Washio, A. Sakurai, K. Nakajima, H. Takeda, S. Tojo, M. Yokoo (Eds.), New Frontiers in Artificial Intelligence. XIII, 484 pages. 2006.

Vol. 4008: J.C. Augusto, C.D. Nugent (Eds.), Designing Smart Homes. XI, 183 pages. 2006.

Vol. 4005: G. Lugosi, H.U. Simon (Eds.), Learning Theory. XI, 656 pages. 2006.

Vol. 4002: A. Yli-Jyrä, L. Karttunen, J. Karhumäki (Eds.), Finite-State Methods and Natural Language Processing. XIV, 312 pages. 2006.

Vol. 3978: B. Hnich, M. Carlsson, F. Fages, F. Rossi (Eds.), Recent Advances in Constraints. VIII, 179 pages. 2006.

Vol. 3963: O. Dikenelli, M.-P. Gleizes, A. Ricci (Eds.), Engineering Societies in the Agents World VI. XII, 303 pages. 2006.

Vol. 3960: R. Vieira, P. Quaresma, M.d.G.V. Nunes, N.J. Mamede, C. Oliveira, M.C. Dias (Eds.), Computational Processing of the Portuguese Language. XII, 274 pages. 2006.

Vol. 3955: G. Antoniou, G. Potamias, C. Spyropoulos, D. Plexousakis (Eds.), Advances in Artificial Intelligence. XVII, 611 pages. 2006.

Vol. 3949: F.A. Savacı (Ed.), Artificial Intelligence and Neural Networks. IX, 227 pages. 2006.

Vol. 3946: T.R. Roth-Berghofer, S. Schulz, D.B. Leake (Eds.), Modeling and Retrieval of Context. XI, 149 pages. 2006.

Vol. 3944: J. Quiñonero-Candela, I. Dagan, B. Magnini, F. d'Alché-Buc (Eds.), Machine Learning Challenges. XIII, 462 pages. 2006.

Vol. 3937: H. La Poutré, N.M. Sadeh, S. Janson (Eds.), Agent-Mediated Electronic Commerce. X, 227 pages. 2006.

Vol. 3932: B. Mobasher, O. Nasraoui, B. Liu, B. Masand (Eds.), Advances in Web Mining and Web Usage Analysis. X, 189 pages. 2006.

Vol. 3930: D.S. Yeung, Z.-Q. Liu, X.-Z. Wang, H. Yan (Eds.), Advances in Machine Learning and Cybernetics. XXI, 1110 pages. 2006.

Vol. 3918: W.-K. Ng, M. Kitsuregawa, J. Li, K. Chang (Eds.), Advances in Knowledge Discovery and Data Mining. XXIV, 879 pages. 2006.

Vol. 3913: O. Boissier, J. Padget, V. Dignum, G. Lindemann, E. Matson, S. Ossowski, J.S. Sichman, J. Vázquez-Salceda (Eds.), Coordination, Organizations, Institutions, and Norms in Multi-Agent Systems. XII, 259 pages. 2006.